T0293350

Financing the Education of Health Workers

Gaining A Competitive Edge

World Scientific Series in Health Investment and Financing

ISSN: 2591-7315

Series Editor: Alexander S. Preker *(Columbia University, USA and Health Investment & Financing Corp, USA)*

Most western developed countries offer universal access to healthcare through mechanisms that provide financial protection against its high cost, either through insurance or government subsidy programs.

In most middle- and low-income countries, financing is often at the center of reforms in the healthcare sector. Success or failure of these reforms can have major impact on the political survival of governments that get involved, and major implications for the dynamics of the healthcare industry and overall economy.

With this series, World Scientific will contribute knowledge about a policy area which is still poorly-understood. The series merges policy and practice, exploring the economic underpinnings of real trends in health investment and financing.

The series will appeal and be accessible to investors, the health insurance industry, healthcare actuaries, business schools with healthcare tracts, healthcare management programs, researchers, graduate students, policy makers and practitioners working in the health sector worldwide.

World Scientific Series in Health Investment and Financing – Vol. 3

Financing the Education of Health Workers

Gaining A Competitive Edge

Alexander S. Preker
Columbia University, USA
The Icahn School of Medicine at Mount Sinai, USA
Health Investment & Financing Corporation, USA

Hortenzia Beciu
Johns Hopkins Medicine International, USA

Eric L. Keuffel
Health Finance and Access Initiative, USA

World Scientific

W JERSEY · LONDON · SINGAPORE · BEIJING · SHANGHAI · HONG KONG · TAIPEI · CHENNAI · TOKYO

Published by

World Scientific Publishing Co. Pte. Ltd.

5 Toh Tuck Link, Singapore 596224

USA office: 27 Warren Street, Suite 401-402, Hackensack, NJ 07601

UK office: 57 Shelton Street, Covent Garden, London WC2H 9HE

Library of Congress Cataloging-in-Publication Data

Names: Preker, Alexander S., 1951– author, editor. | Beciu, Hortenzia, author, editor. | Keuffel, Eric L., author, editor.

Title: Financing the education of health workers : gaining a competitive edge / by Alexander S Preker, Hortenzia Beciu and Eric L Keuffel.

Other titles: World Scientific series in health investment and financing ; v. 3.

Description: New Jersey : World Scientific, 2019. | Series: World Scientific series in health investment and financing ; volume 3 | Includes bibliographical references and index.

Identifiers: LCCN 2019008589 | ISBN 9789813278745 (hc : alk. paper)

Subjects: | MESH: Health Personnel--education | Health Occupations--education | Health Workforce--economics | Education, Medical--economics | Public-Private Sector Partnerships--economics

Classification: LCC RA410.7 | NLM W 18 | DDC 610.69068/1--dc23

LC record available at https://lccn.loc.gov/2019008589

British Library Cataloguing-in-Publication Data

A catalogue record for this book is available from the British Library.

For any available supplementary material, please visit
https://www.worldscientific.com/worldscibooks/10.1142/11225#t=suppl

Desk Editors: Herbert Moses/Shreya Gopi

Typeset by Stallion Press
Email: enquiries@stallionpress.com

Foreword

One hundred years ago, a series of reports transformed the education of health professionals. Starting with the *Flexner Report* in 1910, these reports sparked an enormous burst of creative energy that harnessed the power of science to revamp and improve higher education in the health field. Over 100 years later, with the publication of this book, the spirit of the original Flexner Report remains as relevant as ever.

Building on this rich legacy, a global independent initiative — the Commission on the Education of Health Professionals for the 21st Century — was launched in January 2010. It provided and reviewed the landscape of professional health education, identified gaps and opportunities, and made recommendations for a new generation of research and reforms. I had the privilege of being the Co-Chair of this initiative with Lincoln Chen, and to work with 20 leaders from diverse disciplinary backgrounds, institutional affiliations, and regions of the world. The Commission's work was published as a special Report by *The Lancet* on health education — "Health Professionals for a New Century: Transforming Education for Health Systems in an Interdependent World."

Notable among the new generation of research that followed publication of *The Lancet* report is this book on *Financing the Education of Health Workers* by World Scientific. It is particularly inspirational in its economic approach to analyzing our global challenges in addressing both the health education and human resource challenges of the 21st Century and associated health care reforms.

The book takes a systems approach to analyzing the entire health and education enterprise, rather than focusing on single institutions. This is similar to the approach we took for the earlier report published by *The Lancet*. Many illustrious educational leaders from diverse countries worked diligently and contributed to the research behind this book over the past 10 years, leading to a vision and recommended action plans for the new century and beyond.

We hope this book, like *The Lancet* report, will generate sustained follow-up to further refine and implement our recommendations in multiple sites around the world. Just like human generations with grandparents, parents, and children, we take valuable elements from each generation and build on their legacies. This book focuses on building reforms on evidence, and promoting both change and continuity, as we chart a new direction, based on the interdependence of nations and the power of transformative learning.

Julio Frenk
President, University of Miami
Former Secretary of Health for Mexico
Former Executive Director, WHO Geneva

Preface

The research undertaken for this volume reviews the economic underpinnings and institutional changes needed to scale up education for health workers.

The critical nature of the human resources in health (HRH) crisis has been brought to the forefront of the health debate in the last few years. According to World Health Organization (WHO) needs-based estimates, an additional 1.5 million health workers are required to meet basic health care needs in Africa, at a cost of $2.6 billion a year in training (WHO, 2008). Demand-based estimates indicate a lower but still acute shortage of 800,000 health care workers in 31 African countries by 2015 (Scheffler, 2008). The high cost of expanding the current workforce is related not only to accommodating and retaining the labor force in the current working environment but also to expanding its productivity.

For the past three decades, internal and external investments in developing countries' educational systems have been targeted to the primary and secondary levels of the education sector. As a result, the number of qualified secondary school graduates has increased, leading to a potentially larger pool of higher education students. As many economies continue to grow, new opportunities arise to harness potential gains in human resource development, including scaling up the production of much needed health workers. A way to accomplish this more rapidly is to leverage both public and private health worker production systems simultaneously.

The target audience of the volume is expected to include, policy makers, leaders of health education organizations, private sector investors, donors, and general audience. The volume aspires to move these actors toward concrete policy actions and investment decisions that will further enable the existing public and private sectors to expand the resources available to high-quality private institutions to help address the human resources in health crisis.

Building on Past Reviews

Commission on Health Education
Richard's Articles
Scaling Up Saving Lives: GHWA
World Bank Pre-Investment Studies and Other Work
Tertiary Education and Economic Growth: The World Bank

Roadmap

The remaining part of the preface provides a roadmap for the volume, summarizing some of the key findings from each chapter.

The chapters in this volume provide a broad overview of the global and regional human resources and health education crisis today. The specific challenges in sub-Saharan Africa are highlighted. And links are made with the broader higher education agenda.

Chapter 1. Transformative Learning in Health Education for a New Century by Julio Frenk, Lincoln C. Chen, and Catherine Michaud. A century after the landmark Flexner Report of 1910, a Commission on Education of Health Professionals for the twenty-first century was launched in January 2010 to landscape the field, identify current gaps and opportunities with a focus on quality of health education and its relevance in the current health context, and offer recommendations for health education reform.

The Global Commission on the Education of Health Professionals for the twenty-first century embraced the mission of advancing health, both individual and population-based, through landscaping instructional and institutional innovations in professional education to prepare the next generation for addressing frontier health challenges of the current century. The commissioners, professional leaders from diverse countries developed a shared approach to postsecondary education beyond the confines of national boundaries. Their report presents the first-ever global study of health professional education.

It purposefully encompassed multiple health professions — focusing on medicine, nursing-midwifery, and public health while recognizing the importance of dentistry, pharmacy, and other disciplines — and moving beyond silos to expand space for professional collaboration. And the commission adopted an inclusive approach to both the public and private sectors. A new generation of educational reforms for the twenty-first century should be informed by the increasing interdependence that characterizes the health arena — just as reforms a century ago were propelled by the discovery of the germ theory with the emergence of modern medical sciences.

This chapter summarizes the commission's findings and its views of the future of medical education. It sets the scene for the rest of the volume.

***Chapter 2. Setting the Stage for Scaling Up Health Education* by Hortenzia Beciu and Paul Jacob Robyn.** This chapter presents a synopsis of successes achieved by countries making higher education the gold standard for achieving economic growth and prosperity among their citizens. The higher education policies across the globe emphasized the need for strong leadership and good governance, significant investments, public–private partnerships, and industry cooperation to achieve the stated goals. Higher enrollment rates for both undergraduate and post-graduate education, lower drop-out rates, increased number of publications in peer-reviewed journals, and increased number of university patents per student population were among the indicators to gauge the success of the education reforms.

Important investments were made recently by governments and international partners to increase access to education in low and middle-income countries, over the past several decades. Apart from achieving access in universal primary education, the concerted efforts were also meant to specifically address gender imbalances in school enrollment and to increase the completion rate among students especially at the primary and secondary levels. The results are promising. The World Bank 2020 Education Strategy citing UNESCO sources, highlights some of the achievements made: (1) the increase in net enrollment in primary education from around 60 percent in 1999 to 80 percent in 2008 with completion rates above 60 percent in low-income countries; (2) the increase in gross secondary school enrollment for low-income countries from slightly below 60 percent to nearly 70 percent; and (3) increase girls enrollment and graduation with notable positive changes among Middle East and North African countries.

The increased enrollment and completion at the primary level, lead to an increase in the number of secondary school graduates, expanding the pool of potential higher education students as well. Globally, in 2009, over 165 million students participated in higher education, which is a five-fold increase since 1970 and a three-fold increase since 1980. Sub-Sahara Africa (SSA) had the highest average annual growth rate in tertiary education, 8.4 percent for the past four decades, but its average gross enrollment ratio estimated for 2014 was just 9 percent. This ranks very low in comparison with other regions averages: i.e. fragile and conflict affected situations states (11 percent), South Asia (21 percent), Middle East and North Africa (38 percent), Latin American and Caribbean (45 percent), East Asia and Pacific (39 percent), Europe, and Central Asia (65 percent).

Most of the time demand for higher education exceeds the available entrance slots. Medical education makes no exception. In the US, the data from the Association of American Medical Colleges, 2016–2017 reveals that only 26 percent of the applications were matriculated in the first year of study. A study conducted by Beciu *et al.* in Ghana in 2008–2009, revealed that on average there were 20 times more applicants for one slot than the available positions in the medical schools at that time.

The chapter summarizes lessons learned from success stories about making higher education a worthwhile investment, with a high rate of financial return. The increase demand for higher education can relate to: (1) increased student access to finance; (2) local labor market incentives; (3) regionalization and globalization of the labor markets and ease of labor movement; (4) globalization of the tertiary education; (5) individual curiosity and interest. The supply may be limited by: (1) the current schools capacity and lack of resources to scale-up; (2) regulations of the profession and upstream interests; (3) students access to finance; etc. Many of these topics will be discussed in greater detail in the following chapters.

***Chapter 3. Needs-Based Workforce Analysis for Investing in Health Education* by Daniel R. Arnold and Richard M. Scheffler.** The United Nations' Sustainable Development Goals (SDGs) set an ambitious agenda for achieving better global health by 2030. The agenda includes reducing global maternal and infant mortality, ending epidemics such as AIDS, tuberculosis, and malaria, and achieving universal health coverage. Reaching these goals will require well-functioning health systems.

As health systems are highly labor intensive, the availability and performance of health workers will have a significant impact on whether these goals are achieved. Given the substantial time and resources needed to educate and develop skilled health workers, forecasts of future health worker needed are necessary to enable countries to plan appropriately today.

This chapter explains the methods used for conducting such analyses, includes examples of how these methods have been applied recently, and provides an exercise that allows readers to test their grasp of the material covered. While the methods are explained in the context of global needs-based forecasts, the methods can easily be applied to more local levels (e.g. provinces within countries) assuming data is available.

This chapter also discusses some of the hurdles that may be faced when attempting to implement standards for educating and developing health workers. Countries often face economic and fiscal constraints both in terms of paying the cost of labor and in terms of investing in and paying for the health education system. As such, a more iterative process to labor markets and education institutions may be necessary where countries first set standards based on what is affordable rather than desirable.

***Chapter 4. Bridging the Global Gap in Health Manpower* by Brent D. Fulton, Richard M. Scheffler, Agnés Soucat, Marko Vujicic, and Erica Yoonkyung Auh.** This chapter summarizes the existent literature on unbalances in supply and demand of health workers across the globe, trends in migration of health workers, the overall impact of current shortages, and future perspectives.

The global human resources shortage sets the stage for the targets that health education institutions have to match in terms of numbers, skills, and distribution of health workers globally. It also highlights the interdependence among countries. Scaling up the capacity for educating health workers will be an endless and unaffordable task if 60 percent of those trained in Africa and other low-income regions end up working in Europe and North America. Health education strategies therefore have to be coupled with a better approach to the labor market for health workers globally.

Continuing the story from Chapter 3 on using a needs-based approach to address shortages and skill-mix imbalances of the health workforce in low-income countries, this chapter looks at possible policy interventions. Task shifting is one such approach in addition to scaling up education of skilled health workers that has become popular not just in low-income countries but is also extensively used in the USA today. Task shifting defined as delegating tasks to existing or new cadres with either less training or narrowly tailored training, is a potential strategy to address these challenges in low-income countries.

Countries having fewer than 2.28 doctors, nurses, and midwives per 1,000 population were, on average, unable to achieve an 80 percent coverage rate for deliveries by a skilled birth attendant, according to estimates by The World Health Organization published in its *World Health Report 2006*. Fifty-seven countries fall short of that threshold, resulting in a needs-based shortage of 4.3 million health workers, including 2.4 million doctors, nurses, and midwives. In addition to the workforce shortage, the report emphasizes three other workforce challenges: skill-mix imbalances, urban–rural distribution imbalances, and poor working conditions, including compensation.

The primary objective of task shifting is to increase productive efficiency, that is, to increase the number of health care services provided at a given quality and cost, or, alternatively, to provide the same level of health care services at a given quality at a lower cost. Another objective of task shifting is to reduce the time needed to scale up the health workforce, because the cadres performing the shifted tasks require less training.

The authors use an economics perspective to examine the strength of the evidence on task shifting, to identify gaps in the evidence, and to propose a research agenda. The chapter is organized as follows: the introductory section, "Economic Framework to Evaluate Skill Mix", continues by describing an economic-based conceptual framework to analyze skill-mix policies. The next section, "Methods and Data", describes the methods and data used to select studies to include in the literature review. Then, the section "Results" summarizes the studies' results. Finally, "Discussions" section proposes a research agenda. Appendix A to this chapter summarizes the important elements of each study reviewed in this chapter.

***Chapter 5. Better Governance and Leadership in Health Education* by Peter Walker and Hortenzia Beciu.** This chapter stresses the importance of good governance practices of higher education institutions and systems within the complex milieu of national and international markets that more and more respond to current and potential consumers of their services or products. The chapter summarizes the evolution of higher education from the governance perspective and presents conceptual frameworks used within the past several decades in the quest to define the right governance attributes that will lead to expected performance of systems and organizations. UK, US, and France systems are summarized as a preamble of a more detailed discussion about the evolution of tertiary education in sub-Sahara Africa and what can be done to support its development. Specific references are made to medical and allied health schools and or institutions all the way in this chapter.

The revitalization of governance systems for higher educational institutions is essential in the present time. The very fast pace in which technology provides data, information and analysis, already changed the way we think and apply modern tools and techniques in the learning process. The technology not only changed the access to learning and education, these days the information is delivered and received from almost any corner of the world, but it also brought up an informed and demanding consumer. Communities and or individuals have a voice in what they think and what they demand of both public and private education entities. As the result, more and more people like to tailor their experiences with almost everything including their education.

In medical field, the shift in mindset and application tools, though still its early stages will be important. The practices are moving from a full bed side direct patient contact, as main learning path to more diverse options including virtual learning (i.e. simulation), virtual libraries, and the use of interactive software as learning and maintenance tools. This is not a trivial change in learning and in the years to come technology will continue to advance and play potentially even a higher role in medical education.

Chapter 6. Fiscal Constraints to Investing in Health Education by **Alexander S. Preker, Marko Vujicic, Yohana Dukhan, Caroline Ly, Hortenzia Beciu, Peter Nicolas Materu, and Khama Rogo.** All countries face fiscal constraints in scaling up the education of health workers. The economics of scaling up education for health workers are reviewed in this chapter in the context of the Africa region. The resources likely to be available to the health and education sectors by 2015 are assessed using different assumptions about political commitment to economic growth, spending on health care, and institutional development. The number of additional staff that countries could hire under the different resource envelope scenarios, and the cost of scaling up health worker education in terms of recurrent and capital costs are estimated, country-by-country. Regional estimates are based on the sum of this detailed country-level analysis. Scaling up health education has significant implications for both the health and the education sectors. The cost of employing new staff falls on the health sector while the cost of educating health workers falls mainly on the education sector.

The research presented in this chapter was carried out under the auspices of the Task Force on Scaling up Health Education (TFSHE), established in 2006 under the Global Health Workforce Alliance (GHWA). The data and analysis was based on time series available at the time of the work undertaking for the Task Force on Scaling up Health Education (TFSHE). Although the country rankings and values would be different today, the overall story of the fiscal challenge of financing a significant scaling up of human resources and training in Africa remains a major constraint in achieving heath goals in the Africa region, as it does elsewhere in the world.

The review used a combination of cross-sectional and longitudinal analysis to explore the various dimensions of the economics of scaling up health education in the Africa region. Several economic models were built and tested based on available data on the countries' macroeconomic contexts, sources of financing for the health sector, health expenditure trends, cost of both health education and higher education, and evidence on investment cost of health and higher education today.

Drilling down to the regional level, this chapter reviews the economics of scaling up education for health workers in the context of sub-Saharan Africa. It provides an assessment of the resource envelope likely to be available to the health and education sectors by 2015 under different assumptions about economic growth, political commitment to spending on health care, and institutional development; an estimate of the number of additional staff that countries could hire under the different resource–envelope scenarios; and an estimate of the costs of scaling up the education of health workers in terms of recurrent and capital costs.

***Chapter 7. Investment and Financing in Health Education* by Eric L. Keuffel, Alexander S. Preker, and Caroline Ly.** This chapter looks at an often overlooked topic: investing in health education institutions and the special nature of capital finance in this area. It summarizes both public and private approaches to capital finance, including new and innovative mechanisms such as subsidized debt facilities, condition grants, and equity markets (direct placements and publicly listed stocks). The chapter provides a unique summary of regional and country-level approaches to private financing of capital investment in higher education, including health education institutions.

The critical shortage of physicians, nurses, and health workers (human resources for health, HRH) has been a central policy issue inhibiting developing countries from improving health outcomes for several decades. While substantial resources and efforts have ameliorated and addressed shortages in some contexts, the recently developed United Nations Sustainable Development Goals underscore the continued support which HRH will require to deliver many of the health outcomes anticipated by 2030.

In the past, one of the reasons for limited support of tertiary and health sector specific educational institutions received were the expected higher financial rates of social return across other competing investments for developing countries. For example, with respect to Africa over the past three decades, internal and external investments in the education systems have been targeted to the primary and secondary levels of the education sector. Historically, the focus on the lower levels of education was supported by research indicating that the social rate of financial return for investment in primary and secondary education were higher than returns anticipated from higher education. A comprehensive analysis examining 98 countries over 37 years (1960–1997) estimated socials rate of return from primary schooling at 18.9 percent and tertiary education at 10.8 percent.

However, there is an increasing recognition that the methodologies for evaluating rates of return likely did not capture the full benefit of tertiary education (as usually just wage effects for the individual were evaluated as the benefit) and that, as "knowledge workers" become more important in developing the institutional capacity of countries, the benefits to a strong tertiary education system will likely grow even larger. These are the investment and financing themes that are explored in this chapter.

***Chapter 8. Role of Private Sector in Financing Health Education* by Eric L. Keuffel and Alexander S. Preker.** This chapter reviews the various ways countries can finance higher education and institutions that train health workers, stressing both public and private approaches. In many countries, enrollment in primary and secondary education is often treated as a basic right, but tertiary education is usually voluntary and dependent on some student financial contribution. However, because tertiary education is often seen as a basis for both individual prosperity and a country's competitive edge in the global marketplace, both households and governments are giving higher priority to such education.

The public sector has typically played an extensive role in health personnel training through its provision of institutional support for a wide variety of programs, colleges, and universities in developing countries.

In their current form across numerous countries, the sole use of public finance cannot keep pace with the growing demand for higher education and the scale up required of health workforce to meet health outcome goals, particularly in Africa and Asia. Augmentation of public finance of health institutions with innovative private sector sources, novel public finance approaches, and unique mechanisms of finance for health institutions may help bridge the gap between the demand for health workers in developing countries and the current capacity of the state to fund the production of human capital for health.

The chapter highlights key issues related to private or public sector finance for tertiary health education institutions, examines potential novel sources of funding from various sectors (public, private for-profit, private not-for-profit) and evaluates the costs, benefits, and feasibility of these potential financing solutions. While the lessons in this chapter are broadly relevant across many developing country locales, we will focus particular attention in Africa as the dearth of health workers and resources are particularly acute there. Our analyses are relevant for researchers, students' private sector investors, policy makers, and donors. We aspire to move these actors toward concrete actions to adopt useful financial practices and innovative mechanisms from the public and private sectors in order to address the human resources in health crisis.

Chapter 9. Public–Private Partnerships in Financing Health Education by **Taara Chandani, and Ilana Ron Levey.** Private sector participation in tertiary medical education is gaining prominence in developing countries as a complement to public sector provision and a way to accelerate the production of health workers. Private actors are increasingly entering the health education marketplace, an area that has traditionally fallen under the purview of governments. The explicit partnerships between the public and private sectors that are emerging carry enormous potential to scale up the health workforce, improve efficiencies and quality, and spur innovation.

The term "public–private partnerships" (PPP) carries a range of interpretations according to geographic context, and as donors, governments, and the private sector commonly adopt different definitions. Fundamentally, PPPs are founded on the premise that governments can meet — and potentially enhance — their policy objectives by using service delivery models that go beyond the traditional publicly financed and delivered ones. The World Bank describes a PPP as a partnership between the public and private sector for the purpose of delivering a project or a service that may come in a variety of different legal or contractual forms. Adding more specificity, this chapter defines a PPP as a formal collaboration between government at any level (federal, state, district, city) and the private sector (commercial or non-profit actors) to jointly regulate, finance, or implement the delivery of medical education. While the scope and formality of PPPs may differ substantially in practice, the literature identifies certain common elements that frame these partnerships: involve public and private sectors; entail a formal arrangement with contractual basis; involve sharing of risks and rewards; maintain a focus on outcomes; and recognize complementary role of public and private sectors.

The chapter focuses on PPPs in the tertiary medical education sector. It considers the full range of postsecondary certification and degree programs for medicine, public health, midwifery, nursing, pharmacy, and allied health professions. Institutions that offer these programs are diverse in terms of ownership (public, private, or hybrid), formality, and teaching philosophy, among other factors. For instance, public training institutions may experience varying degrees of autonomy from central ministries, and in some cases, are privately managed. Private institutions may be for-profit or not-for-profit in their operating status, or aligned with faith-based movements (Frenk *et al.*, 2010, p. 22). Beyond these core educational establishments, other actors involved in the supply of medical education include regulatory bodies, professional councils, associations, and research organizations.

***Chapter 10. The Market for Health Education* by Howard Tuckman, Alexander S. Preker, and Eric L. Keuffel.** Although there is a paucity of date on the private sector and markets in health education especially in lower income settings, market exists whenever buyers and sellers come together to engage in trade. Numerous theoretical and empirical studies contribute to the way in which researchers and practitioners define the boundaries for a market, and explore how homogeneous a market will be.

Indeed, there are many different ways to do business within the confines of a market (high-quality versus low-cost product), and this can create disagreements among those who examine the market for health education services. Key to marketplace analysis is the realization that people trade only when it is to their benefit to do so, that trades give rise to valuable information on how both price and quantity are decided by sellers and responded to, and that markets exist at many levels (e.g. local, regional), that the market for labor interacts with the market for goods and services, and that differences among markets in price and quantity will equalize when markets are allowed to operate.

The chapter reviews and analysis understanding of market structure and potential new forms of private organizations that may bolster the capacity to produce health workers, especially in low-income contexts. With some justification, private entrants in health education markets are now generally (but not exclusively) viewed as second-rate institutions aiming to enter high-profit areas (in the case of for-profits) for a "quick return" as a "credentialing shop". But new entrants with different business models are not restricted to competing as low-quality, small-scale entrants.

While novel forms of private education are rapidly emerging in the developed world market for higher education (including some health professions such as nursing or public health), there is proportionally less activity in developing countries and only a share of that naturally occurs in health education markets. The potential of some models to reduce cost and increase output of health workers exists, although the level of technology adoption within country markets (say, Internet access) may have important infrastructure effects on the viability and quality of the several modes for educating health workers. Nevertheless, government and institution decisions will play a crucial role in the extent of development of these models. Based on this initial literature review, recommendations are proposed in four areas: regulation, inputs, models, and finance.

About the Editors

Hortenzia Beciu is the Director for the Middle East and Africa (MEA) region at Johns Hopkins Medicine International. In this capacity, she provides oversight in partnership management, market analysis and business development in MEA. Before joining JHI, she worked for the World Bank Group with foreign governments, bilateral and multilateral development partners, international not-for-profit organizations, and various health industry groups and associations, creating bridges and projects between these stakeholders. While working for the World Bank, she developed a series of works on scaling up education for health workers in middle- and low-income countries. Her notable publications include *The Labor Market for Health Workers in Africa: A New Look at the Crisis* and *Toward Interventions in Human Resources for Health in Ghana: Evidence for Health Workforce Planning and Results*. Hortenzia Beciu holds a master's degree in Public Health, Global Health from The George Washington University, and a medical degree from the University of Medicine and Pharmacy, Carol Davila.

Eric L. Keuffel is a Specialist in health finance and policy with over 20 years of experience in industry, policy and academic roles in health economics, finance and operations. Currently, he serves as the Founder and Principal at the Health Finance and Access Initiative. An expert on international health systems and pharmaceutical policy, he has worked as an Assistant Professor and Instructor at both the Wharton School (University of Pennsylvania) and the Fox School of Business (Temple University). He has publications in both health policy and health economic journals/books and has presented his research at numerous international and domestic conferences. He also served as a Consultant to the World Bank/IFC and has extensive commercial consulting experience advising healthcare industry, government and institutional clients on strategy, policy, and economic issues. He has taught health finance/economics, health policy, and international health systems at graduate and undergraduate levels. His recent consulting engagements include work for multinational pharmaceutical clients, USAID, the World Bank, the World Health Organization (WHO), foundations, and select non-governmental organizations. Prior funding sources include the US National Institutes of Health (NIH) and the National Bureau of Economic Research (NBER). Erick Keuffel earned his bachelor's degree in economics from Princeton University (*Magna cum Laude*), his Master in Public Health (MPH) from the Johns Hopkins University Bloomberg School of Public Health and his doctorate in Applied Health Economics and Managerial Science from the Wharton School (University of Pennsylvania).

Alexander S. Preker is a globally recognized expert on the economics of investing and financing health systems, health care policy, governance and health care reform. He has been an advisor to Ministers of Health and senior policy makers throughout the world on capital investment in the health sector, health financing, health insurance, public–private partnerships, and the political process of health care reform. And he is on the executive board of several private health care companies. He is a Commissioner with the Global Commission on Pollution, Health and Development. He is an honorary member of the International Hospital Federation, a member of the Board of the USA Health Care Alliance and several other organizations that deal with health policy and health reform. He is an Adjunct Associate Professor for Health Care Management at the Mailman School of Public Health at Columbia University in New York. He is an Adjunct Associate Professor of Public Policy at New York University's Robert F. Wagner Graduate School of Public Policy and he is an Executive Scholar at the Icahn School of Medicine at Mount Sinai in New York. He is a prolific writer and has published extensively, having authored and co-authored over 20 books, many scientific articles and has been the primary author of a wide range of institutional reports and policy briefs. While at the World Bank, he was a member of the Editorial Board for the World Bank's External Operations Publication Department and Editor-in-Chief of its health care publications. Currently, he is the Editor-in-Chief for the *Health Investment & Financing* Series of World Scientific and Chair of the Editorial Board for the *World Hospitals and Health Services Journal* of the International Hospital Federation. Alexander Preker holds a PhD in Economics from the London School of Economics and Political Science, a Fellowship in Medicine from University College London, a Diploma in Medical Law and Ethics from King's College London, and an MD from University of British Columbia.

About the Contributors

Daniel R. Arnold is the Research Director of the Nicholas C. Petris Center on Health Care Markets and Consumer Welfare, School of Public Health, University of California, Berkeley. His areas of research include global health workforce, healthcare market concentration, the Affordable Care Act marketplaces, and mental health economics. He has published extensively in academic journals including *Health Affairs*, *Healthcare*, and *Health Economics*, *Policy and Law*. Daniel Arnold holds a PhD in Economics from the University of California, Santa Barbara.

Taara Chandani is an independent Consultant with over 15 years of experience in health sector financing and capacity building. She has worked extensively in brokering public–private partnerships, offering advisory services to government and health care enterprises and building organizational capacity. She has led numerous publications and best practice guidelines for USAID, CGAP, and other donors on improving healthcare systems and access to quality health services. She has worked in and managed programs across Asia and sub-Saharan Africa with development agencies including ACCESS Health International, Banyan Global, and UNDP. Taara Chandani holds a master's degree in Public Administration from Columbia University, New York, and a bachelor's degree from Oberlin College, Ohio. She is currently based in India.

Lincoln C. Chen is the President of the China Medical Board (CMB). After celebrating its 100th anniversary in 2014, the CMB was endowed by John D. Rockefeller as an independent American foundation dedicated to advancing health in China and neighboring Asian countries in an interdependent world. CMB's strategic philanthropy seeks to spark innovation and strengthen partnerships in building university capacity in health policy sciences, health professional education, and global health. He was the Taro Takemi Professor of International Health at the Harvard School of Public Health, Director of the University-wide Harvard Center for Population and Development Studies, and the founding Director of the Harvard Global Equity Initiative. He is currently a member of the HSPH Visiting Committee and Co-Chair of the Harvard FXB Center on Health and Human Rights. He served as the Executive Vice President of the Rockefeller Foundation and Representative of the Ford Foundation in India and Bangladesh. He also served as the Special Envoy of the WHO Director General on Human Resources for Health, founding board Chair of the Global Health Workforce Alliance, and founding member of the Advisory Board to the UN Secretary General of the United Nations Fund for International Partnerships. He currently chairs the Board of Trustees of BRAC USA, an affiliate of the world's largest anti-poverty NGO. He is also a board member of the Institute of Health Metrics and Evaluation (University of Washington), and the Public Health Foundation of India. He is a member of the National Academy of Medicine, the American Academy of Arts and Sciences, and the Council of Foreign Relations. He graduated from Princeton University, Harvard Medical School, and the Johns Hopkins School of Hygiene and Public Health. Lincoln Chen did his internship and residency in internal medicine at the Massachusetts General Hospital.

Yohana Dukhan is a Senior Health Specialist with the World Bank. Prior to joining The Bank, she was a Senior Economist with Management Sciences for Health (MSH) and a Senior Development Officer at the African Development Bank. Prior to that, she consulted for several international organizations and NGOs, such as the World Bank, the International Finance Corporation, the World Health Organization, Medecins du Monde, on health financing and social protection studies.

She has conducted analyses of costing, resource tracking and efficiency, financial planning, cost effectiveness, performance-based financing and health insurance, including costing of health center interventions and development of a costing tool for laboratory services to inform the design of the National Health Insurance benefit package in Uganda; costing of community health interventions for investment purposes in Madagascar and South Sudan; costing of primary health services in the Sahel region (Burkina-Faso, Mali and Niger) aiming to reduce financial barriers to health care access; and costing of the free health care policy in Sierra Leone. Yohana Dukhan holds a PhD in Economics from the University of Auvergne CERDI and a master's degree in Economic Policies and Industrial Economics from the University of Montpellier.

Julio Frenk is the President of the University of Miami since August 2015. He also holds academic appointments as Professor of Public Health Sciences at the Leonard M. Miller School of Medicine, as Professor of Health Sector Management and Policy at the Miami Business School, and as Professor of Sociology at the College of Arts and Sciences. Prior to joining the University of Miami, he served for nearly 7 years as the Dean of the Harvard T. H. Chan School of Public Health and the T & G Angelopoulos Professor of Public Health and International Development, a joint appointment with the Harvard Kennedy School of Government. He was the Minister of Health of Mexico from 2000 to 2006. There he pursued an ambitious agenda to reform the nation's health system and introduced a program of comprehensive universal coverage, known as Seguro Popular, which expanded access to health care for more than 55 million previously uninsured persons. He was the founding Director General of the National Institute of Public Health in Mexico, one of the leading institutions of its kind in the developing world. He also served as the Executive Director in charge of Evidence and Information for Policy at the World Health Organization and as senior fellow in the global health program of the Bill & Melinda Gates Foundation, among other leadership positions. His scholarly production, which includes over 175 articles in academic journals, as well as many books and book chapters, has been cited over 22,000 times. In addition, he has written three best-selling novels for youngsters explaining the functions of the human body. He is a member of the American Academy of Arts and Sciences, the US National Academy of Medicine, the National Academy of Medicine of Mexico, and El Colegio Nacional. Julio Frenk holds a medical degree from the National University of Mexico, as well as a master's degree in Public Health and a joint PhD in Medical Care Organization and in Sociology from the University of Michigan. He has received honorary degrees from 10 universities.

Brent D. Fulton is an Assistant Adjunct Professor of Health Economics and Policy and the Associate Director of the Nicholas C. Petris Center on Health Care Markets and Consumer Welfare, School of Public Health, University of California, Berkeley. His research areas include the health workforce, healthcare market concentration, health insurance markets, accountable care organizations and precision medicine. Brent Fulton holds a doctorate in public policy analysis from Pardee RAND Graduate School and an MBA in Strategy and Finance from the Anderson School at University of California, Los Angeles.

Arthur M. Hauptman is an independent Public Policy Consultant specializing in higher education finance issues since 1981. He has consulted and written extensively on student financial aid, fee-setting policies, and the public funding of higher education in countries around the world. A consistent theme of his work is that public policies in higher education are more effective when these three key elements of financing are linked systematically. In the US, he has consulted with many federal and state agencies as well as higher education associations and institutions. He has helped develop the rationale for a number of federal programs including direct loans, income contingent loans, and tuition tax credits. For states, he has argued for developing counter-cyclical policies, tying public sector tuition levels to general income growth, and creating funding formulas that pay institutions based on their performance and efficiency. Internationally, he has consulted with governments or funding bodies in more than two dozen industrialized and developing countries to develop financing strategies for tertiary education. Arthur Hauptman holds a BA in Economics from Swarthmore College and an MBA from Stanford University.

Ilana Ron Levey is a Consulting Director at Gallup, the global analytics and research firm. At Gallup, Ilana leads complex public sector research and consulting engagements while leading a team of social scientists in the United States and Europe. Prior to joining Gallup, Ilana served as the Co-Director of the qualitative methods center for Abt Associates and specialized in research and program evaluation about the role of the private health sector in the developing world. She has published more than 30 major research reports, book chapters and articles, including articles in Health Policy and Planning and for the World Bank. She is a liaison to the Qual360 North America annual conference for qualitative consumer insights professionals that is co-hosted by Gallup. She has deep expertise in sub-Saharan Africa, and worked in Johannesburg, South Africa for 4 years. She has led research and consulting engagements in the United States, South Africa, Namibia, India, Botswana, Ghana, the Philippines, Nigeria, Malawi, Ethiopia, Swaziland, Zambia, Tanzania, and Uganda. Ilana Levey holds degrees in research methods and political science from McGill University and the London School of Economics.

Caroline Ly is a Health Economist in USAID's Bureau of Global Health. She has over a decade of experience working on health financing issues in Africa, the Middle East, and Asia. This includes work on domestic resource mobilization for health and HIV/AIDS through USAID's Sustainable Financing Initiative. Her notable publications include "The Economic Transition of Health in Africa: A Call for Progressive Pragmatism to Shape the Future of Health Financing" (*Health Systems and Reform*, Volume 3, 2017), "Big-Bang Reforms in Anglophone Africa" (*Scaling Up Affordable Health Insurance*, World Bank, 2013), "Financing Health Care Investments in Developing Countries: The Story of Debt and Equity" (*SSRN Electronic Journal*, 2007). Caroline Ly holds a BA from the University of Chicago, an MA from Johns Hopkins University, and a PhD from the University of Pennyslvania.

Peter Nicolas Materu is the Director of Education and Learning at The MasterCard Foundation. He is in charge of strategy development, program management, new innovations, transformative leadership, partner and counterpart dialogue and engagement, and team leadership. Previously, he was a Sector Manager and Practice Manger with the World Bank, Lead Education Specialist and Program Leader for higher education in the Africa Region, Cluster Leader for 16 countries in West Africa and Task Team Leader of several analytical and lending operations. Before joining the World Bank, he served as the Director for graduate studies and also as Dean of the College of Engineering and Technology at the University of Dar es Salaam, Tanzania. From 1991 to 1997, he was a Professor and Dean of the Faculty of Engineering at University of Dar es Salaam Computing Centre. Peter Materu holds a PhD in Engineering and master's degree in education and engineering. He has an impressive publication record in education and engineering, many with the World Bank.

Catherine Michaud worked in the past as a Senior Research Scientist at the Harvard School of Public Health and the China Medical Board. She has undertaken research over the past 20 years in the following focus areas: Global Burden of Disease, tracking Resource Flows for Health and Health Research, and Health Professional Education. She was the Research Coordinator of *The Lancet* report "Health Professionals for a New Century: Transforming Education to Strengthen Health Systems in an Interdependent World" and the Commission Report Follow-up. She is currently retired. Catherine Michaud holds a medical degree from the University of Geneva Medical School and a master's degree in Public Health from the Harvard School of Public Health.

Paul Jacob Robyn is a Senior Health Specialist at the World Bank, Health Nutrition and Population Division, focusing primarily on operations and impact evaluations for results-based financing interventions in West and Central Africa. He currently manages the World Bank health portfolios for Cameroon and Central African Republic, and is the Principal Investigator for several performance-based financing impact evaluations in the West and Central Africa region. Prior to joining the Bank, Jake coordinated a research program for community-based health insurance schemes in Burkina Faso, and was a US Peace Corps volunteer in Burkina Faso and Malawi. He conducted assessments and impact studies in the field of health systems and public health interventions conducted around the globe. Among these assessments are in-depth analyses spanning from measuring the impact of performance-based financing, such as "Looking into the Performance-Based Financing Black Box: Evidence from an Impact Evaluation in the Health Sector in Cameroon" and "Encouraging Service Delivery to the Poor: Does Money Talk When Health Workers Are Pro-Poor?", to measuring the maternal and child health interventions' effectiveness, such as "Measuring Effective Coverage of Curative Child Health Services in Rural Burkina Faso: A Cross-Sectional Study". Jake Robyn holds a PhD in Public Health, Health Systems Research from University of Heidelberg and Masters of Science in Public Health from Harvard School of Public Health.

Khama Rogo is a Lead Health Sector Specialist with the World Bank and Head of the World Bank Group's USA\$1 billion Health in Africa Initiative (HIA). The HIA initiative is a program that provides capital for the private sector and advice to governments in dealing with the private sector. Its objectives are to "catalyse sustained improvements in access to quality health-related goods and services in Africa and financial protection against the impoverishing effects of illness with an emphasis on the under-served." He is also a Professor in Obstetrics and Gynecology and a prominent advocate and global authority on reproductive health issues. He is a Visiting Professor at several universities and author of over 100 papers and book chapters. He served on the Gender Advisory Panel of WHO, the Advisory Committee of the David and Lucile Packard Foundation, and the board of the Center for African Family Studies. He is currently on the board of INTRAHEALTH, among other responsibilities. Khama Rogo holds a medical degree in obstetrics and gynecology, and an MD and PhD in Gynecologic Oncology from Sweden.

Jamil Salmi is a global Tertiary Education Expert providing policy advice to governments, universities, professional associations, multilateral development banks, and bilateral cooperation agencies. Until January 2012, he was the World Bank's Tertiary Education Coordinator. In the past 25 years, he has provided advice on tertiary education development, financing reforms, and strategic planning to governments and university leaders in about 100 countries all over the world. He is the Emeritus Professor of higher education policy at Diego Portales University in Chile and

Research Fellow at Boston College's Center for Higher Education. His 2009 book addresses the *Challenge of Establishing World-Class Universities*. His 2011 book, co-edited with Professor Phil Altbach, was entitled *The Road to Academic Excellence: The Making of World-Class Research Universities*. His latest book, *Tertiary Education and the Sustainable Development Goals* was published in August 2017. Jamil Salmi holds a master's degree in Public and International Affairs from the University of Pittsburgh and a PhD in Development Studies from the University of Sussex.

Richard M. Scheffler is a Distinguished Professor of Health Economics and Public Policy at the School of Public Health and the Goldman School of Public Policy at the University of California, Berkeley. He is also the Chair Emeritus in Healthcare Markets and Consumer Welfare endowed by the Office of the Attorney General for the State of California in 1999. In addition to directing the Petris Center, he is also the Director of the Global Center for Health Economics and Policy Research. He has been a Visiting Professor at the London School of Economics, Charles University in Prague, at the Department of Economics at the University of Pompeu Fabra in Barcelona and at Carlos III University of Madrid, Spain. He has been a Visiting Scholar at the World Bank, the Rockefeller Foundation in Bellagio, and the Institute of Medicine at the National Academy of Sciences and a Consultant for the World Bank, the WHO, and the OECD. He has been a Fulbright Scholar at Pontifica Universidad Catolica de Chile in Santiago, Chile, and at Charles University, Prague, Czech Republic. He was awarded the Chair of Excellence Award at the Carlos III University of Madrid in 2013. In 2015, he was awarded the Gold Medal for Charles University in Prague for his longstanding and continued support of international scientific and educational collaboration. In 2018, he was awarded the Berkeley Citation, among the highest honors the campus bestows on its community presented on behalf of the Chancellor to individuals whose contributions to UC Berkeley go beyond the call of duty and whose achievements exceed the standards of excellence in their fields. Richard Scheffler holds a PhD in Economics from New York University, Master of Arts in Economics from Brooklyn College, and Bachelor in Economics from Hofstra University.

Agnés Soucat is the Director for Health Systems, Governance and Financing at the WHO in Geneva. Until recently, she was the Global Leader Service Delivery and Lead Economist at the World Bank. She previously was the Director for Human Development for the African Development Bank, where she was responsible for health, education, and social protection for Africa, including 54 countries in sub-Saharan Africa and the Maghreb. She has over 25 years of experience in health and poverty reduction, covering Africa, Asia, and Europe. She was a pioneer of several innovations in health care financing including community-based financing and performance-based financing and authored seminal publications on these topics. She is also the co-author of the World Development Report 2004 "Making Services Work for Poor People" and of *The Lancet* Commission report "Global Health 2035: A World Converging within a Generation". She recently was the commissioner of the recent Lancet and Rockefeller Commission on Planetary Health. She also did extensive work on the health labor market dynamics in Africa. Agnés Soucat holds an MD and a master's degree in Nutrition from the University of Nancy in France as well as a master's degree in Public Health and a PhD in Health Economics from the Johns Hopkins University.

The late **Howard Tuckman** was the Dean of the Fordham Graduate School of Business Administration where he was the George Jean Chair and Professor of Finance and Economics. Prior to joining Fordham, he was the Dean of the Rutgers Business School for 7 years and Dean of the School of Business at Virginia Commonwealth University for 5 years. Under his leadership, Rutgers Business School dramatically rose in the national rankings, expanded into China, undertook a record-setting capital campaign, and advanced its use of innovative technology for research and instruction. A renowned and prolific economics scholar, his works include numerous co-authored books and more than 100 peer-reviewed articles on educational finance, education in developing countries, finance of government and the economies of wealth. He was inducted into the New Jersey High Tech Hall of Fame as an Outstanding Educator and also served as a Distinguished Professor of Economics at the University of Memphis where he received the University Distinguished Teaching Award as well as the University Distinguished Research Award. He received the B'nai

Brith Golden Medallion for his contributions to higher education, and a Brookings Economic Policy Fellowship and a Ford Foundation Graduate Fellowship. He served the Kennedy administration in the Think Tank Program working to develop the Medicare and Medicare health-care systems. He also served as a member of the boards of the New Jersey Center for Nonprofit Management and Leadership, the New Jersey Symphony Orchestra, the New Jersey Chamber of Commerce, the Levi Arthritis Hospital, the Small Business Development Center for New Jersey and the World Affairs Council. The late Howard Tuckman held a bachelor's degree in Industrial and Labor Relations from Cornell University and a doctoral degree in Economics from the University of Wisconsin, Madison.

Marko Vujicic currently serves as the Chief Economist and Vice President of the Health Policy Institute at the American Dental Association. Previously, he was the Senior Economist with The World Bank in Washington D.C. where he focused on health system reforms in developing countries and directed the global health workforce policy program. He was also a Health Economist with the World Health Organization in Geneva, Switzerland. Marko Vujicic holds a PhD in Economics from the University of British Columbia and a bachelor's degree in Business from McGill University in Montreal.

Peter Walker is the Professor of Medicine in the Faculty of Medicine at the University of Ottawa. He is an academic Endocrinologist with a longstanding clinical and research interest in thyroid diseases. He has served in many academic capacities at the University of Ottawa, including Chair of the Division of Endocrinology and Metabolism, Physician-in-Chief of the Department of Medicine at the Ottawa Civic Hospital and Deputy Chair of the Department of Medicine at the University of Ottawa, Assistant Dean, Policy and Planning in the Faculty of Medicine, and Dean of the Faculty of Medicine at the University of Ottawa. He chaired the Council of Faculties of Medicine of Ontario and has chaired or co-chaired a number of Province of Ontario committees and working groups on physician human resources and academic funding programs. He served as the Coordinator of the Technical Working Group for the Task Force for Scaling Up Education and Training for Health Workers of the Global

Health Workforce Alliance of the World Health Organization. He has provided expert advice to Canadian universities on development and implementation of innovative medical education programs. He served as the Chief Scientific Officer and President of the Bruyère Research Institute and was a member of a Canadian Academic of Health Sciences Expert Panel on Team Science. He has been a longstanding member of the Executive of the Board of the International Council for the Control of Iodine Deficiency Disorders, now the Iodine Global Network. Peter Walker received his MD from the University of Ottawa and his postgraduate and research training at Université Laval and the University of California at Los Angeles.

Erica Yoonkyung Auh was an Assistant Professor of Social Welfare at Ewha Womans University in Seoul, Korea. She conducted research as an NIMH postdoctoral fellow in mental health economics at the Petris Center for Health Care Markets and Consumer Welfare at UC Berkeley. Her research interest includes older adults, labor force participation, mental health, and non-profit organizations. Erica Auh holds a PhD in Social Welfare from UC Berkeley with a BA in Economics from Wellesley College.

Acknowledgments

This volume on Financing the Education of Health Workers would not have been possible without earlier research and partner support provided by the World Bank, the International Finance Corporation, the World Health Organization, the Bill and Melinda Gates Foundation, the Clinton's Global Initiative of the Clinton Foundation, the CapacityPlus Project of USAID, the Rockefeller Foundation, the Results for Development Institute, the SHOPS Plus Project of Abt. Associates, the Aga-Khan Foundation, the Aspen Institute and Jhpiego, a Johns Hopkins University Affiliate. Intellectual guidance was provided by experts at Berkeley (University of California), the Fox School of Business (Temple University), and the Wharton School (University of Pennsylvania).

The authors are also grateful to the Dutch and Norwegian Dutch Governments that provided several small research grants to local country experts that were instrumental in them sharing their knowledge and experience with the authors and various research teams.

Special recognition is given to several individuals who over the years have provided leadership at the global level in the area of strengthening human resources in the health sector and the private sector. This includes Lincoln Chen, David De Ferranti, Tim Evans, Amanda Folsom, Julio Frenk, Cecil Fruman, the late Ralph Harbison, Ruth Kagia, Gina Lagomarsino, Khama Odera Rogo, Eric De Roodenbeke, Richard Scheffler, Agnes Soucat, and Kate Tulenko.

Recognition is also given to Sam Adjey, Samuel Gabriel Akyanu, James Antwi, Seth Ayettey, Peter Donkor, Aaron Lawson, Grace Namaganda, Vincent Oketcho, and Sonnia Jabbi who have enlighted us regarding the issues of health human resources in their countries and many other professional leaders who worked with the various research teams on issues of health human resources in their countries. A special thanks go to Dessislava Dimitrova and Marty Makinen who helped deepen understanding resources needed to scale up the production of health workers, and Nicholas Burnett, Harry Anthony Patrinos, and Jamil Salmi on the economics of education.

We would also like to thank Carmelo Cuffari for his valuable contribution in reviewing the final manuscript of the book.

A special note of thanks is provided to Katherine A. Lynch (Kassie) who over the years has provided invaluable editorial help and guidance on the publication of various documents, reports, and books.

Contents

Abbreviations and Acronyms

AIDS	Acquired Immune Deficiency Syndrome
ALOS	Average Length of Stay
ANS	Agencia Nacional de Saude Suplementar, National Agency for Private Health ("Supplementary") Insurance, Brazil
CBI	Community-Based Insurance
CGHS	Central Government Health Scheme, India
CIRC	China Insurance Regulation Commission
CIS	Clinical Information System
CMS	Council of Medical Schemes, South Africa
CVM	Contingent Valuation Method
DHS	Demographic and Health Survey
DOH	Department of Health, South Africa
DRG	Diagnosis-Related Group
EAP	East Asia and Pacific Region, World Bank
ECA	Eastern Europe and Central Asia Region, World Bank
EHHUES	Egypt Household Health Utilization and Expenditures Survey
EIMIC	Egyptian International Medical Insurance Company
EISA	Egyptian Insurance Supervisory Agency
ESIS	Employee State Insurance Scheme, India
EU	European Union
FMIS	Fund Management Information System
FONASA	Fondo Nacional de Salud, National Health Fund, Chile

GIS	Government Insurance Scheme, China
GNI	Gross National Income
GDP	Gross Domestic Product
GNP	Gross National Product
HCE	Health Care Expenditure
HIC	Highly Indebted Country
HIF	Health Insurance Fund for Africa
HMO	Health Maintenance Organization
HSRI	Health Systems Research Institute, Thailand
ILO	International Labour Organization
IRDA	Insurance Regulatory and Development Authority, India
ISAPRE	Institucione de Salud Previsional, Private Health Insurance Scheme, Chile
LCR	Latin America and Caribbean Region, World Bank
LIC	Low-Income Country
LIS	Labor Insurance Scheme, China
LSMS	Living Standard Measurement Survey
MC	Managed Care
MDG	Millennium Development Goal
MENA	Middle East and North Africa Region
MHI	Mutual Health Insurance
MOFE	Ministry of Finance and Economy, Republic of Korea
MOH	Ministry of Health
MOHP	Ministry of Health and Population, Arab Republic of Egypt
MOHW	Ministry of Health and Welfare, Republic of Korea
MOPH	Ministry of Public Health, Arab Republic of Egypt
MSA	Medical Savings Account
NCAER	National Council for Applied Economic Research, India
NCMS	New Cooperative Medical Services, China
NGO	Non-Governmental Organization
NHA	National Health Account
NHIC	National Health Insurance Corporation
NHIS	National Health Insurance Scheme, Nigeria
NHRPL	National Health Reference Price List, South Africa
NHS	National Health Service
NMC	Non-Medical Consumption

NSSO	National Sample Survey Organisation, India
OECD	Organisation for Economic Co-operation and Development
OOP	Out-Of-Pocket
OOPS	Out-Of-Pocket Spending
ORT	Organisation for Educational Resources and Technological Training
PHI	Private Health Insurance
PMB	Prescribed Minimum Benefit
PPO	Preferred Provider Organization
PVHI	Private Voluntary Health Insurance
PVO	Private Voluntary Organization
REF	Risk Equalization Fund, South Africa
SAR	South Asia Region, World Bank
SARS	Severe Acute Respiratory Syndrome
SES	Socioeconomic Status
SHI	Social Health Insurance
SRP	Social Risk Pool, China
SSA	Sub-Saharan Africa Region, World Bank
SSI	Social Security Insurance
SUS	Sistema Unificado de Saude, Unified Health System, Brazil
THE	Total Health Expenditure
VAT	Value-Added Tax
VHI	Voluntary Health Insurance
WHO	World Health Organization
WTO	World Trade Organization
WTP	Willingness To Pay

List of Figures and Tables

Tables in Text

Table in Appendix

Chapter 1

Transformative Learning in Health Education for a New Century: Interdependence in the Education of Health Professionals

Julio Frenk, Lincoln C. Chen, and Catherine Michaud

Introduction

Health professional education is essential to strengthen health systems. This chapter draws on the findings of the Lancet Commission on the Education of Health Professionals for the twenty-first century, which adopted a global approach to multi-professional education in an increasingly interdependent world. Based on an integrated framework of health and educational systems, instructional and institutional design are examined and recommendations made for improvements. The authors conclude that there are important opportunities for the private sector to contribute through leadership, financing, quality assurance, accreditation, certification, and knowledge development.

At the Cross-Roads

Health is all about people. Beyond the glittering surface of modern technology, the core space of every health system is occupied by the unique encounter between one set of people who need services and another that has been entrusted by society to deliver them. This trust is earned through a special blend of technical competence and service orientation, steered by ethical commitment and social accountability, which forms the core of professional work. Developing such a blend requires a prolonged period of education and a substantial investment on the part of both students and society. Through a chain of events flowing from effective learning to high-quality services to improved health, professional education at its best is an essential ingredient for the well-being of persons, families, and communities. Yet, the context, content, and conditions of the social effort to train competent, caring, and committed health professionals are changing at an unprecedented pace.

In our complex and interdependent world, professional education is at the cross-roads. In all countries, rich and poor, the education of health professionals is confronting major challenges in meeting the needs of patients and populations.

Difficult to design and slow to implement, educational reforms in richer countries are attempting to develop professional competencies responsive to changing health needs, overcome professional silos through interprofessional education, empowered learning by harnessing information technology (IT), enhance cognitive skills for critical inquiry, and strengthen professional identity and values for health leadership.

Even more challenging are reforms in poorer countries, constrained by severely limited resources (Public Health Foundation of India, 2008; Ke and Sun, 2010; Lu *et al.*, 2010). Many countries are attempting to extend essential services to patients and populations through the deployment of basic health workers, even as most people resort to un-credentialed providers, both traditional and modern (Bhutta *et al.*, 2010). Mobilizing to achieve national and global health goals, many poorer countries are channeling significant but restricted external donor funding toward implementing disease-targeted initiatives. Consequently, in many countries, post-secondary professional education is low on the policy agenda — overtaken by "crash projects" and considered too costly, insufficiently relevant, or too long-term.

Paradoxically, despite glaring disparities, interdependence in health is growing. All countries are challenged by demographic and epidemiologic transitions, rapid technological change, and greater complexity and higher cost of health systems. Global flows across national borders are accelerating — health workers and patients, diseases and health risks, knowledge and financing. Poor and rich countries alike suffer from workforce shortages, skill-mix imbalances, and maldistribution of professionals[1] (Josiah Macy Jr. Foundation, 2008; Chen, 2010; Chen *et al.*, 2004; Amin *et al.*, 2010). In neither richer nor poorer countries is professional education generating sufficient value for money.

These are the reasons the Global Commission on the Education of Health Professionals for the twenty-first century embraced the mission of advancing health, both individual and population-based, through landscaping instructional and institutional innovations in professional education to prepare the next generation for addressing frontier health challenges of the current century. The commissioners, professional leaders from diverse countries developed a shared approach to post-secondary education beyond the confines of national boundaries. Their report presents the first-ever global study of health professional education (Frenk *et al.*, 2010). It purposefully encompassed multiple health professions — focusing on medicine, nursing-midwifery, and public health while recognizing the importance of dentistry, pharmacy, and other disciplines — and moving beyond silos to expand space for professional collaboration. And the commission adopted an inclusive approach to both the public and private sectors. A new generation of educational reforms for the twenty-first century should be informed by the increasing interdependence that characterizes the health arena — just as reforms a century ago were propelled by the discovery of the germ theory with the emergence of modern medical sciences.

The Vision

Based on research and deliberations, the commission proposed two guiding notions to anchor its vision: (Figure 1.1): transformative learning and interdependence in professional education.

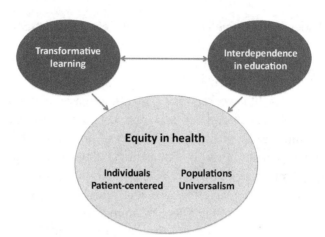

Figure 1.1   Vision for a New Era of Professional Education

Transformative Learning

Transformative learning captures the imperative of generating purposeful change in three directions:

- Transformation through acquisition of information and knowledge in the learning process to develop competent experts.
- Transformation of education in formative learning to develop professional values of responsibility, accountability, and service orientation.
- Transformation of learners as change agents and professional leaders to have an impact on social realities.

Transformative learning can project present and future professionals into a new era of pro-active, patient- and population-centered, competency-based, inter-professional, IT-empowered, and life-long learning. The purpose is to develop competencies effective in local contexts while harnessing global perspectives. The goal is to realize a new professionalism grounded on social accountability for mobilizing evidence and ethical deliberation to solve real-world problems by working with allies and stakeholders.

Interdependence in Professional Education

Interdependence in professional education underscores interactions that harmonize six key linkages:

- Between the local and global spheres of action
- Between the health and education systems
- Between health professionals and their patients and populations
- Across categories of the health workforce, leading to intra-, inter-, and transprofessional collaboration
- Between context and competencies, so that the latter respond to the former
- Between teachers and learners, so that education becomes a pro-active, mutually enriching process.

To realize this vision, the commission proposed instructional and institutional reforms. Curricular reforms should evolve to a competency-driven approach emphasizing local adaptation with global awareness, interprofessional and team-based work, harnessing the power of IT, and developing professional attitudes, values, and behavior. Institutional reforms should include joint planning by education and health authorities, extending learning sites into communities and homes, and development of collaborative networks, consortia, and alliances. Every country, no matter how rich or poor, should increase investments in professional education, and development assistance partners should increase donor financing. It is not enough, however, to increase the level of resources available for health professional education. In addition, financial flows to educational institutions should be reoriented to ensure maximum value for money, creating incentives for improved performance. Accreditation and credentialing systems should be aligned to national health goals, and global learning systems should be built to strengthen the knowledge base for steadily advancing professional education around the world.

Why Now?

Our great grandparents would never have dared to dream that life expectancy of their descendents would double over the course of the twentieth century. Unprecedented in human history, these advances were knowledge-based and socially driven (Frenk, 2009; Chen and Berlinguer, 2001; Pablos-Mendez *et al.*, 2005). Scientific knowledge not only produces new technologies but also empowers citizens to adopt healthy lifestyles, improve care-seeking strategies, and become proactive citizens conscious of their rights. In addition, knowledge translated into evidence can guide practice as well as health policy and systems improvements. Alongside the centrality of knowledge, health progress is also socially driven through the determining effect that multiple social factors have on health, the social forces that historically shape national health systems, and the power of social movements for health.

Coming on the heels of the discovery of the germ theory that began in Europe in the nineteenth century, the twentieth century witnessed many reform efforts in professional education. In the United States, such reports as by Flexner (1910), Welch and Rose (1915), Goldmark Committee for the Study of Nursing Education (1923), and Gies and Pritchett (1926) transformed post-secondary education to equip physicians, public health workers, nurses, and dentists, respectively, to play key health roles — as brokers of knowledge, providers of care and services, team members, systems leaders, and agents for social change. Parallel developments were instituted in Europe and other regions. Through these roles, health professionals around the world can rightly claim some credit for the spectacular health achievements of the twentieth century (Anand and Barninghausen, 2004).

While much can be applauded, weaknesses in professional education also developed, especially the growing mismatch of competencies to patient and population priorities due to narrowly conceived and outdated static curricula producing ill-equipped graduates from underfinanced institutions (Institute of Medicine, 2002, 2003; Josiah Macy Jr. Foundation, 2008; UK General Medical Council, 2009; Benner *et al.*, 2010; Cooke *et al.*, 2010; AFMC, 2010; The Prime Minister's Commission on the Future of Nursing and Midwifery in England, 2010; Joint Learning Initiative 2004; WHO, 2006; Global Health Workforce Alliance, 2008). While the original reports issued recommendations for developed countries, they were rapidly disseminated to developing nations where their uncritical adoption led to educational programs that were grossly unresponsive to local requirements. Not uncommonly, all public financing for professional education would be consumed by one or two national medical schools without balance of other professionals and the deployment of basic health workers. Partly as a result, the opening of a new century revealed an unfinished agenda of glaring health gaps affecting left-behind populations, alongside daunting new challenges posed by dynamic demographic, epidemiologic, and health care transitions (Institute of Medicine 2005, 2009; Commission on Social Determinants of Health, 2008).

Yet new opportunities are also emerging. The most important propelling forces are the changing expectations of patients and populations, especially the spreading global norm of health as a fundamental human right. Health has assumed political salience in both the national and global arenas. At the same time, there are new ways of harnessing the power of interdependence and mutual learning across countries that can capitalize on the global flow of information and knowledge while preserving local sensitivities and effectiveness (Frenk, 2009; Crisp, 2010). The digital revolution portends unprecedented transformation in professional education and practice. Not only can instructional and institutional innovations enhance learning across borders but cross-cultural educational experiences can also equip professionals with the tools and sensitivities to become even more effective domestically and internationally in a globalized world.

The Systems Framework

The Commission report adopted a systems approach to bring together the spheres of education and health. Opening the "black box" of the educational system, it considered aspects of both institutional and instructional design. Adopting such a comprehensive perspective was inspired by the original reports of the twentieth century, which sought to answer not only the question of what and how to teach, but also where to teach, in the sense of recommending the type of organization that should carry out the programs of instruction. However, in contrast to the original reports, the Commission report considers institutions not as individual organizations, but as part of an interrelated set of organizations charged with

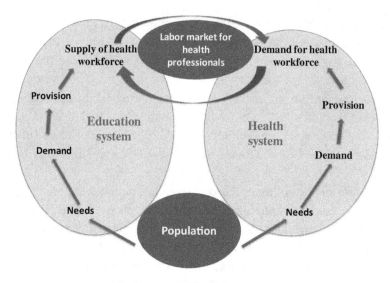

Figure 1.2   Systems Framework

carrying out the diverse functions of an educational *system*: stewardship and governance (including such critical aspects as certification and accreditation), financing, provision of the educational service itself, and generation of essential resources like faculty and information. In this systemic perspective, institutional structures interact with instructional processes to generate educational outcomes.

Figure 1.2 (systems framework) is a graphic representation of the systems framework. In this figure, professional education is the product of two systems — education and health. The population is the base and the driver of these systems. Indeed, people are not exogenous to the systems. It is, after all, people who generate needs in both education and health, which in turn, may be translated into demand for educational and health services. The provision of educational services generates the *supply* of an educated workforce to meet the *demand* for professionals to work in the health system.

To have a positive impact on the functioning of health systems and, ultimately, on health outcomes of patients and populations, educational institutions must be designed to generate an optimal instructional process. Figure 1.3 shows the interaction of the two critical dimensions of education.

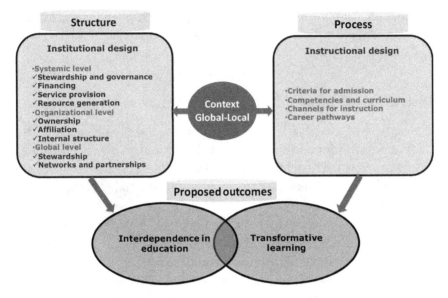

Figure 1.3   Key Components of the Educational System

Instructional design involves what can be presented as four C's: (1) criteria for admission; (2) competencies (not as they are attained, which is part of educational outcomes, but as they are defined in the process of designing programs of instruction); (3) curriculum; and (4) channels of instruction, defined here as the set of didactic methods and teaching technologies.

In contrast to the more limited scope of the twentieth century reports, today's interdependent world requires a global dimension to institutional design. Given current personnel shortages and resource constraints, it is impossible to conceive that every developing country will be able to train on its own the full required complement of health professionals. For this reason, the framework includes regional and global consortia as a crucial part of institutional design in the twenty-first century.

Educational outcomes from instructional and institutional designs are deeply influenced by contexts, both local and global. While many commonalities may be shared globally, there is local distinctiveness and richness. Whereas some professionals are being trained to manage sophisticated technologies in tertiary hospitals, others may be trained to improvise with rudimentary equipment in rural community centers. Such diversity offers great opportunities for shared learning across countries at all levels of economic development.

Instructional Innovations

The authors of the present study of instructional design adopted a case study approach informed by literature review. Based on historical analyses of instructional and institutional innovations, three generations of reform in the past century, leading to five frontier instructional challenges, were identified.

To improve understanding, the commission developed a typology of three generations of reforms (Figure 1.4). Like all classification schemes, this one simplifies multidimensional realities. Yet, it has heuristic value. The word "generation" conveys the notion that this is not a linear succession of clear-cut reforms. Instead, elements of each generation persist in the following ones, in a complex and dynamic pattern of innovation. Innovation in medical learning has long and deep historical roots around the world that started well before the past century. Early systems of medical education were reported in India around the sixth century BCE in a classical text called *Susruta Samhita* (Filliozat, 1964) and in China from around the second to fourth centuries CE during the Wei and Jin Dynasties

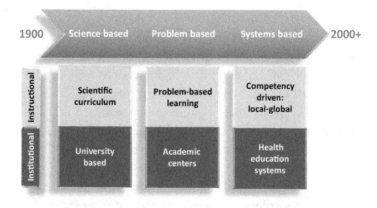

Figure 1.4   Three Generations of Reform

(Zhu, 1998). Arabic civilization had flourishing medical learning systems as did the Greek and the Mesoamerican civilizations (Bonner, 1996; Porter, 1997). In the UK, the General Medical Council was established by the Medical Act of 1858 (Irvine, 2006), and similarly early roots may be found in Latin America and Africa.

Spurred by scientific advances in Europe during the second half of the nineteenth century, reforms introduced the modern medical sciences into classrooms and laboratories in medicine, nursing, and public health in the early twentieth century. These reforms in North America — usually sequencing biomedical sciences to clinical and public health practice — were joined by similar reforms in other countries. Curricular reform was linked to institutional transformation — university bases, academic hospitals linked to universities, closure of weak proprietary schools, and linking of education to research. The goals were to advance scientifically based professionalism with high technical and ethical standards.

A second generation of reforms witnessed the growth of schools after World War II, both in industrialized countries and in developing nations, many of them having just gained independence from colonialism (Rosenberg, 2007). Breakthrough innovations were problem-based learning and integrated curriculum, shifting learning from top-down into student-centered processes (Pickering, 1978; Papa and Harasym, 1999; Neville, 2009). Disciplinary expansion and interdisciplinary work characterized public health curricular change, and nursing-midwifery education pursued advanced graduate programs. The continuum from classroom to clinical training in medicine was linked through earlier student exposure to patients, including broadening training sites beyond hospitals into the community and home (Seipp, 1963; Wyon and Gordon, 1971; Kark, 1981; Chen and Bunge, 1989). The goals were to promote pro-active learning with stronger social accountability.

Recent reform efforts in the past two decades may be considered the beginnings of the third generation. Reforms have emphasized patient and population centeredness, competency-based curriculum, interprofessional and team-based education, IT-empowered learning, and policy and management leadership skills. While all countries are testing practical solutions by delegating authority and responsibility to more briefly trained workers, poorer countries — many without large cadres of professionals — have by necessity been experimenting and demonstrating how non-professionals can master new knowledge and techniques at lower cost. Global perspectives and relationships have enriched learning through institutional connectivity and international collaboration. The goals are greater sharing of resources and development of partnerships within and across countries.

Instructional Challenges

With few exceptions, there is little hard evidence to demonstrate conclusively the superiority of any single individual innovation on educational outcomes. Most countries have mixed patterns of instruction, and no country has a single uniform generation of instructional design. There are no apparent barriers for institutions to "leap frog" from earlier to later generations. In the end, for this study, the authors selected five issues they considered frontier challenges in instruction: competencies and curriculum, adaptation to diverse contexts, interprofessional education, IT-empowered learning, and preparing for the professions.

Competencies and Curriculum

Competence-based education is an approach to design and conduct instruction that focuses on the desired performance characteristics of graduates. It is a disciplined approach to specify the health problems to be addressed, to identify the requisite competencies required of graduates, to tailor the curriculum to achieve competencies, and to assess achievements and shortfalls (Figure 1.5) The competency approach can promote reforms that better align education to health priorities — differing from the traditional model where a given curriculum anchored by historical legacies drives learning objectives.

Adaptation to Diverse Contexts

Striking a balance between global norms and transnational learning versus locally adapted competencies is a major challenge for every country. The world's richest and poorest countries demonstrate a 100-fold

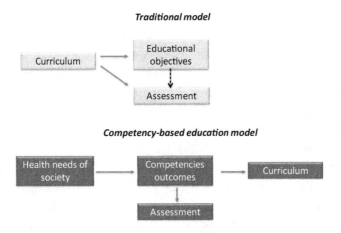

Figure 1.5   Competency-Based Education

differences in national income and a 1000-fold differences in health care expenditures. Indiscriminate adoption of curriculum and competencies can generate mismatches. It should be recognized, however, that many resource-poor institutions suffer from faculty and curriculum insufficiencies irrespective of competencies desired. The adaptation process can benefit from engaging stakeholders in addition to education professionals.

Interprofessional Education

Health has always been about team work, and the silos of individual professions hamper health system performance. Interprofessional education entails students of two or more professions learning together, especially about each other's roles, by interacting with each other on a common educational agenda. Though simple in concept, interprofessional education is difficult to implement. As argued later, transprofessional teamwork, involving also non-professional health workers, may be of equal importance for health system performance.

IT-Empowered Learning

The impact of e-learning is likely to be revolutionary, albeit how precisely e-learning will revamp professional education remains uncharted.

E-learning traditionally has included computer-assisted instruction to facilitate the delivery of standalone multimedia packages and distance learning for delivering instruction to learners in remote locations (Ruiz *et al.*, 2006). Explosive growth of the internet has brought power, speed, and versatility to both approaches.[2] And, in many cases, the uptake of new digital technologies has been faster and more widespread in poorer than in richer countries. As with all technologies, the drivers of constructive change are not the hardware and software by themselves, but rather the institutional transformation that the technologies enable, including what has been called "humanware." IT-empowered learning is already a reality for the younger generation in most parts of the world. Educational institutions must now be reengineered to ride this wave of transformation, or else they risk being drowned by it. One particularly promising aspect of the revolution in information and communication technologies lies in the open education resources movement, with its potential to expand global access to didactic materials. Another exciting area of development is the application of information and communication technologies to build global consortia of educational institutions, in order to leverage their resources, realize synergies, and transform educational opportunity into a global public good. While much more experimentation and evaluation are required, the most promising approaches seem to be those that combine full exploitation of digital resources with the human interaction that is the very essence of true education.

Preparing for the Professions

Professionalism "signifies a set of values, behaviors, and relationships that underpin the trust" of the public (Royal College of Physicians, 2005: 14). Professional education must inculcate responsible professionalism, not only by developing explicit knowledge and skills, but also by aligning the "hidden curriculum" so that the learning environment is made consistent with professional rhetoric and values (Cooke *et al.*, 2010). Students should learn of different traditions of medicine, ethical dilemmas, and brighter and darker sides of professionalism. Far from being an exclusionary force that erects artificial barriers to entry, protects privileges, and promotes practice monopolies through "credential creep" (Starr, 1982), a new professionalism for the twenty-first century should promote quality, embrace teamwork, uphold a strong service ethic, and be centered on the interests of patients and populations.

Institutional Landscaping

The commission undertook a quantitative landscaping of institutions and graduates in medicine, nursing-midwifery, and public health, the first-ever mapping of health professional education around the world. After showing the patterns of institutions and graduates globally, it focused on four frontier challenges as key levers for institutional and systems improvement — investment and financing, accreditation and stewardship, skill and labor markets, and collaborative and learning systems.

In 2008, an estimated 2,420 medical schools produced close to 389,000 medical graduates annually for a world population of 7 billion people (Table 1.1). Noteworthy are the large number of medical schools in India, China, Asia, Western Europe, and Latin America and the Caribbean, in contrast with the paucity of schools in Central Asia, Central and Eastern Europe, and sub-Saharan Africa. Data were insufficient to disaggregate these data into public and private institutions.

There also were an estimated 467 schools of public health, only 20 percent the number of medical schools. The count of public health schools is problematic because their definition varies — from entirely independent faculties to departments within medical schools with variable authority for degree granting. Nursing and midwifery school counts are even more difficult because of heterogeneity. While nursing and midwifery have many post-graduate programs, there are also many vocational schools offering certificates rather than post-secondary schooling.

Figure 1.6 shows density of medical schools. The best-endowed regions are Western Europe, North Africa and the Middle-East, and Latin America and the Caribbean; the lowest density is found in sub-Saharan Africa and parts of Southeast Asia.

The top four countries (India, China, Brazil, and the United States), each having more than 150 schools, comprise 35 percent of world's total. Thirty-one countries have no medical school whatsoever (including 9 in

Table 1.1   Institutions, Graduates, and Workforce, by Region

Region	Country	Population (millions)	Estimated number of schools		Estimated graduates per year (thousands)		Workforce (thousands)	
			Medical	Public health	Doctors	Nurses/midwives	Doctors	Nurses/midwives
Asia	China	1,371	188	72	175	29	1,861	1,259
	India	1,230	300	4	30	36	646	1,372
	Other	1,075	241	33	18	55	494	1,300
	Central	82	51	2	6	15	235	603
	High-income Asia Pacific	227	168	26	10	56	409	1,543
Europe	Central	122	64	19	8	28	281	670
	Eastern	212	100	15	22	48	840	1,798
	Western	435	282	52	42	119	1,350	3,379
Americas	North America	361	173	65	19	74	793	2,997
	Latin American/Caribbean	602	513	82	35	33	827	1,099
Africa	North Africa/Middle East	450	206	46	17	22	540	925
	sub-Saharan Africa	868	134	51	6	26	125	739
World		7,036	2,420	467	389	541	8,401	17,684

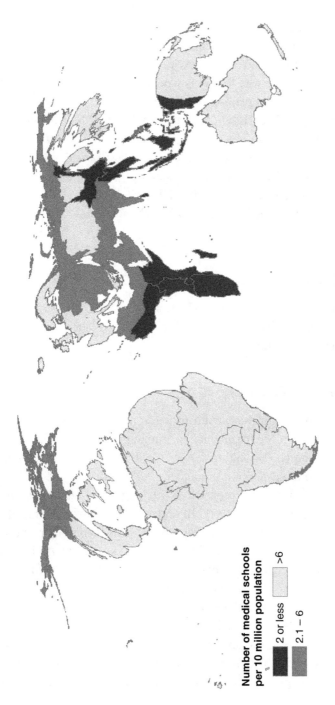

Figure 1.6   Density of Medical Schools, by Region

Number of medical schools per 10 million population

>6

2 or less

2.1 – 6

sub-Saharan Africa), and 44 countries have only one medical school (including 17 sub-Saharan Africa).

There is a major mismatch between the density of medical schools and the burden of disease. Whereas world population is weighted toward Asia, the global burden of disease, as measured in disability-adjusted life years (DALYs), is heavily concentrated in Africa. Medical school numbers and distribution do not correspond well to either population size or disease burden. There are many schools in India, Brazil, North Africa, and the Middle East. These production capacities, modified by international migration, translate ultimately into the global stock of the workforce, which is heavily concentrated in Asia, North America, and Western Europe.

Institutional Challenges

Four areas present institutions with major challenges: investment and financing, accreditation and stewardship, skills and labor market, and collaboration and learning.

Investment and Financing

Total yearly expenditure in health professional education is estimated at about US$100 billion for medicine, nursing, public health, and allied health professions. Education of medical graduates is estimated at US$47.6 billion and nursing graduates at $27.2 billion (Table 1.2). The figures for these individual professions are roughly inflated, in the absence of detailed information, to $100 billion by inclusion of public health and other related professions. This represents less than 2 percent of the $5.5 trillion that is spent globally on health — clearly an insufficient amount given the crucial role played by health professionals in determining the effectiveness and efficiency of those expenditures.

Altogether, there were 389,000 medical graduates in 2008, costing an average of $122,000 per graduate. There is, however, huge variation in production and costs. Larger production of medical graduates is found in China and India, and also in Western Europe and in Latin America and the Caribbean, compared to lower production in Central Asia, Central Europe,

Table 1.2 Financing of Medical and Nursing Graduates, by Region

Region	Country	Doctors			Nurses/midwives		
		Graduates per year[a] (thousands)	Expenditure per graduate[a] (US$ thousands)	Total expenditure (US$ billions)	Graduates per year[a] (thousands)	Expenditure per graduate[a] (US$ thousands)	Total expenditure (US$ billions)
Asia	China	175	14	2.5	29	3	0.1
	India	30	35	1.0	36	7	0.2
	Other	18	85	1.6	55	20	1.1
	Central	6	74	0.4	15	13	0.2
	High-income Asia Pacific	10	381	3.8	56	75	4.2
Europe	Central	8	181	1.4	28	39	1.1
	Eastern	22	151	3.4	48	29	1.4
	Western	42	400	17.0	119	82	9.8
Americas	North America	19	497	9.7	74	101	7.5
	Latin America/Caribbean	35	132	4.6	33	26	0.9
Africa	North Africa/Middle East	17	113	1.9	22	24	0.5
	sub-Saharan Africa	6	52	0.3	26	11	0.3
World		389	122	47.6	541	50	27.2

Note: [a] Estimated.

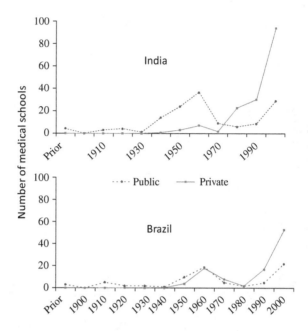

Figure 1.7   New Medical Schools (Public and Private) in India and Brazil

and sub-Saharan Africa. The range in cost goes from a high of $497,000 per graduate in North America to a low of $14,000 in China. Surprisingly, sub-Saharan Africa exhibits a moderate $52,000 per graduate, due most likely to small graduating cohorts.

Trend data for new schools are mostly unavailable. However, a few countries, like India and Brazil, show dramatic expansion, mostly of commercial for-profit schools (Figure 1.7). Similarly marked growth is also reported in China, but there it is financed by the government. In many developing countries, professional educational institutions must rely on external donor funding. While data are imprecise, most development partners have not ranked professional education as a major claimant for external donor funding.

Despite the data limitations, it is safe to conclude that investments in professional education are modest throughout the world. Particularly alarming is the fact that global investment in health professional education represents less than 2 percent of a global health care industry with an annual turnover estimated at more than $5.5 trillion yearly. Even in the United States, such investments represent a mere 0.3 percent of total health expenditures.

Beyond aggregate financial estimates, more detailed studies are needed on the way educational institutions receive investment flows and subsidies. Understanding the set of incentives that each financial model generates is particularly important. For example, many educational institutions receive public subsidies that are insensitive to their performance. In contrast, it is possible to empower students by providing scholarships that they can direct to the educational institution of their choice based on their perception of quality.

In light of the observed imbalances, the world as a whole is clearly not getting enough value for the money it invests in health professional education. To the insult of insufficient funding, many countries add the injury of inefficient expenditure.

Accreditation and Stewardship

Accreditation is the "control knob" of professional education as an instrument for good stewardship and as a pathway to individual certification and licensure. Currently, there are no global standards, many countries have weak or limited processes, and authority may vary between government, professional bodies, or independent councils. Lack of transparency in accreditation has been criticized by many seeking greater "social accountability".

Skills and Labor Markets

Educational institutions determine how many of what kind of professionals are produced. Ideally, they do so in response to labor market signals generated by health institutions. Also ideally, those signals correctly respond to the needs of the population. In reality, though, there are several forms of imbalance: undersupply, quantitative underemployment (meaning professionals working less than full time), qualitative underemployment (meaning professionals working in jobs that require lower levels of knowledge and skill), unemployment, and qualitative inadequacy (meaning a mismatch with population health needs).

To avoid such imbalances, the educational system must respond to quantitative requirements of the health system. Also critical are the delivery models, which define rules and roles for the various personnel categories. In this respect, the skill mix of health workers would be expected to differ between richer countries with more professionals and poorer countries with more basic health workers. In both cases, transprofessional education is essential for teamwork among professional, basic, and other non-medical staff.

In addition, the incentives created by different processes of personnel management take into account, including recruitment, retention, and remuneration. There is also a political dimension, since health professionals do not act in isolation but are usually organized as interest groups.

Last, the fact that labor markets for health professionals are not only national but also global must be kept in mind. Among professionals with internationally recognized credentials, migration is a major challenge for countries that educate them, especially considering the chronic deficits in many importing countries and growing numbers of countries producing professionals for export. The only way of addressing this complex problem is through international cooperation, as exemplified by the global code of conduct for international migration recently adopted by the World Health Assembly.[3]

Collaboration and Learning

Positive synergies in professional education can be achieved through alliances and networks of two kinds. The first are educational collaborations that can pool resources, share information, and promote joint work. The second are cross-institutional collaborations between education and government, business, non-governmental agencies, and the media. Sharing and learning can also be enhanced by data, monitoring, and evaluation to strengthen the knowledge base in professional education.

Commission Recommendations

The vision of the commission calls for a new era of professional education that advances transformative learning and harnesses the power of interdependence in education. Just as reforms in the early twentieth century rode on the wave of the germ theory and the establishment of the modern medical sciences, so too the commission believes that the future will be shaped by adaptation of competencies to specific contexts, drawing upon the power of global flows of information and knowledge. The vision is global rather than parochial, multi-professional and not confined to one group, committed to building sound evidence, encompassing of both individual and population-based approaches, focused on instructional and institutional innovations, and attempts to mobilize both the public and private sectors.

Ten major recommendations were prioritized. Six of them are instructional reforms and four are institutional reforms.

Proposed Instructional Reforms

Instructional reforms should encompass the entire range from admission to graduation, to generate a diverse study body with a competency-based curriculum that, through the creative use of information technology prepares students for the realities of teamwork, to develop flexible career paths that are based on the spirit and duty of new professionalism.

1. Adoption of competency-based curricula that are responsive to rapidly changing needs rather than being dominated by static coursework. Competencies should be adapted to local contexts and be determined by national stakeholders, while harnessing global knowledge and experiences.
2. Promotion of interprofessional and transprofessional education that breaks down professional silos while enhancing collaborative and non-hierarchical relationships in effective teams.
3. Exploitation of the power of IT for learning through development of evidence, capacity for data collection and analysis, simulation and testing, distance learning, collaborative connectivity, and management of the increase in knowledge.
4. Adaptation locally but harnessing of resources globally in a way that confers capacity to flexibly address local challenges while using global knowledge, experience, and shared resources, including faculty,

curriculum, didactic materials, and students linked internationally through exchange programs.

5. Strengthening of educational resources, since faculty, syllabuses, didactic materials, and infrastructure are necessary instruments to achieve competencies.

6. Promote a new professionalism that uses competencies as the objective criterion for the classification of health professionals, transforming present conventional silos, and developing a core set of attitudes, values, and behaviors.

Proposed Institutional Reforms

Institutional reforms should align national efforts through joint planning especially in the education and health sectors, engage all stakeholders in the reform process, extend academic learning sites into communities, develop global collaborative networks for mutual strengthening, and lead promotion of the culture of critical inquiry and public reasoning.

1. Establishment of joint planning mechanisms in every country to engage key stakeholders, especially ministries of education and health, professional associations, and the academic community, to overcome fragmentation by assessment of national conditions, setting priorities, shaping policies, tracking change, and harmonizing the supply of and demand for health professionals to meet the health needs of the population.

2. Expansion from academic centers to academic systems, extending the traditional discovery-care-education continuum in schools and hospitals into primary care settings and communities, strengthened through external collaboration as part of more responsive and dynamic professional education systems.

3. Linking together through networks, alliances, and consortia between educational institutions worldwide and across to allied actors, such as governments, civil society organizations, business, and media.

4. Nurturing of a culture of critical inquiry as a central function of universities and other institutions of higher learning, which is crucial to mobilize scientific knowledge, ethical deliberation, and public reasoning and debate to generate enlightened social transformation.

Mobilizing the Private Sector

Educational reform is not easy anywhere, and there will be many obstacles. Large numbers of students in classes, poor teacher-to-student ratios, compromised faculty time for teaching, and overwhelming expansion of the knowledge base all favor the status quo and the well-known lecture-based method of teaching with passive learning. In many places, faculty members, eager to see their specific fields of expertise reflected in the curriculum, may generate strong resistance to change. Accreditation bodies also may be conservative — preserving the status quo, seeking financial advantage, and promoting "tribalism" of individual professions. In most settings, incentives are insufficient to reward quality and innovation. Educational reform is a long and difficult process that cries for leadership and requires changing mindsets, work styles, and relationships among all actors. The commission called on the most important constituencies to embrace the imperative for reform through dialogue, open exchange, discussion, and debate over these recommendations. Professional educators are key players since change will not be possible without their leadership and ownership. So too are students and young professionals who have a stake in their own education and careers. Other stakeholders include professional bodies, universities, non-governmental organizations, international agencies, and donors and foundations.

The private sector, both non-profit and commercial, can and should play a vital role in this reform process. The private sector often has the financial and managerial capacity to innovate through the development of public–private partnerships for reform of health professional education. Indeed, the broad engagement of leaders from all sectors will be crucial to energize instructional and institutional reforms. While health professional education serves societal purposes, the private sector can be an important catalyst and leader in the reform process.

The private sector obviously is critically important for enhancing investments. Public financing is rarely sufficient. The private sector can be engaged across the full spectrum of professional education, although commercial investments are more likely to be forthcoming for degrees that are linked to well-paying jobs such as clinical medicine. Attention should be paid to balanced educational investments, as community-based workers and certain other professional groups may not be similarly attractive to commercial investors. Here, public financing, non-profit private funding, and donor funding may be deployed to balance commercial investments.

As Flexner (1910) proposed a century ago, setting standards for accreditation and certification helps to ensure quality, in addition to establishing a level playing field for all actors.

Finally, private sector engagement may not simply be the establishment of more and better educational institutions. The private sector is active across the range of learning activities. For example, instruction is being transformed by IT innovations, simulation services, and new learning pedagogy that come mostly from private investments. Similarly, institutional networking recommended by the commission depends mostly on private sector provisioning of internet and other connectivity services. Opportunities for private sector contributions, therefore, extend far beyond the establishment of private schools.

The work of the commission has opened up many questions that require more detailed studies addressing the requirements of specific institutions and professions. It has also revealed promising avenues for innovation that need to be explored in greater depth through experimentation and evaluation, including that carried out by the private sector. Yet enough information and insights have been generated to guide concrete action along the lines suggested by the recommendations in this chapter.

Most important, implementation of the recommendations can be propelled by a global social movement engaging all stakeholders as part of a concerted effort to strengthen health systems. The result would be a more enlightened professionalism that can lead to better services and consequent improvements in the health of patients and populations. In this way, professional education would become a crucial component in the shared effort to address the daunting health challenges of the twenty-first century, and the world would move closer to new era of passionate, participatory, and people-centered action to progressively realize the right to the highest attainable standard of health.

Endnotes

1. World Health Organization, *Increasing Access to Health Workers in Remote and Rural Areas through Improved Retention*, Geneva, 2010, accessed at

www.who.int/hrh/retention/guidelines, http://www.who.int/hrh/migration/
code/practice/en/guidelines/en/index.html.
2. OECD, *Policy Brief: E-learning in Tertiary Education*, 2005, accessed at
    http://www.cumex.org.mx/archivos/ACERVO/ElearningPolicybriefenglish.
    pdf.
3. World Health Organization, *WHO Global Code of Practice on the
    International Recruitment of Health Personnel*, Geneva, 2010, accessed at
    http://www.who.int/hrh/retention/guidelines/en/index.html.

References

AFMC (Association of Faculties of Medicine of Canada), *The Future of Medical
Education in Canada (FMEC): A Collective Vision for MD Education*.
Ottawa: AFMC, 2010.

Amin, Z., W. P. Burdick, A. Supe, and T. Singh, "Relevance of the Flexner Report
to contemporary medical education in South Asia", *Academic Medicine*, **85**,
333–339, 2010.

Anand, S. and T. Barnighausen, "Human resources and health outcomes: Cross-
country econometric study", *Lancet*, **364**, 1603–1609, 2004.

Bhutta, Z., Z. Lassi, G. Pariyo, and L. Huicho, "Global experience of community
health workers for delivery of health-related millennium development goals:
A systematic review, country case studies, and recommendations for
integration into national health systems." Global Health Workforce Alliance,
2010.

Benner, P., M. Sutphen, V. Leonard, and L. Day, *Educating Nurses: A Call for
Radical Transformation*, Stanford, CA: Carnegie Foundation for the
Advancement of Teaching, 2010.

Bonner, T. N., *Becoming a Physician: Medical Education in Britain, France,
Germany, and the United States* 1750–1945, New York: Oxford University
Press, 1996.

Chen, L. C., "Striking the right balance: Health workforce retention in remote and
rural areas", *Bulletin of the World Health Organization*, **88**, 323, 2010.

Chen, L., T. Evans, S. Anand, J. I. Boufford, H. Brown, M. Chowdhury, M. Cueto,
L. Dare, G. Dussault, G. Elzinga, E. Fee, "Human resources for health:
overcoming the crisis", *Lancet*, **364**, 1984–1990, 2004.

Chen, L. and G. Berlinguer, "Health equity in a globalizing world", In
Challenging Inequities in Health: From Ethics to Action, (eds.). T. Evans,

M. Whitehead, F. Diderichsen, A. Bhuiya, and M. Wirth, New York, NY: Oxford University Press, pp. 35–44, 2001.

Chen, C. C. and F. M. Bunge, *Medicine in Rural China*, Berkeley: University of California Press, 1989.

Commission on Social Determinants of Health, *Closing the Gap in a Generation: Health Equity through Action on the Social Determinants of Health*, Geneva: World Health Organization, 2008.

Committee for the Study of Nursing Education *Nursing and Nursing Education in the United States*, New York: Rockefeller Foundation, 1923.

Cooke, M., D. M. Irby, B. C. O'Brien, and L. S. Shulman, *Educating Physicians: A Call for Reform of Medical School and Residency*, Stanford, CA: Carnegie Foundation for the Advancement of Teaching, 2010.

Crisp, N., *Turning the World Upside Down: The Search for Global Health in the 21st Century*, New York: New York University Press, 2010.

Filliozat, J., *The Classical Doctrine of Indian Medicine*, Delhi: Munshiram Manoharlal, 1964.

Flexner, A., *Medical Education in the United States and Canada: A Report to the Carnegie Foundation for the Advancement of Teaching*, New York: Carnegie Foundation for the Advancement of Teaching, 1910.

Frenk, J., "Globalization and health: The role of knowledge in an interdependent world", David E Barmes Global Health Lecture, National Institutes of Health. Bethesda, MD, 2009.

Frenk, J., L. Chen, Z. A. Bhutta, J. Cohen, N. Crisp, T. Evans, H. Fineberg, P. Garcia, Y. Ke, P. Kelley, and B. Kistnasamy, "Health professionals for a new century: Transforming education to strengthen health systems in an interdependent world", *Lancet*, **376**(9756), 1923–1958, 2010.

Gies, W. J. and H. S. Pritchett, *Dental Education in the United States and Canada: A Report to the Carnegie Foundation for the Advancement of Teaching*, New York: Carnegie Foundation for the Advancement of Teaching, 1926.

Global Health Workforce Alliance, *Scaling Up, Saving Lives*, Geneva: World Health Organization, 2008.

Institute of Medicine, "Global issues in water, sanitation, and health", Workshop Summary. Washington, DC: National Academy Press, 2009.

Institute of Medicine, *Microbial Threats to Health: Emergence, Detection and Response*. (eds.). M.S. Smolinski, M.A. Hamburg, and J. Lederberg. Washington, DC: National Academy Press, 2005.

Institute of Medicine, *Who will keep the Public Healthy: Educating Public Health Professionals for the 21st Century*, (eds.). K. Gebbie, L. Rosenstock, and L. M. Hernandez. Washington, DC: National Academy Press, 2003.

Institute of Medicine, *The Future of the Public's Health in the 21st Century*, Washington, DC: National Academy Press, 2002.

Irvine, D., "A short history of the general medical council", *Medical Education*, **40**, 202–211, 2006.

Joint Learning Initiative, *Human Resources for Health: Overcoming the Crisis*, Cambridge, MA: Harvard University Press, 2004.

Josiah Macy Jr. Foundation, *Revisiting the Medical School Educational Mission at a Time of Expansion*, Charleston: Josiah Macy Jr. Foundation, 2008.

Kark, S., *The Practice of Community-Oriented Primary Health Care*, New York, NY: Appleton-Century-Crofts, 1981.

Ke, Y. and B. Z. Sun, "Challenges in China's health professional education", Presentation at Commission's second meeting, April 26, 2010, Peking University, Beijing, China.

Lu, C., M. T. Schneider, P. Gubbins, K. Leach-Kemon, D. Jamison, and C. J. Murray, 2010, "Public financing of health in developing countries: A cross-national systematic analysis", *Lancet*, **375**, 1375–1387, 2010.

Neville, A. J., "Problem-based learning and medical education forty years on. A review of its effects on knowledge and clinical performance", *Medical Principles and Practice*, **18**, 1–9, 2009.

Pablos-Mendez, A., S. Chunharas, M. A. Lansang, R. Shademani, and P. Tugwell, "Knowledge translation in global health", *Bulletin of the World Health Organization*, **83**, 723, 2005.

Papa, F. J. and P. H. Harasym, "Medical curriculum reform in North America, 1765 to the present: A cognitive science perspective", *Academic Medicine*, **74**, 154–164, 1999.

Pickering, G., *Quest for Excellence in Medical Education: A Personal Survey*, Oxford, UK: Oxford University Press, 1978.

Porter, R., *The Greatest Benefit to Mankind: A Medical History of Humanity*, New York: W.W. Norton & Company, 1997.

Prime Minister's Commission on the Future of Nursing and Midwifery in England, *Front Line Care: The Future of Nursing and Midwifery in England*, London: the Prime Minister's Commission on the Future of Nursing and Midwifery in England, 2010.

Public Health Foundation of India, *Report of the International Conference on New Directions for Public Health Education in Low- and Middle-Income Countries*, Hyderabad, India, 2008.

Rosenberg, C. E., *Our Present Complaint: American Medicine Then and Now*, Baltimore, MD: Johns Hopkins University Press, 2007.

Royal College of Physicians, *Doctors in Society: Medical Professionalism in a Changing World*, London: Royal College of Physicians, 2005.

Ruiz, J. G., M. J. Mintzer, and R. M. Leipzig, "The impact of e-learning in medical education", *Academic Medicine*, **81**, 207–212, 2006.

Seipp, C., (ed.). *Health Care for the Community*, Baltimore, MD: Johns Hopkins University Press, 1963.

Starr, P., *The Social Transformation of American Medicine*, New York: Basic Books, 1982.

UK General Medical Council, *Tomorrow's Doctors: Outcomes and Standards for Undergraduate Medical Education*, London: General Medical Council, 2009.

Welch, W. H. and W. Rose, *Institute of Hygiene: A Report to the General Education Board of Rockefeller Foundation*, New York: Rockefeller Foundation, 1915.

WHO (World Health Organization), *The World Health Report: Working Together for Health*, Geneva: WHO, 2006.

Wyon, J. B. and J. E. Gordon, *The Khanna Study: Population Problems in the Rural Punjab*, Cambridge: Harvard University Press, 1971.

Zhu, Y.-P., *Chinese Materia Medica: Chemistry, Pharmacology, and Applications*, Amsterdam: Harwood Academic Publishers, 1998.

Chapter 2

Setting the Stage for Scaling Up Health Education

Hortenzia Beciu and Paul Jacob Robyn

Introduction

Important investments were made by governments and international partners to increase access to education in low- and middle-income countries, over the past several decades. Apart from achieving access in universal primary education, the concerted efforts were also meant to specifically address gender imbalances in school enrollment and to increase the completion rate among students especially at the primary and secondary levels. The results are promising. The World Bank 2020 Education Strategy citing UNESCO sources, highlights some of the achievements made: (1) the increase in net enrollment[1] in primary education from around 60 percent in 1999 to 80 percent in 2008 with completion rates above 60 percent in low-income countries; (2) the increase in gross secondary school enrollment[2] for low-income countries from slightly below 60 percent to nearly 70 percent; and (3) increase girls enrollment and graduation with notable positive changes among Middle East and North African countries[3] (World Bank, 2011).

The increased enrollment and completion at the primary level, lead to an increase in the number of secondary school graduates, expanding the pool of potential higher education students as well. Globally, in 2009, over

165 million students participated in higher education, which is a five-fold increase since 1970 and a three-fold increase since 1980 (UNESCO Institute for Statistics, 2012).[4] Sub-Sahara Africa (SSA) had the highest average annual growth rate in tertiary education, 8.4 percent for the past four decades, but its average gross enrollment ratio estimated for 2014 was just 9 percent. This ranks very low in comparison with other regions averages: i.e. fragile and conflict affected situations states (11 percent), South Asia (21 percent), Middle East and North Africa (38 percent), Latin American and Caribbean (45 percent), East Asia and Pacific (39 percent), Europe and Central Asia (65 percent) (World Bank, 2016), etc.[5]

Most of the time demand for higher education exceeds the available entrance slots. Medical education makes no exception. In the US, the data from the Association of American Medical Colleges, 2016–2017 reveal that only 26 percent of the applications were matriculated in the first year of study. A study conducted by Beciu *et al.* in Ghana in 2008–2009, revealed that on average there were 20 times more applicants for one slot than the available positions in the medical schools at that time.

The increase demand for higher education can relate to: (1) increased student access to finance; (2) local labor market incentives; (3) regionalization and globalization of the labor markets and ease of labor movement; (4) globalization of the tertiary education; and (5) individual curiosity and interest. The supply may be limited by: (1) the current schools capacity and lack of resources to scale-up; (2) regulations of the profession and upstream interests; and (3) students access to finance; etc.

For the health market, the need for medical personnel across the globe is growing and so the current shortages of medical personnel raises legitimate concerns. The Global Disease Burden Study published by the Institute for Health Metrics and Evaluation states that while the biggest contributor to the world's health burden used to be premature mortality, driven by deaths in children under the age of five, now the disease burden is caused mostly by chronic diseases and injuries such as musculoskeletal disorders, mental health conditions, and injuries. The report also emphasize that the disease burden intensifies as people live longer (IHME, 2010).[6] These facts in turn put pressure on the governments to stimulate an increase in the capacity of their medical schools and or to compensate and cover the national gaps by attracting labor from other countries.

Internal demands and international pressure to address the international migration of health workers lead to many governments to take actions. In 2015, the Association of the American Medical Colleges stated that in the US, medical schools are on target to reach a 30 percent increase in enrollment by 2019.[7] Despite this positive move, the US labor market continues to relay on international medical graduates.[8] In other countries too, the government and or the private sector players are scaling-up medical education capacity. However, resources are paramount in such endeavors.

The 2008 Global Financial Crisis coupled with an extended period of low commodity prices, nuanced the story of economic growth among many low- and middle-income countries by influencing the availability of resources for growth. Predictions are that as a continent, SSA will slow down from 3 percent economic growth in 2015 to an estimated 1.6 percent in 2016, the lowest level in over two decades in accordance with a World Bank Report (World Bank, 2016). Since SSA has the lowest tertiary education enrolment rates and the lowest proportion of adult population (+25) having completed a tertiary education degree (Salmi, 2017),[9] the prospects of economic growth through education and innovation are not as good as they could have been. Good Governance manifested by strategic vision, political stability, accountable and efficient public organizations, and economic diversification is needed for the countries[10] to lift their citizens from poverty as well as create a larger and robust middle class. Further creating opportunities for upper secondary and tertiary education graduates to pursue and materialize their ideas will be invaluable.

For students in low-income countries interested in starting their studies in medicine, the reality of higher education system can be disappointing. Underfunded and over-enrolled, many of the tertiary-level medical training programs in low and some middle-income countries do not support the right environment and infrastructure for quality education, nor do they keep pace with the advancements in curricula approaches and build the competencies of a twenty-first century medical personnel. In these countries, education reform is needed. Whether it is a reinvestment in the administrative capacity of the institution, in education and learning technology, a revamping of the curriculum to align with the competency-based learning processes, establishing new financing mechanisms to increase the schools' capacity, hiring more teachers, and provide equitable access for students, many medical training programs are in need of change. Strategic vision, investment in and better use of technology, and innovative collaborations to increase financial resources are needed to prepare for more and better health workforce.

In recent years, numerous innovations in the tertiary education sector have been implemented around the world. Whether it is the expansion and privatization of higher education in countries throughout South and East Asia, innovations in financing mechanisms throughout Latin America and Europe, or experiments with student-centered learning in Southeastern Europe and the technology-driven and guided self-learning in the US, there are lessons to be learned from these recent reforms. The higher education training methodology is evolving rapidly: from academic lectures and passive listening to interactive, guided self-learning and self-assessment milestones with ubiquitous use of available technology (apps, games, internet, open learning resources, etc.). The same evolution, though not as widespread, is true for medical education. Improving the twenty-first century skilled-based learning, coupled with a broader and better understanding of the social and economic environment of individuals and families is the new norm for general medicine trainees.

This chapter will highlight key components of tertiary medical education systems and describe current global trends in approaches to tertiary medical education.

Training and Education for Human Resources for Health

A country's framework for building the health workforce should appropriately address the changing health needs and the culture of the generations that it will serve. A stronger relationship between health professionals, communities, knowledgeable consumers, and technology is building up.

Health professionals play a central and critical role in improving access to quality health care. They provide services that promote health, prevent diseases, and deliver health care services to individuals, families, and communities. For this to occur, a nation's health education system should produce an appropriately skilled workforce to address its current

Table 2.1 Health Worker Training Institutions by WHO Regions, 2006

WHO region	Medical 2006	Medical 2013	Nursing and midwifery	Dental	Public health	Pharmacy
Africa	66	179	288	34	50	57
Americas	441	—	947	252	112	272
Southeast Asia	295	—	1,145	133	12	118
Europe	412	—	1,338	247	81	219
Eastern Mediterranean	137	—	225	35	8	46
Western Pacific	340	—	1,549	72	112	202
Total	1,691	—	5,492	773	375	914

Note: These data underestimate the current number of schools because of the time elapsed since this information was collected and concerning the availability of the information on middle-level schools, financed by government investments (public schools) or private funds (private schools).
Source: WHO (2006) and FAIMER (2017).

health priorities while been cognizant of the future needs. Since the 2006 WHO effort to collect data on estimated numbers of medical, dental, pharmacy, nursing, midwifery schools in different regions of the world, there has not been any similar or reiterative process to update this information to this extent (Table 2.1).

According to the Foundation for Advancement of International Medical Education and Research (FAIMER), the total number of medical schools increased from 1691 in 2006 to 2357 in 2013. In Africa, estimates for the number of medical schools increased from 66 in 2006 (WHO estimates) to 179 in 2013 (FAIMER, 2013).

We assume that since 2006 similar or even higher increases took place among nursing, dental, pharmacy, and public health schools around the globe.

Key Functions of Training Institutions

The World Health Organization (2006) defines health-training institutions as having six key functions: stewardship and institutional governance; provision of educational services; selection and employment of staff members; financing of training; development and maintenance of infrastructure and technology; and generation of information and knowledge.

When looking at medical education on a global scale, using a general model for evaluation may assist in cross-regional and systematic comparisons. One such framework is the World Federation for Medical Education (WFME) Global Standards for Quality Improvement, which Bossert *et al.* (2007) highlight as a grounded starting point for identifying indicators of quality health professional education. WFME identifies nine areas of quality assessment and potential improvement of health professional education: mission and outcomes; educational programs; assessment of students; academic staff/faculty; educational resources; program evaluation; governance and administration; and continuous renewal (Bossert *et al.*, 2007).

The focus of this book is on understanding how to think of the factors influencing the supply and demand for medical education, the role of market, governance and innovative financing in shaping the future of medical education.

Levels of Medical Training within a National Education System

Although the focus of this chapter is on tertiary medical education, higher levels of medical training are only one type of professional training that builds a nation's health workforce. The Global Health Workforce Alliance (2008a,b) divides a national health workforce into three major levels: the community level, including community health workers; mid-level professionals such as enrolled or auxiliary nurses and midwives, pharmaceutical/lab, and radiology technicians, clinical officers, and medical assistants; and high-level professionals, comprised of registered nurses/midwifes, pharmacists, and medical doctors as shown in Figure 2.1 (Task Force for Scaling Up Education and Training for Health Workers, 2008).

There is an important difference in the education and therefore the roles of community health workers in developed and developing countries. While the final aim maybe the same, to address the health and psychosocial needs of the communities by knowing and understanding these needs and bridging between these communities and different organizations, the community health workers in developed countries are many

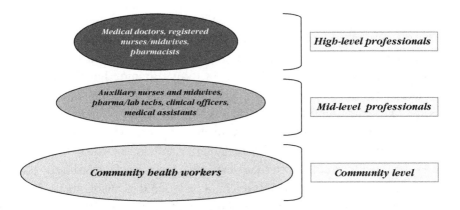

Figure 2.1   Three Tiers of a National Health Workforce
Source: Task Force for Scaling Up Education and Training for Health Workers, 2008.

times frontline public health professionals or social workers who are conducting outreach activities meant to educate, inform, counsel, follow-up on individuals and their families after an episode of care or other encounter. Though the qualifications of community health workers vary in developed countries, the minimum required education is often a high school diploma. In developing countries, the roles of community health workers are most of the time fulfilled by less educated or even unschooled individuals. As in developed countries, important variations in education and roles exists as well often due to variability in purpose, availability and interest, and the agency financing the training (either government or development partners).

For mid-level professionals and up (formal education) in many developing countries, health trainees follow the same curriculum as previous or successive cohorts, with little or no flexibility in the way trainees can learn or the pace of learning (Robson, 2005). One classic model is that of pre-service curricula for high-level health workers overemphasizing theoretical knowledge and practices in well-resourced tertiary hospitals, with less emphasis on the competencies and the disease profile of that country. Training or primary care doctors is either overlooked and or not fully equipped with adequate resources and the right settings for students to truly learn primary care skills. As a result, a graduates' ability to deal effectively with real-life health needs may be compromised — particularly where resources are few, access to equipment and technology is limited and the referral system is not within any performance parameters. The educational system may also fail to ensure that competencies fulfill accepted intervention standards, both in formal training but also in less formal endeavors such as the training of traditional birth attendants (Task Force for Scaling Up Education and Training for Health Workers, 2008).

In low-income countries, many medical training programs concentrate too much on western disease patterns without an equal focus on prevalent health problems in their respective countries. Accordingly, the skills of the young professionals may not be tailored to handle many day-to-day cases. Due to epidemiological transition in disease profiles of low-income countries (such as an increased prevalence of non-communicable diseases, substance abuse, mental health, etc.), training programs should be streamlined cautiously and so the need to train health workers need to be kept broad (communicable and non-communicable disease" with a focus on most prevalent conditions.

Globally, the minimum curriculum for medical education is 4 years, and the maximum length varies from 5–8 years and even 10 years (in the US) especially for students willing and interested to pursue dual degrees programs like MD and PhD.

Although the efficiency of medical training is improving throughout SSA, the wastage rates[11] ranged between 10 percent and 40 percent annually (Task Force for Scaling Up Education and Training for Health Workers, 2008) raised the question concerning the length of medical training. One idea is that efficiencies can be achieved through further streamlining of training programs, resulting in more focused curriculum and a shortening of the overall duration of pre-service and post-service education programs.

Recruitment and Training of Human Resources for Health: The Education Funnel

Bossert and associates (2007) asserts an education system's capacity to provide an adequately trained workforce and appropriate number of health workers can be viewed as an "education funnel," beginning with the available pool of applicants and ending with labor market entry rate (Figure 2.2).

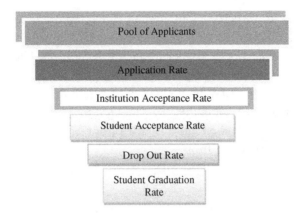

Figure 2.2   Education Funnel for Human Resources for Health
Note: The student acceptance rate measures the number of admitted students who accept invitations to study at training institutions.
Source: Bossert *et al.* (2007).

Bossert *et al.* (2007) also note that the pool of applicants and application rate can be constrained by the levels and quality of a country's secondary education system as well as the labor market incentives. In contrast, the institutional acceptance rate can be regulated by the institutions themselves (e.g. by limiting the number of medical school places), while the dropout rate has been shown to be affected by choice of pedagogical methods, the length of education, the resources needed, the academic background of the students admitted, students psychological characteristics, and other personal aspects.

Students with weak academic background, especially in science, often have a higher dropout rate than those with a solid foundation. This seems consistent in different other studies conducted at different universities around the world (Maher *et al.*, 2013). In a retrospective 10-year study conducted by Maher *et al.* (2013) at University College Cork using qualitative and quantitative measures among five medical cohorts revealed that among different nationalities who were enrolled, the country of student origin matters. "Male students were also more likely to drop out than females but this was not statistically significant. Absenteeism was documented in 30 percent of students, academic difficulty in 55.7 percent, social isolation in 20 percent, and psychological morbidity in 40 percent" (Maher *et al.*, 2013).[12]

In the US, a study of the association of the American Colleges revealed the following data concerning the graduation rates: "for only Medical Doctor programs the four-year graduation rates fell from 90 percent in late 1970 to around 83 percent in the 1980s and it remained the same throughout; the five-year graduation rate has fallen from 97 to 94 percent, and the eight-year graduation rate from 98 to about 97 percent for the same time period". Joint programs, MD PhD, have the highest graduation rates (AAMC, 2014).[13]

Although content selection and the quality of teachers and teaching methods influences the knowledge, skills, and aptitudes of students, there has been a worldwide trend in education for the health professionals to emphasize academic knowledge over the skills needed to work in clinical settings (Bossert *et al.*, 2007). Western institutions have evolved more quickly out of this paradigm currently embarking in trial programs such as the US American Medical Association project "Accelerating Change in Medical Education." In this trial, 11 US Medical Schools formed a consortium to share their ideas and experiment with programs that will equip medical students with tools to support lifelong learning, self-assessment, knowledge about health care systems, technology use, while continuing to provide individualized patient center care.[14] Other new medical education models have already been established in some of the traditional schools in the United States such as the Johns Hopkins "Gene to Society" model or Harvard "New Pathway Curriculum," whereby clinical practice and basic sciences are integrated and introduced early on, together with competencies that spans from multi-culturality, health disparities, and other general integrating disciplines.[15] A more traditional model still exists in the US whereby the division of didactic and practical training can be found within a traditional four-year medical school curriculum.

Global Numbers in Tertiary Medical Education

The World Health Organization annually publishes the *World Directory of Medical Schools,* now part of the Global Directories of Education Institutions for Health Professions, a partnership of WHO and the

University of Copenhagen. Databases are also compiled by the Institute for International Medical Education (IIME), the Association of American Medical Colleges (AAMC), and the Foundation for Advancement of International Medical Education and Research (FAIMER), which produces the *International Medical Education Dictionary* (IMED).

As of September 2013, according to a study conducted by Duvivier and Boulet combining data from multiple resources, the authors estimated 2,597 operating medical schools worldwide. The study revealed that there are discrepancies between different databases. The IMED database listed 2,335 medical schools (FAIMER, 2013), whereas the Avicenna Directories have 2,165 entries. According to the authors, of the world's 207 independent states, 183 have at least one medical school, 24 have no medical schools, and 50 have only one medical school (Duvivier *et al.*, 2014).

According to the latest data from the World Directory of Medical Schools, the countries with the largest numbers of medical schools are India (380), Brazil (209), the USA (182), China (184), and Pakistan (99). Globally one-third of all medical schools are located in five countries and nearly half are located in 10 countries (World Director of Medical Schools, 2014–2015).[16]

Asia has the most medical schools, 1,188, but it also have 60 percent of the world's population which comes to one medical school for every 3.5 million people. China, with the world's largest population, has one school per 9.3 million inhabitants. There are approximately 382 medical schools in South America (Duvivier *et al.*, 2014) with one medical school for every 1.1 million people. The Caribbean has the highest density of medical schools per population: one medical school per 0.56 million inhabitants though this is not as relevant as in the case of other regions given that these schools mostly train students for the international market (Duvivier *et al.*, 2014). In Europe, there is one medical school for every 1.8 million people and Africa has one school per 5.0 million population. (Duvivier *et al.*, 2014).

Between 1950 and 1999, the highest rates for medical school growth were in Latin America, but from 2000 to present the highest growth rate has shifted to Asia. The official languages for medical schools is dominated by English and Spanish, comprising 22 percent and 21 percent of the medical schools' official languages, respectively. Chinese is the official language for 12 percent of medical schools, with French (8 percent), Portuguese (8 percent), Japanese (7 percent), and Russian (6 percent) (Boulet *et al.*, 2007).

The Latin American and Caribbean Region (LAC) has experienced dynamic reforms in higher education, due to elevated numbers of qualified secondary school students aspiring to continuation at the tertiary level. For the last two decades, Latin American governments have increased public investments in lower levels of education. One significant result is that this has led to improved graduation rates for primary and secondary education, enlarging the pool of qualified students and an intensifying demand for tertiary education. Since 1985, enrollment in higher education has been increasing annually by 2 percent throughout Latin America. Nonetheless, in 2001, the average tertiary education gross enrollment rate[17] was only 23 percent in the Latin America and Caribbean Region as compared with 56 percent in high-income countries. In 2014, the average enrollment rate reached 39.6 percent at par with MENA but still lower in comparison with other regions (Salmi, 2017).[18] Why have the enrollment numbers remained lower in the LAC Region than in high-income countries? According to a World Bank report (Murakami, 2008), depressed enrollment rates are a result of affordability barriers and lack of financing for tertiary education; low equity, leading to insufficient and unequal access to tertiary education; and low expectations of attending tertiary education from low-income families (Murakami, 2008).

An analysis by Salmi,[19] that took into account households' socioeconomic status, reveals that Latin American and the Caribbean, rank third concerning mean disparity ratio in access to tertiary education[20] after MENA and SSA with the second highest disparity range after SSA. In a different type of analysis by the same author, that correlate the family educational attainments and their socioeconomic status with the probability to enroll in tertiary education, Latin America continues to reveal a high disparity in comparison with countries from OCED, Eastern and Central Europe (ECA), and Southeast Asia (SEA) regions. Data were not available for Africa and Middle East for this analysis (Salmi, 2017).

The World Bank (2013) cites low quality of education as an additional reason for low enrollment rates in LAC. The LAC regional average share of tertiary education expenditure to total education expenditure was 21 percent, while the proportion was 26 percent in Western Europe and 29 percent in East Asia. Finally, Latin America and Caribbean higher education institutions remain unresponsive to changes in evolving labor markets. Studies conducted by Holm-Nielsen *et al.* (2003) and Wit *et al.* (2005) reveals a mismatch between higher education programs and the labor market needs. However, the regional average does not speak about different countries' individual performance. In the study conducted by the World Bank, Chile and Colombia performed better than the LAC average in "degree to which university education is perceived to meet the needs of a competitive economy while Mexico, Brazil, and Argentina were below average at that time" (Wit *et al.*, 2005).

The number of medical schools does not necessary correlate with access to medical services and the performance of a health care systems. There are many factors leading to population access and overall good quality of the medical services. To name a few, these are: (a) the capacity of the schools to provide quality education so that medical workers have the knowledge and the skills to correctly identify and treat conditions; (b) the regulatory environment allowing medical schools to expand; (c) the availability of the sources of finance for post-graduate education; (d) the market incentive to retain the medical personnel in the country/region where they were graduating from. All these factors need to be taken into account when looking at what needs to be in place for better population health.

Private Sector of Tertiary Education

An important and growing phenomenon in higher education is the expansion of the role of the private sector in tertiary education, with varying rates of growth in different regions. The average OECD (Organisation for Economic Cooperation and Development) countries in 2012 had 85 percent of lower secondary students and 80 percent of upper secondary students enrolled in public schools.[21] Over 80 percent of tertiary-level students in OECD member countries and partner countries were enrolled in public schools in 2004. However, in other parts of the world, according to Salmi, the growth of private tertiary education has been so significant that more students are enrolled in private institutions than public ones. This is the case in some Latin American countries such as Brazil, Chile, Costa Rica, Dominican Republic, El Salvador, Paraguay, and in East Asian countries, Cambodia, Indonesia, South Korea, and the Philippines. Salmi citing Bloom *et al.* (2014) states that in SSA between 1990 and 2014, the number of private institutions grew from 30 to about 1,000, compared to a fivefold increase of public universities for the same time period.[22] Accordingly, the enrollment in private education increased significantly. For Example, in Chad, Congo, Côte d'Ivoire, and Uganda, private sector enrollment has tripled or quadrupled in the past decade.

In South east Asia, at the time of its independence in 1945, Indonesia had only 1,000 tertiary-level students. In 2015, it was reported that Indonesia had 4,384 tertiary education institutions, 91.5 percent privately run and 8.5 percent public.[23]

The private sector dominates the tertiary education system in Belgium, Brazil, South Korea, and the Philippines. Private higher education institutions outside the United States, especially in developing countries are usually narrow in scope, smaller in size, focusing on market-oriented vocational programs such as business and information technology, and employ teaching staff from public universities on a part-time basis. "A major reason for the expansion of the private sector is the inability of public finances to keep pace with the growing demand for higher education, dissatisfaction with the quality of public education (large class sizes, teacher absenteeism, lack of supplies), the existence of more modern and job-relevant curricula in the private sector, the politicization of public education, and favorable policy changes that facilitate the growth of private higher education" (Bjarnason *et al.*, 2009).

Since education is part of a country's economic and social development, private education makes no exception. Governments should observe who has access and graduates from tertiary education institutions as they do for public schools. The governments can also steer and or use private investments for societal benefits to larger societal groups.

According to Fielden and LaRocque (2008), the expansion of the private education sector can produce several positive effects on a country's higher education system. First, the private education sector can supplement the limited capacity of government institutions to absorb growth in school and higher education enrollments. Private education also provides opportunities for government to support publicly funded students in private schools. Examples of such a strategy exist in Pakistan, the Philippines, and Uganda. More schools lead to more competition, and competition introduced through the expansion of the private sector often results in an increase in both the efficiency and quality of education delivery for both public and private sectors. With its possible greater management flexibility, the private sector can respond to market changes more quickly than public institutions by developing appropriate curricula for the evolving needs of the country (Fielden and LaRocque, 2008). In the Democratic Republic of the Congo, the number of medical and nursing graduates doubled between 2001 and 2003, due largely to the private sector-led increase in health worker education and training (World Health Organization, 2006).

The International Finance Corporation (IFC) has estimated that with the public sector's resource constraints there is a private investment opportunity of $1.7 billion in medical education in Africa (IFC, 2007). Yet there exists a list of common regulatory barriers for development of higher education's private sector. "Barriers include confused, unclear national policies; cumbersome, complex higher education registration processes; outdated criteria for accreditation; prohibition of foreign-owned private education institutions; limits on the private sector's freedom to set tuition fees at market rates and earn profit; and restrictions on religion/political aspects of curriculum. 'Lengthy and complex registration processes may reduce access by deterring new providers or increasing their costs to such a degree that these institutions become unaffordable to their clientele' (Bjarnason *et al.*, 2009). National governments can provide support in the form of guidebooks on the registration process for higher education institutions. Examples of such strategies exist, such as the Commission for Higher Education in China, the Ghanaian National Accreditation Board, and the Tanzanian Commission for Universities" (Fielden and LaRocque, 2008).

Fielden and LaRocque (2008) also provide specific recommendations for a healthy development and expansion of the private higher education sector. First, national governments should provide a sound policy framework for the operation of private education sector including a strong oversight. Second; clear, objective, streamlined criteria for establishing private education institutions should be developed together with market or direct incentives to allow for a true contribution of the private sector. "Countries like Malaysia and Mexico have mandated a minimal proportion of low-income students to whom private providers should provide financial support" (see Endnote 9). Other countries offer students access to loans to support their enrollment in private institutions.

Accreditation Systems for Tertiary Medical Education

According to the Accreditation Council on Graduate Medical Education (ACGME), *accreditation* is defined as "a voluntary process of evaluation and review based on published standards and following a prescribed process, performed by a non-governmental agency of peers" (ACGME, 2008). It is a process for discerning and publicly recognizing good educational processes. Globalization of the production and trade, efforts to harmonize and standardize the education at the regional and global level, workforce mobility, e-learning, brought about a stringent need to reanalyze the role of programs accreditation. In medical education, the outcomes and the relationship between the medical practitioners and the community he/she serves shall be emphasized in an accreditation process (WHO, 2013).[24]

According to Phillips, in a 2016 conference in Washington DC stated that accreditation is meant to advance academic quality, to demonstrate accountability, and to encourage purposeful change and needed improvement. Accreditation, however, reflects all that is tried and true, and what is agreed upon as emerging in the profession, but it does not quite reach the visionary and imaginative thinking that leads the way at a certain point in time.

New aims of the accreditation process can relate to facilitate interprofessional learning, competency-based training, improve quality, processes, and outcomes.[25]

In the United States, the Liaison Committee on Medical Education (LCME) is the nationally recognized accrediting authority for medical education programs leading to the MD degree in US and Canadian medical schools. The LCME is sponsored by the Association of American Medical Colleges and the American Medical Association. The usual full accreditation period lasts for 8 years. US medical residency programs (post-graduate education) are accredited by the Accreditation Council on Graduate Medical Education (ACGME). The ACGME and the organization of certifying boards (the American Boards of Medical Specialists), have agreed on six areas in which all physician residents should be competent, and which should be covered in Graduate Medical Education programs: patient care, medical knowledge, practice-based learning, and improvement, professionalism, interpersonal skills and communication, and systems-based practice as shown in Figure 2.3 (Batalden *et al.*, 2002). Each **competency** consists of different

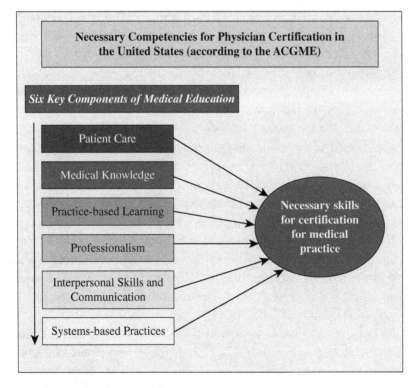

Figure 2.3   ACGME Requirements for Physician Certification
Source: Batalden *et al.* (2002).

milestones which residents are required to master at key stages of their medical training. In the United States, residency programs must be ACGME-accredited to receive government funding and to enable their graduates to qualify for specialty certification. Increasingly, certification is a required qualification for employment as a physician.

Graduate medical education is specifically focused on the progression of medical students through the "Dryfus" competency stages (knowledge and skills acquisition), designated novice, advanced beginner, competent, proficient, and expert. This is seen in the progression from advanced beginners (medical school graduates) to fully competent physicians. Residency offers training to move from proficient to expert (Batalden *et al.*, 2002).

Europe has developed an innovative approach to accreditation of institutions and portability of the qualifications. Formally launched as a non-binding agreement at European level (with the 1999 Bologna Declaration), the "Bologna Process" culminated in the creation of a European Higher Education Area (EHEA) in 2010 (Bologna Process, 2008).[26] The overarching aim of the EHEA is to promote mobility, be internationally competitive, and attract students and staff from Europe and beyond. It aims to do this by facilitating greater comparability and compatibility between the diverse higher education systems and institutions across Europe, as well as by enhancing their quality. Today, 48 countries participate in the Bologna Process (European University Association). The first organization to develop the Bologna process was the European Quality Assurance Register for Higher Education (EQAR). Currently, EQAR lists 24 agencies in 23 countries compliant with the European Standards and Guidelines. The current status within the EU space allows for Basic medical training and general practitioner training to be automatically recognized throughout the EU, entitling a EU practitioner to work in any EU country. Some specialist doctors' qualifications are also automatically recognized in certain EU countries.[27]

In India, accreditation of medical schools by the Medical Council of India (MCI) is compulsory. The information requested emphasizes documentation of infrastructure and human resources more than measures the quality of medical education and outcomes. Information comes solely from the medical school administration. Information from faculty, students, or patients is not used in the accreditation process (Supe and Burdick, 2006).

In Chile, under the auspices of the Ministry of Education, institutions are accredited in one of four categories: full autonomy, accredited, examined, or supervised. Full autonomy institutions have the freedom to plan and organize programs, designate personnel, and administer the budget. The 25 traditional councils of the rector universities have been granted full autonomy. "Since 1999, provisionary national accreditation commissions have set standards and granted formal recognition to programs at the graduate and undergraduate levels based on self-assessments and external peer-review processes" (Holm-Nielsen *et al.*, 2004). Since 2006, there is a unique National Commission for Accreditation for both undergraduate and graduate programs. The accreditation of medical schools programs is mandatory. Other programs functions on a voluntary basis (Rolwing and Clark, 2013).[28]

Accreditation organizations are also present in many SSA countries. In Sudan, the Sudan Medical Council and the Ministry of Higher Education are the two regulatory bodies of medical education. They have developed standards for medical education and accreditation systems for medical institutions and programs, as well as self-evaluation and quality assurance units in various medical schools. They have also adopted the Trilogy of World Federation of Medical Education (WFME) of Global Standards for quality improvement in medical education (Fahal, 2007). Other examples of national accreditation bodies include the Ghana Medical and Dental Council, the Medical and Dental Council of Nigeria's National Universities Commission, the Health Professions Council of South Africa, the Medical Council of Zambia, and the Tanzanian Commission for Universities. In Ethiopia, the Ministry of Health manages the medical school accreditation system (FAIMER, 2008).

In West Africa, national and regional bodies oversee accreditation. The West African Health Organization (WAHO) has established regional health colleges that act as accreditation agencies for post-graduate training and education. These include the West African College of Physicians, the West African College of Surgeons, and the West African College of Nursing. Both the College of Physicians and the College of Surgeons are part of the West African Post-Graduate Medical College (WAPMC), which is the largest agency providing certification for medical specialization in the region. Licensed medical practitioners from WAHO member states are eligible for placement through fellowship examinations (WAHO, 2008).

Certification and Licensing

In many countries, certification and licensing examinations are required upon completion of tertiary medical training programs. In the United States, medical school students must pass three stages of the United States Medical Licensing Examination (USMLE) for certification to practice medicine (it is the most general medical practice model in the United States).[29] In the US, all doctors are required to complete residency training. The USMLE is supervised and implemented by the National Board of Medical Examiners. The third step of the USMLE exam is usually taken during the first or second year of post-graduate training. Apart from USMLE in the US, step three physicians can also take the specialty board exams. These exams are voluntary and because they vary among different states, they restrict medical practice to that states that have commonalities or agreements with.

American Medical Association (AMA) defines certification as "the process which involves to provide assurance to the public that a certified medical specialist has successfully completed an approved educational program and an evaluation, including an examination process designed to assess the knowledge, experience, and skills requisite to the provision of high-quality care in a particular specialty" (American Medical Association, 2008).

In many Central and Eastern European countries, there is a general medicine exam upon graduation of the bachelor in medicine, which most of the time is designed by each university center. Residency exams can take the form of national exams for entering into a particular specialty (post-graduate). At the end of the residency, training specialty exams are compulsory for a person to practice in that specialty. There is a certification process at the end of the residency by either the Ministry of Health or Ministry of Education and a license provided by the professional association allowing physicians to practice medicine within their areas of specialty. Within the EU, the licensing exams is recognized at the national level and recently at the regional level. This allows many physicians to practice medicine without geographical boundaries or constraints of a country or region.

In France, until 2005, the university diploma awarded at the end of training functioned as the certification that authorizes clinical practice. Recent reforms have introduced a law, making continuing to advanced training a requirement for practice, as well as a set of competencies programs and practice evaluation procedures (Segouin, 2007).

"In other parts of the world fewer than 60 percent of developing countries require graduating medical students to pass national certification exams, and in Africa and Southeast Asia, the figure drops below 40 percent" (Evans *et al.*, 2016; Task Force for Scaling Up Education and Training for Health Workers, 2008).

Financial Flows in Tertiary Education

Most governments in developing countries retain control over health worker training, and one instrument of regulation is financial control of training institutions. (Financing methods for tertiary medical education are discussed below.) "In 2001, African heads of state, meeting in Abuja, committed themselves to devoting a minimum of 15 percent of government funds to the health sector in order to address the massive burden of ill-health facing countries in Africa, particularly within the context of a growing burden of HIV/AIDS, TB, and malaria" (Govender *et al.*, 2008). WHO notes, 10 years after that, only one country, Tanzania, reached that target. Twenty-six countries have increased the proportion of total government expenditures allocated to health while 11 countries reduced their relative contributions of government expenditures to health during the period. In the other nine countries, there is no obvious trend upwards or downwards (WHO, 2011).[30]

For the education sector, there was no such numeric target set. In this sector, the goal of the governments and international community was to increase access and reach universal education at primary levels. The past decades made clear to the governments that the next steps on their development agenda was to support secondary and tertiary education, to stimulate, generate, and capture the potential of these graduates for the society.

In *Innovations in Tertiary Education Financing: A Comparative Evaluation of Allocation Mechanisms,* Salmi and Hauptman (2006) present various forms of innovative financing mechanisms for higher education. There is a current evolution in public transfer mechanisms, diverging from recurrent expenditures and capital investment, via the more traditional negotiations of budgets between governments and public institutions, toward more sophisticated funding formulas. A few examples include: the creation of "demand-side" voucher systems, in which vouchers are given to all students for institution operating subsidies; the implementation of performance-based allocation mechanisms; financing university-based research separate from instruction; the substantial expansion of financial aid for students with high level financial need; and the growth of student loans (Salmi and Hauptman, 2006).

Investment in tertiary education has increased globally both from the public but even more notably from the private sector. Models are now intertwined between the public and private sector. Students supported through public funds can study in private schools. Public schools are now charging small tuition fees or enrolled students as private students beyond a certain admission quota. Private schools can be for-profit and not-for-profit. They can be secular or under a religious denomination. The connection between the labor markets (industry) and academics is becoming stronger. Industry can support capital investments in private schools (i.e. laboratories), student scholarships, and or research programs. Increase in tertiary education enrollment but mostly innovations is seen as an asset and a valuable investment by both the governments and the private sector. Although the degree of investment and interest varies between developed, middle-income and low-income countries, it is apparent that economic growth as well as individual prosperity is related to skills and knowledge in the new millennium, where new ideas are valued and innovation prevails.

For international students, choosing to study abroad on their own without government support, the tuition fees can make a difference in their decision of the place of study. An OCED report reveal that there are countries where tuition fees are higher for international students in comparison with domestic students for non-EU students, i.e. Australia, Austria,*[31] Belgium,* Canada, the Czech Republic,* Denmark,* Estonia,*

Iceland,* Ireland, the Netherlands,* New Zealand, Poland,* the Russian Federation, Sweden,* Turkey, the United Kingdom,* and the United States. Other countries such as Finland, Norway have no tuition fees for either domestic or international students. France, Germany, Italy, Japan, Korea, Mexico, Spain, and Switzerland have the same tuition fees irrespective of the student's country of origin (OECD, 2013).[32]

Tertiary Medical Education and the Labor Market

While some countries face the challenge of increased numbers of health professionals immigrating to other countries for better working and living conditions, others face the paradox of having a relatively adequate number of health workers while confronting difficulties in keeping those workers in the places where they are most needed, particularly in remote and rural areas.

Labor markets are shaped by supply and demand for health workers. Demand for health workers can be driven by public-sector budgets based on historical levels and political forces, private sector participation in care delivery, wage differentials, working conditions, direct and indirect benefits to individuals and families, other incentives. When policy interventions are implemented to increase the supply of labor and bring it closer to country needs, care must be taken to ensure that new workers encounter a job market that can effectively deploy them. This requires creating appropriate fiscal space for employment and the finances to do so. Training alone, without the corresponding correctives on the demand side, is likely to have no effect or backfire. Also equally important, mismatches between the education provided and the capabilities required in the job market contribute to high graduate unemployment rates in certain sectors. In Africa, the unemployment exceeding 20 percent in nine of the 23 countries in which labor market data are available (World Bank, 2008). Among OCED countries, the unemployment rate among tertiary-educated adults stood at an average 5.0 percent; among 25–34 year-old, it was 7.4 percent. By comparison, the unemployment rate for 25–34 year-old without an upper secondary education reached 19.8 percent in 2012.[33]

Recruitment from public delivery system to the private sector may play a substantial role in the labor market. Losses to other sectors run between 15 percent and 40 percent a year according to estimates from Ghana, Malawi, Mozambique, Tanzania, Zambia, and Zimbabwe (Robson, 2005).

In the US, a study conducted by IHS for the Association of American Medical Colleges reveal that demand for physicians will continue to grow faster than supply, leading to a projected shortfall of between 61,700 and 94,700 physicians by 2025. The highest impact on these estimates is brought by the change in population demographics. For certain categories of health workers such as advanced practice nurses (APRNs), if the labor force participation patterns remain unchanged, then the supply of APRNs will grow more rapidly than is needed to keep pace with growth in demand for services at current APRN staffing levels. Similarly, the supply of physician assistants (PAs) is projected to increase substantially between 2013 and 2025 (IHS, 2015, 2016).[34] If these two categories of health providers, APRNs and PAs stay as projected the move toward home base-community base care can alter the need for general practitioners and thus influence market demand and ultimately the supply of physicians. Surgical specialties will not be affected by the labor skill mix and currently are in high demand across the US. The same study suggests that in the US the new payment methodologies, including bundled payments and risk-sharing arrangements, and innovations in technology, may significantly restructure the way we deliver care in the coming years (IHS, 2015).

In Ethiopia in 2007/2008, the training of health education workers was being combined with a simultaneous expansion of the primary health care infrastructure, with health posts being built or upgraded to absorb new graduates. The cost of salaries, incentive packages, and training for these workers was included in the government, program budget.

In Kenya during the same period, the presence of unemployed health workers was being used to the advantage of the Emergency Hiring Plan, a fast-track hiring, training upgrade and deployment programs. The plan was to redistribute 800 health workers to work in public facilities on three-year contracts. The Ministry of Health led the program, with involvement from the U.S. President's for AIDS Relief (PEPFAR) and other partners (Scaling Up, Saving Lives, World Health Organization, 2008).

In Uganda, for every additional year of tertiary education, earnings have been found to increase by eight percent (Liang, 2004). This can be translated into a high social return of 13 percent and a private return of 24 percent for tertiary education. At the time of the study in 2004 (Liang, 2004), the School of Hygiene Mbale (Makerere University) had maintained a five-year 100 percent employment record as almost all of its graduates go to work for government hospitals and health facilities, while other schools such as teachers' colleges have employment rates as low as 20 percent (Liang, 2004).

Student Mobility versus International Migration

Student mobility has become a topic of much discussion on the policy agenda of international organizations. On one hand, the discussion is sparked by the globalization of education, technology advances with good online learning platforms at 10 percent of the cost of traditional education and market demand of the skill-sets rather than education background which are now being sought by employers. Student mobility is also a strategic approach that many countries and or university centers are pursuing in the quest to increase and attract talents and also support the sustainability of their education system. For small countries that have resources, it maybe more cost-effective to send students abroad rather than build their own tertiary education system at the level of specialization that already exists in other parts of the word (UIS, 2010).[35]

On the other hand, attracting increased attention in Africa and some parts of Southeast Asia, given the challenges with which these continents are confronted regarding the development of human capital and the achievement of sustainable development for themselves. While the overall mobility of the students within the African continent increased, both regionally among the cluster of countries that have regional bodies or regional treaties, i.e. Southern Africa, Western Africa Councils, but also internationally, students from Europe and the US studying abroad, have a higher probability to return and contribute to their countries in comparisons with other international students.

For several decades, many countries around the world have implemented policies and/or programs supporting the increase in the outflow of students going to pursue a post-secondary degree abroad (outbound students) and/or the inflow of foreign students coming to pursue degree programs in the host country (inbound students). For each individual, these programs were beneficial as labor mobility around the globe increased. UNESCO Institute for Statistics estimated that in 2008, 223,000 students from SSA were enrolled in tertiary education institutions outside their own country. "This number represented 4.9 percent of the total number of domestic students from that year, a number three times greater than a global average of 1.9 percent" (see Endnote 35). It was also noted that many countries in SSA spend a lot more public funds for tertiary students as percentage of GDP per capita than more developed countries. Since the gross enrollment ratios are not still very low in SSA, it means that more resources are spend by government to support students to study at the tertiary level. Maybe the return-on-investment would still be better if these future workers will stay or come back in their home countries (UIS, 2010).[36] For low- and middle-income countries, this story maybe different: countries struggling to educate and train sufficient numbers of a relevant health workforce experience a further loss of trained health workers to other countries.

A recent upsurge in nurse migration has worsened the situation, as inflows from training schools cannot maintain even the existing poor staffing levels. A World Health Organization study in 2004 showed a general reduction in the availability of nurses, in some countries having as much as 12 percent decline over a three-year period (cited by Dovlo, 2007). High-cadre health professionals often leave their country of training and residence for external markets that they see as offering more attractive working and living conditions. The situation is worst in SSA. For example, in Malawi, 114 of the 190 registered nurses (60 percent) left a tertiary hospital between 1999 and 2001 (Martineau, 2004). In 2000, more than 500 nurses left Ghana for work, in western industrial countries — more than twice the number of new graduates of nursing programs that year (Buchan and Sochalski, 2004).

To address this situation, in July 2004, the World Health Assembly adopted Resolution WHA57.19, calling for the development of a Code of Practice on the International Recruitment of Health Personnel. The WHO has also requested that member states put in place mechanisms to improve the retention of their own health workers. Following the Kampala Declaration which called on governments to ensure "adequate incentives" and "an enabling and safe working environment for effective retention and equitable distribution of the health workforce" (WHO, 2008), the adoption in 2010 of the Global Code of Practice was a step forward toward dialogue and shared responsibility. As of March 2014, 85 countries had successfully designated a national authority to monitor the data on workforce migration and 56 countries, mostly in Europe, have completed and returned their National Reporting Instrument (NRI) to WHO.

By understanding and responding to the problem, the governments of Australia and Norway increased the number of Australian and Norwegian graduate students respectively, and also addressed labor incentives by improving the work conditions and consolidating part-time jobs into full-time jobs in their respective markets. The Norwegian government has formally stopped recruiting health personnel from countries facing critical shortages in the health workforce (Taylor, 2011).[37]

Increases in the education expenses in the west allowed for some reverse trends of students from developed countries studying in middle-income countries. Known cases are among American students studying medicine in Caribbean countries and Eastern European countries. While most Americans studying in Caribbean islands return home to practice medicine, the situation is not that clear for the students studying in Eastern Europe and, since this last trend is increasing, it remains to be seen if these students will not choose to remain in Europe to practice medicine or return to the US (Schuetze, 2013).[38]

Cuba is one example of a medical education system in the LAC Region that produces enough for itself while also targeting making their manpower available for international markets. About 24,950 Cuban health professionals serve in 68 countries, and 12,000 international students are enrolled on full scholarship in Cuban medical education institutions (Frank and Reed, 2005). Since the early 1960s, almost 70,000 Cuban health workers have participated in structural cooperation programs in 37 Latin American countries, 33 African countries, and 24 Asian countries. For international students that opt to study in Cuba registration is organized by Cuban diplomatic missions, and academic requirements for entrance are comparable to those of other medical schools in the LAC Region (De Vos *et al.*, 2007). The ELAM Medical School in Cuba, which opened its first international medical education program in 1998, graduated more than

25,000 doctors from 84 countries since its beginning, according to the information provided on the school website.

For tertiary education, countries which have historically been popular destinations for international students (i.e. Australia, France, Germany, the United Kingdom, and the United States) increased their market share in time, hosting higher numbers of overseas students seeking foreign academic credentials. In addition to these groups, other countries have emerged as new popular destinations for international students, such as China, Malaysia, the Republic of Korea, South Africa, and Eastern Europe. OECD data reveal that between 2000 and 2011, the number of international students more than doubled. Almost 4.5 million tertiary students are enrolled outside their country of citizenship. The largest numbers of international students are from China, India, and Korea with Asian students accounting for 53 percent of all students studying abroad worldwide (OECD, 2014).[39]

Teaching Strategies in Tertiary Medical Education

Curriculum content and approaches to medical training vary across the globe. Typically, academic training centers have a three-part mission: teaching, research, and service delivery. These three aspects should ideally receive equal attention and institutional resources, with staff being encouraged to contribute to each. However, it is seldom that all three pillars are addressed at the same time. In the US, incentives are often heavily weighted in favor of research and service delivery, to the detriment of teaching (WHO, 2006). The imperative to generate income to support overhead costs through service, delivery or research leaves education and teaching short of resources and attention. "In Southeast Asia, the trend toward following the money is steering teaching toward more lucrative fields within specialty medicine, potentially decreasing the capacity of the health workforce to respond to basic public health needs" (WHO report, 2006).

There are various approaches to teaching strategies found in tertiary medical institutions. Practice-based teaching aims to bridge the gap between academia and practice; benefit students, schools, agencies, and communities; involve and develop critical thinking and problem-solving skills; be interdisciplinary, multidisciplinary, and multidimensional; and incorporate experimental education, including observation, critical reflection, self-assessment, and learning-by-doing. Problem-based learning complements practice-based learning through identifying problems, exploring pre-existing knowledge, generating hypotheses and possible mechanisms, identifying learning issues and objectives, and using self-study and group learning. Patient-focused practice: integrates teaching and learning with clinical practice; shares experience of illness, disease and recovery with patients; understands varying needs for care; and observes and participates in the ways in which different service providers work together to meet the patients' needs (WHO report, 2006).

Core Curricula

The core of medical education is that part of the curriculum that is common to all students independent of their specialty. It can be defined at institutional, national, or international levels. According to Harden and Davis,[40] mastery of the core curriculum, covering knowledge, skills and attitudes, ensures the maintenance of standards among all students. As mentioned earlier in this chapter, current practice of medical education supports the development of competency-based curricula. The ACGME six core competencies for resident education that were described earlier, medical knowledge, patient care, professionalism, interpersonal and communication skills, practice-based learning, and systems-based practice, have been embraced by medical schools in the US and around the globe, as the building blocks necessary for becoming an accomplished practicing physician. Students will incrementally acquire these competencies as they advance in their education.

An example of one strategy used to define core curricula can be found at Ankara University Faculty of Medicine in Turkey. In 2004, the decision was made to replace the traditional curriculum with an integrated, problem-based and student-centered one. The Department of Medical Education oversaw developing the process by which the new curriculum would be developed. Once the vision and mission of the medical school was determined, the aims and objectives of undergraduate medical education were concretely established. The core curriculum was defined as the knowledge, skills, and attitudes that will be common to all medical students who eventually enter the workforce. During the process, each department proposed topics and was asked to write down its aims and objectives for undergraduate medical education. Each topic was expected to fulfill three basic criteria: the topic should be in accordance with the aims and objectives of the relative department; the topic should be in accordance with the aims and objectives of the undergraduate education of the Faculty of Medicine; and the topics should prepare the student to function as a competent general practitioner, whose duties have been described by the Ministry of Health (Kemahli *et al.*, 2004).

Problem-based Learning

Problem-based learning has become a common approach to medical education teaching. The approach is understood to mean an instructional strategy in which students identify issues raised by specific situations to help develop an understanding of underlying concepts and principles. The problem-based learning aims to promote critical thinking, teamwork, and communication skills. Many problem-based learning programs are based on the Maastricht Model of problem-based learning. Maastricht University, in the Netherlands, is well known for its adoption of problem-based learning as the educational approach in all seven of its faculties. In 2003–2004, Ondokuz Mayis University Medical School in Turkey adopted problem-based learning according to the Maastricht Model. The first-year curriculum consisted of 60 problem-based tutorials. Problem-based learning groups of 7–8 students meet twice a week for 2- to 3-hour sessions to discuss a problem. Students investigate on their own, the issues that emerge, synthesize the knowledge, and apply it to the problem discussed. When compared to a control program using traditional didactic teaching, the students from the problem-based learning group showed significant progress between post- and pre-test results in scientific thinking skills, improved problem-solving skills (self-reported), and greater conflict resolution skills. Some studies suggested that problem-based learning students have less pre-clinical knowledge than traditionally taught students, but a study by Yalcin and Associates (2006) shows otherwise.

In India, any significant reforms to the Bachelor of Medicine, Bachelor of Surgery (MBBS) curricula must be approved by the Medical Council of India, which stipulates in great detail, the rules for medical school curriculum structure and content. "Medical training has been established as a three-phase framework of pre-clinical or first MBBS (12 months), pre-clinical or second MBBS (18 months), and clinical or third MBBS (24 months), plus a one-year internship. Mandated summative assessment for each MBBS phase is composed of external, university-based exams uniformly required for all medical colleges" (Supe and Burdick, 2006). The Medical Council of India also regulates time allocation among disciplines. "These regulations for medical school curricula were revised in 1997 in order to promote small-group learning, greater emphasis on health and community, problem-based learning approaches, and horizontal and vertical integration" (Medical Council of India, 1997). Discipline-based teaching nonetheless remains the dominant mode of education. Medical internships have a mandated three-month community medicine block (six-weeks urban, six-weeks rural). Interns must also spend two months in each discipline; medicine, surgery, and obstetrics and gynecology; one month of casualty, and half a month in family planning welfare. "Only 29 percent of medical school graduates are able to enter post-graduate education positions in a clinical specialty, the remainder enter directly into non-specialty medical practice or emigrate" (Supe and Burdick, 2006).

In South Africa, the medical faculty at the University of Transkei (Unitra), now Walter Sisulu University, was established in 1985 with a program of Bachelor in Medicine, Bachelor in Surgery/Chirurgery (*MBChB*). The Unitra Council formulated and, in 1988, published Council Guidelines for the medical faculty based mainly on community-based medical education (CBME) and problem-based learning. By the first semester of 1989, (when problem-based learning was introduced) there were obvious obstacles to the implementation of the curriculum. Insufficient preparation of the envisaged curriculum, insufficient preparation of the academic and support staff, insufficient preparation of the learners, and insufficient preparation of local opinion and policy makers all led to problems by the end of the year. A lack of academic coordination existed between faculties. The medical faculty had relied on the Faculty of Science to provide pre-medical courses, yet it became clear that the science faculty was prepping the students for degrees in B.Sc. instead of MBChB. Therefore, in 1991, students were admitted to MBChB I, and the courses were designed for students with weak science backgrounds.

Semester I would be didactic, and Semester II would be problem-based learning. In 1992, a better-planned problem-based learning, CBME was introduced, and has remained successful. In 1996, the South African National Department of Health introduced compulsory community service after the one-year internship, and as a result Unitra's program is directed at rural and underserved areas (Kwizera *et al.*, 2005).

At the Malawi College of Medicine, 25 percent of the curriculum is allotted to community health in all five years of the course. The district hospital in Mangochi, 190 km from Blantyre on Lake Malawi, was adopted as the base for community health training because the lakeshore reflected the medical problems of a rural environment. Community health remains a cornerstone of the curriculum. The college had introduced problem-based learning as one of the core principle of learning. The college has received several international accolades for its innovative undergraduate teaching program. For example, the department of Community Health received the Association of the African Universities Prize in 1994; in successive years, students won first or second prizes in Tropical Health Education Trust (Muula and Broadhead, 2001). Some students are drawn from neighboring countries that have no medical school of their own. A major obstacle for student recruitment is Malawi's low literacy rate (62.7 percent in 2008) (CIA, 2008), as well as the limited opportunities for secondary and tertiary education, limiting the number of potentially eligible students (Muula and Broadhead, 2001).

Against the disadvantages of excessive demands on staff time, set-up and maintenance costs, and increased stress for both students and staff, advocates of problem-based learning assert that it promotes deep understanding, improves collaboration between disciplines, and increases knowledge retention by both students and staff. Reviews of controlled evaluation studies, however, found limited evidence that problem-based learning in continuing medical education increased participants' knowledge and performance and improved patients' health (Yalcin *et al.*, 2006).

Focusing on Primary Health Care

In various academic surroundings, there are many different approaches to adopting a primary health care-oriented curriculum. In Sudan, the

Educational Development Center (EDC) for medical and health professionals was established at the Faculty of Medicine, University of Khartoum in 1980, in response to the growing demand in both the Sudan and the region for qualified medical teachers. "The center trained a target group of medical and health staff to support the implementation of Primary Health Care Programs with emphasis on Mother and Child Health Care and Family Planning. This training staff included nursing staff, health visitors, midwives, and medical assistants. 'The EDC produces medical and health materials for education, training, and health promotion, and in Khartoum it has developed a clinical skill laboratory where high-fidelity simulation is used for teaching and learning clinical skills'" (Fahal, 2007).

Team-based learning at Jimma University in Ethiopia has operated since 1990, where teams of 20–30 final year students in medicine, nursing, pharmacy, laboratory science, and environmental health are posted to district health centers. They become familiar with other member's fields and learn how to work in teams. The program is managed by a central office within the university. The Millennium Medical School, also in Ethiopia, tailors its education program to meet the country's health needs and reduce education and training time from 3.5 to 4 years from 6 years (Ethiopia Human Resources for Health Program). In Nigeria, community-based education and service (COBES), developed at the Ilorin University in the 1960s, prepared students to address the priority needs of communities, as they progress gradually from basic health education activities to the provision of clinical health interventions (Task Force for Scaling Up Education and Training for Health Workers, 2008).

At the Aga Khan University in Pakistan, community health sciences account for 20 percent of the curriculum. The five-year teaching–learning sequence follows a problem-solving process known as the community health planning cycle: community assessment, problem identification and prioritization, vertical and then integrated planning, implementation, and evaluation. The curriculum is divided into pre-clinical and clinical phases, each accounting for 2.5 years. Community health sciences are taught in the pre-clinical terms, while clinical skills are learned at several field sites. The Aga Khan University School of Nursing in Kenya, devotes

15 percent of its curriculum to community health. Since 1988, a two-year post-baccalaureate Bachelor of Science in Nursing has been introduced (Bryant *et al.*, 1993).

Primary health care is also a priority in tertiary medical education in Latin America. The Latin American Medical School (ELAM) in Cuba offers a six-year program, the Comprehensive Health Program (CHP). ELAM enrolls international students mostly coming from low-income countries, low-income families, providing full scholarships for the duration of the study.[41] Curriculum for the program includes a six-month to one-year pre-med bridging course, with Spanish for those who need it, two years of basic science, and four years of clinical rotations, when students are sent out to all 14 provinces to train alongside Cuba's future physicians. The graduates make a commitment to serve in underserved communities upon graduation, which is reinforced by a summer program devised by students themselves, in which they spend part of their vacations serving in their home communities under the supervision of Cuban professors (Frank and Reed, 2005). According to the University Website, more than 25,000 doctors from 84 countries have graduated from ELAM.[42]

In Mexico, the Xochimilco health sciences modular program at Mexico's Universidad Autonoma Metropolitana prepares students for work in primary care settings. It features a common intake year that focuses on general knowledge starting with, for example, the history of science, introduction to scientific inquiry and methodology, before students opt for a specific focus on medicine, dentistry, nursing, or nutrition.[43] Post-secondary education programs are usually longitudinal, but a modular approach was put in place, enabling students to acquire increasingly complex competencies while gaining skills and experience providing services. The modular approach focuses on interdisciplinary studies, has an interactive teaching approach using small groups of students assigned to a teacher and promote research experience from the onset of the program. At Xochimilco (one of the four main university campuses), links exist between course modules and field placements, so that placement reinforces the lessons of one module and introduces new issues to be explored in the upcoming modules (Task Force for Scaling Up Education and Training for Health Workers, 2008).

In the US, in 2017, the University of Washington was ranked number one concerning primary care residency program (US News and World Report, 2017). The school is organized into six colleges, each college with its own mentor who counsel students throughout their four years in medical school. Through partnerships between the school and nearby states, students complete several six-week clerkships in Washington, Wyoming, Montana, Alaska, and Idaho. The medical students are encouraged to get involved in service-learning projects like the Community Health Advancement Program, and Student Providers Aspiring to Rural and Underserved Experience (US News and World Report, 2017).[44]

At Johns Hopkins University, the primary care track of the Osler Medical Residency, "Urban Health Internal Medicine Primary Care Leadership Track," trains residents to be primary care leaders who improve the health of vulnerable, urban populations. The program produces graduates who are experts in enhancing patient's self-management and care-seeking behaviors. The program brings together internal medicine, public health, adolescent medicine, psychiatry, together with experiences and learning from local organizations such as Baltimore City Health Department and Health Care for the Homeless.[45]

Conclusion: Lessons Learned from International Experience

Medical education institutions will thrive only in higher education systems that support core principles that proved to be certain in sustainability and success of an organization. These include: sufficient autonomy, governments providing clear oversight and policy directions but avoiding day-to-day management; "explicit stratification, allowing institutions to play to their strengths, while competing for funding, faculty and students; cooperation as well as competition within the system" (Bloom *et al.*, 2007); increased awareness of the evolving community and population needs; openness with the business field, health industry, venture capital and any other forms that will support innovation in health care. On its own, the market will not provide these qualities. Governments need to develop a new role as stewards, rather than managers of higher education (Bloom *et al.*, 2007; Task Force on Higher Education and Society, 2000).

Recently, there has been a shift from traditional teacher-centered didactic, lecture-based teaching which characterized most medical learning up to the first half of the twentieth century, to a student-centered, problem-oriented community-based medical training in the twenty-first century. Problem-based learning has gained worldwide popularity. Efforts are being made to tailor modern educational methods to local needs. Two examples of such efforts are the success of community-based medical education (CBME) and problem-based learning used to train doctors for rural South Africa, as well as schools in Nigeria that have significant CBME components in their medical curriculum. In addition, more recently the focus had been to address and strengthen the medical students' capacity to support lifelong learning, self-assessment, knowledge about health care systems, and technology use. These are experimental models such as the US American Medical Association project "Accelerating Change in Medical Education." Eleven US Medical Schools formed a consortium to share their ideas and experiment with programs that will equip medical students with the tools mentioned previously.

Mostly using the internet as a platform, for the past several years many education technologies were developed. These technologies such as simulations meant for virtual learning, educational games, open sources knowledge repositories, social networks and blogs to describe issues and community problems have facilitated the process of learning, especially through learner-centered methods of education. While these tools that currently come at an affordable price in developed and middle-income countries and therefore are used intensely, they don't have the same availability and affordability in low-income countries. To attempt such a transformation within rural Africa and South Asia, for example, where electricity alone can be a problem, basic infrastructure becomes a major obstacle. The transformation will require a concerted effort and the government vision toward economic development and diversification by supporting and nurturing openness to the world of knowledge and ideas that are already there.

There has also been a movement toward emphasizing the knowledge about the communities comprising individuals, families, education and social organizations that the communities are engaged in. In many countries, the primary care training already includes visits to local communities, discussions to better understand the behavior, the social needs, and the disparities that may exist in a community. Communication skills and teamwork are also emphasized during medical training, so that physicians will be able to listen to the patients' view and negotiate treatment plans and options, with the patient following clear explanation of problems and their solutions.

It has been noted that the current practice of health care delivery is best delivered by teams of professionals, rather than individuals. Inter-professional learning has become a strong component of the curriculum at many medical schools. Primary and secondary care teams can be very different in SSA, with varying roles and levels of responsibility, calling for more innovative inter-professional courses in undergraduate education in Africa (Gukas, 2007). A local teacher development program, such as the FAIMER Regional Institutes, where more than 100 faculties have participated in programs in India and Brazil, may be best tailored to the specific needs of regional groups of faculty (Burdick, 2007). Other areas of change include: a new accent on behavioral medicine (comprised of prevention and rehabilitation); the development of more valid systems of assessment and performance-standard setting; increased attention given to management of medical education and faculty education; and adherence to international standards in medical education (Gukas, 2007).

As has been noted throughout this chapter, many constraints exist to strengthen and improve the higher education sector. During the past three decades, investments in primary and secondary education around the globe have led to an increase in the number of secondary education candidates, thus increasing the numbers of potential high-level health workers. Investments in higher education institutions will be a necessary response to such gains, as developing countries must grasp their human resource potential to its fullest. Lessons can be learned at the global and regional level, as countries continue to respond to changes in the economic and social systems that guide their higher education policies. In ways that are organic to their own region, governments, civil society, students and teachers have all continued to thrive and evolve within continually evolving environments. Countries in less developed regions must do the same, as the current situation in higher education presents opportunities for growth and success that have never been realized before. Tertiary medical training will hopefully seize these opportunities, and in return build and strengthen human resources networks across the globe.

Endnotes

1. Net enrollment rate, "Total number of students in the theoretical age group for a given level of education enrolled in that level, expressed as a percentage of the total population in that age group", UNESCO Glossary, accessed at http://uis.unesco.org/en/glossary-term/net-enrolment-rate.
2. Gross secondary enrollment rate, The number of children enrolled in a level (primary or secondary) regardless of age, divided by the population of the age group that officially corresponds to the same level, UNICEF Education, accessed at https://www.unicef.org/infobycountry/stats_popup5.html.
3. The World Bank Group, "Education Strategy 2020: 'Learning for All' Investing in People's Knowledge and Skills, to Promote Development", 2011.
4. UIS Information, Bulleting Number 7, accessed at http://www.uis.unesco.org/Education/Documents/ib7-student-mobility-2012-en.pdf.
5. World Bank, 2016, Gross enrolment ratio, tertiary, both sexes (%), Gross enrollment ratio, tertiary both sexes (%) all countries and economies, accessed at http://data.worldbank.org/indicator/se.ter.enrr.
6. Institute for Health Metrics and Evaluation, Global Burden of Diseases Study, 2010, accessed at http://www.healthdata.org/news-release/global-burden-disease-massive-shifts-reshape-health-landscape-worldwide.
7. Association of American Colleges, *"The 2014 Medical Schools Enrollment Survey"*, Center for Workforce Studies, April 2015, accessed at https://www.aamc.org/download/459890/data/2014medicalschoolenrollmen treport.pdf.
8. International Medical Graduates are physicians with degrees (undergraduate and or graduate from foreign medical schools) practicing medicine in the US.
9. Salmi, J., *The Tertiary Education Imperative*: *Knowledge, Skills and Values for Development*, "Sense Publishers, Rotherdam/Botson/Taipei, 2017, https://www.hopkinsmedicine.org/gim/training/Osler/Med_Urban_Health/over-view.html.
10. Open Knowledge Repository, Africa's Pulse, No. 14, October 2016, accessed at https://openknowledge.worldbank.org/handle/10986/25097.
11. *Wastage rate* is defined as "the drop-out rate from a company, college, or other organization, especially before they have completed their education or training". Collins (2013), Collins English Dictionary, accessed at https://www.collinsdictionary.com/us/dictionary/english/wastage-rate.

12. Maher, B., H. Hynes, C. Sweeney, S. Khashan Ali, M. O'Rourke, K. Doran, A. Harris, and S. O' Flynn, "Medical school attrition-beyond the statistics: A ten year retrospective study", *BMC Medical Education*, 2013, accessed at https:// bmcmededuc.biomedcentral.com/articles/10.1186/1472-6920-13-13.
13. Analysis in Brief, Association of the American Colleges, **14**(5), May 2014.
14. Accelerating Change in Medical Education — Creating the Medical School of the Future, American Medical Association, accessed at https://www.ama-assn.org/sites/default/files/media-browser/public/about-ama/ace-mono-graph-interactive_0.pdf.
15. "Gene to society: A curriculum for the Johns Hopkins University, School of Medicine," accessed at hopkinsmedicine.org; "Pathways", Harvard Medical School, accessed at https://hms.harvard.edu/departments/medical-education/md-programs/pathways.
16. World Directory of Medical Schools, accessed at https://search.wdoms.org.
17. *Gross Enrolment Rate* is defined as the number of pupils enrolled in ISCED [International Standard Classification of Education 5 and 6] regardless of age, expressed as a percentage of the population in the five-year age group following on from the secondary school-leaving age (UNESCO, 2008).
18. See Endnote 9.
19. See Endnote 9.
20. The mean disparity ratio is calculated as enrollment rate of the top income quintile divided by the enrollment rate of the lowest quintile); the range of disparity ratios comprises best-to-worst countries in each region.
21. OCED "Education at a Glance — 2014 OECD Indicators", accessed at https://www.oecd.org/edu/Education-at-a-Glance-2014.pdf.
22. See Endnote 9.
23. Global Business Guide — Indonesia, accessed at http://www.gbgindonesia.com/en/education/article/2015/higher_education_indonesian_academia_must_open_up_11276.php.
24. Accreditation of Institutions for Health Professional Education, WHO, 2013.
25. Phillips D. Susan, "Accreditation: Realities, Challenges, and Opportunities", presentation in Washington DC at the Forum Exploring the Role of Accreditation in Enhancing Quality and Innovation in Health Professions Education — Global Forum on Innovation in Health Professional Education, National Academy of Sciences, 2016.
26. European Higher Education Area, "Bologna Process", 2010, accessed at http://www.ehea.info/.

27. European Commission, "Growth: Internal Market, Industry, Entrepreneurship and SMEs," accessed at http://ec.europa.eu/growth/single-market/services/free-movementprofessionals/qualifications-recognition/automatic_en.

28. Rolwing, K. and Clark, N., "Americas, Higher Education in Chile" World Education News and Reviews, December 2013, accessed at http://wenr.wes.org/2013/12/introduction-to-the-higher-education-system-of-chile.

29. United States Medical Licensing Examination, accessed at http://www.usmle.org/step-3/.

30. WHO, "The Abuja Declaration: Ten Years On", 2011, accessed at http://www.who.int/healthsystems/publications/abuja_report_aug_2011.pdf?ua=1.

31. *Higher for non-EU students and or non-European Economic Area students.

32. OECD, 2013, "Education Indicators in Focus", accessed at https://www.oecd.org/education/skills-beyond-school/EDIF%202013--N%C2%B014%20(eng)-Final.pdf.

33. OECD, "Education at a Glance-2014", accessed at https://www.oecd.org/edu/Education-at-a-Glance-2014.pdf.

34. IHS Inc., 2015, 2016 "The Complexities of Physician Supply and Demand: Projections from 2013 to 2025", accessed at https://www.aamc.org/download/426242/data/ihsreportdownload.pdf?cm_mmc=AAMC_ScientificAffairs_PDF_ihsreport and accessed at https://www.aamc.org/download/458082/data/2016_complexities_of_supply_and_demand_projections.pdf.

35. UNESCO Institute for Statistics, "Trends in Tertiary Education: Sub-Sahara Africa", Fact Sheet, December 2010, No 10.

36. See Endnote 35.

37. Taylor, A. L., Hwenda L. and Larsen Bjørn-Inge, D. N., "Stemming the Brain Drain — A WHO Global Code of Practice on International Recruitment of Health Personnel", *New England Journal, N Engl J Med*, **365**:2348–2351, 2011.

38. Schuetze, F. C., "Medical Students Head to Eastern Europe", New York Times, 2013, accessed at http://www.nytimes.com/2013/08/12/world/europe/medical-students-head-to-eastern-Europe.html.

39. See Endnote 21.

40. Harden, R. M. and Davis M. H., "AMEE Medical Education Guide No. 5. The core curriculum with options or special study modules", *Journal of Medical Teacher*, **17**(2), 1995, accessed at http://www.tandfonline.com/doi/abs/10.3109/01421599509008301?journalCode=imte20.

41. The Latin American Medical School website, accessed at http://instituciones.sld.cu/elam/historia-de-la-elam/.

42. See Endnote 21.
43. The Universidad Autonoma Metropolitana, Mexico, accessed at http://www. uam.mx/licenciaturas/licenciaturas_por_unidad.html.
44. US News and World Report, "Best Medical Schools: Primary Care", accessed at https://www.usnews.com/best-graduate-schools/top-medical-schools/university-of-washington-04122.
45. Johns Hopkins Urban Health Track: Program Overview, accessed at http://www.hopkinsmedicine.org/gim/training/Osler/Med_Urban_Health/overview.html.

References

ACGME (Accreditation Council for Graduate Medical Education). "Glossary of terms", 2008, accessed at http://www.acgme.org/acWebsite/about/ab_ACGMEglossary.pdf.

American Medical Association (AMA), "State Medical Licensure Requirements and Statistics", 2008, p. 147.

Amin, Z., K. H. Eng, M. Gwee, K. D. Rhoon, and T. C. Hoo, "Medical education in Southeast Asia: Emerging issues, challenges and opportunities", *Medical Education*, **39**(8): 829–832, 2005.

Association of the American Colleges, "Accelerating change in medical education — Creating the medical school of the future", Report 2015, accessed at https://www.ama-assn.org/sites/default/files/media-browser/public/about-ama/ace-monograph-interactive_0.pdf.

Barzansky, B. and S. I. Etzel, "Educational programs in US medical schools, 2002–2003", *Journal of the American Medical Association*, **290**(9), 1190–1196, 2003.

Batalden, P., D. Leach, S. Swing, H. Dreyfus, and S. Dreyfus, "General competencies and accreditation in graduate medical education", *Health Affairs*, **21**(5), 103–111, 2002.

Bjarnason, S., H. A. Patrinos, J.-P. Tan, "The evolving regulatory context for private education in emerging economies", World Bank working Paper No. 154, Discussion Paper and Case Studies, 2009, p. 7.

Bloom D., M. R. Agosin, G. Chapelier, and J. Saigal, "Solving the ridddle of globalization and development", Routledge Taylor and Francis Group, UNDP, 2007, Chapter 7, p. 185.

Bologna Process, Bologna Process Official Website, 2008; accessed at http://www.ond.vlaanderen.be/hogeronderwijs/bologna/.

Bossert, T., T. Barnighausen, D. Bowser, A. Mitchell, and G. Gedik, *Assessing Financing, Education, Management and Policy Context for Strategic Planning of Human Resources for Health.* Geneva: World Health Organization, 2007.

Brieger, W. R. and R. J. Adeniyi, "Self-treatment in rural Nigeria: A community health education diagnosis", *Hygiene*, **5**(2), 41–46, 1986.

Bryant, J. H., D. R. Marsh, K. S. Khan, R. D' Souza, K. Husein, A. Aslam, A. F. Qureshi, V. DeWit, and R. M. Harnar, "A developing country's university oriented toward strengthening health systems: Challenges and results", *American Journal of Public Health*, **83**(11), 1537–1543, 1993.

Buchan, J. and J. Sochalski "The migration of nurses: Trends and policies", *Bulletin of the World Health Organization*, **82**(8), 587–594, 2004.

Burdick, W., "Challenges and issues in health professions education in Africa", *Medical Teacher*, **29**(9), 882–886, 2007.

CIA (Central Intelligence Agency) "CIA World Factbook: Malawi, 2008." 2008, accessed at https://www.cia.gov/library/publications/the-world-factbook/geos/mi.html

De Vos, P., W. De Ceukelaire, M. Bonet, and P. Van der Stuyft, "Cuba's international cooperation in health: An overview", *International Journal of Health Services*, **37**(4), 761–776, 2007.

Dovlo, D., "Migration of nurses from Sub-Saharan Africa: A review of issues and challenges", *Health Services Research*, **42**(3 Pt 2), 1373–1388, 2007.

Duvivier, R., J. Boulet, C. Bede, A. Opalek, M. Van Zanten, and J. Norcini, "An overview of the world's medical schools: An update", 2014 John Wiley & Sons Ltd., *Medical Education*, **48**, 860–869, 2014.

European University Association, accessed at http://eua.be/eua-work-end-policy-area.

Fahal, A. H., "Medical education in the Sudan: Its strengths and weaknesses", *Medical Teacher*, **29**(9), 910–914, 2007.

Fielden, J. and N. LaRocque, "The Evolving Regulatory Context for Private Education in Emerging Economies." *Education Working Paper 14*, World Bank/International Finance Corporation, Washington, DC, 2008.

Frank, M. and G. Reed, "Doctors for the (Developing) World", *Medicc Review*, **7**(8), 2–7, 2005.

Fredriksen, B. and T. J. Peng, (eds.), *An African Exploration of the East Asian Education Experience*, Washington, DC: World Bank, 2008.

Global Health Workforce Alliance, "Scaling Up, Saving Lives", Task Force for Scaling Up Education and Training for Health Workers, World Health Organization, 2008a.

Global Health Workforce Alliance, Taskforce on Scaling Up Education and Training for Health Workers, Ethiopia Human Resources for Health Program, Country Case Study, 2008b.

Govender, V., D. McIntyre, and R. Loewenson, "Progress towards the Abuja target for government spending on health care in East and Southern Africa", Equinet Discussion Paper No. 60, 2008.

Gukas, I. D., "Global paradigm shift in medical education: Issues of concern for Africa", *Medical Teacher*, **29**(9), 887–892, 2007.

Harvard Medical School, "Pathways", accessed at https://hms.harvard.edu/departments/medical-education/md-programs/pathway.

Holm-Nielsen, L. B., A. Blom, and P. Garcia, "Providing skills for the knowledge economy: The World Bank in tertiary education in Latin America and the Caribbean", Washington, DC: World Bank, 2003.

Holm-Nielsen, L., J. S. Jeppesen, and K. Thorn, "Approaches to results-based funding in tertiary education: Identifying finance reform options for Chile", Washington, DC: World Bank, 2004.

IHS Inc., "The complexities of physician supply and demand: Projections from 2013 to 2025", 2015–2016, accessed at https://www.aamc.org/download/426242/data/ihsreportdownload.pdf?cm_mmc=AAMC_ScientificAffairs_PDF_ihsreport; https://www.aamc.org/download/458082/data/2016_complexities_of_supply_and_demand_projections.pdf.

Institute for Health Metrics and Evaluation (IHME), "Global burden of diseases study", 2010, accessed at http://www.healthdata.org/news-release/global-burden-disease-massive-shifts-reshape-health-landscape-worldwide.

Johns Hopkins University, School of Medicine, "Genes to Society", accessed at hopkinsmedicine.org.

Kemahli, S., F. Dokmeci, O. Palaoglu, T. Aktug, B. Arda, Y. E. Demirel, T. Karahan, F. Ozyurda, H. Akan, and I. H. Ayhan, "How we derived a core curriculum: From institutional to National — Ankara University experience", *Medical Teacher*, **26**(4), 295–298, 2004.

Kwizera, E. N., E. U. Igumbor, and L. E. Mazwai, "Twenty years of medical education in rural South Africa — Experiences of the University of Transkei medical school and lessons for the future", *South Africa Medical Journal*, **95**(12), 920–922, 924, 2005.

Liang, X., "Uganda tertiary education sector report", *Africa Region Human Development Working Paper*, Washington, DC: World Bank, 2004.

Linden, T., N. Arnhold, and K. Vasiliev, "From fragmentation to cooperation: Tertiary education, research and development in South Eastern Europe", Washington, DC: World Bank, 2008.

Mahal, A. and M. Mohanan, 2006. "Growth of private medical education in India", *Medical Education*, **40**(10), 1009-1011, 2006.

Martineau, T., "'Brain drain' of health professionals: From rhetoric to responsible action", *Health Policy*, **70**, 1–10, 2004.

Medical Council of India. "Salient features of regulations on graduate medical education", 1997. Accessed at http://www.mciindia.org/know/rules/rules_mbbs.htm, July 17, 2006.

Murakami, Y., "Accessibility and Affordability of Tertiary Education in Brazil", Colombia, Mexico and Peru within a Global Context, World Bank, 2008.

Muula, A. S. and R. L. Broadhead, "The first decade of the Malawi College of Medicine: A critical appraisal", *Tropical Medicine and International Health*, **6**(2), 155–159, 2001.

Preker, A. S. and C. Ly, "Capital financing in health professional education", World Bank, 2007.

Robson, J., "Scaling up health and education workers: Systems for training", London: Department of International Development, 2005.

Salmi, J. and A. M. Hauptman, "Innovations in tertiary education financing: A comparative evaluation of allocation mechanisms", *Education Working Paper No. 4*, Washington, DC: World Bank, 2006.

Segouin, C., "Country report: Medical education in France", *Medical Education*, **41**, 295–301, 2007.

Supe, A. and W. Burdick, "Challenges and issues in medical education in India", *Academic Medicine*, **81**(12), 1076–1080, 2006.

Task Force for Scaling Up Education and Training for Health Workers, "Scaling up, saving lives", Geneva: World Health Organization, 2008.

Task Force on Higher Education and Society, "Higher education in developing countries: Peril and promise", Washington, DC: World Bank, 2000.

UNESCO Institute for Statistics, UIS Information, Bulleting Number 7, 2012, accessed at http://www.uis.unesco.org/Education/Documents/ib7-student-mobility-2012-en.pdf.

UNESCO, "Beyond 20/20 WDS", accessed at http://stats.uis.unesco.org/unesco/TableViewer/document.aspx?ReportId=136&IF_Language=eng&BR_Topic=0.

United States Medical Licensing Examination, accessed at http://www.usmle.org/step-3/.

WHO (World Health Organization) Report, 2006, Chapter 3, p. 49 in The PLoS Medicine Editors, "Improving Health by Investing in Medical Education", PLoS Med 2(12): e424, 2005.

WHO (World Health Organization) "Health workforce migration and retention", 2008, accessed at http://www.who.int/hrh/migration/en/.

Wit, H., *et al.*, "Higher education in Latin America: The international dimension", World Bank, 2005.

World Bank, "Accelerating catch-up: Tertiary education for growth in Sub-Saharan Africa", Washington, DC: World Bank, 2008.

World Bank, "African economies need deeper diversification and better policies", The World Bank, Africa's Pulse, No. 14, 2016.

World Bank, "Gross enrolment ratio, tertiary, both sexes (%), Gross enrollment ratio, tertiary both sexes (%), all countries and economies", 2016, accessed at http://data.worldbank.org/indicator/se.ter.enrr.

World Bank, "Higher Education in Brazil — challenges and options", Washington, DC: World Bank, 2002.

World Bank, "Higher education in developing countries, Peril and Promise", 2000, accessed at http://elibraary.worldbank.org.

World Bank, Africa Region Human Development Working Paper Series, "Uganda Tertiary Education Sector Report" March 2004, accessed at http://documents.worldbank.org/curated/en/916401468318016857/pdf/328070UG0Tertiary0education0AFHDno150.pdf.

World Health Organization (WHO), "Accreditation of institutions for health professional education", 2013.

World Health Organization (WHO), "The World Health Report 2006: Working together for health", Geneva: World Health Organization, 2006.

Yalcin, B. M., T. F. Karahan, D. Karadenizli, and E. M. Sahin, "Short-term effects of problem-based learning curriculum on students' self-directed skills development", *Croatian Medical Journal*, **47**(3), 491–498, 2006.

Chapter 3

Needs-Based Workforce Analysis for Investing in Health Education

Daniel R. Arnold and Richard M. Scheffler

The United Nations' sustainable development goals (SDGs) set an ambitious agenda for achieving better global health by 2030. The agenda includes reducing global maternal and infant mortality, ending epidemics such as AIDS, tuberculosis, and malaria, and achieving universal health coverage. Reaching these goals will require well-functioning health systems. As health systems are highly labor intensive, the availability and performance of health workers will have a significant impact on whether these goals are achieved.

Given the substantial time and resources needed to educate and develop skilled health workers, forecasts of future health worker needs are necessary to enable countries to plan appropriately today. This chapter explains the methods used for conducting such analyses, includes examples of how these methods have been applied recently, and provides an exercise that allows readers to test their grasp of the material covered. While the methods are explained in the context of global needs-based forecasts, the methods can easily be applied to more local levels (e.g. provinces within countries) assuming data is available.

This chapter also discusses some of the hurdles that may be faced when attempting to implement standards for educating and developing health workers. Countries often face economic and fiscal constraints both in terms of paying the cost of labor and in terms of investing in and paying for the health education system. As such, a more iterative process to labor markets and education institutions may be necessary where countries first set standards based on what is affordable rather than desirable.

Introduction

The High-Level Commission on Health Employment and Economic Growth recently released its report to the United Nations Secretary-General (World Health Organization, 2016c). The motivation for the formation of the commission, and a focus of its deliberations, is the global mismatch between supply, need, and demand for health workers to 2030. The report of the High-Level Commission is the latest addition to a series of reports and articles that has expressed concern about the shortage of health workers (e.g. Evans *et al.*, 2016; Cometto and Campbell, 2016; Campbell *et al.*, 2013).

Given the resources and time needed to increase the training of health workers, countries must plan appropriately today to stave off future workforce shortages. The two types of health labor market shortages that are most often discussed are demand-based shortages and needs-based shortages (see Bruckner *et al.* (2016) for a detailed account of the differences between the two). Both shortages require an underlying estimate of health worker supply: demand-based shortages are calculated as demand minus supply, while needs-based shortages are calculated as need minus supply. The demand for health workers in a country is derived from the willingness and ability to pay of its purchasers of health care (e.g. the government, private sector firms). The need for health workers does not consider a country's ability to pay for health workers. Estimates of need are based on a country's disease burden profile and resulting estimates of need are fully dependent on how need was defined. Different definitions of need would lead to different estimates of need and ultimately different estimates of needs-based shortages. Because of this, needs-based shortages are not true shortages in the typical labor economics sense of the word — they simply represent shortfalls in health workers relative to a particular benchmark of what need means. Nevertheless, needs-based shortages are helpful for gaging which countries could most use additional health resources. For instance, low-income countries often do not exhibit demand-based shortages due to their demand being low from their inability to pay (Liu *et al.*, 2016). However, low-income countries often exhibit the largest needs-based shortages due to a combination of facing significant health epidemics (e.g. AIDS and malaria) and having a low supply of health workers because of underdeveloped education systems or as a result of losing significant numbers of health workers to countries offering higher wages (Scheffler *et al.*, 2016). While we discuss the demand-based approach at times, the focus of this chapter is needs-based health workforce planning. As we proceed through the chapter, the reader should keep in mind that there are many factors — such as politics and professional protectionism — that will play a large role in the way health labor markets ultimately work and the way future health workers will be trained. An extended discussion of these issues is beyond the scope of this chapter, but it is important to keep them in mind when applying the methods presented in this chapter.

The purpose of this chapter is to show analysts tasked with planning for the future: (1) how to estimate current health worker need, (2) how to forecast the need for health workers into the future, and (3) how to calculate needs-based shortages. The methods presented here have recently been applied to country level data to produce global estimates of health worker need and needs-based shortages (Scheffler *et al.*, 2016), but the same methods could easily be applied to state or province level data to produce estimates of health worker need for regions within countries.

The chapter proceeds as follows. A conceptual framework for thinking about the health labor market is discussed in the section, "Health Labor Market Framework". The next section "Skilled Birth Attendant Benchmark" shows the analyst how to use the skilled birth attendant benchmark to estimate health worker need. The following section "SDG Composite Index" presents the sustainable development goals (SDG) composite index approach for estimating health worker need. The next section "Forecasting Need" shows the analyst how to use estimates of health worker need to forecast future health worker needs. The next section "Estimated and Forecasted Workforce Shortages" presents recent estimates and forecasts of global health worker needs-based shortages and the final section concludes. An exercise that analysts can use to test their grasp of the methods presented in this chapter is available in the Appendix.

Health Labor Market Framework

To conceptualize how needs-based and demand-based shortages are calculated, we discuss the health labor market as it exists in many countries. We start by defining need, demand, and supply. Need is defined generally as the number of health workers required to attain the objectives of a health system (Scheffler *et al.*, 2016; Bruckner *et al.*, 2016; Scheffler, 2009). Often a defined threshold is used to estimate a country's need for health workers. For instance, a country's need for health workers could be estimated based on the minimum number of health workers needed to address priority population health issues.

Demand for health workers is derived from the willingness and ability to pay of purchasers of health care (e.g. the government, private firms). The more purchasers are willing to pay for health care, the larger the demand for health workers capable of delivering the demanded health services. A country's demand for health workers is influenced by household income, the fiscal capacity of the government to employ public sector workers, and demographic features of the country's population (e.g. age), and the level of financial protection available to consumers for accessing the health care services they need (Liu *et al.*, 2016; Scheffler *et al.*, 2008).

Forecasts of needs-based and demand-based shortages require a measurement of the supply of health workers, namely, the number of health workers that are available in a country (Serneels *et al.*, 2016). Labor economics predicts that as wages increase for health workers, more workers will be willing to become employed as health professionals. Additionally, higher wages encourage students to pursue medical training, thus increasing the future supply of health workers (Tulenko *et al.*, 2016). In global labor markets, worker skills are often transferable across countries, making migration important in determining a country's supply of health workers. Migration is a particular problem for low- and middle-income countries who lose their health workers to countries (often high-income countries) with better compensation (Chen *et al.*, 2004, Vujicic

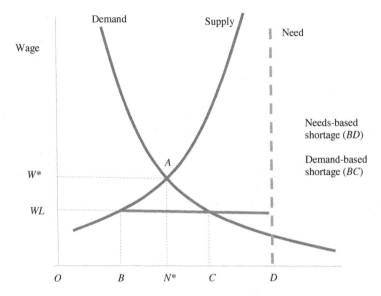

Figure 3.1   The Health Labor Market

and Zurn, 2006). The WHO Global Health Workforce Statistics database provides health worker counts per 1,000 population for 193 countries (Global Health Workforce Statistics database, 2016).

Figure 3.1 graphically depicts the health labor market. In a perfectly functioning labor market, the market reaches equilibrium when the supply of health workers equals the demand at point *A*. When this happens, the wage would be *W** and *N** doctors would be employed. However, low- and middle-income countries often face binding constraints on the amount of financing that is available to pay health workers and rigidities such as government salaries that are set by law across civil servant categories, often do not fully relate to the value of a health worker's productivity. Thus, the wage offered will be lower, *WL* rather than *W**, resulting in a shortage of doctors represented by length *BC* as shown in Figure 3.1. The supply of doctors willing to work at *WL* is *B* while the demand for doctors at this wage is *C*. If the lack of government policies or resources prevent wages from rising to *W**, the shortage will persist.

The need for doctors is represented by the vertical line which passes through point *D*. At a wage *WL*, the number of doctors employed will be

B but the need is *D*, so the needs-based shortage is length *BD*. In this case, the needs-based shortage is larger than the demand-based shortage by *CD* (*BD* minus *BC*). Needs-based shortages being larger than demand-based shortages is common in low- and middle-income countries. For high-income countries and upper-middle-income countries, the situation is often reversed. The need line moves to the left (past point *C*) and demand-based shortages become larger than needs-based shortages.

Figure 3.1 depicts the basic dynamics underlying the labor market for health workers. Box 3.1 presents an example of how task shifting, a much discussed method for dealing with shortages (see Fulton *et al.*, 2011, for a review), could change the level of shortages in the health labor market.

Box 3.1 Task Shifting

Task shifting refers to changing who performs various health care services. For instance, tasks normally performed by surgeons could be shifted to surgery technicians, or tasks performed by doctors could be shifted to nurses. The amount of task shifting is often restricted in countries due to licensing requirements that limit the performance of certain services to certified groups. Relaxation of these requirements or the development of new professions (e.g. nurse practitioners) could increase the amount of task shifting in the future.

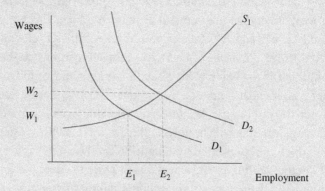

Figure 3B.1   Labor Market for Surgery Technicians

(*Continued*)

Box 3.1 (*Continued*)

Figure 3B.1 shows how task shifting to surgery technicians would affect their employment and wages in a freely-functioning labor market. Since surgery technicians are paid less than surgeons, task shifting increases the demand for surgery technicians (D_1 to D_2), which increases their wages (W_1 to W_2) and the number of technicians employed (E_1 to E_2). The wages and employment of surgeons would necessarily fall, unless there had been excess demand for surgeons, which is often the case in low-income countries. Excess demand means demand is greater than supply (i.e. a shortage exists). When there is excess demand for surgeons, there exists a level of increase in surgery technicians that would not cause a decrease in the level of surgeon employment; all that would happen is that the shortage of health workers performing surgery would decrease (see Scheffler, 2016, for details).

Skilled Birth Attendant Benchmark

With a conceptual framework in place, we now move to a description of how to go about estimating the need line that is depicted in Figure 3.1. We start with the skilled birth attendant benchmark approach that was developed in 2006 by WHO (World Health Organization, 2006). This approach defines need as the number of health workers to ensure that 80 percent of all births occur with a skilled birth attendant present. Reduction of infant and maternal mortality has been, and continues to be, a top health priority for most low- and lower-middle-income countries. WHO calculated that 2.28 health workers per 1,000 population were necessary to reach the threshold of 80 percent coverage of births by skilled birth attendants. WHO arrived at this number by fitting a curve to data from countries on their density of health workers and percentage of births with a skilled birth attendant. The curve that was fit is shown in Figure 3.2.

The fitted curve in Figure 3.2 was the result of estimating the following regression model:

$$\% \text{ Births Covered}_i = \beta_0 + \beta_1 \ln (\text{health worker density}_i) + \varepsilon_i, \quad (3.1)$$

where % Births Covered$_i$ is the percent of births with a skilled birth attendant for country i, β_0 is a constant, ln(health worker density$_i$) is the natural

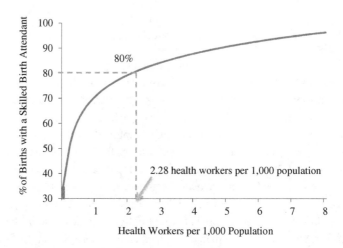

Figure 3.2   Population Density of Health Care Professionals Required to Ensure Skilled Attendance at Births
Source: WHO, "The world health report 2006: Working together for health", Geneva: World Health Organization, 2006, accessed at http://www.who.int/whr/2006/en/.

log of health worker density for country i, β_1 is the slope of the health worker density variable, and ε_i is a normally distributed error term. Health worker density is defined as the number of doctors, nurses, and midwives per 1,000 population. After estimating the coefficients of this regression (i.e. β_0 and β_1), an analyst could then insert his chosen threshold for births covered (e.g. 60 percent) and solve for the number of health workers per 1,000 population necessary to achieve that threshold. The WHO's chosen threshold of 80 percent coverage leads to 2.28 health workers per 1,000 population.

The shape of the curve in Figure 3.2 is consistent with the notion of diminishing returns to additional health workers. Diminishing returns is the concept that as inputs are added, the additional output created form the next input will be less than the output created by the previous unit. In this case, the inputs are health workers and the output is births covered. To make this point another way, the curve in Figure 3.2 shows that a relatively small increase in health workers can increase coverage by five percent at low levels of coverage (e.g. 10–15 percent coverage).

An analyst wishing to build on this model could do so by adding variables that allow geographic factors to influence a country's need for health workers. Research has shown that urban and rural composition may drive health care access (Scheffler and Fulton, 2013). Given this, variables such as percentage of the population living in an urban area or population per square kilometer could be added to Equation (3.1) (Bruckner *et al.*, 2016). The World Bank's Health, Nutrition, and Population database contains data on both these population variables (World Bank, 2016). After including the new variables into (1), the analyst would estimate the new regression equation to obtain new coefficient estimates. To then find the number of health workers needed, the analyst would solve the following equation:

$$
\begin{aligned}
\text{Desired \% Births Covered Threshold} \\
= \widehat{\beta_0} + \widehat{\beta_1} \ \ln(\text{health worker density}) \\
+ \widehat{\beta_2} \ \overline{\text{\% living in an urban area}} \\
+ \widehat{\beta_3} \ \overline{\text{population per square kilometer}}
\end{aligned}
\quad , \qquad (3.2)
$$

where the $\widehat{\beta}$s are the estimated coefficients from the regression and the bars over the % living in an urban area and population per square kilometer variables represent the sample means for those two variables. In multivariate regressions such as Equation (3.2), the health worker density per 1,000 population solved for represents the number of health workers needed when the other variables in the equation are set to their means. A different number of health workers would be needed if the additional variables were set at their medians, or some other number of interest. After the analyst substitutes his desired threshold into Equation (3.2), he will be left with an equation with one unknown (health worker density) which can be solved for with some simple algebra.

There is an obvious limitation to model (1): it only accounts for one population health goal — reducing infant and maternal mortality. How many health workers would be needed if we were also concerned about meeting other populations health goals, such as ending the AIDS epidemic or reducing the number of death and illnesses from water pollution/infestation? The next section proposes an answer to this question.

SDG Composite Index

A recent WHO report has extended the skilled birth attendant approach to address more population health goals (Scheffler *et al.*, 2016). The premise of the report was that all countries should strive to attain workforce goals that enable universal health coverage (UHC) (Evans *et al.*, 2016). With UHC in mind, the WHO specified 12 tracer conditions listed in SDG 3[1] for which countries should achieve 80 percent coverage. Table 3.1 lists the 12 tracer indicators used in the analysis.

Estimating need proceeded as follows (see the Appendix of Scheffler *et al.*, 2016, for details). First, a country was assigned a score from 0 to 12. Countries received one point for each indicator where they attained coverage of greater than 80 percent of the population. Next, each category was weighted by the global burden of disease that it addresses to arrive at a

Table 3.1   **The 12 Selected Tracer Indicators in the SDG Index Threshold and their Primary Classification**

SDG tracer indicator	Classification
Antenatal care	MNCH
Antiretroviral therapy	ID
Cataract	NCD
Diabetes	NCD
DTP3 immunization	ID
Family planning	MNCH
Hypertension	NCD
Potable water	ID
Sanitation	ID
Skilled birth attendance	MNCH
Tobacco smoking	NCD
Tuberculosis	ID

Note: Abbreviations: Maternal, Newborn, Child Health (MNCH), Infectious Disease (ID), Non-communicable Disease (NCD).
Source: Scheffler *et al.* (2016).

Table 3.2   The Global Burden of Disease for the 12 SDG3 Tracer Indicators

SDG3 tracer indicator	DALYs (in 1,000s)	Analytical weight
Antenatal care	85,576	0.10
Antiretroviral therapy	91,897	0.10
Cataract	16,329	0.02
Diabetes	41,368	0.05
DTP3 immunization	12,018	0.01
Family planning	85,576	0.10
Hypertension	191,461	0.21
Potable water	67,010	0.07
Sanitation	67,010	0.07
Skilled birth attendance	85,576	0.10
Tobacco smoking	112,142	0.12
Tuberculosis	43,613	0.05
Total	899,576	1.00

Source: Scheffler *et al.* (2016).

score between 0 and 1. Table 3.2 shows the global burden of disease (measured in disability-adjusted life years (DALYs)) for each of the 12 indicators and the analytical weights used for each indicator.[2] As an example of how the weighting works, if a country only achieved 80 percent coverage for antenatal care, diabetes, and sanitation, its weighted score would be 0.22 (1 × 0.10 + 1 × 0.05 + 1 × 0.07). Achieving 80 percent coverage in all 12 indicators would lead to a score of 1. We refer to this 0–1 score as the SDG composite index in what follows. The 889,576,000 total DALYs addressed by the 12 indicators are notable in that they account for roughly one-third of the global burden of disease (World Health Organization, 2016a). This is a significant improvement over the global burden of disease accounted for by skilled birth attendant benchmark approach.

The WHO report computed a SDG composite index for 210 countries with sufficient data across the 12 tracer conditions. A curve was then

fit that related the health worker density of countries to the SDG index —
very similar to the skilled birth attendant benchmark approach. Specifically,
the following regression equation was estimated

$$\text{SDG composite index}_i = \beta_0 + \beta_1 \ln(\text{health worker density}_i) + \varepsilon_i. \quad (3.3)$$

Taking the natural log of the independent variable will produce a curve
that exhibits diminishing returns, just as in the skilled birth attendant
benchmark approach. The solid curve in Figure 3.3 is the fitted curve that
comes from estimating Equation (3.3). The two dashed curves surrounding the solid curve show the 95 percent confidence interval.

Figure 3.3 also shows that 4.45 health workers per 1,000 population
are necessary to achieve a SDG index score of 0.25. A score of 0.25 corresponds to the median SDG composite index of the 210 countries used to
estimate Equation (3.3). This threshold of 0.25 was used by WHO to

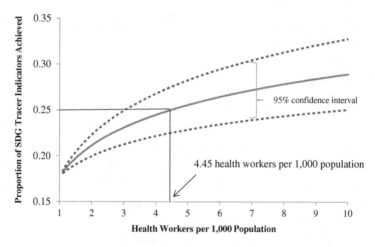

Figure 3.3   Results from the SDG Index Composite Needs-Based Method

Notes: Proportion of 12 selected SDG tracer indicators achieved as a function of health workers per
1,000 population (n = 210 countries and territories). The solid curve shows the regression coefficient
of health workers; the dashed curves show the upper and lower 95 percent confidence interval of
health workers. Skilled health workers are defined as doctors and nurses/midwives. The SDG tracer
indicators were weighted by the global burden of disease each tracer intends to address. The resulting
target number is 4.45 workers that achieve the median score (25 percent) of SDG tracer indicator
attainment for all countries analyzed.

Source: Scheffler *et al.* (2016).

define a country's need. Specifically, WHO's definition of need in this analysis is the number of health workers necessary to achieve the median level of coverage across the 12 indicators (i.e. a score of 0.25).

An analyst wanting to perform this type of analysis can modify the previous model in several ways. First, a threshold other than 0.25 could be chosen. Second, a different set of indicators could be used to compute the SDG composite index. Third, there is no reason 12 indicators need to be used. Depending on the data availability in one's country, it may be necessary to use fewer than 12 indicators. And fourth, additional independent variables could be added to the analysis, such as % living in an urban area as in Equation (3.2).

Importantly, with sufficient data, this analysis could easily be done within a country as opposed to across countries. Instead of 210 countries, Equation (3.3) could be estimated using data from 40 provinces inside a country. The analyst could calculate the median SDG composite index across the 40 provinces and use it as the new threshold, in place of 0.25. This approach would identify which provinces are in most need of extra health resources.

Forecasting Need

The previous sections have focused on estimating current health worker needs-based shortages. This section presents a framework for thinking about how the health worker needs of a country can evolve over time. In what follows we assume that the productivity of doctors remains constant over time. If the productivity of doctors were to increase over time, the forecasted number of doctors needed in the future would decrease relative to a projection that assumes doctor productivity remains constant into the future.

Figure 3.4 presents a diagram that can assist in following the dynamics of the health labor market. Start at point A1 in quadrant I. Quadrant I relates time to percent coverage. A1 says that in year 2013, the country we're examining has a coverage level of 40 percent. Staying at the level of 40 percent coverage, we move to Quadrant II to see how many doctor visits are necessary to achieve this coverage level. At point A2, coverage level is 40 percent and the number of visits associated with this coverage level is V_{2013}. Moving to Quadrant III, we then ask the question: How

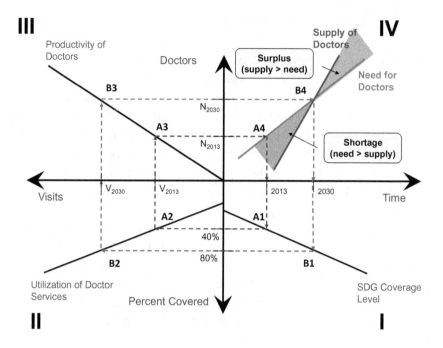

Figure 3.4   Health Worker Need Dynamics

many doctors are needed to conduct V_{2013} visits? The answer is given by point A3. At A3, V_{2013} visits correspond to N_{2013} doctors. Finally, we move to Quadrant IV and add the first point to the need for doctors' line. In year 2013, N_{2013} doctors are needed. As countries improve on their coverage levels, the need for doctors will increase, and thus the need for doctors' line slopes upward. The path from B1 to B4 confirms that at a higher coverage level (80 percent) the need for doctors is greater (N_{2030}).

The supply of doctors has been superimposed on to Quadrant IV. It is upward sloping under the assumption that the supply of doctors will increase into the future. Figure 3.4 was drawn using straight lines for simplicity of exposition, but it is likely that the lines would actually be curves when empirically estimated. In particular, we've already shown previously that diminishing returns set in at high levels of SDG coverage.

In practice, need has often been forecasted into the future under an assumption that the *status quo* prevails (e.g. doctor productivity remains the same into the future). Scheffler *et al.* (2016) used 4.45 health workers per 1,000 population benchmark and populations estimates for 2030 to forecast health worker need to 2030.

Estimated and Forecasted Workforce Shortages

Before presenting the shortage numbers that emerge from the SDG composite index method, we must spend some time discussing the supply of health workers. Estimates of supply underlie all reported shortage figures: needs-based shortages are defined as the difference between need and supply while demand-based shortages are defined as the difference between demand and supply.

The method we present here for estimating and forecasting supply follows the method used in Scheffler *et al.* (2016). Start by collecting health workforce figures from the WHO Global Health Observatory (World Health Organization, 2016b). Choose a base year to estimate supply for. We'll use 2013 in this example to match the base year used in Scheffler *et al.* (2016). Then, for each country, calculate the population density of doctors and nurses/midwives for the most recent year for which data is available. Adjust this number using 2013 populations if the country's most recent year of data is prior to 2013. For countries with missing data on health workers, impute the number of doctors and nurses/midwives for each of the four World Bank-designated income groups. Next, use available "other cadres" data to estimate for each World Bank-defined income level a cadre multiplier that when multiplied by the total number of doctors and nurses/midwives in the country will provide an estimate of "all other cadres" supply. This process yielded the following "other cadres" multipliers in Scheffler *et al.* (2016): high income (0.373), upper-middle income (0.406), lower-middle income (0.549), and low income (0.595). With these multipliers and totals for doctors and nurses/midwives, the total supply of health workers (doctors + nurse/midwives + all other cadres) can be calculated at the country level for 2013.

To forecast supply to 2030, proceed as follows. First, obtain historical data on the increase in densities of doctors and nurses/midwives in each country. To forecast supply from this data, employ a linear growth rate model (see Annex 2 of Scheffler *et al.* (2016) for details). This model assumes that the historical growth rate of doctor and nurse/midwife densities will continue into the future at the same rate of growth.

With estimates of supply in hand, shortages can now be calculated. Table 3.3 presents needs-based and demand-based shortages across 165 countries for 2013 and 2030. We present demand-based shortages in conjunction with needs-based shortages to show the reader how they compare. While this chapter has been focused on how to go about estimating and forecasting need, Liu *et al.* (2016) is a good source for learning how to estimate and forecast demand. We refer the reader to that paper to obtain the tools necessary to compute the demand-based shortages presented in Table 3.3.

There is an important distinction in the methods used to calculate demand-based shortages versus needs-based shortages. The demand-based shortages presented in Table 3.3 follow the method used in Liu *et al.* (2016): shortages and surpluses are added up and a net result is calculated. Scheffler *et al.* (2016) use a very different method where surpluses of health workers are not considered in the global needs-based shortage estimates, only countries with shortages are included in the totals. As was the case in World Health Organization (2006), this method is also correct in the sense that the calculated surpluses only reflect the fact that in most cases high- and middle-income countries have exceeded the 4.45 per 1,000 benchmark. Thus, they are not actual surpluses; they just indicate that some countries have exceeded the benchmark, reflecting a more comprehensive service delivery profile and corresponding health workforce.

The stark differences between needs-based and demand-based shortages are evident from the first row of Table 3.3: low-income countries had a needs-based shortage of over four million health workers in 2013 which is projected to increase to six million by 2030, whereas they had a slight demand-based surplus in 2013 which is projected to become a slight demand-based shortage of 15,000 workers by 2030. Low-income countries lack the financial resources to generate the demand to meet population health needs and thus have relatively low demand-based shortages.

Table 3.3   Estimated and Projected Global Shortages of Health Workers, by World Bank Income Group and WHO Region, 2013 and 2030 [Shortages are Positive, Surpluses are Negative]

	Needs-based shortages (Need-supply)		Demand-based shortages (Demand-supply)	
	2013	2030	2013	2030
World Bank Income Group (# of countries)				
Low (29)	4,202,379	5,746,161	−55,173	15,498
Lower-middle (44)	9,003,163	6,495,262	1,029,616	3,723,638
Upper-middle (46)	3,658,626	1,746,981	5,276,413	11,929,697
High (46)	81,361	74,838	305,367	−167,623
WHO Region (# of countries)				
Africa (43)	4,194,741	6,088,186	−768,647	−661,859
Americas (28)	708,021	503,870	441,453	2,545,754
Eastern Mediterranean (15)	1,569,814	1,508,924	367,081	1,590,107
Europe (50)	78,394	57,749	1,485,608	1,355,508
Southeast Asia (8)	6,661,765	4,547,443	192,068	2,038,195
Western Pacific (21)	3,732,794	1,357,071	4,838,663	8,633,507
World (165)	16,945,529	14,063,242	6,556,224	15,501,211

Notes: Health worker refers to doctors, nurses/midwives, and other health workers. For demand-based shortages, positive totals represent shortages while negative totals represent surpluses. The total needs-based shortages reported in this table are lower than the totals reported by Scheffler *et al.* (2016) because this table computes needs-based shortages for 165 countries (to correspond with the demand estimates in Liu *et al.* (2016)) whereas Scheffler *et al.* (2016) computed needs-based shortages for 210 countries.
Sources: Scheffler *et al.* (2016) and Liu *et al.* (2016).

Conclusion

The current global health worker needs-based shortage is estimated to be close to 17 million. Assuming the *status quo* prevails into the future, the global health worker needs-based shortage is forecasted to be over 14 million in 2030. Investments in health care today can help reduce the future needs-based shortage. Health planners could benefit from knowledge of the regions in their countries that are most in need of additional resources. This chapter gives planners the tools to identify these regions. With regional data, planners can modify the country-level analysis presented in this chapter in order to perform a more localized analysis on their country or province of interest.

The appropriateness of applying a needs-based analysis versus a demand-based analysis to particular countries will vary. The needs-based analysis is useful for determining which countries are in most need of health workers based on their disease burden profile and their current level of supply. This approach says nothing about whether a country has the financial resources to meet this need. But the approach does a good job at identifying countries where additional health resources are likely to be of most use. As low-income countries generally have low demand for health workers due to their lack of financial resources, they generally do not have large demand-based shortages. Thus, an approach that used demand-based shortages as the measure for deciding which countries needed additional health resources would direct little attention to low-income countries.

On the other hand, demand-based analyses are typically more appropriate for richer countries. Using the SDG composite index approach presented in this chapter, richer countries are generally above the 4.45 health workers per 1,000 population benchmark. As stressed earlier, this does not mean these countries have surpluses in the typical labor economics sense of workers wanting to work, but not being able to find employment. These countries have simply exceeded the benchmark, reflecting a more comprehensive service delivery profile and corresponding health workforce. Needs-based analyses become somewhat meaningless for countries above the benchmark.

Ultimately, the many factors mentioned in the introduction as important factors to keep in mind while applying the methods of this chapter — such as politics and professional protectionism — can vary widely across countries. Incorporating the idiosyncratic features of a particular country into the models we presented in this chapter could go a long way in improving the accuracy of needs-based and demand-based forecasts for these countries.

We hope that this chapter will inspire analysts to undertake building and estimating richer models that incorporate the features of their country of interest.

Appendix

Exercise

The following set of questions mimic the procedure used to estimate and forecast needs-based shortages using the SDG composite index approach outlined in this chapter. Table 3A.1 contains data on SDG indices, population, and supply for 30 hypothetical countries. An analyst wishing to calculate needs-based shortages for provinces/states/regions instead of countries would first compute SDG indices and estimate/forecast supply for each province/state/region following the methods presented in this chapter. From there, the analyst could then work through the questions below to arrive at estimates and forecasts of need and needs-based shortages for his provinces/states/regions of interest.

1) Using 2013 data from Table 3A.1, estimate model (A1).

   $$\text{SDG Composite Index}_i = \beta_0 + \beta_1 \ln(\text{health worker density}_i) + \varepsilon_i,$$

   $$\text{where health worker density}_i = \frac{\text{all health workers}_i}{\text{population (in 1,000 s)}_i}. \qquad \text{(A1)}$$

   Plot the data points used in the estimation along with the fitted regression line.
   What is the equation of the fitted regression line?
2) How many health workers per 1,000 population are needed in 2013? Use 0.25 as the benchmark SDG index.
3) What is the total need for health workers in 2013?
4) What is the total health worker needs-based shortage in 2013?
5) Forecast the total need for health workers in 2030.
6) What is the total health worker needs-based shortage for 2030?
7) Repeat (1)–(6) for doctors instead of all health workers.

Table 3A.1   Exercise Data

Country	SDG index	Population (in 1,000s) 2013	Population (in 1,000s) 2030	2013 supply Doctors	2013 supply All health workers	2030 supply Doctors	2030 supply All health workers
1	0.29	6,982	6,150	27,652	87,666	30,860	112,513
2	0.29	4,408	4,090	13,311	53,478	13,215	58,121
3	0.21	821	1,058	353	1,646	436	1,395
4	0.29	87,653	121,814	234,525	769,132	363,916	1,526,122
5	0.29	1,283	1,188	4,155	16,955	4,504	20,471
6	0.30	58	58	176	747	202	938
7	0.19	1,748	2,435	124	1,853	1,586	7,646
8	0.19	753	843	173	914	243	1,310
9	0.33	320	369	1,070	8,226	1,378	9,025
10	0.23	1,291,920	1,557,054	914,314	4,845,192	1,424,302	8,388,002
11	0.30	8,196	10,035	27,395	91,891	39,189	152,670
12	0.30	6,478	7,334	11,987	75,537	21,005	107,667
13	0.27	2,025	2,038	5,328	19,017	6,686	34,415
14	0.17	17,202	28,362	1,321	11,977	1,453	14,000
15	0.27	125,851	155,127	244,273	761,880	187,565	1,090,450
16	0.34	37	40	267	1,217	373	1,584
17	0.30	608	604	1,281	6,675	641	5,771
18	0.22	32,290	41,652	20,035	79,502	42,211	183,219
19	0.16	25,291	40,989	999	18,205	2,976	36,537
20	0.22	180,843	263,812	73,702	519,582	247,838	1,007,545
21	0.34	5,010	6,166	22,199	155,201	23,765	142,974
22	0.30	40,214	37,082	83,090	431,177	44,920	367,445
23	0.24	189	212	90	679	267	1,289
24	0.31	33	34	156	595	180	746
25	0.23	11,862	17,079	4,623	26,590	17,524	92,484
26	0.32	8,088	9,345	31,471	117,994	47,574	269,559
27	0.30	1,405	1,408	4,276	16,244	3,190	14,272
28	0.26	79,997	86,929	131,940	427,164	193,207	705,068
29	0.29	5,020	6,435	7,597	38,437	32,869	141,032
30	0.30	64,301	67,771	171,407	972,914	240,461	1,219,297

Solutions

1) Using 2013 data from Table 3A.1, estimate model (A1).

$$\text{SDG Composite Index}_i = \beta_0 + \beta_1 \ln(\text{health worker density}_i) + \varepsilon_i,$$

where health worker density $_i = \dfrac{\text{total health workers}}{\text{population (in 1,000s)}}$.   (A1)

Plot the data points used in the estimation along with the fitted regression line.

What is the equation of the fitted regression line?

SDG Composite Index = 0.1807 + 0.0465 ln(health worker density)

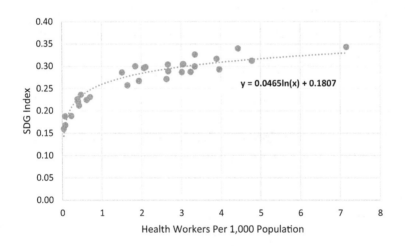

2) How many health workers per 1,000 population are needed in 2013? Use 0.25 as the benchmark SDG index.

0.25 = 0.1807 + 0.0465 ln(health worker density),
health worker density = 4.4 health workers per 1,000 population

3) What is the total need for health workers in 2013?

Total population (in 1,000 s) for the 30 countries listed in A1 is 2,010,885.
2,010,885 × 4.4 = 8,847,894 health workers needed in 2013.

4) What is the total health worker needs-based shortage in 2013?

Need – supply = needs-based shortage. Only countries with shortages are counted.
Needs-based shortage in 2013 = 1,370,695.

5) Forecast the total need for health workers in 2030.

Total population (in 1,000 s) for the 30 countries listed in A1 is 2,477,515.
2,010,885 × 4.4 = 10,901,064 health workers needed in 2030.

6) What is the total health worker needs-based shortage for 2030?

Need – supply = needs-based shortage. Only countries with shortages are counted.
Needs-based shortage in 2030 = 416,612.

7) Repeat (1)–(6) using doctors instead of total health workers.

1) **SDG Composite Index = 0.2595 + 0.0358 ln(health worker density)**

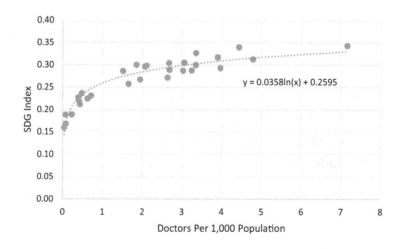

2)   0.25 = 0.2595 + 0.0358 ln (health worker density),
    health worker density = 0.8 doctors per 1,000 population

3)   **Total population (in 1,000 s) for the 30 countries listed in A1 is 2,010,885.**
    2,010,885 × 0.8 = 1,608,708 doctors needed in 2013.

4)   **Need – supply = needs-based shortage. Only countries with shortages are counted.**
    Needs-based shortage in 2013 = 234,599.

5)   **Total population (in 1,000s) for the 30 countries listed in A1 is 2,477,515.**
    2,010,885 × 0.8 = 1,982,012 doctors needed in 2030.

6)   **Need – supply = needs-based shortage. Only countries with shortages are counted.**
    Needs-based shortage in 2030 = 52,256.

Endnotes

1. See http://www.un.org/sustainabledevelopment/health/ for details on the goals put forth in SDG 3.
2. See http://www.healthdata.org/gbd/about for more information on the global burden of disease and the Appendix of Scheffler *et al.* (2016) for details on how DALYs were assigned to indicators where there is a lack of consensus among researchers on the direct correspondence to specific causes of DALYs. For example, skilled birth attendance, family planning, and antenatal care coverage all address a portion of maternal mortality during childbirth, but assigning a specific contribution of each of these to reducing maternal mortality is challenging.

References

Bruckner, T., L. Jenny, and M. S. Richard, "Demand-based and needs-based forecasts for health workers." In *Health Labor Market Analyses in Low- and Middle-Income Countries: An Evidence-Based Approach*, (eds.). R. M. Scheffler, C. H. Herbst, C. Lemiere, and J. Campbell, 2016, pp. 49–67. Washington, DC: International Bank for Reconstruction and Development/ The World Bank, 2016, December 8, accessed at https://openknowledge. worldbank.org/handle/10986/25137.

Campbell, J., G. Dussault, J. Buchan, F. Pozo-Martin, M. G. Arias, C. Leone, A. Siyam, and G. Cometto, "A universal truth: No health without a workforce", 2013, Geneva: Global Health Workforce Alliance and World Health Organization, 2016, December 8, accessed at http://www.who.int/workforcealliance/knowledge/resources/hrhreport2013/en/.

Chen, L., T. Evans, S. Anand, J. I. Boufford, H. Brown, M. Chowdhury, M. Cueto, L. Dare, G. Dussault, and G. Elzinga, "Human resources for health: Overcoming the crisis", *The Lancet*, **364**(9449), 1984–1990, 2004.

Cometto, G. and J. Campbell, "Investing in human resources for health: Beyond health outcomes", *Human Resources for Health*, **14**(1), 51, 2016, doi: 10.1186/s12960-016-0147-2.

Evans, T., E. C. Araujo, C. H. Herbst, and O. Pannenborg, "Addressing the challenges of health professional education: Opportunities to accelerate progress toward universal health coverage", Doha, Qatar: World Innovation Summit for Health, 2016, December 8, accessed at http://www.wish-qatar.org/wish-2016/forum-reports.

Fulton, B. D., R. M. Scheffler, S. P. Sparkes, E. Yoonkyung Auh, M. Vujicic, and A. Soucat, "Health workforce skill mix and task shifting in low income countries: A review of recent evidence", *Human Resources for Health*, **9**(1), 1, 2011.

Global Health Workforce Statistics database, Geneva: World Health Organization, 2016, December 8, accessed at http://www.who.int/hrh/statistics/hwfstats/.

Liu, J. X., Y. Goryakin, A. Maeda, T. Bruckner, and R. Scheffler, "Global health workforce labor market projections for 2030", Washington, DC: World Bank Group, 2016, December 8, accessed at: http://documents.worldbank.org/curated/en/546161470834083341/Global-health-workforce-labor-market-projections-for-2030.

Scheffler, R., G. Cometto, K. Tulenko, T. Bruckner, J. Liu, E. L. Keuffel, A. Preker, B. Stilwell, J. Brasileiro, and J. Campbell, "Health workforce requirements for universal health coverage and the Sustainable Development Goals — Background paper N.1 to the WHO Global Strategy on Human Resources for Health: Workforce 2030." Geneva: World Health Organization, 2016, December 8, accessed at http://www.who.int/hrh/resources/health-observer17/en/.

Scheffler, R. M. "A labor market framework for human resources for health for low- and middle-income countries", In *Health Labor Market Analyses in Low- and Middle-Income Countries: An Evidence-Based Approach*, (eds.). R. M. Scheffler, C. H. Herbst, C. Lemiere and J. Campbell, Washington, DC: International Bank for Reconstruction and Development/The World

Bank, 2016, pp. 49–67, 2016, December 8, accessed at https://openknowledge.worldbank.org/handle/10986/25137.

Scheffler, R. M. and B. D. Fulton, "Needs-based estimates for the health workforce", In *The Labor Market for Health Workers in Africa: A New Look at the Crisis*, (eds.). by Agnes Soucat, R. M. Scheffler and Tedros Adhanom Ghebreyesus, Washington, DC: The World Bank, 2013, pp. 15–31, 2016, December 8, accessed at http://elibrary.worldbank.org/doi/abs/10.1596/978-0-8213-9555-4.

Scheffler, R. M., J. X. Liu, Y. Kinfu, and M. R. Dal Poz, "Forecasting the global shortage of physicians: An economic-and needs-based approach", *Bulletin of the World Health Organization*, **86**(7), 516–523B, 2008.

Scheffler, R. M., C. B. Mahoney, B. D. Fulton, M. R. Dal Poz, and A. S. Preker, "Estimates of health care professional shortages in Sub-Saharan Africa by 2015", *Health Affairs*, **28**(5), w849–w862, 2009, doi: 10.1377/hlthaff.28.5.w849.

Serneels, P., T. Lievens, and D. Butera, "Health worker labor supply, absenteeism, and job choice", In *Health Labor Market Analyses in Low- and Middle-Income Countries: An Evidence-Based Approach*, (eds.). R. M. Scheffler, C. H. Herbst, C. Lemiere and J. Campbell, Washington, DC: International Bank for Reconstruction and Development/The World Bank, 2016, pp. 85–134, 2016, December 8, accessed at https://openknowledge.worldbank.org/handle/10986/25137.

Tulenko, K., A. E. Maghraby, A. Soucat, A. Preker, and T. Bruckner, "Measuring and analyzing production supply", In *Health Labor Market Analyses in Low- and Middle-Income Countries*, (eds.). R. M. Scheffler, C. H. Herbst, C. Lemiere, and J. Campbell, Washington, DC: International Bank for Reconstruction and Development/The World Bank, 2016, pp. 69–84, 2016, December 8, accessed at https://openknowledge.worldbank.org/handle/10986/25137.

Vujicic, M. and P. Zurn, "The dynamics of the health labour market", *The International Journal of Health Planning And Management*, **21**(2), 101–115, 2006.

World Bank, World Bank Health, Nutrition, and Population Database, Washington, DC: World Bank, 2016, December 8, accessed at http://datatopics.worldbank.org/hnp/.

World Health Organization, "The world health report 2006: working together for health", Geneva: WHO, 2016, December 8, accessed at http://www.who.int/whr/2006/en/.

World Health Organization, DALY estimates, 2000–2012, Geneva: WHO, 2016a, 2016, December 8, accessed at http://www.who.int/healthinfo/global_burden_ disease/estimates/en/index2.html.

World Health Organization, Global health observatory data, Geneva: WHO, 2016b, 2016, December 8, accessed at http://www.who.int/gho/en/.

World Health Organization "Working for health and growth: Investing in the health workforce", Geneva: WHO, 2016c, 2016, December 8, accessed at http://www.who.int/hrh/com-heeg/en/.

Chapter 4

Bridging the Gap in Medical Manpower*

*Brent D. Fulton, Richard M. Scheffler, Agnés Soucat,
Marko Vujicic, and Erica Yoonkyung Auh*

Background

The needs-based shortages and skill-mix imbalances of the health workforce in low-income countries are significant health workforce challenges. *Task shifting,* defined as delegating tasks to existing or new cadres with either less training or narrowly tailored training, is a potential strategy to address these challenges in low-income countries.

Countries having fewer than 2.28 doctors, nurses, and midwives per 1,000 population were, on average, unable to achieve an 80 percent coverage rate for deliveries by a skilled birth attendant, according to estimates by The World Health Organization published in its *World Health Report,* 2006. Fifty-seven countries fall short of that threshold, resulting in a needs-based shortage of 4.3 million health workers, including 2.4 million doctors, nurses, and midwives. In addition to the workforce shortage, the report emphasizes three other workforce challenges: skill-mix imbalances, urban–rural distribution imbalances, and poor working conditions, including compensation. With regard to skill mix, the report states that the skills of expensive professionals are not well matched to local health

---

*This chapter originally appeared in the *Journal of Human Resources for Health,* **9**(1), 2011.

needs (p. xviii). As a result, health care services become less accessible, and even when they are accessible, they become less affordable.

Dovlo (2004) describes various task-shifting scenarios, such as shifting tasks from higher- to lower-skilled health workers (e.g. from a nurse to a community health worker). Task shifting also includes the creation of new professional or non-professional cadres, whereby tasks are shifted from workers with more general training to workers with specific training for a particular task (e.g. assistant medical officers trained in obstetrics in Mozambique).

The primary objective of task shifting is to increase productive efficiency, that is, to increase the number of health care services provided at a given quality and cost, or, alternatively, to provide the same level of health care services at a given quality at a lower cost. The efficiency gain from changing the skill mix of health workers could result in a number of improvements, such as increased patient access, a reduction in health worker training and wage bill costs, and a reduction in the health workforce needs-based shortage. Another objective of task shifting is to reduce the time needed to scale up the health workforce, because the cadres performing the shifted tasks require less training. While task shifting has been occurring for decades, it is seen by some as becoming more urgent, because of health care needs for HIV/AIDS patients and overall health worker needs-based shortages (Lehmann *et al.*, 2009).

In this review, the authors use an economics perspective to examine the strength of the evidence on task shifting, to identify gaps in the evidence, and to propose a research agenda. The chapter is organized as follows: the introductory section continues by describing an economic-based conceptual framework to analyze skill-mix policies. The section, "Economic Framework to Evaluate Skill Mix," describes the methods and data used to select studies to include in the literature review. The "Results" section summarizes the studies' results. The next section proposes a research agenda. Appendix A summarizes the important elements of each study reviewed in this chapter.

Economic Framework to Evaluate Skill Mix

The skill mix of health workers within a health workforce significantly impacts the delivery of health care services. At a given facility, the optimal skill mix is the combination of health workers that produce a given level of health care services at a particular quality for the lowest cost. In economic terms, this mix of workers is defined as "productively efficient".

Palmer and Torgerson (1999) distinguish among technical efficiency, productive efficiency, and allocative efficiency. Technical efficiency refers to the relationship between inputs and outputs, whereby a technically efficient relationship produces the maximum output, given the inputs. Productive efficiency extends technical efficiency to incorporate input costs. Productive efficiency is achieved when the maximum output is produced with a given budget for inputs, or alternatively, it is achieved when a given level of output is produced with the least costly mix of inputs. Productive efficiency implies technical efficiency, although the converse is not necessarily true. Allocative efficiency extends productive efficiency to incorporate the output's value to society. Allocative efficiency is achieved when economic social welfare is maximized, which occurs when the marginal social benefit of the output (i.e. its price, under free market conditions) equals the marginal social cost to produce the output. Allocative efficiency implies productive efficiency, although the converse is not necessarily true. Note that allocative efficiency does not consider equity.

Figure 4.1 provides a stylized health care production process to illustrate the factors that influence the productively efficient mix of workers. This optimal mix of health workers is influenced by (1) the other health care inputs that are used; (2) the production processes that utilize the inputs to create health care services; and (3) the type and quality of services that are produced. The types of health workers include both health care service providers (e.g. physicians, pharmacists, nurses, midwifes, assistant medical officers, assistant pharmacists, and community health workers [see dotted interior box]) and health management and support workers (e.g. administrative, computing, and maintenance personnel). Other health care inputs include facilities, equipment, information systems, supplies, and pharmaceuticals, as well as non-health care inputs such as transportation infrastructure and patients' education levels. The production processes use these inputs to produce health care services, and the processes are affected by organizational structure, organizational norms, management, technology, incentives, and regulations. The type of service provided (e.g. primary care, birth deliveries, HIV/AIDS

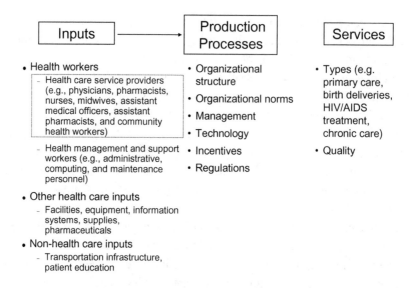

Figure 4.1   Health Care Services Production Process

antiretroviral therapy, chronic care) and its level of quality will also influence which mix of workers is productively efficient. Because the above factors vary within and across countries, the external validity of many of the studies is relatively weak because the productively efficient skill mix depends on these local factors.

Many combinations of health worker skill mixes could produce a health care service in a particular setting. Figure 4.2 illustrates the lowest-cost skill mix that can be used to produce a particular quantity of a given health care service at a given level of quality. It assumes a scenario in which two health worker types are available, physicians and nurses, but the same approach could be used to determine the productively efficient number of other health workforce cadres as well as non-human resource inputs for various health care services. In the figure, the horizontal axis represents the number of physicians, and the vertical axis represents the number of nurses. The straight line that intersects each axis represents a fixed budget constraint along which total staffing costs are equal. The budget constraint intersects the horizontal axis where the entire budget is used for physicians (i.e. the number of physicians will be the total budget divided by the physician wage); and the budget constraint intersects the

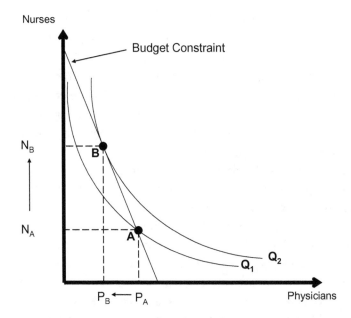

Figure 4.2   Productively Efficient and Inefficient Skill Mixes
Note: This figure was based on well-known figures illustrating productive efficiency in economics textbooks such as Ehrenberg and Smith (2000).

vertical axis where the entire budget is used for nurses (i.e. the number of nurses will be the total budget divided by the nurse wage). The budget constraint could incorporate amortized training costs. The curved line Q_1 is an isoquant that represents a particular quantity of the health care service that is produced by different mixes of physicians and nurses. The second curved line Q_2 represents another particular quantity that is greater than Q_1. The figure shows a productively inefficient skill mix (Point A) and a productively efficient skill mix (Point B). Point A is not productively efficient because the service provider could decrease the number of physicians from P_A to P_B and simultaneously increase the number of nurses from N_A to N_B. This skill-mix change would not increase costs, but would produce a higher quantity of health care services ($Q_2 > Q_1$). The productively efficient mix of workers is the point where the budget constraint is tangent to the isoquant, where the quantity of services at a given quality is maximized, subject to the available budget. Alternatively, the productively efficient mix can be thought of as the mix for which a given quantity of services at a particular quality is produced for the lowest cost.

Studies point to evidence that countries may not be operating at the productively efficient mix. For example, in 2003, the ratio of nurses to doctors was 8 to 1 in Africa and 1.5 to 1 in Western Pacific countries (WHO, 2006). Hongoro and McPake (2004) show low- and middle-income countries that have a physician-to-nurse ratio greater than the global average (0.43), including Brazil (4.04), Bangladesh (0.96), and India (0.83). Zurn *et al.* (2004) show skill-mix variation within countries with similar economic development. Zurn *et al.* (2004) and Gupta *et al.* (2003) show skill-mix variation within and between developed and transitional-economy countries. Even with the difficulties in comparing cadre definitions across countries with different health care systems, such variations clearly suggest that countries operate at different efficiency levels in terms of skill mix. However, the productively efficient skill mix varies across and within countries because of the different health care services provided and because of different contextual factors, such as the health system, payment scheme, workforce training, and management culture.

If the skill mix is not at the productively efficient point, the potential inefficiencies are significant. For example, Fulton and Scheffler (2010) examined 84 low- and middle-income non-African countries, and estimated that 12 countries would experience a needs-based shortage of doctors, nurses, and midwives in 2015, totaling 581,000 health care professionals, costing $1.8 billion (2007 US dollars) per year to eliminate. Based on simulations, they estimated the percent reduction in the additional wage bill resources required to fill these shortages under three different scenarios of substituting community health workers (CHW) for nurses and midwives.

All three scenarios increased the needed number of nurses and midwives relative to doctors. In the first, or baseline, scenario, no nurses and midwives were replaced with CHWs. In the second and third scenarios, 10 percent and 20 percent, respectively, of each country's needed nurses and midwives were replaced with CHWs. For each scenario, the number of doctor equivalents was the same, whereby nurses, midwives, and CHWs were converted into doctor-equivalents. A nurse's or midwife's productivity was assumed to equal 0.8 of a doctor's, based on estimates in the United States, because there are few reliable estimates of this relative productivity factor in low- and middle-income countries (Scheffler, 2008; Scheffler *et al.*, 1996; Record *et al.*, 1980). A CHW's productivity was assumed to equal 0.3 of a nurse's or midwife's, and a CHW's wage was assumed to be 0.2 of a nurse's or midwife's. Because of the lack of CHW studies estimating productivity and wages, the relative CHW productivity and wage as compared to a nurse or midwife were based on the authors' preliminary assessment, which they acknowledge will vary across countries. The relative productivity factor could be estimated at a facility level using time and motion studies (e.g. Kurowski *et al.*, 2003). When the needed nurse-plus-midwife-to-doctor ratio was increased by 50 percent in each of the 12 countries, the overall reduction in the annual wage bill shortage was four percent. Under that new ratio, when 10 percent of the needed nurses and midwives were replaced with CHWs, the annual wage bill reduction grows to 10 percent; when 20 percent of the needed nurses and midwives were replaced, the annual wage bill reduction grows to 15 percent.

Economic factors are not the only influence governing skill-mix decisions. Health care worker associations and licensure requirements define workers' scope of practice and can influence the extent to which the ratio of, for example, doctors-to-nurses can be altered (Scheffler, 2008).

If sufficient data exist, the facility or firm-level studies can be aggregated up to the country level to determine the productively efficient skill mix for a country. This type of aggregation is important, as the determination of the optimal mix of health worker cadres has important implications on country-level budgetary planning and training.

Methods and Data

The authors examined different methods of conducting their literature review. A systematic literature review is a common method, but it is better suited for a narrowly defined research question (CRD, 2009; Petticrew and Roberts, 2006). Because their research scope was broad, they followed the steps based on the guidelines for a systematic literature review by the Centre for Reviews and Dissemination and adjusted for their work:

(1) Determine research areas.
(2) Determine eligibility criteria for study selection.
   - search Google scholar using keywords
   - limit studies to primarily include low-income countries
   - limit time range to primarily between 2006 and September 2010
   - select studies based on strength of evidence (i.e. research design, methods, and statistical significance of results).
(3) Conduct search based on the above eligibility criteria to select studies.
(4) Evaluate studies, primarily based on research design, methods, and health care topic.
(5) Extract key information from selected studies, such as research design, methods, and results.
(6) Summarize results with suggestions for future research.

Steps (1), (2), and (5) are discussed in further detail next. The research area included skill mix, with an emphasis on task shifting among health care service providers in low-income countries. The skill-mix studies examined health outcomes, health care utilization, and budget impacts of different skill mixes of workers.

Using Google Scholar, the authors searched for studies on skill mix with the following keywords: skill mix, task shifting, assistant medical officer, assistant clinical officer, assistant nurse, auxiliary nurse, enrolled nurse, auxiliary health worker, health care assistant, assistant pharmacist, and community health worker, as well as various combinations of these keywords. Google Scholar's ranking system heavily weights an article's citation count (Beel and Gipp, 2009). To supplement the Google Scholar search, the authors used PubMed to search for additional articles. Additional studies were obtained from the authors' knowledge of relevant studies and from bibliographies of recent studies. Thirty-one studies were selected for critical analysis based on the strength of evidence presented (i.e. research design, methods, and statistical significance of results) and how recently they were published. The authors searched for studies published mostly between 2006 and September 2010, but earlier studies were included when there was a compelling reason (e.g. high strength of evidence).

The elements used to describe the studies included the following: research question(s), population studied, study design, analytic method, and key results. These elements are presented for each of the 31 studies in Appendix A to this volume. The research question(s) included the study's primary research questions, whether a health workforce intervention was tested, and related policy questions.

The population studied was defined along several dimensions, including the geographical location, year(s), unit of analysis (e.g. patient, health worker, health facility); data source (e.g. survey, administrative records, or a trade association); data structure (e.g. cross-section, repeated cross-section, and longitudinal); and sample size.

There were seven study designs, ordered by the strength of evidence: randomized controlled trial (known as an experimental design), quasi-experimental, multi-group comparison, forecast, case study, descriptive study, and literature review. A study was considered to be a randomized controlled trial if treatments (e.g. skill mixes) were randomly assigned to patients. Quasi-experimental studies included those for which the skill-mix assignment was the result of an exogenous policy not directly related to the outcome of interest (e.g. patient outcomes; see Barber *et al.*, 2007). Multi-group comparison studies included those involving comparisons of two or more groups of workforce cadres, based on measures such as patient outcomes or costs; however, the patients were not randomly assigned to the workforce cadre, so the potential for confounding factors biasing the estimated results is high. Forecast studies included those for which forecasts were prominent. A study was considered to be a case study if it used formal case study protocols (Yin, 2009). A study was considered descriptive if it did not use formal protocols and relied primarily on qualitative assessment rather than quantitative evidence. The descriptive studies usually examined a specific health workforce issue, and in many cases argued for a particular viewpoint based on the author(s)' expertise and judgment. We included literature reviews as part of our review, but primarily relied on original research.

The two types of analytic methods were quantitative and qualitative. A quantitative method was denoted when data analysis strongly influenced the findings. A qualitative method, typically used for a descriptive evaluation, was denoted when the author's/authors' findings were based on key-informant interviews and their own expertise and judgment. When quantitative methods were used, the authors noted whether the method involved descriptive statistics, comparing means, or multivariate regression analysis. For a literature review, the analytic methods included systematic review (e.g. meta-analysis), structured review (i.e. protocols for study selection were documented), and unstructured review (i.e. protocols for study selection were not documented).

Results

Many of the health workforce skill-mix studies examined whether patient health outcomes, quality of care, and costs differed among different skill mixes of health care service providers. The studies examined task shifting, particularly the development of new professional cadres designed to increase productive efficiency and reduce the time needed to scale up, resulting in increased patient access and a reduction in health worker training and wage bill costs.

Task shifting includes various scenarios, such as substituting tasks among professionals, delegating tasks to professionals with less training, including creating a new cadre, delegating tasks to non-professionals, or a combination of these (Dovlo, 2004). For example, the work can shift from specialist physicians to general practitioners, nurses, midwives, or assistant medical officers. Other cadre titles that participate in task shifting include clinical officer, assistant clinical officer, assistant nurse, auxiliary nurse, enrolled nurse, auxiliary health worker, health care assistant, assistant pharmacist, and community health worker.

The work can also be redistributed according to new categories of health workers. There are many examples of new professional cadres being developed, from health extension workers being trained in one year in vocational schools in Ethiopia, to assistant medical officers being trained in obstetrics in Mozambique, to physician assistants being trained in the United States (Teklehaimanot *et al.*, 2007; Pereira *et al.*, 1996; Hooker, 2006). Task shifting, including the development of new professional cadres, has been occurring for decades in both high-income countries (e.g. in the USA, see Hooker, 2006) and low-income countries, but is seen by some as becoming more urgent in low-income countries because of health care needs for HIV/AIDS patients and overall health worker needs-based shortages (Lehmann *et al.*, 2009; Hooker, 2006; Mullan and Frehywot, 2007).

The review produced three main findings. First, the studies provide substantial evidence that task shifting is an important policy option to help alleviate health workforce shortages and skill-mix imbalances, whether the shortages and imbalances are needs-based or economic demand-based. This finding is supported by other recent reviews of task shifting, including HIV/AIDS treatment and care provided by lay and community health workers in Africa, maternal and child health care as well as the management of infectious diseases by lay health workers, and doctor–nurse substitution in primary care in developed countries (Callaghan *et al.*, 2010; Lewin *et al.*, 2010; Laurant *et al.*, 2004). As discussed below, the reviews emphasized that the success of task shifting depends on local contextual factors. Although the studies that evaluated task shifting were typically not based on an experimental design such as a randomized controlled trial (e.g. as noted by Buchan and Dal Poz, 2002 and by Zurn *et al.*, 2004), there is substantial evidence from non-experimental studies.

Several example studies are discussed next; the first two are based on randomized controlled trials. In Kenya, no significant clinical differences were found between HIV/AIDS patients who received clinic-based antiretroviral therapy care versus primarily community-based care delivered by people living with HIV/AIDS (Selke *et al.*, 2010) who received pre-programmed personal digital assistants with decision support. In Uganda, non-physician clinicians (NPC) and physicians had considerable strength of agreement for HIV/AIDS patient assessment, particularly with the final antiretroviral therapy (ART) recommendation, WHO clinical stage assignment, and tuberculosis status assessment (Vasan *et al.*, 2009). Surgically trained assistant medical officers (*técnicos de cirurgia,* TCs) and physician specialists, i.e. obstetricians and gynecologists in Mozambique obtained similar patient outcomes, but the TC's cost of surgery was estimated to be one-quarter of a physician specialist's costs, and TCs provided more than 90 percent of obstetric surgery delivered in district hospitals (Pereira *et al.*, 1996; Kruk *et al.*, 2007). Clinical officers and medical officers providing obstetric surgery in Malawi obtained patient outcomes (Chilopora *et al.*, 2007). Huicho *et al.* (2008) found that the number of years of pre-service training was generally not associated with the appropriate assessment, diagnosis, and treatment of young children in Bangladesh, Brazil, Tanzania, and Uganda. Lekoubou *et al.* (2010) reviewed the evidence of nurses' managing chronic conditions, specifically hypertension and diabetes mellitus in sub-Saharan Africa, and concluded that they are a potentially promising cadre to efficiently manage these chronic conditions. While nurse-led care is common in sub-Saharan Africa, nurse-led care with a specific application to chronic diseases is relatively new.

In a mental health example, which used an experimental design, Rahman *et al.* (2008) found that lady health workers (community health workers) in Pakistan trained in cognitive behavior techniques significantly lowered depression prevalence among new mothers more than lady health workers without the training. While outcomes were not compared to physician specialists and other psychosocial care providers, the study demonstrates the potential to train CHWs in mental health treatments (also see Patel, 2009). This is important, considering the large needs-based shortage of mental health workers in low- and middle-income countries (Scheffler *et al.*, 2011; Bruckner *et al.*, 2010).

Second, while the evidence is substantial that task shifting has the potential to increase productive efficiency and reduce the time needed to scale up, there are a number of challenges, and results have not always been favorable. In task shifting in HIV/AIDS in sub-Saharan Africa, Zachariah *et al.* (2009) note quality and safety concerns, professional and institutional resistance, and the need to sustain motivation and performance. For example, quality of care may decrease if CHWs are given complex tasks. In Kenya, where CHWs had broad responsibilities in diagnosing and treating children, 80 percent of all guideline-recommended procedures were performed correctly, but only 58 percent of ill children were prescribed all potentially life-saving treatments (Rowe *et al.*, 2007). The same is true in high-income countries: Buchan and Calman (2005) found that many questions remain on the efficacy of nurses' replacing doctors before a patient receives a diagnosis. In a systematic review of CHW studies in the United States, Viswanathan *et al.* (2010) found mixed evidence on participant behavioral change and health outcomes.

Supervision and training is an important component for quality of care. Barber *et al.* (2007) found quality improvements at public health facilities in Indonesia that had at least one physician versus those that had none. The Ministry of Health (MOH) in Mozambique suspended training of non-physician clinicians providing antiretroviral therapy until the training program could be revised, because of poor quality of care results (Brentlinger, 2010). However, the particular type of supervision and training is sometimes difficult to measure and replicate in other settings.

The third finding is conceptual. When tasks have been shifted from traditional professional cadres (e.g. specialists, doctors or nurses) to new professional cadres, most studies compare the new cadre's productivity and patient outcomes to the traditional cadre's. The parallel comparison occurs between higher- and lower-skilled workers. However, the appropriate comparison is between the results from the care received by the new cadre and the results from the care the patient would have received — if any care at all — had the new cadre not been available. Verteuil articulated this point well in his response to the Mozambique study by Kruk *et al.* (2007: 1260): "An appropriate comparator to *técnicos de cirurgia* would be a 'do nothing' comparator as opposed to using formally trained surgeons ... a more realistic alternative for patients treated by *técnicos de cirurgia* would be no formal treatment at all, which would, it is presumed, result in far worse outcomes for the patients." Additionally, the opportunity cost of task shifting needs be incorporated into an evaluation, because a cadre that has shifted tasks will no longer be able to perform its original tasks.

The use of cost effectiveness analysis helps ensure that appropriate comparisons are made. For example, Hounton *et al.* (2009) found newborn case fatality rates after a caesarean section in Burkina Faso were highest among those performed by clinical officers (198 per 1,000) versus general practitioners (125 per 1,000) and versus obstetricians (99 per 1,000). By calculating the incremental cost-effectiveness ratio, they found that the cost per avoided newborn fatality was only $200 when 1,000 caesarean deliveries were performed by a general practitioner instead of a clinical officer, but the cost per avoided newborn fatality increased to $11,757 when 1,000 caesarean deliveries were performed by an obstetrician versus a general practitioner (2006 US dollars).

To generalize potential savings from task shifting, Scheffler *et al.* (2009) use simulations to illustrate how skill-mix changes can mitigate overall wage bill gaps in sub-Saharan Africa in 2015 (Scheffler *et al.*, 2009). They estimate that 31 sub-Saharan Africa countries will experience needs-based health workforce shortages in 2015, and estimate the annual wage bill to eliminate them at about $2.6 billion (2007 US dollars). Their simulations show this wage bill could be reduced, for example, by between two percent and five percent by increasing the needed nurse-plus-midwife-to-doctor ratio by 50 percent, assuming a nurse or midwife is between 0.7 and 0.9 as productive as a doctor. Fulton and Scheffler (2010) extend this simulation to include CHWs, and Babigumira *et al.* (2009) used a time-motion survey of CHWs and other workforce cadres to estimate savings from task shifting. The simulations provide a framework for policy makers to assess their own health workforce mix in the context of resource constraints.

Discussion

Proposed Research Agenda

Based on these three key findings, the research agenda should include studies that evaluate the impact of skill-mix changes, particularly task shifting, on productive efficiency. It is important that the studies use an appropriate research design to estimate the effect of skill-mix changes on patient health outcomes, quality of care, and costs. The particular areas of study should be based on local conditions, driven by the burden of disease and the areas in which task shifting could have the most benefit, such as HIV/AIDS, malaria, tuberculosis, maternal health including obstetric surgery, children's health, and chronic conditions (e.g. Lopez *et al.*, 2006). These areas closely align with the health-related United Nations Millennium Development Goals (MDGs). The studies should seek to determine whether health care services of a given quality are being produced at the lowest cost. For example, Walker and Jan (2005) critically review cost-effectiveness studies involving community health workers.

The role of new technologies, including e-health and telemedicine, needs to be considered (e.g. Chandrasekhar and Ghosh, 2001). Information and communication technology (ICT) can influence the geographical need and training requirements for health workers. For example, in Kenya, community-based antiretroviral therapy care was augmented with pre-programmed personal digital assistants with decision support (Selke *et al.*, 2010). For complicated HIV/AIDS cases in Zambia, health workers consulted HIV clinicians in the United States, Canada, and South Africa via the internet (Morris *et al.*, 2009). Technology can profoundly modify the skills required, for example, by shifting the need for invasive and life-threatening surgical skills in favor of medical treatment or non-invasive procedures that can be performed by technicians.

A randomized trial is the best research design to estimate the causal effect of a particular policy intervention — in this case, a skill-mix change — on a particular outcome. However, randomized controlled trials tend to lack external validity, because the study is testing a specific intervention within a specific context, defined by factors such as the health system, payment scheme, workforce training, and management culture. Therefore, it is important to not only estimate the main effect of task-shifting policy, but to also estimate how the effect is influenced by contextual factors. Because of ethical, logistical, and political economy issues, randomized controlled trials are sometimes not feasible, so quasi-experimental designs need to be utilized, but they carry the same external validity concerns. Ideally, multi-country studies should be conducted using a similarly rigorous experimental design. This would be a priority area for the international community to support.

Case studies, including the comparison of different health care providers, are another important research design. For example, a provider group or facility that produces high-quality health care at low costs can be studied to better understand the management, supervision, skill mix, training, incentives, and processes that produce these results. These findings can also inform the skill-mix interventions that should be tested with a randomized controlled trial. More emphasis needs to be given to these contextual and enabling factors that determine whether task shifting will be effective (e.g. for community health workers, see Lehmann and Sanders, 2007; for community health workers providing HIV services, see Celletti *et al.*, 2010 and Hermann *et al.*, 2009). These contextual factors include patients' acceptance of the cadre's new role, such as a community health worker (Hermann *et al.*, 2009).

Two case studies from Pakistan and Ethiopia are discussed to illustrate the importance of contextual and enabling factors. A recent review of the Pakistan Lady Health Worker program suggests contextual factors are important in determining the success or failure of a skill-mix policy change (GHWA, 2008: 2–7). There was high-level political support for this program — at the level of prime minister. The lady health workers had to be residents of the community in which they work. Each lady health worker was attached to a government health facility from which she received training, a small allowance, and medical supplies. Candidates had to be recommended by the community and meet a set of criteria, including having a minimum of eight years of education. Further study is needed to determine which of these factors were most important relative to their cost in enabling the program to achieve better health outcomes than the control population.

Similarly, the community-based health extension workers (HEW) within Ethiopia's Health Extension Program offer insight into the potential importance of contextual factors, particularly the use of HEWs in remote areas (Teklehaimanot *et al.*, 2007). Some of the factors identified include leadership and training (e.g. mentoring, continuing education, supervision, monitoring), workplace infrastructure (e.g. buildings, equipment, supplies, reference material), and living conditions (e.g. housing, transportation, relationship with community). Given that the Health Extension Program has a limited budget, it is important for future studies to identify which factors are most important relative to their cost.

Study Limitations

This article includes four limitations that warrant discussion. First, the literature review focused on studies published in 2006 or later, but included some studies with strong evidence prior to 2006. While the review may have omitted particular studies, the authors do not think their inclusion would change the main findings in this chapter, given the substantial evidence presented by the included studies. Second, there is a bias for investigators to submit, and editors to publish, studies based on the direction or strength of the findings, which is known as publication bias (Dickersin, 1990). Within published studies, there is a bias to selectively report these same types of outcomes, known as outcome reporting bias (Dwan *et al.*, 2008). It is difficult to estimate the effect of this potential bias, but it is likely be present given its pervasiveness. However, its effect is somewhat mitigated in studies involving task shifting, where a finding of no significant differences (e.g. on patient quality-of-care measures or outcomes) between workforce cadres is an important finding that will likely be published. Third, many of the included studies involved small sample sizes, limiting their ability to detect differences between workforce cadres. Larger-sample studies in the future will add important information. Fourth, countries have different entry and education requirements for health workers (e.g. non-physician clinicians) and the included studies used different training interventions for cadres (Mullan and Frehywot, 2007). Comparisons across countries and studies need to control for these differences.

Information Gaps

Recent evidence in developing countries shows that the major information gaps in health policy are not on "what to do" but rather on implementation — "how to do it" (Peters *et al.*, 2009). The "how to do it" depends on contextual factors, and WHO (2008) developed a series of research questions to be asked, including the following:

- What are the country-specific factors that will guide decision making in the implementation of task shifting?
- What preconditions must be met for the safe, efficient, and effective implementation of task shifting?
- How can countries create enabling conditions for task shifting through an appropriate regulatory framework?
- What measures must be taken to ensure quality of care under the task-shifting approach?
- How can task shifting be implemented in a way that is sustainable (both politically and fiscally)?

Some of these questions, however, suggest that there is strong evidence that the current skill mix and task allocation are the most productively efficient, implying that task shifting represents a risk. However, in many cases, the evidence either does not exist or is based on weak research designs. Current task allocation is often influenced by tradition and the political power of health worker cadres. In many low-income countries, task shifting may be an essential strategy to improve service delivery, because of health worker shortages, low productivity, and low quality of care. Therefore, some other questions could be added to the above list, such as:

- What is the evidence that shows the current skill mix is productively efficient?
- Is the current skill mix responding to the country's needs?
- What skill mix is needed to improve the country's health indicators?
- Which skill profiles provide more productively efficient care delivery?
- What are the constraints to introduce flexibility into education and training policies to adjust the skill mix and each cadre's activities and tasks to evolving needs and technology?
- What informal task shifting is occurring outside the scope of practice regulations?

While studies can identify the primary contextual factors that influence which skill mix is most productively efficient in a particular setting, there are too numerous combinations of factors to test them all. Therefore, it is important that the health care system include the necessary incentives for health care administrators to use the most productively efficient skill mix in their local setting.

Conclusion

In summary, by providing health care services at the productively efficient skill mix — the mix that produces the maximum number of health care services at a given quality and cost — more health care services are going to be accessible and affordable to populations seeking care. Task shifting is a policy option that should be considered to help achieve productive efficiency and provide access to services that otherwise might not be available. A more productively efficient skill mix will partially dampen the effect of health workforce needs-based shortages and better enable countries to meet the health-related United Nations Millennium Development Goals.

Acknowledgments

The authors are grateful to Mario Dal Poz (Coordinator, Human Resources for Health, World Health Organization) and to Mistique Felton (Senior Research Associate, Global Center for Health Economics and Policy Research, School of Public Health, University of California, Berkeley) for their helpful comments on a draft of this study. This study was funded by the Global Health Workforce Economics Network, a joint collaboration among the Global Center for Health Economics and Policy Research in the School of Public Health at the University of California-Berkeley, The World Bank, and the World Health Organization. The findings, interpretations, and conclusions expressed in this chapter are the authors' and do not necessarily reflect the views of their affiliated institutions.

This chapter has been adapted from Fulton *et al.* (2011).

Author Contributions

BF participated in the study concept and design, acquisition and interpretation of studies, and drafting the manuscript. RS participated in the study concept and design, interpretation of the studies, and critically revising the manuscript for important intellectual content. SS participated in the acquisition and interpretation of the studies and drafting the manuscript. EA, AS, and MV participated in the study concept and design, and drafting the manuscript. All authors read and approved the final manuscript.

APPENDIX A

Medical Skill Mix and Task Shifting: Summary, Case Study Analysis

Brent D Fulton, Richard M Scheffler, Susan P Sparkes, Erica Yoonkyung Auh, Marko Vujicic, and Agnes Soucat

Table 4A.1 summarizes salient details of the 31 studies analyzed in Chapter 4. The studies are grouped under the following topics: health care (various types), primary care, maternal care and obstetric surgery, HIV/ AIDS, children, and mental health. Each numbered row in the table represents a study, and the columns present the elements used to describe and evaluate the studies.

Table 4A.1   Elements of the 31 Studies that were Analyzed

Case no.	Type of health care	Authors and year published	Research questions	Population studied	Study design	Analytic method	Key results and comments
1	Health care (various types; hospitals)	Herbertson *et al.* (2007)	Can trained clinical support workers reduce junior doctors' workloads in teaching hospitals while maintaining the same quality?	United Kingdom, 2000–2001, Nottingham City Hospital; n = 1264 cannulations; n = 1513 venepunctures; n = 5 clinical support workers	Multi-group comparison (non-random assignment)	Quantitative: descriptive statistics	Clinical support workers did significantly reduce the number of cannulations and venepunctures performed by junior doctors. The clinical support workers had a cannulation success rate of 94 percent and a venepuncture success rate of 95 percent. Authors state that these rates did not compromise patient care. One limitation is that only five clinical support workers were included in the study.
2	Health care (various types)	Mullan and Frehywot (2007)	In what countries do non-physician clinicians (NPCs) practice and what are their roles?	47 sub-Saharan Africa countries, 2007, key informant interviews	Case study	Qualitative	NPCs practice in 25 of 47 sub-Saharan Africa countries, but comprehensive data are lacking on NPCs. NPC definitions vary across countries with respect to pre-service education, training, and tasks. NPCs provide a wide array of clinical services, including specialty activities such as caesarean

(Continued)

Table 4A.1   (*Continued*)

Case no.	Type of health care	Authors and year published	Research questions	Population studied	Study design	Analytic method	Key results and comments
							section, ophthalmology, and anesthesia. NPCs are less costly and take less time to train than physicians. Their training is highly practical and localized to the specific needs of the community in which they serve, but there is a lack of standardization of training and roles within and across countries.
3	Health care (various types)	Buchan and Dal Poz (2002)	What is the evidence base and limitations of skill-mix studies?	Global, 1986–2000; meta-analyses, single site, and large-scale data surveys, 41 references	Literature review	Structured	The literature on skill mix was primarily descriptive and had methodological weaknesses. Most of the studies were USA-focused, and those findings might not be applicable to other contexts. Although increased use of less-qualified health workers will not necessarily be effective in all contexts; there is evidence that increasing the scope of nurses and midwives may be beneficial in some contexts.

4	Health care (various types)	Dovlo (2004)	What is the evidence base on substitute health workers with respect to education, regulation, scope of practice, and cost-effectiveness?	World Health Organization (WHO) documentation, ministry of health documents and internet search focused on sub-Saharan Africa, 1987–2003, 22 references	Literature review	Structured	Substitute health workers were cost-effective in African health systems. Studies found similar quality between doctors and clinical officers. Retention of substitute health workers is higher than professional workers, particularly in rural areas. The authors conclude that to make the most effective use of substitute health workers, it is important to understand the various roles and conditions under which each cadre is most effective. Professional scopes of practice will need to change to permit effective substitution among cadres.
5	Health care (various types)	Hongoro and McPake, 2004	How can skill-mix changes reduce the needs-based shortage in human resources for health?	Low-income countries, 1978–2004	Descriptive study	Qualitative	The capacity to train doctors and nurses in low-income countries is highly constrained. The increased use of auxiliary health workers, such as nurse aides, medical assistants, and clinical officers, has been successful. Moreover, the demand for these workers in

(Continued)

Table 4A.1   *(Continued)*

Case no.	Type of health care	Authors and year published	Research questions	Population studied	Study design	Analytic method	Key results and comments
							high-income countries is less than for doctors and nurses. More research is needed to better understand effectiveness and document the roles of auxiliary health workers.
6	Health care (various types)	Hooker (2006)	How many physician assistants (PAs) and nurse practitioners (NPs) are in the United States, and what are their roles?	United States, 2006, NPs and PAs	Case study	Qualitative	In 2006, 110,000 PAs and nurse practitioners comprised one-sixth of the United States of America's medical workforce, with an additional 11,200 graduating each year. They can provide almost 90 percent of the services a primary care physician can provide. PAs and NPs are employed by more than one-quarter of all group practices, and are major sources of patient access in rural areas and in large health maintenance organizations.

7	Health care (various types)	Scheffler et al. (2009)	What will be the estimated health workforce needs-based shortage in 2015, and how would skill-mix changes reduce the wage bill shortage?	39 sub-Saharan African countries, 2015; physicians, nurses, and midwives	Forecast	Quantitative: multivariate regression and simulations	Of the 39 sub-Saharan African countries analyzed, 31 will experience a needs-based shortage of doctors, nurses, and midwives in 2015. The estimated annual wage bill required to eliminate these shortages is about $2.6 billion (2007 US dollars). This wage bill could be reduced, for example, by between 2 percent and 5 percent by increasing the needed nurse-plus-midwife-to-doctor ratio by 50 percent, assuming a nurse or midwife is 0.7 to 0.9 as productive as a doctor.
8	Primary care	Kinnersley et al. (2000)	What are the differences between care from NPs and general practitioners (GPs) for patients seeking "same-day" consultations in primary care?	Wales and England, 1999; 10 general practices in South Wales and South West England. Same-day consultations requested by 1368 patients	Randomized controlled trial. Patients seeking same-day consultations were randomly assigned to an NP or a GP, sometimes in blocks.	Quantitative	Most patients reported at 2 weeks after their consultation that their symptoms had improved and their concerns were reduced, but there was no statistical difference between patients who were treated by a GP versus an NP. For children, mean satisfaction level was statistically higher for NP

(Continued)

Table 4A.1 *(Continued)*

Case no.	Type of health care	Authors and year published	Research questions	Population studied	Study design	Analytic method	Key results and comments
							(80.4) versus GP (75.6), based on a 100-point scale. For adults, mean satisfaction level was statistically higher for NPs versus GPs in 3 of 10 practices; no statistical differences were found in other practices. Consultation times were shorter for GPs, even after accounting for time taken by NPs to get prescriptions signed. In the 10 practices, the consultation time GP: NP ratio ranged from 0.57 to 0.92, eight of which were statistically different from 1. Patients were significantly more likely to receive particular information from NPs versus GPs, including cause of illness (81 percent versus 72 percent), how to relieve symptoms (86 percent versus 68 percent), and what to do if the problem persists (93 percent versus 88 percent).

#	Topic	Author (year)	Research question	Setting/sample	Design	Analysis	Findings
9	Primary care	Gary et al. (2009)	What are clinical characteristic differences and emergency room utilization differences between Type 2 diabetes mellitus patients assigned to minimal intervention care versus minimal intervention care plus individualized, culturally tailored care provided by a nurse case manager (NCM) and a community health worker (CHW)?	United States, 2001–2003; managed care organization in Baltimore, Maryland; n = 542 African Americans with Type 2 diabetes mellitus	Randomized controlled trial. Patients randomly assigned to either minimal intervention care or minimal intervention care plus individualized, culturally tailored care provided by a NCM and a CHW (i.e. intensive intervention group).	Quantitative, multivariate regression	At 24 months, patients who had more visits with a CHW and NCM approached having a statistically significant decline in HbA1c levels (−0.43 percent) as compared with the minimal group ($p = 0.12$). At 24 months, patients in the intensive intervention group were 23 percent less likely than the minimal intervention group to have emergency room visits.
10	Primary Care	Barber et al. (2007)	What are the contributions of physicians, nurses, and midwives to the quality of primary health care?	Indonesia; 1993 and 1997; nationally representative health facilities (n = 992 in 1993; n = 915 in 1997)	Quasi-experimental	Quantitative: multivariate regression	Quality of care was found to depend on the availability, type, and number of health workers. There was significant evidence that quality of care depends on physician presence at a facility. For example, prenatal care quality was 4.5 percentage points higher

(Continued)

Table 4A.1   (*Continued*)

Case no.	Type of health care	Authors and year published	Research questions	Population studied	Study design	Analytic method	Key results and comments
							in a facility with one versus zero physicians, and 6.3 percentage points higher in a facility with two versus zero physicians found larger impacts on improvements in curative care the addition of a nurse was found to have a greater impact on quality of care than the addition of another physician or midwife.
11	Primary care	Lewin *et al.* (2010)	What is the effect of using lay health workers (LHW: e.g. CHWs) on primary care, particularly maternal and child health as well as infectious disease care?	Global review, 1975–2010, n = 82 studies, including 55 studies in six high-income countries (many of these focused on low-income and minority populations), 12 studies in eight middle-income countries, and 15 studies in 10 low-income countries	Literature review of randomized controlled trials	Systematic, meta-analysis	Moderate-quality evidence was found that LHWs promote immunization uptake and breastfeeding and improve tuberculosis treatment outcomes, as compared to usual care. Low-quality evidence was found for LHWs' reducing child morbidity and child/neonatal mortality and increasing the likelihood of seeking care for childhood illness, as compared to usual care.

| 12 | Primary care (and hospitals) | Buchan and Calman (2005) | What are the implications of skill-mix changes between physicians and nurses in primary care and hospitals? | OECD countries, with 16 responses to a survey; literature review (139 references); US and UK (case study); 1990–2004 | Literature review, case study | Unstructured, qualitative | For this review, "low-quality evidence" means that further research is very likely to have an important impact on the estimated effect, because, for example, the estimate did not have a *p-value* less than 0.05, although it was typically less than 0.10, and because heterogeneous effects were found across the studies. "Moderate-quality evidence" means that further research is likely to have an important impact on the estimated effect. "High-quality evidence" means that further research is very unlikely to have an important impact.

The evidence regarding the effectiveness of replacing doctors with nurses was mixed in the USA, UK and Australia. Many studies examined the possible benefits of replacing doctors with nurses after diagnosis but many questions remained on its efficacy prior to diagnosis. Of the 16 OECD |

(Continued)

Table 4A.1 (*Continued*)

Case no.	Type of health care	Authors and year published	Research questions	Population studied	Study design	Analytic method	Key results and comments
							countries that responded to the OECD survey, eight reported using nurses in advanced practice, with three additional countries undergoing pilots in this area. In the USA and the UK, the key drivers of the increased use of nurses in advanced roles included value (cost savings), insufficient doctors, and the introduction of new treatments. More support for the increased use of nurses in the USA than in the UK was noted.
13	Maternal care and obstetric surgery	Kruk *et al.* (2007)	What are the cost differences between surgically trained assistant medical officers and surgical specialist physicians to perform major obstetric surgeries in Mozambique?	Mozambique, 2002, 47 specialist physicians (5264 major obstetric surgeries) and 53 assistant medical officers (6914 major obstetric surgeries)	Multi-group comparison (non-random assignment)	Quantitative: descriptive statistics	The cost per major obstetric surgery (caesarean sections, obstetric hysterectomies, and laparotomies for ectopic pregnancy) by assistant medical officers ($38.90) is about one-quarter of a surgical specialist physician's ($144.10) costs. These costs include training and wages over a 30-year career. Costs are reported in 2006 US dollars. One limitation is that the non-surgical tasks were not included.

14	Maternal care and obstetric surgery	Pereira *et al.* (2007)	What shares of major obstetric surgeries in Mozambique are done by surgically trained assistant medical officers versus surgical specialist physicians, and where do these cadres work?	Mozambique, 12 178 major surgical obstetric operations in 2002: 59 medical officers and 34 surgically trained assistant medical officers	Multi-group comparison (non-random assignment)	Quantitative: descriptive statistics	Assistant medical officers performed 57 percent of all major obstetric surgical interventions in Mozambique, including 92 percent of the interventions in district (rural) hospitals. After 7 years, no medical officers initially assigned to district (rural) hospitals remained there, while 88 percent of assistant medical officer graduates remained there.
15	Maternal care and obstetric surgery	Hounton *et al.* (2009)	What is the cost-effectiveness of caesarean sections provided by clinical officers, general practitioners, or obstetricians?	Burkina Faso, 2004–2005; 2305 caesarean sections	Multi-group comparison (non-random assignment)	Quantitative: descriptive statistics	Newborn case fatality rates after a caesarean section in Burkina Faso were highest among those performed by clinical officers (198 per 1,000) versus general practitioners (125 per 1,000) versus obstetricians (99 per 1,000). Based on the incremental cost-effectiveness ratio, the cost per avoided newborn fatality was only $200 when 1,000 caesarean deliveries were performed by a general

(Continued)

Table 4A.1 (*Continued*)

Case no.	Type of health care	Authors and year published	Research questions	Population studied	Study design	Analytic method	Key results and comments
							practitioner versus a clinical officer, but the cost per avoided newborn fatality increased to $11,757 when 1,000 caesarean deliveries were performed by an obstetrician versus a general practitioner (2006 US dollars).
16	Maternal care and obstetric surgery	Chilopora *et al.* (2007)	What were patient outcome differences between patients receiving obstetric surgery from clinical officers versus medical officers?	Malawi, 2005; n = 2131 obstetric surgeries	Multi-group comparison (non-random assignment)	Quantitative: descriptive statistics (chi-square test)	No post-operative differences were found between patients receiving obstetric surgery from clinical officers versus medical officers, for the occurrence of pyrexia, wound infection, or dehiscence, reoperation need, neonatal outcome, or maternal death.
17	Maternal care and obstetric surgery	McCord *et al.* (2009)	What were patient outcome and quality of care differences between patients receiving obstetric surgery from assistant medical officers versus medical officers?	Tanzania, 2006; mothers who had major surgery by assistant medical officer (n = 945) and by medical officer (n = 142).	Multi-group comparison (non-random assignment)	Quantitative, mostly compared means	No significant differences were found between assistant medical officers and medical officers regarding patient outcomes and quality of care. Patient outcomes included maternal death, perinatal death, and major post-operative complications. Quality of care measures included whether surgery was performed without an absolute

maternal indication or clear fetal indication; delay of surgery by more than three hours; and absence of a blood transfusion when needed. One limitation was that a multivariate regression model was not estimated to account for maternal and fetal risk indicators simultaneously with the hospital's attributes, likely because of the relatively small sample size of surgeries performed by medical officers.

| 18 | Maternal care and obstetric surgery | De Brouwere et al. (2009) | What was the effect of task shifting on the numbers and rates of major obstetrical surgical interventions as well as its effect on maternal and perinatal outcomes? | Senegal, 2001–2006. n = 3 districts. Task shifting included training non-specialists (general practitioners, anesthetists, and surgical assistants) in emergency obstetric surgery. | Case study, hospital records reviewed; key informant interviews | Quantitative | Caesarean-section rates increased in district hospitals with a functioning surgical team, with positive outcomes for newborns as well. The district of Bakel had the greatest increase in intervention rate, a 2.6-fold increase between 2001 and 2006. However, across the districts studied, varying availability of surgical teams jeopardized these positive effects, and there were never enough surgical teams to meet the need. |

(Continued)

Table 4A.1   *(Continued)*

Case no.	Type of health care	Authors and year published	Research questions	Population studied	Study design	Analytic method	Key results and comments
19	HIV/ AIDS	Selke *et al.* (2010)	What were HIV/AIDS patient outcome differences between those treated with clinic-based care versus community-based care delivered by people living with HIV/AIDS who had pre-programmed personal digital assistants with decision support?	Kenya, 2006–2008, patients in clinic-based care (n = 112), patients in community-based care (n = 96)	Randomized controlled trial. Randomization unit was at the sublocation level within the Kosirai Division. Clinic-based care included monthly clinic visits, while community-based care included monthly community-based visits plus one visit every three months to a clinic.	Quantitative, multivariate regression	No significant differences in clinical outcomes were found after one year between patients treated in the clinic versus the community. The outcomes included detectable viral load, mean CD4 count, decline in Karnofsky score, change in ART regimen, new opportunistic infection, and pregnancy rate. One noted limitation is the study's limited power to detect differences, given the small sample size. During the one-year study period, the community-based care group had fewer visits per patient (6.2) than the clinic-based care group (12.4).
20	HIV/AIDS	Samne *et al.* (2010)	What were HIV-infected patient outcome differences between those assigned to nurse- versus doctor-monitored antiretroviral therapy (ART) care?	South Africa, 2005–2009, two primary care sites in Cape Town and Johannesburg: n = 404 HIV patients assigned to nurse-monitored ART care; n = 408 HIV patients assigned to doctor-monitored ART care	Randomized controlled trial: patients were randomly assigned nurse- or doctor-monitored ART care	Quantitative, regression analyses	After a median follow-up of 120 weeks, patients in the nurse-versus doctor-led care groups had similar outcomes: deaths (10 versus 11), virological failures (44 versus 39), toxicity failures (68 versus 66), and program losses (70 versus 63). Results support feasibility of appropriately trained nurses to monitor ART care.

| 21 | HIV/AIDS | Vasan et al. (2009) | What is the degree of agreement between physicians and non-physicians to start ART in Uganda? | Uganda, 2006: 254 patients seen by a nurse and a physician; additional 267 patients seen by a clinical officer and a physician; locations included 12 government ART sites | Randomized controlled trial: patients were first randomly assigned to be seen by a nurse or clinical officer; patients were then seen by a physician | Quantitative, Kappa analysis | Both nurses and clinical officers agreed strongly with physicians, particularly with final ART recommendation, WHO clinical stage assignment, and tuberculosis status assessment. Clinical officers and physicians had more agreement (weighted Kappa = 0.76) on final ART recommendation than did nurses and physicians (weighted Kappa = 0.62). However, nurses and physicians had more agreement on WHO clinical stage than did clinical officers and physicians. |
| 22 | HIV/AIDS | Brentlinger et al. (2010) | How well did NPCs perform on ART clinical practice quality against norms they were taught in their two-week course, as determined by two clinical observers? | Mozambique, 2007; public sector health facilities; n = 127 patients; n = 44 NPCs | Multi-group comparison (non-random assignment), where comparison group is a norm | Quantitative: descriptive statistics | The NPCs' agreement rates with the clinical observers were as follows: staging (37.6 percent), cotrimoxazole management (71.6 percent), ART therapy management (75.5 percent), adverse drug reaction management (69.7 percent), and diagnosis of opportunistic infections and other infectious |

(Continued)

Table 4A.1 (*Continued*)

Case no.	Type of health care	Authors and year published	Research questions	Population studied	Study design	Analytic method	Key results and comments
							diseases (49.1 percent). These low agreement rates caused the Ministry of Health to suspend training until the ART training program could be revised.
23	HIV/AIDS	Wools-Kaloustian et al. (2009)	How well did community care coordinators (CCCs) with personal digital assistants (PDAs) perform on patient monitoring and ART-dispensing tasks for HIV patients?	Kenya, Kosirai Division, 2006–2008: n = 133 and n = 88 patient evaluations in years 1 and 2, respectively; n = 8 CCCs	Multi-group comparison (non-random assignment), where comparison group is a norm	Quantitative: descriptive statistics	The CCCs performed well. On the patient evaluations, they received superior evaluations at the following rates for years 1 and 2, respectively: summary score (88.7 percent, 94.3 percent), obtaining vital signs (90.8 percent, 100 percent), taking histories (91.9 percent, 98.8 percent), using the PDA (90.6 percent, 100 percent), making clinical judgments (83.1 percent, 98.8 percent), displaying humanistic qualities (86.4 percent, 95.5 percent), and interacting with staff (89.1 percent, 92 percent).

| 24 | HIV/AIDS | Shum-busho et al. (2009) | How well did nurse-centered ART compare with national guidelines for ART eligibility and prescription, and what were the key patient outcomes? | Rwanda, 2005–2008, HIV/AIDS patients in rural health centers (n = 1076) | Case study, retrospective examination of patient records | Quantitative, descriptive statistics | Nurses achieved high compliance with national guidelines for ART eligibility and prescription and had excellent patient outcomes. Of the 622 patients determined ineligible for treatment, none had been started on treatment. Of the 451 patients determined eligible for ART, 435 had started treatment; the remaining 16 had not started treatment for various reasons, none attributed to the nurse. All prescriptions were consistent with national guidelines, except one patient was given efavirenz without prior exclusion of pregnancy. Of the 435 patients initiating ART, 90 percent were alive at assessment. One limitation was the lack of an explicit comparison group of health workers. |

(Continued)

Table 4A.1 *(Continued)*

Case no.	Type of health care	Authors and year published	Research questions	Population studied	Study design	Analytic method	Key results and comments
25	HIV/AIDS	Callaghan *et al.* (2010)	What is the effect of task shifting in HIV treatment on patient access, cost, and quality of care?	Sub-Saharan Africa, searched databases from inception to May 2009 (n = 25 original studies), 80 references	Literature review	Structured	The literature review revealed that task shifting effectively addresses health worker shortages in HIV treatment and care, because it provides high-quality care to more patients than a physician-centered model. Task shifting is cost effective, but may not be cost saving, because a greater number of people will be able to access services. Noted challenges include training, support, and integration of staff into new roles, and compliance with regulatory bodies.
26	HIV/AIDS	Zachariah *et al.* (2009)	What are the primary opportunities and challenges for task shifting in ART in sub-Saharan Africa?	Malawi, South Africa and Lesotho; 2004–2007, National ART scale up plan (Médecins sans Frontières), 57 references	Case study; literature review	Qualitative; unstructured	Both opportunities and challenges presented by task shifting for ART are highlighted in the study. Opportunities include improving the workforce skills mix and health-system efficiency; enhancing the role of the community; cost advantages; and reducing

					attrition and international "brain drain". The challenges include maintaining quality and safety; addressing professional and institutional resistance; and sustaining motivation and performance.
27	HIV/AIDS	McCourt and Awases (2007)	How has Namibia managed its health workforce, focusing on skill mix/ hierarchy, employee selection, performance appraisal, and training?	Namibia; 2005, 22 key informant interviews	Case study Qualitative	While a general scaling up is needed, a focus on increasing number of low- and middle-level cadres of health workers will create a more efficient allocation of resources, the authors conclude. They cite the use of job analysis and competence development to identify the precise skills that the new treatments will require, and to provide them to trainees at the lowest possible level, equivalent to Namibia's enrolled nurses and community counselors. Additional higher-level cadres will need management training to supervise these workers.

(Continued)

Table 4A.1 (*Continued*)

Case no.	Type of health care	Authors and year published	Research questions	Population studied	Study design	Analytic method	Key results and comments
28	HIV/AIDS	Kober and Van Damme (2004)	What are the primary constraints and solutions to scale up ART in Africa?	Malawi, Mozambique, Swaziland, and South Africa, January, 2004; interviews with country officials	Case studies	Qualitative	The primary barrier to scaling up antiretroviral treatment was not a lack of financial resources, but rather a scarcity of health workers to deliver the treatment. To meet these needs, countries are scaling up medical schools, improving secondary schools to expand the number of applicants, and using lower-skilled cadres.
29	Children	Rowe *et al.* (2007)	How well did CHWs diagnose and treat ill children in Siaya District of Kenya?	Kenya (Siaya District), 2001, 192 ill-child consultations performed by 114 CHWs	Multi-group comparison (non-random assignment)	Quantitative: descriptive statistics	CHWs performed correctly 80 percent of all guideline-recommended procedures, but only 58 percent of ill children were prescribed all potentially life-saving treatments. The CHWs were evaluated by physicians who were experts with CARE Management of Sick Child (MSC) Guidelines; therefore, physicians were the comparison group.

| 30 | Children | Huicho *et al.* (2008) | How does quality of care of children under age 5 differ among health workers (physicians, nurses, midwives, clinical officers) with different number of years of pre-service training, but who received in-service Integrated Management of Childhood Illness (IMCI) training? | Bangladesh (2003, n = 272 children).Brazil (2000, n = 147 children), Uganda (2002, n = 612 children), Tanzania (2000, n = 231 children) | Multi-group comparison (non-random assignment). Within each country, health workers were classified into either shorter or longer duration training, based on the number of years of pre-service training they had received. | Quantitative, t-tests, chi-square tests, multivariate regression | Among the 12 comparisons (three outcomes by four countries), pre-service training was not found to be significant for 9 of the comparisons. The three outcomes included an index of integrated assessment of children (continuous measure), children correctly classified/ diagnosed (binary measure), and children correctly managed/treated (binary measure). However, in Tanzania, workers with longer-duration pre-service training had better assessment index scores than those with shorter-duration pre-service training: 0.94 versus 0.88, adjusted difference equal to 0.06. In contrast, in Uganda and Brazil, workers with longer duration pre-service training had worse management/treatment results than those with shorter duration pre-service training: Uganda (23.1 percent versus 32.6 percent, adjusted odds ratio equal to 0.59) and Brazil (57.8 percent versus 83.7 percent, adjusted odds ratio equal to 0.11). |

(Continued)

Table 4A.1   (*Continued*)

Case no.	Type of health care	Authors and year published	Research questions	Population studied	Study design	Analytic method	Key results and comments
31	Mental health	Rahman *et al.* (2008)	What is the change in depression prevalence among depressed, pregnant women treated by lady health workers routinely trained versus specially trained using the Thinking Healthy Programme (cognitive behavior therapy techniques)?	Pakistan, 2005–2006, women aged 16 to 45 in third trimester of pregnancy who had clinical depression, based on the Diagnostic and Statistical Manual of Mental Disorders, Fourth Edition (DSM-IV). Women were visited by a lady health worker during and for 10 months following pregnancy. Control group (n = 463); treatment group (n = 4 40). Randomization occurred at Union Council level (population of 15,000–20,000). 40 Union Councils participated.	Randomized controlled trial	Quantitative, multivariate regression	Women who were clinically depressed during pregnancy had better mental health outcomes than women in the control group if visited by Lady Health Workers trained with the Thinking Healthy Programme. Specifically, women in the treatment group had lower depression prevalence (23 percent) than women in the control group (53 percent) 6 months after giving birth. Similarly, women in the treatment group had lower depression prevalence (27 percent) than women in the control group (59 percent) 12 months after giving birth. The results remained statistically different when independent variables were included in the model, such as mother's baseline depression score, age, education, and socioeconomic status.

Source: Chapter 3, this volume.

References

Babigumira, J. B., B. Castelnuovo, M. Lamorde, A. Kambugu, A. Stergachis, P. Easterbrook, and L. P. Garrison, "Potential impact of task shifting on costs of antiretroviral therapy and physician supply in Uganda", *BMC Health Services Research*, 192, 2009.

Barber, S. L., P. J. Hertler, and P. Harimurti, "The contribution of human resources for health to the quality of care in Indonesia", *Health Affairs*, **26**(3), w367–w379, 2007.

Beel, J. and B. Gipp, "Google Scholar's ranking algorithm: An introductory overview", In Proceedings of 3rd International Conference on Research Challenges in Information Science (RCIS '09). Institute of Electrical and Electronics Engineers (IEEE); 2010, April 8, accessed at http://www.beel. org/files/papers/asestestpapers/Google%20Scholar%27s%20Ranking%20 Algorithm%20--%20An%20Introductory%20Overview%20--%20prepri. pdf.

Brentlinger, P. E., A. Assan, F. Mudender, A. E. Ghee, J. V. Torres, P. M. Martínez, O. Bacon, R. Bastos, R. Manuel, L. R. Li, C. McKinney, and L. J. Nelson, "Task shifting in Mozambique: Cross-sectional evaluation of non-physician clinicians' performance in HIV/AIDS care", *Human Resources for Health*, **8**(23), 2010.

Bruckner, T. A., R. M. Scheffler, G. Shen, J. Yoon, D. Chisholm, J. Morris, B. D. Fulton, M. R. Dal Poz, and S. Saxena, "The mental health workforce gap in low- and middle-income countries: A needs-based approach", *Bulletin of the World Health Organization*, **89**: 184–194, 2010; accessed December 6, 2010, at http://www.who.int/bulletin/online_first/10-082784.pdf.

Buchan, J. and L. Calman, "Skill-mix and policy change in the health workforce", *OECD Health Working Papers*, No. 17, Paris, OECD, 2005.

Buchan, J. and M. R. Dal Poz, "Skill mix in the health care workforce: Reviewing the evidence", *Bulletin of the World Health Organization*, **80**(7), 575–580, 2002.

Callaghan, M., N. Ford, and H. Schneider, "A systematic review of task shifting for HIV treatment and care in Africa", *Human Resources for Health*, **8**(8), 2010.

Celletti, F., A. Wright, J. Palen, S. Frehywot, A. Markus, A. Greenberg, R. A. T. de Aguiarc, F. Campos, E. Buche, and B. Samba, "Can the deployment of community health workers for the delivery of HIV services represent an effective and sustainable response to health workforce shortages? Results of a multicountry study", *AIDS*, **24** Suppl 1:S45–S57, 2010.

Chandrasekhar, C. P. and J. Ghosh, "Information and communication technologies and health in low-income countries: The potential and the constraints", *Bulletin of the World Health Organization*, **79**(9), 850–855, 2001.

Chilopora, G., C. Pereira, F. Kamwendo, A. Chimbiri, E. Malunga, and S. Bergstrom, "Postoperative outcome of Ceasarean sections and other major emergency obstetric surgery by clinical officers and medical officers in Malawi", *Human Resources for Health*, **5**(17), 2007.

CRD (Centre for Reviews and Dissemination) 2009. "Systematic reviews: CRD's guidance for undertaking reviews in health care", New York, UK: University of York.

De Brouwere, V., T. Dieng, M. Diadhiou, S. Witter, and E. Denerville, "Task shifting for emergency obstetric surgery in district hospitals in Senegal", *Reproductive Health Matters*, **17**(33), 32–44, 2009.

Dickersin, K., "The existence of publication bias and risk factors for its occurrence", *Journal of the American Medical Association*, **263**(10), 1385–1389, 1990.

Dovlo, D., "Using mid-level cadres as substitutes for internationally mobile health professionals in Africa: A desk review", *Human Resources for Health*, **2**(7), 2004.

Dwan, K., D. G. Altman, and J. A. Arnaiz, "Systematic review of the empirical evidence of study publication bias and outcome reporting bias", *PLoS ONE*, **3**(8): e3081, 2008.

Ehrenberg, R. G. and R. S. Smith, *Modern Labor Economics: Theory and Public Policy*, 7th ed. Reading, MA: Addison-Wesley.

Fulton, B. D. and R. M. Scheffler, "Health care professional shortages and skill-mix options using community health workers: New estimates for 2015", In *The Performance of a National Health Workforce*, (eds.). J. M. Moore, M. R. Dal Poz, G. Perfilieva, H. Jaccard-Ruedin, and B. D. H. Doan. Paris: Centre de Sociologie et de Démographie Médicales.

Fulton, B. D., R. M. Scheffler, S. P. Sparkes, E. Y. Auh, M. Vujicic, and A. Soucat, "Health workforce skill mix and task shifting in low-income countries: A review of recent evidence", *Human Resources in Health*, **9**(1), 1, 2011.

Gary, T. L., M. Batts-Turner, H. C. Yeh, F. Hill-Briggs, L. R. Bone, N. Y. Wang, D. M. Levine, N. R. Powe, C. D. Saudek, M. N. Hill, M. McGuire, and F. L. Brancati, "The effects of a nurse case manager and a community health worker team on diabetic control, emergency department visits, and hospitalizations among urban African Americans with type 2 diabetes mellitus: A randomized controlled trial", *Archives of Internal Medicine* **169**(19), 1788–1794, 2009.

GHWA (Global Health Workforce Alliance), "Global health workforce alliance task force on scaling up education and training for health workers: Country case study: Pakistan's Lady Health Worker Programme", 2008, Geneva: GHWA; 2010, September 25, accessed at http://www.who.int/workforcealliance/knowledge/case_studies/Pakistan.pdf.

Gupta, N., K. Diallo, P. Zurn, and M. R. Dal Poz, "Assessing human resources for health: What can be learned from labour force surveys?" *Human Resources for Health*, **1**(5), 2003.

Herbertson, R., A. Blundell, and C. Bowman, "The role of clinical support workers in reducing junior doctors' hours and improving quality of patient care", *Journal of Evaluation in Clinical Practice*, **13**, 272–275, 2007.

Hermann, K., W. van Damme, G. W. Pariyo, E. Schouten, Y. Assefa, A. Cirera, and W. Massavon, "Community health workers for ART in sub-Saharan Africa: Learning from experience — Capitalizing on new opportunities", *Human Resources for Health*, **7**(31), 2009 doi:10.1186/1478-449.

Hongoro, C. and B. McPake, "How to bridge the gap in human resources for health", *Lancet*, **364**, 1451–1456, 2004.

Hooker, R., "Physician assistants and nurse practitioners: The United States experience", *Medical Journal of Australia*, **185**, 4–7, 2006.

Hounton, S. H., D. Newlands, N. Meda, and V. De Brouwere, "A cost-effectiveness study of Caesarean-Section deliveries by clinical officers, general practitioners and obstetricians in Burkina Faso", *Human Resources for Health*, **7**(34), 2009.

Huicho, L., R. W. Scherpbier, A. M. Nkowane, and C. G. Victora, "The multi-country evaluation of IMCI Study Group. How much does quality of child care vary between health workers with differing durations of training? An observational multicountry study", *Lancet*, **372**, 910–916, 2008.

Kinnersley, P., E. Anderson, K. Parry, J. Clement, L. Archard, P. Turton, A. Stainthorpe, A. Fraser, C. C. Butler, and C. Rogers, "Randomised controlled trial of nurse practitioner versus general practitioner care for patients requesting 'Same Day' consultations in primary care", *British Medical Journal*, **320**(7241), 1043–1048, 2000.

Kober, K. and W. Van Damme, "Scaling up access to antiretroviral treatment in Southern Africa: Who will do the job?", *Lancet*, **364**, 103–107, 2004.

Kruk, M., C. Pereira, F. Vaz, S. Bergstrom, and S. Galea, "Economic evaluation of surgically trained assistant medical officers in performing major obstetric surgery in Mozambique", *British Journal of Obstetrics and Gynaecology*, **114**, 1253–1260, 2007.

Kurowski, C., K. Wyss, S. Abdulla, N. Yémadji, and A. Mills, "Human resources for health: requirements and availability in the context of scaling up priority interventions in low-income countries: Case studies from Tanzania and Chad. Department for International Development (DFID)", LSHTM Health Economics and Financing Programme, 2003.

Laurant, M., D. Reeves, R. Hermens, J. Braspenning, R. Grol, and B. Sibbald, "Substitution of doctors by nurses in primary care", *Cochrane Database of Systematic Reviews*, **4**, 2004.

Lehmann, U. and D. Sanders, "Community health workers: What do we know about them? The state of the evidence on programmes, activities, costs and impact on health outcomes of using community health workers", Geneva: World Health Organization, 2007.

Lehmann, U., W. Van Damme, F. Barten, and D. Sanders, "Task shifting: The answer to the human resources crisis in Africa?", *Human Resources for Health*, **7**(49), 2009.

Lewin, S., S. Munabi-Babigumira, C. Glenton, K. Daniels, X. Bosch-Capblanch, B. E. van Wyk, J. Odgaard-Jensen, M. Johansen, G. N. Aja, M. Zwarenstein, and I. B. Scheel, "Lay health workers in primary and community health care for maternal and child health and the management of infectious diseases", *Cochrane Database Syst Rev.* **17**(3), CD004015, 2010.

Lekoubou, A., P. Awah, L. Fezeu, E. Sobngwi, and A. P. Kengne, "Hypertension, diabetes mellitus and task shifting in their management in sub-Saharan Africa", *International Journal of Environmental Research and Public Health*, **7**, 353–363, 2010.

Lopez, A. D., C. D. Mathers, M. Ezzati, D. T. Jamison, and C. J. L. Murray, "Global and regional burden of disease and risk factors, 2001: Systematic analysis of population health data", *Lancet*, **367**, 1747–1757, 2001.

McCord, C., G. Mbaruku, C. Pereira, C. Nzabuhakwa, and S. Bergstrom, "The quality of emergency obstetrical surgery by assistant medical officers in Tanzanian District Hospital", *Health Affairs*, **28**(5), w876–w855, 2009.

McCourt, W. and M. Awases, "Addressing the human resources crisis: A case study of the Namibian Health Service", *Human Resources for Health*, **5**(1), 2007.

Morris, M. B., B. T. Chapula, B. H. Chi, A. Mwango, H. F. Chi, J. Mwanza, H. Manda, C. Bolton, D. S. Pankratz, J. S. A. Stringer, and S. E. Reid, "Use of task shifting to rapidly scale up HIV treatment services: Experiences from Lusaka, Zambia", *BMC Health Services Research*, **9**(5), 2009, doi:10.1186/1472-6963.

Mullan F. and S. Frehywot, "Nonphysician clinicians in 47 sub-Saharan African countries", *Lancet*, **370**, 2158–2163, 2007.

Palmer, S. and D. J. Torgerson, "Definitions of efficiency", *British Medical Journal Publishing Group*, **318**, 1136, 1999.

Patel, V., "The future of psychiatry in low- and middle-income countries", *Psychological Medicine*, **39**(11), 1759–1762, 2009.

Pereira, C., A. Bugalho, S. Bergstrom, F. Vaz, and M. Cotiro, "A comparative study of Caesarean deliveries by assistant medical officers and obstetricians in Mozambique", *British Journal of Obstetrics and Gynaecology*, **103**, 508–512, 1996.

Pereira, C., A. Cumbi, R. Malalane, F. Vaz, C. McCord, A. Bacci, and S. Bergstrom, "Meeting the need for emergency obstetric care in Mozambique: Work performance and histories of medical doctors and assistant medical officers trained for surgery", *British Journal of Obstetrics and Gynaecology*, **114**(12), 1530–1533, 2007.

Peters, D. H., S. El-Saharty, B. Siadat, K. Janovsky, and M. Vujicic, (eds.), *Improving Health Service Delivery in Developing Countries: From Evidence to Action*, Washington, DC: World Bank, 2009.

Petticrew, M. and H. Roberts, *Systematic Reviews in the Social Sciences: A Practical Guide*, Malden, MA: Blackwell Publishing, 2006.

Rahman, A., A. Malik, S. Sikander, C. Roberts, and F. Creed, "Cognitive behaviour therapy-based intervention by community health workers for mothers with depression and their infants in rural Pakistan: A cluster-randomised controlled trial", *Lancet*, **372**(9642), 902–909, 2008.

Record, J. C., M. McCally, S. O. Schweitzer, R. M. Blomquist, and B. D. Berger, "New health professions after a decade and a half: Delegation, productivity, and costs in primary care", *Journal of Health Politics, Policy and Law*, **5**(3), 470–497, 1980.

Rowe, S. Y., J. M. Kelly, M. A. Olewe, D. G. Kleinbaum, J. E. McGowan, D. A. McFarland, R. Rochat, and M. S. Deming, "Effect of multiple interventions on community health workers' adherence to clinical guidelines in Siaya District, Kenya", *Transactions of the Royal Society of Tropical Medicine and Hygiene*, **101**, 188–202, 2007.

Sanne, I., C. Orrell, M. P. Fox, F. Conradie, P. Ive, J. Zeinecker, M. Cornell, C. Heiberg, C. Ingram, R. Panchia, M. Rassool, R. Gonin, W. Stevens, H. Truter, M. Dehlinger, C. van der Horst, J. McIntyre, and R. Wood, "Nurse versus doctor management of HIV-infected patients receiving antiretroviral therapy (CIPRA-SA): A randomised non-inferiority trial", *Lancet*, **376**(9734), 33–40, 2010.

Scheffler, R. M., *Is There a Doctor in the House? Market Signals and Tomorrow's Supply of Doctors*, Palo Alto, CA: Stanford University Press, 2008.

Scheffler, R. M., N. Waltzman, and J. Hillman, "The productivity of physician assistants and nurse practitioners and health work force policy in the era of managed health care", *Journal of Allied Health*, **25**(3), 207–217, 1996.

Scheffler, R. M., C. B. Mahoney, B. D. Fulton, M. R. Dal Poz, and A. S. Preker, "Estimates of health care professional shortages in sub-Saharan Africa by 2015", *Health Affairs*, **28**(5), w849–w862, 2009.

Selke, H. M., S. Kimaiyo, J. E. Sidle, R. Vedanthan, W. M. Tierney, C. Shen, C. D. Denski, A. R. Katschke, and K. Wools-Kaloustian, "Task-shifting of antiretroviral delivery from health care workers to persons living with HIV/ AIDS: Clinical outcomes of a community-based program in Kenya", *Journal of Acquired Immune Deficiency Syndromes*, **55**(4), 483–490, 2010.

Shumbusho, F., J. van Griensven, D. Lowrance, I. Turate, M. A. Weaver, J. Price, and A. Binagwaho, "Task shifting for scale-up of HIV care: Evaluation of nurse-centered antiretroviral treatment at rural health centers in Rwanda", *PLoS Medicine*, **6**(10), 2009.

Teklehaimanot, A., Y. Kitaw, A. G. Yohannes, S. Girma, A. Seyoum, H. Desta, and Y. Ye-Ebiyo, "Study of the working conditions of health extension workers in Ethiopia", *Ethiopian Journal of Health Development*, **21**(3), 246–259, 2007; 2010, September 25, accessed, at http://ejhd.uib.no/ejhd-v21-n3/246%20Study%20of%20the%20Workeing%20Conditions%20 of%20Health%20Extension%20Workers%20in%20Ethiopia.pdf].

Vasan, A., N. Kenya-Mugisha, K. J. Seung, M. Achieng, P. Banura, F. Lule, M. Beems, J. Todd, and E. Madraa, "Agreement between physicians and non-physician clinicians in starting antiretroviral therapy in rural Uganda", *Human Resources for Health*, **7**(75), 2009.

Viswanathan, M., J. L. Kraschnewski, B. Nishikawa, L. C. Morgan, A. A. Honeycutt, P. Thieda, L. N. Lohr, and D. E. Jonas, "Outcomes and costs of community health worker interventions: A systematic review", *Medical Care*, **48**(9), 792–808, 2010.

Walker, D. G. and S. Jan, "How do we determine whether community health workers are cost-effective? Some core methodological issues", *Journal of Community Health*, **30**(3), 221–229, 2005.

WHO (World Health Organization) 2008. "Task Shifting: Global Recommendations and Guidelines." Geneva: WHO; 2010, September 25, accessed at http:// www.who.int/healthsystems/TTR-TaskShifting.pdf.

WHO, *Working Together for Health: The World Health Report 2006*. Geneva: WHO, 2006.

Wools-Kaloustian, K. K., J. E. Sidle, H. M. Selke, R. Vedanthan, E. K. Kemboi, L. J. Boit, V. T. Jebet, A. E. Carroll, W. M. Tierney, and S. Kimaiyo, "A model for extending antiretroviral care beyond the rural health centre", *Journal of the International AIDS Society*, **12**(1), 22, 2009.

Yin, R. K., *Case Study Research: Design and Methods*, 4th ed., Thousand Oaks, CA: Sage Publications, 2009.

Zachariah, R., N. Ford, M. Phillips, S. Lynch, M. Massaquoi, V. Janssens, and A. D. Harries, "Task shifting in HIV/AIDS: Opportunities, challenges and proposed actions for sub-Saharan Africa", *Transactions of the Royal Society of Tropical Medicine and Hygiene*, **103**, 549–558, 2009.

Zurn, P., M. R. Dal Poz, B. Stilwell, and O. Adams, "Imbalance in the health workforce", *Human Resources for Health*, **2**(13), 2004.

Chapter 5

Better Governance and Leadership in Health Education

Peter Walker and Hortenzia Beciu

This chapter stresses the importance of good governance practices of higher education institutions and systems within the complex milieu of national and international markets that more and more respond to current and potential consumers of their services or products. The chapter summarizes the evolution of higher education from the governance perspective and presents conceptual frameworks used within the past several decades in the quest to define the right governance attributes that will lead to expected performance of systems and organizations. UK, US, and France systems are summarized as a preamble of a more detailed discussion about the evolution of tertiary education in sub-Sahara Africa and what can be done so support its development. Specific references are made to medical and allied health schools and/or institutions all the way in this chapter.

The revitalization of governance systems for higher educational institutions is essential in the present time. The very fast pace in which technology provides data, information, and analysis, already changed the way we think and apply modern tools and techniques in the learning process. The technology not only changed the access to learning and education, these days the information is delivered and received from almost any corner of the world, but it also brought up an informed and demanding consumer. Communities and/or individuals have a voice in what they think and what they demand of both public and private education entities. As the result, more and more people like to tailor their experiences with almost everything including their education.

In medical field, the shift in mindset and application tools, though still its early stages, will be important. The practices are moving from a full bed side direct patient contact, as main learning path to more diverse options including virtual learning (i.e. simulation), virtual libraries, and the use of interactive software as learning and maintenance tools. This is not a trivial change in learning and, in the years to come, technology will continue to advance and play potentially even a higher role in medical education.

In medical education systems, there is an increase appetite for students to live in cultures different from their native ones, which can overturn traditional players in favor of players who offer flexible, technology driven, and less expensive programs.

What will all amounts to? At the national/government level, a need to continuously oversee the assessment and certification of the new tools and means that prove to be truly beneficial in the learning process. At the organizational level, a visionary, flexible with self-assessment capabilities but also cost conscious governance of the organizations of higher learning.

To produce the future health professionals, this impetus is driven by the need to create on one hand integrated, technology based, efficient and effective system of higher education, and on the other hand, providers that can easily embrace the technology and critically reflect and self-assess their performance.

Introduction

There has been increased attention to the importance of good governance and many reports and books have been written about what ingredients are necessary for a good governance. Nowadays in an era of multiple opportunities and consumer-driven demand, the higher education institutions are facing pressure from these stakeholders who for most of the previous century were passive receiver of what was available and/or prescribed to them. It is said that the tertiary education organizations are functioning in a complex environment, with a degree of complexity that increases by year, coming from both horizontal but also vertical stakeholders.

The horizontal stakeholders: connect local actors (which can be unilateral but also coming from other sectors such as environment, labor, and social services) with the organizations of tertiary education. The organizations themselves are complex systems which horizontal and vertical structures, formal and informal networks.

The vertical stakeholders can be different: local, regional, and national organizations that are responsible of oversight, certification, and/or accreditation of the institutions and/or its programs. Also at the national level, federal countries add another degree of complexity while the one that are not federal can have regional and local bodies in charge of the oversight.

The interactions between organizations of higher education and the many actors in the system are therefore many and with different interests.

Fielden (2008) has emphasized the critical importance of the governance of tertiary education sector by governments as stewards of the system. At present time, the systems continue to move from the direct state control of universities to stewardship that supports and encourages the universities' autonomy, while insisting on the development of measurable accountabilities. The move from state control to state oversight has been dictated by several factors: (1) the need for additional resources and know-how needed to support a viable, competitive higher education system; (2) a recognition that higher education in a knowledge-based society plays a vital role in economic development; (3) the increasing complexity of the sector with a growing number of multidisciplinary institutions; (4) the development of a vibrant private sector; (5) the increasing complexity of the higher education institution itself; (6) the increase in demand from individuals and communities for a tailored, and at the same time, flexible learning experience. All these factors require an increased autonomy for the management of higher education institutions, new ways to finance the education, new ways to deliver the education and the development of a better, more encompassing, governmental policy setting for, and oversight of, the higher education sector.

The works of Salmi (2009)[1] and Aghion *et al.* (2008) focus on those qualities that define world-class universities. For them, there are two challenges or aims of the higher education systems: to provide (1) high-quality education to all who want it, regardless of their geographical location; and (2) at affordable cost to improve equity in access. Both authors underscored the importance of national policies in support of tertiary education, and on the need for autonomy of institutions. Salmi (2009) identifies four essential components for success in his analysis of the challenges of world-class universities: (1) favorable and supportive government frameworks and processes in tertiary education; (2) favorable institutional governance; (3) abundant talent; and (4) abundant resources.

Figure 5.1 illustrates these features as they relate to the expected outcomes at the national level of a university education system, with

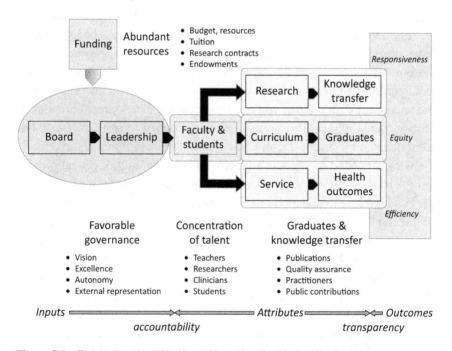

Figure 5.1   Determinants of Tertiary Education Institution Performance
Source: Adapted from Salmi (2008).

particular relevance to higher education organizations that are responsible for the education and training of health workers. The additional component — which goes beyond just a practicum requirement, like in other disciplines — the clinical services, are specific for medical and allied health training institutions. Therefore, the institutions of medical higher education are expected to contribute to the communities and society by improving and/or maintaining health status within these communities.

Mikkelson-Lopez *et al.* (2010)[2] characterize the three principal areas of their health system governance framework as inputs, attributes, and outcomes. In this model, the main attributes that lead to a successful transformation of inputs into outcomes are accountability and transparency (Figure 5.1).

Concerning the principle of favorable (good) governance, the model suggests that strategic vision, excellence in teaching and research, autonomy and having external representation in the organization's boards, are the main ingredients for success. However, none of these factors alone are sufficient to predict success.

The degree of autonomy of an organization can correlate with the organizational performance in a direct relationship but this is not always sufficient. For a good performance, accountability and transparency are also attributes of essence (Aghion *et al.*, 2008). An OECD report "Governing Education in a Complex World" also finds accountability a key element for effective governance and successful reform of the health education system, together with capacity building and strategic thinking (Burns and Köster, 2016).

As mentioned before in a tertiary institution that educates and trains health professionals, there is an additional dimension beyond education and research. This additional dimension relates to provision of health services by teachers, clinicians, and school graduates residents and fellows. Together, they represent a significant contribution to the community's health and well-being while at the same time they require additional regulatory and oversight.

Combining the above viewpoints we can state that the model suggests that the main ingredients for a successful tertiary education performance are favorable governance, alignment of goals and interests at all levels of the system, concentration of talents and abundant resources.

To mirror the expected patients and community good health outcomes, the systems of higher education needs to also have organizations that will put the public and patients' interests first.

Because health education encompasses everything from Certificate to PhD level, in many countries, the oversight responsibility for health professional worker education is split between different government ministries. Therefore, differing from other sectors, the health sector brings in additional complexities. In most countries, the responsibility for national policy direction for the higher education sector resides with an education ministry. The health care worker's education, however, has a mixed model in most countries with the two ministries (education and health) playing a role in the education of medical professionals. Physician, pharmacy, and dental education, for example, occurs within the university, and the university is governed by policies dictated by the ministry of higher education. Responsibility for nursing education or technicians, on the other hand, may derive from the ministry of health and be carried out in colleges that have little interaction with the university sector. To meld their policies into one national strategy, the complex interactions among these different actors require an integrated or at least coordinated stewardship and governance at the national level.

For optimum planning, there must be a close collaboration between the education ministry and the ministry of health that oversees the health system and is responsible for the provision of health services thus for hiring health workers. In only a few countries, does the governance of education and training of health professionals resides with one ministry (i.e. in Iran "The Ministry of Health and Medical Education").

In addition to government stewardship, many other organizations are designated to regulate the standards of education and the professional practice.

Comparing the governance of undergraduate and graduate medical education, the Chapter 4 of the book, *Graduate Medical Education That Meets the Nation's Health Needs*, by Jill Eden, Donald Berwick, and Gail Wilensky (Institute of Medicine, 2014) mention that assessing "the principles of good governance in the context of graduate medical education (GME) is challenging". The governance of GME is perhaps best described as an intricate puzzle of interlocking, overlapping, and sometimes missing pieces". The report builds on previous evidence to emphasize the lack of stringent criteria for allocation and monitoring mechanisms for graduate medical education public financing. The only straightforward allocation is the one that relates to residency programs accreditation by different bodies such as Council on Podiatric Education or the Accreditation for Graduate Medical Education (ACGME) (MedPAC, 2010). Previous data suggests that more than US$15 billion are spent annually, from public funds, for GME (GME financing, 2014). The magnitude of this spending requires specific, measurable, achievable, realistic and timely milestones together with a legal framework for accountability of the resource allocation and its results (Institute of Medicine, 2014).

Setting the Stage

Many studies have demonstrated a significant shortage of highly trained health workers in developed and developing countries. The shortage is perhaps most severe in sub-Saharan Africa where the burden of illness is acutely high, the production of health workers is low and attrition rates among students and health workers are high. In low-income countries, despite continued overall progress toward the health-related Millennium Development Goals and more recently Sustainable Development Goals, maternal and infant mortality rates remain high, and access to medicines and quality health care services is problematic overall and even more acute for the poor and rural populations (Millennium Development Goals, 2011).

Anand and Barnighausen (2004, 2007) showed that healthy birth outcomes and vaccination coverage were related to physician and nursing density per population (counted together). The Joint Learning Initiative went on to estimate that to achieve the health worker numbers which would provide just 80 percent coverage of the basic population's needs, there is a global shortage of 4.5 million; and in sub-Saharan Africa, the shortage was estimated at 2.5 million (JLI, 2004). The World Health Organization dedicated its 2008 World Health Report to the goal of scaling up the education and training of health workers (WHO, 2008) and many other further works.

A direct result of this series of initiatives, the Global Health Workforce Alliance (GHWA) was created in 2006 with the vision of "access for all to a skilled, motivated and supported health worker" (GHWA, 2008). The alliance created several task forces, each directed to a specific aspect of strengthening the health system of developing countries to increase the size and rebalance the skill mix of the health workforce.

In 2010, an international commission has led the cry for a new approach to professional education, one that must move to a new systems-based approach to meet national and global health goals (Lancet, 2010).[3] Notably, while the principle for standards should be global in scope to ensure accountability, it should also be contextually specific to allow adaptation to address local needs and opportunities for innovation. While much has been accomplished in the sub-Saharan health education schools,[4] more needs to be done.

The drive to a health education systems approach — including service provision — means that autonomous higher education organizations must act together with government, health organizations, patients associations and local, regional, national, and international communities to design educational programs focusing on the types of conditions each country encounters and with adequate numbers of health workers to respond to these conditions.

Such an endeavor will require dedicated and far-sighted leadership. Leadership that will exceed and overcome traditional perspectives of system requirements and therefore contributing to the betterment of society and community.

The centrality of good leadership in development decreases corruption attracts investment and increases system efficiency, laying the foundation for the formation of new networks, furthering the development of institutions and local markets. In several developing countries, the leadership and the organizational environment for good governance is still weak. It is therefore critical for developing countries to establish effective and responsible institutions and organizations to support and promote good governance. As Nigerian writer, Chinua Achebe asked: "How do we begin to solve these problems where the structures are present but there is no accountability?" (Achebe, 2011).

Given the importance of higher education and health to development (McKechnie, 2009)[5] and the massive size of the anticipated spending, it is vital that principles of stewardship of the health system and good organizational governance be firmly in place with the focus on patient-centered education, accreditation of organization and programs, and accessibility. This chapter examines the issues related to stewardship and governance in higher education in general and in institutions that have programs for the education of health professionals specifically. The chapter addresses governance from the macro, meso, to micro levels and cites examples from developed and developing countries with a focus on sub-Sahara Africa. Finally, an attempt will be made to relate the findings to the kind of transformation considered by Frenk *et al.* (2010).

The Different Types of Governance

At its most basic level, governance is the system by which a country's operations, organization, and business are directed and controlled. Governance encompasses the dual process of making and executing decisions. As the multitude of stakeholders that relate to or are affected by operations increased over time so the governance structure and aims evolved. Theisen's define governance as "the processes of establishing priorities, formulating and implementing policies and being accountable in complex networks with many different actors" (Theisens *et al.*, 2017; Pierre and Peters, 2005).

This chapter considers four approaches to stakeholder involvement in health education governance, each of them the subject of a significant body of literature and empirical research. More importantly, when applying a systemic approach to health professional education in developed and developing countries, a sustained commitment is essential at every level to engage, respect, and support each of the different forms of governance. This multi-prong dynamic recognizes that no single level of governance can alone achieve the objectives of the transformed health education and health care delivery system of the future.

The four governance sectors are public sector, corporate sector, health systems sector, and higher education sector. The chapter concludes with a brief discussion of the need to bring the different sectors, and actors, together to enable a systemic response to the need for more and better-trained health professionals to meet the health care needs of their communities and the world.

As stated in the OECD paper, "Governing Education in a Complex World", "there is no one right system of governance. The complexity of the system is not necessary what breaks it or makes it.

Rather, it is the strength of the alignment, the involvement of actors, and the processes involved in governance and reform that makes for good results" (Burns and Köster, 2016).

Public Sector Governance

Before discussing the concept of governance in the public sector, it is important to recall the concept of stewardship proposed by the WHO (2000). *Stewardship* in the health sector was defined as a "careful and responsible management of the well-being of the population, being an expression of the governance arrangements in a system and an organization". Stewardship has three main roles: to provide vision and directions (formulating policies), to exert influence, and to collect and use intelligence (data and information). While this chapter touches on the stewardship function of the different governmental and para-governmental organizations and institutions, the chief aim remains the operational level governance. Governance at the systemic level is the process of guiding and directing through public policy networks that include both public and private sector actors (Lemieux, 2000).

Governance is the means; "The traditions and institutions by which authority in a country is exercised".[6] "Governance comprises the complex mechanisms, processes, and institutions and the exercise of economic, political, and administrative authority through which individuals and other interest groups articulate their wishes, either through formal or informal channels, mediate their differences, and exercise their legal rights and obligations".[7]

Governments are responsible for and accountable to their citizens (Figure 5.2). Elected or appointed officials are viewed as the sacred guardians of the public sector and are held accountable for its governance.

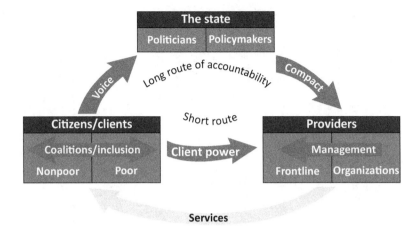

Figure 5.2   Linkages Defining Governance and Accountability Mechanisms in the Public Sector
Source: World Bank (2004).

The overarching public sector objective is to lead the country for the achievement of national objectives. In this regard, it is important for the government to build reliable governance structures at every level of the public sector. The central government has the responsibility for providing a strategic platform and setting policy objectives, usually through a legislature and making sure that sector ministries work toward the attainment of these policy objectives. Successful public governance is when the regulatory frameworks are aligned with the desired goals that create favorable incentives to allow both autonomy and accountability within tertiary institutions.

A 2012 World Bank review selects five key features of a successful system-wide governance based on a review of high performance systems. The key features are: (a) the capacity of the state to guide and direct the development of tertiary education; (b) the presence of a strong and favorable regulatory framework; (c) reliance on performance-based funding allocation mechanisms; (d) a comprehensive quality assurance system for public and private institutions; and (e) a solid accountability framework (World Bank, 2012).

Table 5.1 presents a summary of some of these models analyzed in different studies for the past two decades looking at the key knobs of good

Table 5.1   Elements of Good Governance in the Public Sector

Australia[a]	European Union[b]	United Kingdom[c]	Gottret and Scheiber[d]	Welch and Nuru[e]	OECD Principles of modern governance
Efficiency and effectiveness	Effectiveness	Effectiveness			
		Purpose and outcomes	Coherent decision-making structures	Strategic direction	Strategic vision
Transparency	Openness	Transparent decision making	Transparency and information	Transparency	Open dialogue
Rule of law			Supervision and regulation	Rule of law	
Participation	Participation	Stakeholder engagement	Stakeholder participation	Participation	Stakeholder engagement
	Accountability		Accountability	Accountability	Accountability–Trust
	Coherence	Behavior and values	Stability and consistency		
Responsiveness				Responsiveness	
Equitable and inclusive		Capacity to govern and inclusiveness			Capacity building

Sources: (a). World Bank (2004); (b). EU (2001); (c). Independent Commission on Good Governance in Public Services (2004); (d). Gottret and Scheiber (2006); UNDP (2006); OECD, Principles of Modern Governance, Burns, and Köster (eds.) OECD (2016).

public sector governance. To these models, we added the recent OECD findings of the project lead by The Centre for Educational Research and Innovation (CERI). The project entitled "Governing Complex Education Systems" focused on which models of governance are effective in complex education systems and which knowledge systems are needed to support them (Burns and Köster, 2016). Table 5.1 summarizes the elements of good public sector governance.

Accountability is considered a core, intrinsic value in several of the proposed good governance models together with stakeholder participation and transparency.

Accountability can be defined as "representing the ethical and managerial obligation to report on their activities and results, explain their performance, and assume responsibility for unmet expectations" (World Bank, 2012).

To balance against risk/incidents/corruption, other elements such as transparency, efficiency, and inclusiveness must be in place and intertwined. For effective decision-making, adequate and proper measures must be in place for monitoring, supervision, control, participation, and stability. In return, consumers and clients exert influence, albeit indirectly, by expressing their satisfaction or dissatisfaction, usually during the election season.

The OECD 2016 report, "Governing Education in a Complex World" defines accountability as addressing the challenge of holding different actors at multiple levels (national, regional, individual organization) responsible for their actions. The report also introduces the term "constructive accountability", which is viewed as "balancing the monitoring and pressure required ensuring efficient system functioning, with support for continuous system improvement". The same report defines, capacity building, as "identifying gaps, skill needs and dynamics of implementation on individual, institutional and system level". Lastly, strategic vision pertains to the "development of a long-term plan and set of common goals for the educational system among a broad array of actors" (Burns and Köster, 2016).

The nature and measure of accountability, however, depends on the aims of the organization (Brinkerhoff, 2004). For example, in setting policy, a government wishes to ensure that its funds are used wisely, effectively, and consistent with the policy objectives. At the provider level, the major accountability measures are providing educational services at the best possible quality for the student population. Encouraging tertiary education institutions to develop a strategic plan by which they set their own policies and direction that align their operations with public policy goals is a desirable outcome of public sector governance (World Bank, 2012).

Corporate Sector Governance

The Organisation for Economic Cooperation and Development (OECD) defines *corporate governance* as "a set of relationships between a company management, its board, its shareholders and other stakeholders. Corporate governance also provides the structure through which the objectives are set, and the means of attaining those objectives and monitoring performance are determined" (OECD, 2004).

Corporate governance is usually a term that relates to private sector governance, either for-profit or not-for-profit. However, some public entities, around the globe, are also using some of the organizational structures used in corporate governance, to govern their public affairs. Corporate governance principles are seen as a better, more efficient and transparent way to manage public sector entities.

Corporate sector governance principles differ from those of the public sector. In the private sector, non-governmental institutions (NGOs) and private for-profit organizations, good governance arrangements tend to protect the interests and values of specific constituents (shareholders). Members of corporate boards regarded as the guardians of private sector governance and protectors of assets, profits or both. Corporate governance changed over the past decade or so. The space accorded to social responsibility and accountability has been improving. Yet, it is not necessarily considered one of the main duties or features of private sector governance.

The Conference Board of Canada (1999) identifies the following principles of corporate governance: (a) leadership and stewardship (this principle recalls the public sector principle of strategic direction and coherence of decision making); (b) empowerment (equivalent to autonomy, authority, and accountability); (c) communication (in the corporate sector, information accrual and distribution are paramount); (d) transparency (effectiveness and clarity is imperative); (e) service (although initially dedicated to customer service, this principle increasingly relates to social accountability), and the principle of service also equates to responsiveness in the public sector; (f) accomplishment (this principle equates to efficiency and effectiveness in the public sector principles); and (g) continuous learning and growth (this principle would best resemble Gottret and Scheiber's principle of stability and sustainability).

It should not be understood that, for example, just having a more representative board and better communication tools means that private sector corporate governance is achieving the stated core results, which is measured by increased market share and profit for shareholders. Establishing good corporate governance that optimizes the company's position can be also challenging in the private sector and it is not without problems and wrongdoing. Learning from mistakes and therefore models of good corporate governance are also needed and thought through in the private sector. When in place, there can be a relationship between the ranking/rates corporate governance and organizational outcomes. Though this relationship seems not to be as straightforward, a study conducted by Renders *et al.* reveal that corporate-governance ratings are relevant in measuring company's performance and that in "adhering to good corporate-governance practices, companies can significantly improve their performance in the private sector" (Renders *et al.*, 2016).

There is also another dimension of the private sector corporate governance borough from the public sector that increases the social and ethical responsibility of the private sector. The Encyclopedia of Corporate Social Responsibility, 2010, provide the concepts and standards of how organizations can strive to balance their aims with foreseen and unforeseen externalities of their business. The standards guide clients to take a balanced approach between people, planet, and profit (the three Ps) (3Ps) with the purpose of enhancing sustainability and responsibility of the organization. Corporate responsibility and thus corporate governance need to look into the impact of their organization on society, environment, and economy. The goal again is to be aware, measure, and implement new directions for business sustainability and positive contribution to society (Encyclopedia of Corporate Social Responsibility, 2010).

The Role of the Private Sector in Public Governance

Though well established in several jurisdictions, notably in the United States, private sector engagement in higher education is also growing significantly in many parts of the world including developing countries. Countries like Indonesia, Japan, the Philippines, and the Republic of Korea continued to encourage and further develop their already existent private sector education organizations. In 2011, 80 percent of students in Republic of Korea and Japan were enrolled in private institutions; 60 percent of students in Cambodia, Indonesia and 40 percent of student in Bangladesh and the Islamic Republic of Iran (UNESCO Institute for Statistics, 2014).

Collaborating with the private sector is seen as a solution for the insufficient and inefficient management of the resources that sometime exists in the public sector. The public sector retains the role of oversight and/or establishing regulation that will allow the private sector to function within certain parameters at desirable standards. In some regions, i.e. sub-Saharan Africa, the concern has been raised about standards and the risk of diploma factories at the private enterprises. However, the role of the private not-for-profit sector, particularly faith-based organizations, is a well-established and long-standing model, both in terms of quality and achieving previously unmet needs in health care and education.

Increasingly, corporate governance practices and principles encompass those of the public sector, as indicated previously the corporate social responsibility policies (Porter and Kramer, 2006; Encyclopedia of Corporate Social Responsibility, 2010) that allows for a shared responsibility and sustainable business between public and private sector.

Many public–private partnership (PPP) models already exists in different industries including the education sector (UNECE, 2008) and as the model continue to grow they are seen as innovative approaches to provide education (Verger and Moschetti, 2016). PPPs are arrangements between public and private sector for building facilities and running operations, delivery of goods, etc., in different settings (UNESCO, 2017). Public–private sector governance adds to, or modifies, the principles of good corporate governance by focusing on policy; putting people first; capacity-building; legal framework; risk sharing; procurement and the environment. In education, the PPPs are not as new as in the delivery of health services, for example. Enough experience has been accumulated about PPPs to also discuss their challenges. PPPs are resource intense, demand very good management of the legal arrangements, they can be lengthy, longer than expected, more expensive than predicted and sometime even without the expected outcomes. A UNESCO working paper, "Public-Private Partnership, As an Education Policy Approach", states that not all PPPs are appropriate to achieve expected results given their costs, potential equity issues, and uncertain innovative approaches (Verger and Moschetti, 2016).

Health Sector Governance

In the health sector, governance occurs at different levels of political organization and involves substantive goals — the values a society has and the objectives the society wants to achieve, and mechanisms — how the society organizes the pursuit of these objectives. These goals and mechanisms provide structure to governance (Fidler, 2007).

Good governance in the health sector is essential for effective delivery of services. Good governance begets improved performance; conversely, in its absence, inefficiencies occur and inequities arise. Lack of appropriate standards, incentives, information, and accountability leads to poor provider performance and often corruption (Lewis and Pettersson, 2009). The degree to which poor performance is due to corruption is not clear but performance is certainly improved in conditions of good governance.

Gottret and Schieber (2006) emphasize the importance of national good governance for the support of the health system in developing countries. They also point out to the need for multi-sectoral approaches to achieve maximum leverage and impact. In the health sector, the core ministers that needs to closely collaborate are: health, education, labor, and environment. As stated by Ramalingaswami paper in 1989 citing

Parry, Health of the people is inseparable from the health of the land and the environment (Ramalingaswami, 1989). Ministry of Labor and Ministry of Health need to work closely on the gaps in health workforce and align incentives and improve labor policies to make health profession attractive to more potential candidates. In addition, more and more the health of the employees constitute a concern to the employers. From insurance to healthy eating habits and spaces for the employees to stay fit, the way the organizational governance embraces the health of the organizational environment and its employee's start counting in organizational ratings and the decisions to take a job or not.

Taking the idea further in Constantin Popescu's book, *About Life and Economy* and later on in the *Economic Mode of Thinking — A Holistic Perspective*" the author, developing concepts from multiple sources, states that health, as a consumption and a production good, has no substitute. The production of "health" is the responsibility of the individual who through self-reflection and responsible autonomy need not live outside the consciousness of the whole living beings. The organizations need to reflect that and therefore shall not be allowed to build systems and create environments against human beings. Organizations should not be seen as an unmanageable given that they are built by people. In order to make sure that we are not building unhealthy organizations that in turn will educate and/or produce unhealthy individuals or unhealthy products, the organizations need to conduct multidisciplinary assessments and build indicators that measure the health of the organizations on a continuous basis. We want to make sure that the leadership and governance are geared toward/start with a healthy organization (Popescu, 2011, 2017).

In aligning incentives and making information readily available and transparent, rules or dimensions for good governance are as follows: coherent decision-making structures; diverse stakeholder participation; transparency; supervision and regulation aligned with the goals; and consistency and stability (Savedoff and Gottret, 2008). Savedoff (2009) provides further clarity on governance determinants and performance. He defines governance as "the combination of political, social, economic and institutional factors that affect the behavior of organizations and individuals and influence their performance".

Higher Education Governance

In higher education, university governance is described as "the constitutional forms and processes through which universities govern their affairs".[8]

The OECD (2003) considers governance in higher education to comprise a "complex web including the legislative framework, the characteristics of the organizations and how they relate to the whole system, how money is allocated to organizations and how they are accountable for the way it is spent" (OECD, 2003). The new OECD report, reconsidering the increase in consumer demands through formal and informal networks, along with an overall increase in system's complexity states that the relationships "between governance levels, is moving away from a hierarchical relationship to a division of labor, interdependence and self-regulation. Education systems are now characterized by multi-level governance where the links between multiple actors operating at different levels are to a certain extent fluid and open to negotiation" (Burns and Köster, 2016).

Government exerts significant legislative influence and authority over the higher education sector arguing, with justification, that higher education is a public good that deserves public investment. Therefore, government is poised to regulate higher education, in both the public and private sectors. Governments exercise strategic leverage with their checks and balances, i.e. authority and regulation versus organizational autonomy and accountability. At the same time, government's interest in the quality of higher education has evolved, partly, because of concerns about migration and equivalence of qualifications, so they now insist on more rigorous accountability and standardization.

The approach taken by most countries has evolved significantly from one of ownership to one of devolution of autonomy. This change has occurred as the result of the recognition of the importance of the higher education sector in knowledge-based societies[9] and the advantages of institutional autonomy on improved efficiency and effectiveness. In addition, the demand for a more tailored and user friendly education experience coming from the millennials and the society overall lead to innovative platforms (i.e. Coursera), tools, and methods that are used by institutes of higher education to spread knowledge and/or advertise for their programs.

Historically, higher education governance has been collegial in nature. Over time, however, several factors have motivated significant changes in the sector. They are based on increased mobility of students and faculty members, the demand for a tailored experience, the significant increase in access to information, the drive to massification (mass participation), the need for increased efficiency and effectiveness, and the need for comparability and transportability of qualifications. In many jurisdictions, these factors also have created the opening for increasing private sector involvement in higher education provision.

The result, higher education governance at the highest levels, now more closely resembles corporate governance with governance boards comprising external representatives who can provide community, private and public sector expertise and perspectives and strengthen links to the economy and to the broader community-based issues.

The increasing norm of governance of higher education organizations is "shared" or bicameral where overall institutional governance, represented by a governing board, deals with the institution's legal and financial standing and overall academic direction. In contrast, academic governance, represented by a senate or academic council, is concerned with all substantial aspects of governance that relate directly to the academic life of the institution: education, research, and quality.

The justification for shared governance is nicely encapsulated in the following quote: "An organization (such as a company) exists to get something done and requires management while an institution (such as a university) is less concrete and is largely held together by people in the mind as part of their frame of reference. An institution is composed of the diverse fantasies and projections of those associated with it. These ideas are not consciously negotiated or agreed upon, but they exist".[10]

Although there is considerable variation from jurisdiction to jurisdiction, budgets are now largely given as block grants as opposed to line-item budgets, and universities may manage their budgets to meet their specific needs. Funds allocation from an outside entity are more and more based either on the organization outcomes (performance) or are provided with a clear stated designation and expected results.

Universities also have the right to raise money from external sources, either in the form of fund-raising (e.g. donations, endowments), development of philanthropic or commercial partnerships, and research grants and contracts. In exchange for this increasing autonomy, governments have insisted on more stringent accountability, notably in the form of performance against indicators and targets and quality assessment. Quality assessment is a planned and systematic review process to determine whether an institution or a constituent program meets acceptable standards of education, research, and infrastructure. In some countries, public funds were at least partially linked to the organization's performance as set by the public payer.

Budgetary management includes the right to set tuition and ancillary fees and the authority to manage human resources. In some countries where the state exerts significant ownership of the university, faculty and staff may be public employees and subject, not to university policies, but to public service policies.

Quality assessment can be internally managed but may include external peer assessment, and is usually less burdensome than accreditation. For organizational overall compliance with education standards, quality assessment may be incorporated within an accreditation process that assesses quality against standards established by an external body and involves self-assessment, peer review, and site visits. Failure to achieve or maintain accreditation may result in financial penalty to the institution. Success may result in enhanced funding as well as greater recognition.

Quality assurance instruments vary widely across countries. In OECD countries, quality assurance agencies are autonomous. For each subsector in many countries there is a single national quality assurance agency; others have several. While most accreditation bodies are relatively recent, for almost a century the United States has had accreditation bodies for higher education, including medicine, public health, and nursing.

Higher Education Governance in Developed Countries

Education reforms that began in earnest in the 1960s and 1970s were founded on the core principle of mass participation — *massification* — in higher education on one hand, and the obligation of the state to provide opportunities for personal advancement on the other. Massification, in turn, had two objectives: (1) to promote research, development, and liberal thinking and; (2) to bring affluence to middle- and lower-income families. Consequently, the higher education sector had undergone significant expansion. With this expansion, the need for more efficient forms of governance in higher education was warranted. In general, governments have responded by progressively devolving authority from the government to the institutions and adopting a more supervisory and steering role.

For the purposes of this discussion, reference will be made to countries with special mention of the regional efforts to harmonize and standardize higher education in the European Community through the Bologna Process, the *Agence Universitaire de la Francophonie* and the Association of Commonwealth Universities. The countries examined are the United Kingdom and France; most sub-Saharan countries' models for their governance approaches to their public and higher education sectors; and because of its unique set of governance structures, the United States, to which many countries are now looking to for higher education sector partnership and guidance.

Higher Education Governance in the United States

The United States has perhaps the most diversified higher education sector in the world with a varied mix of public, private not-for-profit and private-for-profit institutions.

Higher education in the United States is almost the exclusive province of the states, which are responsible for governing universities and colleges (Eckel and King, 2004). The role of the federal government has been limited to research funding for the development of specific legislation guaranteeing access, and for student financial aid. Among the states, there are many different types of control varying from creating universities as separate branches of government, to government-appointed oversight boards, to advisory buffer bodies to locally elected trustees.

Although governments exert significant financial and audit oversight over public institutions, they prefer to leave quality assessment of academic programming to independent accreditation bodies. In the United States, accreditation bodies perform many of the oversight functions required by the government to ensure standards and quality. Accreditation bodies are independent, and members agree to carry out institutional and program accreditation by these third parties on a voluntary or sometimes compulsory basis, depending on the states. In some states, an accreditation is necessary for some organizations to operate while in other states a license is sufficient. Currently 21 states require non-public organizations to be accredited. Also for the same organization that may want to open education programs in a different state, they will need to conform with the regulations of the new states they enter in, independent of their status in the state they originally started. Sometime to receive public funds, the not-for-profit organizations need to subject themselves to an accreditation process. Finally, there are special accrediting organizations that evaluate programs within a specific medical field: Medicine (LCME, 2010), nursing (ANA, 2010), dentistry (ADA, 2010), and pharmacy (ACPE, 2007) are examples of the latter accrediting organizations (Council for Higher Education Accreditation, 2011).

Accrediting organizations establish minimum standards that institutions must meet in a range of areas such as the curricula, faculty qualifications, and student learning outcomes, co-curricular student services, and financial strength. Accrediting organizations do not, however, mandate how institutions go about meeting those standards.

Because accreditation measures the institutions against a set of standards, it generally does not provide a gauge of how well an institution is performing relative to other comparable institutions.

Accreditation is accomplished through institutional self-study and a peer-review process to determine whether the institution has achieved the organization's standard.

Among the newest education innovations that started in US and UK that promises to increase access at very affordable prices among professionals but also undergraduate students is the 100 percent use of e-learning platforms by reputable universities around the world. The pioneers were the Udacity (for-profit startup launched by Stanford), Coursera (founded by Stanford University computer science professors Andrew Ng and Daphne Koller), and FutureLearn (the UK's Open University venture into MOOCs, which overtook Coursera in 2015). It was estimated that in 2016, in the United States 400 universities have produced 2,400 such online courses. Worldwide estimates indicate a total of 35 million students participating in MOOCs in 2015 (Salmi, 2017). Though access to these courses is easy, the graduation rates are still low in comparison with the number of initial students enrolled. These courses have the potential to be recognized by employers especially if the employees will prove their benefits.

Higher Education Governance in the United Kingdom

Universities and colleges in the United Kingdom are independent and self-governed (HCFE, 2004). There have been four stages of university development, starting in the twelfth and thirteenth centuries with the creation of Oxford and Cambridge Universities.[11] Oxford and Cambridge adopted an exclusively internal form of academic governance.[12]

This was followed by the development of three Scottish universities in the fifteenth century. In contrast to England's Oxford and Cambridge, these universities were governed at the highest level by a board of local leaders to ensure that the university reflected its local roots and was integrated into the local community.

With changing societal expectations of the university as an active participant in economic development, and following the German experiment of the research university — also to take hold in the United States — several "civic" universities were created in the nineteenth century. The civic or state universities were the first to develop bicameral governance structures. At the highest level, the governing board with external membership took responsibility for financial and other policy matters. Academic issues were governed by an academic senate comprising internal academic leaders. The bicameral governance approach spread to the expanding higher education sector in North America and remained the dominant form of governance in the United Kingdom throughout the twentieth century.

In the 1960s and 1970s, the United Kingdom awarded full university status to a significant number of polytechnic institutions. These institutions were governed by predominantly lay boards and did not have any form of academic governance since they were largely founded on their mission of education and training (as opposed to scholarship and research for the traditional universities). The creation of these new universities ushered in the period of corporatization. The governance process in the United Kingdom continues to evolve with universities such as Oxford University comprising a bicameral form of governance, the congregation, and the council.

In the United Kingdom, government funding of universities and colleges is managed by the Higher Education Funding Council or equivalent for each of the constituent parts: England, Northern Ireland, Scotland and Wales. These arms-length councils, funded by and accountable to Parliament, allocate funding for research and teaching, promote high-quality teaching and research, ensure access and participation, encourage interactions with business and the community and ensure the proper use of public funds.

The General Medical Council organizes the education standards around five themes that they expect organizations responsible for educating and training medical students and doctors to meet their objectives: (i.e. learning environment and culture, educational governance and leadership, supporting learners, supporting educators, curricula development, and assessment) (General Medical Council, 2016). However, governance cannot function in a vacuum. It needs to work hand-in-hand with regulatory environment in order to align desired goals with the right incentives that will be conducive to obtaining these results. Therefore, not a single characteristic is as the same time necessary and sufficient, to accomplish the aims of a tertiary education organization.

Accountability for quality is managed by the Quality Assurance Agency for Higher Education. As in the United States, higher education institutions are obliged to carry out their own internal quality assurance audits and undergo external peer review on a regular cycle. The external peer review is preceded by an internal self-assessment.

The Quality Assurance Agency works closely with other organizations, notably members of the professional statutory and regulatory bodies play an important role in the quality assurance assessment.[13] Representation from the General Medical Council, the Nursing and Midwifery Council, the General Dental Council, and the Royal Pharmaceutical Society of Great Britain play an important role in quality assurance of professional education programs.

Higher Education in France

The higher education sector in France differs from that of many other countries. It comprises the elite *grandes écoles*, schools that have relatively large resources and small numbers of students. The *grandes écoles* prepare graduates for leadership in business, public service, and the military. The *école polytechnique* prepares graduates for engineering and physics.

Compared to universities, which receive less funding, some *grandes écoles* rank highly in international comparisons: the *école nationale supérieure* is first in France and 59th in the world and the *école polytechnique* ranked second in France and 63rd in the world, followed by Université Pierre et Marie Curie, 84th rank.[14] In contrast, no French university ranks among the top 100 universities worldwide (Université Pierre et Marie Curie, at 84th, is the highest-ranked French university).

There is significant direct state control over the universities in France, more so than in the United States and the United Kingdom. Recently however, there has been a significant movement toward devolution of autonomy to French universities.

The *loi relative aux libertés et responsabilités des universités*, passed in 2007, allows French universities to exercise considerable authority over budgets, strategic planning, property management, and hiring. The new university therefore is an independent and autonomous institution.[15] An earlier law, promulgated in 2006, reinforced the links between government funding and results (Eurydice, 2008). The law obligates the universities to undergo regular evaluation by the *Agence d'évaluation de la recherché et de l'enseignement* supérieur, an independent organization charged with the mandate of quality assessment of universities.[16]

The overall authority for internal governance of the university is vested in a governing body that comprises academic members, students, and external representatives. The external representatives are chosen by the president who chairs the governing body.

The Impact of the Bologna Process on the External Higher Education Dimension

The Bologna Process, although still incomplete, is a significant attempt by members of the European Community to improve, modernize, and standardize higher education. Among the initiatives are standardization of degrees, reciprocal recognition of academic achievement, the fostering of student and graduate mobility, and a common framework for quality assurance.

The Bologna Process has led to the creation of the European Higher Education Area. As Europe sought to make its education offerings more competitive through excellence, it recognized the need to externalize or internationalize its activities. One aim of the Bologna process was to standardize cycles of study to increase the students and faculty mobility, creating a sense of European citizenship among students and teachers. By offering students the opportunity to choose among different EU programs, this in turn was expected to increase competition between organizations. The EU also expects that it increase its attractiveness among non-EU students by allowing a multinational education within the EU space. Another aim of the European framework was to decrease the length of the education cycles — 3 years bachelors, 2 years masters, and 3 years doctorate degrees (The EU and the Bologna Process, 2015).

Notwithstanding this laudable objective, one continues to think in terms of the British system, the French system, or the German system, rather than the European system. While several European countries were already engaged in internationalization activities, many of these were related to exchanges with developing countries through development aid programs.

Concerns about the Bologna Process and its attendant internationalization have been expressed regarding the future of sub-Saharan African higher education.[17] Specifically, while higher education institutions in Anglophone countries appeared to be closer to some of the Bologna Process recommendations, institutions in Francophone and Lusophone countries would have greater difficulty.

Nevertheless, the Association of African Universities and UNESCO are beginning to explore the Bologna recommendations as a model to promote regional collaboration in quality assurance, accreditation, and recognition of qualifications.[18]

Higher Education Governance in the African Context

Good governance is viewed as essential to achieving the country's economic development strategies with an emphasis on poverty reduction, achievement of equity and prosperity of individuals, families, and entire communities.[19] Unfortunately, in many instances, governance in sub-Saharan Africa has been considered problematic (World Bank, 2007; Transparency International, 2009). Higher education in sub-Saharan Africa, as in other developing regions, is subject to several imperatives and constraints. These conditions are not unique to health worker education since they have been discussed in the context of law, accountancy, and engineering (World Bank, 2010).

The Impact of Massification

In addition to the recognition that higher learning contributes to the development of a meritocratic open society,[20] better individual income on average, growth or massification of higher education is perhaps the single most important proximate driver of the need for expansion of the higher education sector (World Bank, 2000; Mohamedbhai, 2008).

In fact, over the past few decades, there has been a major drive to improve literacy in sub-Saharan Africa. While a major emphasis has been on primary and secondary education, the number of institutions of higher education has also increased dramatically. Coordination and planning for the higher education sector, however, has been problematic (Ng'ethe *et al.*, 2008). Equally important, while many countries have increased resource allocations to primary education as part of Education for All, they have decreased their contributions to the higher education sector.

The Economist magazine observed, "If more and more governments are embracing massification, few of them are willing to draw the appropriate conclusion from their enthusiasm: they should either provide the requisite funds (as the Scandinavian countries do) or allow universities to charge realistic fees. Many governments have tried to square the circle through tighter management, but management cannot make up for lack of resources" (The Economist, 2005).[21]

The net effect of increasing the demand for higher education in sub-Saharan countries has been a dramatic increase in numbers of students in small, ill-equipped classrooms with small numbers of teachers, also often poorly qualified. Teaching methods are outdated and rely on rote and passive learning.

Higher education infrastructure is generally poor. Student residences, for example, are frequently in extremely poor condition.

Satisfaction with the training experience also speaks to significant problems. Ferrhino *et al.* (2010) compared two cohorts of medical students in Mozambique. Overall levels of satisfaction decreased substantially in the more recent cohort. They cited poor infrastructure support, notably in library resources, computer facilities, and other learning supports.

According to Salmi starting with 1980, Africa was the last region to see private sector development in tertiary education. Since then, the increase has been spectacular. Between 1990 and 2014, the number of private institutions rose from 30 to about 1,000, compared to a growth of 100–500 for public universities (Bloom *et al.*, 2014). In Chad, Congo, Côte d'Ivoire and Uganda, private sector enrollment has tripled or quadrupled in the past decade (Salmi, 2017). The expansion of the private sector in the education market has a positive mark with the condition that quality of the programs that are offered is at expected standards. Also an important element of the private sector participation in delivering education is that it will not substitute the public sector education for citizens that cannot afford access to private universities, unless their access in the private sector is somehow subsidized (Salmi, 2017).

The Impact of Poor Institutional Governance and Lack of Autonomy

Organizations of higher education, owing to poor oversight or interference from government, frequently lack full autonomy to generate and distribute resources appropriately. This lack of autonomy has led to an inability to recruit and reward qualified faculty members if the organization cannot manage its own appointments and promotion processes. Failure to invest in infrastructure results in unsafe living conditions and contributes significantly to attrition.

Alternatively, organizations may lack the necessary authority to distribute their financial resources in a timely manner to meet their objectives or priorities. The result can be a failure to pay faculty on time resulting in teachers carrying two or more jobs at a time to make ends meet or leaving the profession entirely; or an inability to invest in new infrastructure and equipment.

The Impact of Poor Governmental Governance

As the demand for access to higher education — and the need for skilled human capital — has grown, governments have responded by allowing growth of the higher education sector. In part, this growth has occurred through the expansion of existing institutions, by the limited creation of new institutions, and by the entry of private providers.

Growth of a quality-based higher education sector is justified on the following grounds (Bloom *et al.*, 2005).

- Education spending has a significant effect on economic outcomes and growth.
- A skilled and educated workforce serves as the basis for increased innovation and competitiveness.
- Higher education institutions may form strong linkages with industry for research and access to technology.
- Higher education institutions that are attuned to market demands are better able to provide students with the skills required for employment.

Unfortunately, much growth has occurred where quantity has trumped or diluted quality, where linkages with industry are non-existent. There is ample evidence that graduates cannot find employment (Fernandes and Mattoo, 2009; O'Brien and Gostin, 2008). Furthermore, many countries have seen decreases in government transfers to the higher education sector as a function of total education spending even as the size and importance of the sector increase.

Quality also has been an issue as policy directives have emphasized the need for differentiation in the higher education sector — promoting increased access by increasing the numbers and types of providers in the market. Scaling up access, however, has not been coupled with the provision of appropriate resources in the public sector.

Two surveys have examined the legal frameworks for higher education of sub-Saharan countries (Saint *et al.*, 2009). There is a general move toward increased autonomy in return for greater accountability as a reflection of institutional responsiveness:

- Withdrawal of the state from institutional control
- Creation of buffer bodies for system-wide functions and services
- Greater flexibility in institutional funding mechanisms
- Establishment of external agencies to measure quality
- Creation of performance and outcome measures
- Affirmation of the institutional governing body as the highest decision-making authority
- Withdrawal of the state from appointments of key governing and academic leaders.

Table 5.2 summarizes the higher education environment in 42 sub-Saharan nations, focusing on the presence or absence of legislative governance and the principal loci of governance jurisdiction, that is, the degree of autonomy given to the higher education institutions.

Of these countries, 86 percent have legal frameworks governing higher education. Governmental oversight of higher education functions was exercised largely through the Ministries of Education (12/42) or Higher Education (16/42). In 14 instances, governments have created intermediary or buffer bodies for system oversight. Buffer bodies are more prevalent in English-speaking countries while Ministries of Higher Education tend to be favored in Francophone countries. Smaller countries tend to leave oversight for higher education within a sector-wide Ministry of Education.

In general, there is a trend toward devolution of authority to the institutions even though many governments continue to exert significant control over the most senior decision-making points in the university: governing councils, chief academic officer, and senior academic posts.

Organizational governance differs between Anglophone and non-Anglophone countries. In Francophone and Lusophone countries, the governing council or board is usually comprised of institutional insiders. The benefit of this arrangement is that the board is intimately

Table 5.2   Higher Education, 42 Sub-Saharan Countries

Country	Yes	Date	MOE	MOHE	Buffer	Internal	Mix	Board	Chief officer	Deans, etc.
Angola	Y	1991	X			X		X	G	—
Benin	Y	1975		X		—		—	G	?
Botswana	Y	1982			X		X	G	G	?
Burkina Faso	Y	1991, 1991, 1996		X		X		X	G	?
Burundi	Y	1988, 1989	X			—				—
Cameroon	Y	1993, 1995, 1999, 2001		X		—		—	—	—
Central African Republic	Y	1969, 1985		X						—
Chad	Y	1969, 1994		X			X	G	G	X
Congo, Republic of	Y	1971, 1995		X		—		—	—	—
Congo, Democratic Republic of	Y	1981, 1982		X		—		X	—	—
Côte d'Ivoire	Y	1995		X		—		—	G	G
Djibouti	N		X				X	G	—	G
Eritrea	N		X					—	—	—
Ethiopia	Y	1977, 1993, 1994, 1999, 2003	X					—	—	—
Gabon	N			X						—
Gambia	Y	1963		X		—		—	—	—
Ghana	Y	1961, 1969, 1983, 1991			X		X	G	X	X
Guinea	N			X						—
Guinea–Bissau	Y	1999	X			—		—	—	—
Kenya	Y	1985, 1989			X		X	G	G	X

Country		Year(s)								
Lesotho	Y	2004			X	X		G	X	?
Liberia	N				X	—		—	—	—
Madagascar	Y	1992, 1995		X		—		—	—	—
Malawi	Y	1963		X		—		—	—	—
Mali	Y	1986	X			X		X	G	X
Mauritania	Y	1970, 1986, 1995		X			X	X	G	X
Mauritius					X	X		G	G	X
Mozambique	Y	1990, 1993, 2003		X		X		X	G	X
Namibia	Y	1985			X	X		X	X	X
Niger	Y	1995, 1998	X			—		—	—	—
Nigeria	Y	1993			X	X		G	G	X
Rwanda	Y	1985, 2005			X	X		G	G	X
Senegal	Y	1970, 1971, 1991	X			?		?	G	?
Sierra Leone	Y	1972			X	X		X	X	X
South Africa	Y	1997			X	X		X	X	X
Sudan	Y	1991	X			-		—	—	—
Swaziland	Y	1983		X		—		—	—	—
Tanzania	Y	1978			X	X		G	G	X
Togo	N		X			—		—	—	—
Uganda	Y	2001			X	X		G	G	X
Zambia	Y	1973, 1987		X		X		G	G	X
Zimbabwe	Y	1990			X	X		G	G	X

Note: — no data; X indicates the presence or level of authority for governance decisions; G indicates governmental authority, vested in either the head of state, prime minister, or minister.

Source: Authors.

knowledgeable about the workings of the institution. The drawback is that many of the members owe their appointment to the government and are less likely to respond quickly and objectively to changing circumstances. The governing council or board in Anglophone countries, on the other hand, tends to involve external members who bring an objective viewpoint to the board's deliberations and can build greater responsiveness to external constituencies. In many circumstances, students also are represented.

The degree of organizational autonomy can be gauged by the proportion of governing council members who are appointed by government compared to the number chosen by the board itself. This also extends to the selection of the chief academic officer and senior academic officers of the institution itself. In only four countries — Ghana, Lesotho, Namibia, and South Africa — are the governing councils given the authority to appoint the chief academic officer. Deans, however, are usually chosen democratically by their peers.

Increasingly, African institutions are being given the authority to manage their own budgets and financial affairs; although in many circumstances, ultimate budget control is in the hands of the minister. Some universities can set their own tuition fees, for example, but transactions involving sale of assets or land frequently require ministerial approval.

Interestingly, African organizations appear to have significant autonomy over hiring and setting terms of employment for faculty and other employees. In many situations, however, the institution must respect public service legislation guidelines. This latter point indicates that faculty members, once hired, move ahead based on seniority rather than merit. Saint *et al.* (2009) indicate higher education organizations in Anglophone countries and appear to have greater autonomy than do their counterparts in Francophone or Lusophone countries.

With autonomy also comes accountability, whether strategic, financial, or academic. A key accountability measure for institutions of higher education is accreditation or quality assurance.

Health Professional Schools in Africa

One of the principal difficulties in sub-Saharan Africa is the lack of coordination between the ministries responsible for higher education and those responsible for the health sector. In some, but not all, countries, ministries of health, in addition to their management of health care are responsible for nursing and allied health professional education programs; these programs are usually delivered in non-university institutions. Ministries of education, however, take responsibility for medical education since medical schools are generally nested within universities. In addition to the lack of coordination between the two ministries, there is a wasted opportunity to align and optimize educational programs for the instruction and training of all health workers. An additional difficulty is the failure to link education planning and delivery with the labor markets' needs. Health professional education must be aligned with population needs, on the one hand, and with the health system's ability to pay, on the other.

The recent study by Mullan *et al.*[22] reveals the presence of 168 medical schools on the African continent. This estimate significantly exceeds those previously reported by WHO,[23] and slightly underestimates the International Institute for Medical Education,[24] and the Foundation for Advancement of International Medical Education and Research 2013 data which counts 179 medical schools.[25] There are no reliable data on the number of nursing schools in sub-Saharan Africa. Most data describe the medical school situation only.

These schools are estimated to graduate between 10,000 and 11,000 students annually with retention rates through to graduation of approximately 80 percent. Many schools are expanding and new schools are coming on line. Difficulties in maintaining standards are not uncommon on the continent and can result in withdrawal of accreditation, especially for the private sector schools.[26]

Table 5.3 summarizes the results of a web search of sub-Saharan African universities with health science education programs. The table indicates whether aspects of university governance were presented on the website as well as the health science education programs offered by the institution.

In sub-Saharan Africa, of the 128 universities with medical schools, 71 presented details of their institutional governance structures. In several instances, names of members of governing boards and of university senates were identified. In general, Anglophone universities were more likely to present governance details (66 percent) than were Francophone and

Table 5.3   Sub-Saharan African Universities with Health Science Education Programs

Country	Number of medical schools	Governance identified	Other health science programs[a]		
			Public health	Nursing	Other
Angola	1			1	
Benin	2	2			1
Burkina Faso	1	1			1
Burundi	1				
Cameroon	4	3	3	1	2
Central African Republic	1				
Chad	1	1	1		
Congo, Democratic Republic (Zaire)	13	5	1		3
Congo, Republic	1	1			
Côte d'Ivoire	2	1			
Ethiopia	6	5	2	4	4
Gabon	1				
Ghana	3	3	1	2	1
Guinea	3	1			
Guinea-Bissau	1				
Kenya	2	2	1	1	1
Madagascar	2	1			1
Malawi	1		1		
Mali	2	2			1
Mauritania	1	1			
Mauritius	1				
Mozambique	4	3		1	1
Namibia	1	1	1	1	
Niger	1	1			
Nigeria	23	14		9	11
Rwanda	1	1	1		

(*Continued*)

Table 5.3 (*Continued*)

Country	Number of medical schools	Governance identified	Other health science programs[a]		
			Public health	Nursing	Other
Senegal	2				
Seychelles	1				
Sierra Leone	1	1			
Somalia	2	1			
South Africa	9	7	2	8	8
Sudan	20	6	3	4	9
Tanzania	4	3	1	4	2
The Gambia	1		1	1	
Togo	1				1
Uganda	3	2	1	2	1
Zambia	1	1		1	
Zimbabwe	2		1		1
Total	**127**	**70**	**21**	**39**	**49**

Notes: This summary of distribution of medical schools by country encompasses only universities whose websites were obtainable were shown. [a]Other = pharmacy, dentistry, and allied health professions such as physiotherapy and radiographers.

Sources: This table draws upon data from the following sources: WHO[43]; IIME[44]; FAIMER[45]; Association of African Universities[27]; South African Regional Universities Association[28]; Inter-University Council for Eastern Africa[29]; Conférence internationale des doyens et des Facultés de médecine d'expression française[30]; Agence universitaire de la francophonie[31]; International Colleges and Universities[32]; Africa south of the Sahara.[33]

Lusophone universities (54 percent and 50 percent, respectively). Universities from Arabic jurisdictions discussed governance details in 32 percent of cases.

Quality Assurance in Sub-Saharan Africa

Quality assurance in sub-Saharan Africa began in the 1960s in Nigeria. Later, Kenya established its national quality assurance enterprise in the 1980s, followed by South Africa in the 1990s. Following the Arusha

Convention (UNESCO, 2002), there have been significant developments in quality assurance on the continent. In 2007, more than 15 sub-Saharan African countries had national quality assurance agencies (Materu, 2007; Association of African Universities, 2007).[34]

In the past decade, progress has been impressive and today on the entire Africa continent there are about 23 countries with a national quality assurance agency (Jamil, 2015).

National quality assurance agencies are funded by the government, and board members and senior officials are usually government appointees, which raises questions about their autonomy. Most professional bodies have specific descriptions of their role in standards and undergraduate training. They also have authority to make direct representation to the minister. The result is that professional bodies are increasingly included in national quality assurance evaluations. For example in Nigeria, the Nigerian Medical Association, the Nigerian Dental Association, and the Nursing and Midwifery Council of Nigeria are engaged in national quality assurance activities.

The benefits of engaging professional bodies in quality assurance exercise are that their legal mandates include the standards and quality of professional education, their members are frequently engaged in undergraduate education and can therefore provide expert opinion and advice, and they provide needed manpower for the complex undertaking of quality assurance visits. At the same time, the tendency of the professional body to act as an advocate of the profession's interests as opposed to those of the public, through achievement of the highest standards of education, must be kept in mind. If the latter prevails, the professional body is in an enviable position to exert significant influence on the competitive quality of educational programs, particularly in countries where students have a choice of school.

Because of the difficulties of managing complex quality assurance activities in small countries with few higher education institutions and because of the need for comparability, the African Union, in partnership with the Association of African Universities, the World Bank, and UNESCO, has supported the development of regional approaches to quality assurance. A fourth partner, the *Conférence international des doyens et des facultés de médecine d'expression française* (CIDMEF), provides quality assurance advice to members of Francophone Africa.

These four quality assurance collaboratives embrace a significant number of sub-Saharan countries (Table 5.4). However, none of the organizations publishes the results of its quality assurance schedules, deliberations or findings and recommendations. In fact, CIDMEF's philosophy explicitly disavows the use of sanctions; quality assurance activities are to be used as a continuous improvement tool and on a voluntary basis.

Professional bodies are also engaged in regional quality assurance activities. One notable example is the involvement of the national medical societies in the undergraduate medical programs in East Africa.[38] In West Africa, the organization in charge of facilitating regional harmonization concerning standards of education and care, regional partnerships in research, epidemics and health emergencies, etc. The WAHO — West Africa Health Organization — also promotes medical specialty training especially among countries that are lacking residency and fellowship programs as well as other types of medical training for nurses and allied health personnel (http://www.wahooas.org).

While the advantages of quality assurance in higher education are clear, there are significant disadvantages and difficulties, particularly in resource-scarce situations. The difficulties include: the need for strong political support from the highest levels of government and from higher education organizations; the need for autonomy and freedom from political interference; stable and predictable funding to support administrative, consultative, and infrastructure costs; and access to sufficient numbers of qualified assessors and consultants.

The development of robust quality assurance bodies will take time, resources, and patience. Consequently, all parties — governments, institutions, donors — should recognize the long-term nature of the investment required. Additionally, activities and interventions of the new and developing bodies should be approached incrementally to create a culture of quality assurance. A recognition that the long-term outcomes of quality assurance are better educational programming and more effective health care professionals imbued with the love of lifelong learning and service.

Table 5.4   The Sub-Saharan African Regional Organizations Mandated for Strengthening Quality in Higher Education Institutions

CAMES	CIDMEF	IUCEA	SARUA
Objective: Develop and promote policy dialogue to coordinate systems of higher education and research to align programs and recruitment levels in the various institutions of higher education and research, promote cooperation between different institutions, and exchange information.	*Objective*: Ensure the coherence between the needs of society, the objectives of the program of study, the pedagogical approaches used in the program of study and student outcomes.	*Objective*: Develop a regional quality assurance framework to build and maintain high and comparable standards in higher education in East Africa with special emphasis on the promotion of quality assurance.	*Objective*: Strengthen the leadership and institutions of Higher Education in the Southern African region, thereby consolidating a Southern African Agenda for higher education which results in a significant contribution by Higher Education to national and regional development.
Benin	Angola	Burundi	Angola
Burkina Faso	Benin	Kenya	Botswana
Burundi	Burkina Faso	Rwanda	Congo, Democratic Republic
Cameroon	Burundi	Tanzania	Lesotho
Chad	Cameroon	Uganda	Madagascar

Congo Brazzaville	Chad	Malawi
Côte d'Ivoire	Congo, Democratic Republic	Mauritius
Guinea	Congo Brazzaville	Mozambique
Guinea-Bissau	Côte d'Ivoire	South Africa
Madagascar	Gabon	Swaziland
Mali	Guinea	Tanzania
Niger	Madagascar	Zambia
Rwanda	Mali	Zimbabwe
Senegal	Mauritania	
Togo	Niger	
	Rwanda	
	Senegal	
	Togo	

Sources: see notes: *Conseil Africain et Malgasche pour l'Enseignement Supérieur* (CAMES),[35] the Inter-University Council for East Africa (IUCEA),[36] the South African Regional Universities Association (SARUA),[37] *the Conférence international des doyens et des facultés de médecine d'expression française* (CIDMEF).

Toward A Systems View of Governance in Health Care and Health Professional Education

In its landmark paper, the Commission on Education of Health Professionals for the twenty-first century, echoed calls from the Joint Learning Initiative and the Task Force for Scaling Up Education and Training for Health Workers to take a systemic view of health professional education (Figure 5.3).

In planning and monitoring the activities of health professionals in response to population health needs, it is essential to consider three inter-dependent vectors: the health care delivery sector, the labor market, and the supply vector. If these vectors are not considered as a system, each trajectory fails to intersect appropriately with the others.

System governance is essential to success for the production, deployment, and maintenance of the health workforce. A recent survey of the

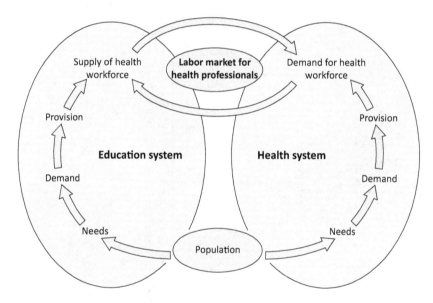

Figure 5.3   Systems View of Health Professional Education in the Twenty-first Century
Source: Mikkelson-Lopez, I., C. Baez-Carmago, K. Wyss, and D. de Savigny, "Towards a new approach for assessing health systems governance", *Geneva Health Forum*, 2010, April 19, accessed at http://www/ghf10.org/ghf10/files/presentations/ps24 Mikkelsen-Lopez Inez.pdf.

health workforce literature in low- and middle-income countries shows, however, that governance — using the definitions employed in this chapter — is infrequently addressed (Dieleman *et al.*, 2011).

Consideration of the health needs of the population should allow needs or gaps in health professional coverage to be measured and assessed. Modeling of the needs, in turn, allows for decisions about accessibility to services and the design of optimal primary care configurations, the appropriateness of task substitution and referral mechanisms to secondary and tertiary care levels, and the staffing requirements at each.

The labor market includes staffing norms, compensation and benefits, and measuring the numbers of actual participants in the workforce against targets. Many sub-Saharan countries measure health professionals working in the public sector since they are the majority; they have the evidence from their paychecks, and to certain extend their performance. However, there is less than sufficient oversight of the private sector.

The consequences of this relative lack of oversight are significant. Vertical programs, such as HIV/AIDS, malaria, etc., and/or private health care systems that are funded from outside sources rather than the country's system compete for health professionals who would ordinarily work in the public sector. In an environment characterized by significant shortages, this ultimately conspires to create difficulties in access and coverage; the public system finds itself compromised at the expense of vertical programs/interventions.

Gaps in coverage can be addressed in several different ways. Health professionals in the field represent an untapped resource for coverage and for quality. In many situations, however, the quality of care is below standard. Field professionals can also be approached over a reasonable timeframe and at reasonable cost because they are already within the workforce. In some countries, health workers have left the health care system, either because of lack of employment opportunities or because of underemployment and migration (both internal and external). These workers represent a potential workforce that can be mobilized within a reasonable period provided the motivational factors are addressed.

For the longer term, the education system requires significant sustained investment and capacity development. Investments are needed at two levels, secondary and university-post-grad. The first group of investments must be directed toward the secondary level. The number of students in higher education has grown substantially, but the transition rate from secondary school to universities and colleges remains low. In some countries, the situation continues to deteriorate, as the mass enrollment in secondary education has not been coupled with the needed resources for a quality educational system. The supply of qualified teachers and proper learning materials is still challenging, and to date, alternative teaching and learning methods cannot be applied at the needed scale due to the resource constraints described here. Accordingly, to turn out many highly qualified graduates who will vie for placements in the health professional schools, greater investment is required at the secondary school level.

Since evidence suggest that graduates who grow up in small towns and rural areas are more likely to decide to practice there than are city dwellers, particular attention must be paid to make sure the former have access to quality secondary school education so as to enlarge the pool of qualified applicants from smaller communities and rural environs who will feel comfortable returning there.

The second major stream of investment must be aimed directly to universities and colleges. The magnitude of investment will vary from country to country and from institution to institution, but must include substantial contributions to infrastructure and resources needed to support the teaching and administrative personnel. This investment is essential to prepare future health professionals with the skills and competencies they will need in the new health care system. As Frenk *et al.* (2010) point out, the new education system must fundamentally re-engineer and transform itself to meet these objectives. New didactic approaches geared toward promoting life-long learning are essential. Teachers steeped in this philosophy also are imperative.

The new health professionals also will be the leaders of the future. But they must be educated for jobs that exist, whether public or private, and not for a labor market that needs, but cannot sustain, them. So then, planning at all levels — health care service, labor market, and higher education — must be integrated, and the principals must work together collaboratively and collectively. Governance issues are key to this new-shared model.

Table 5.5 illustrates how governance principles might apply to the future sub-Saharan African health professional education system using the principles outlined by Gottret and Scheiber (2006). While immediately evident at the national or subnational level, these principles and their resolution are equally valid at the national and continental levels.

At the organizational level, coherent educational programming that is consistent with the needs of the population and the health workforce is urgently needed. Although there is some evidence of differentiation among organizations of higher education in sub-Saharan Africa, there is little in the way of mechanisms that allow students to move from one organization to another.

One of the recommendations in scaling up, saving lives was the ability to create modular learning ladders and career pathways where a student could enter the health education stream at a given level, e.g. physician assistant or practical nurse, and with time and experience, develop the competencies needed to enter education programs that would result in the M.D. or B.Sc.N degree. At present, it is not likely that such a route would be possible. Much remains to be done to promote academic progression.

Education programming for health professionals needs to take a more systems-based approach. In the drive to competency-based education, Dieleman, Shaw, and Zwanikken (2011) observe that the development of educational platforms for medicine and nursing, for example, are desirable. These platforms would allow the creation of role- and task-specific objectives that promote team learning, the resolution of health issues, self-assessment and self-reflection. Introduced right these platforms (portfolios) can be successful, especially at the undergraduate levels (provide citations) (Driessen *et al.*, 2007).

The traditional locus for learning — the academic health sciences center, the schools of medicine, nursing, and the like — must also adapt. Because of the inseparable linkages between health professional education and health care, learning should occur where the services are required, namely community-based, in support of primary care. One of the fundamental difficulties in achieving this necessary learning transformation is

Table 5.5   Application of Governance Principles to the Future Health Education System in Sub-Saharan Africa

Principle	Issue	Resolution
Coherent decision-making structures	At present, each jurisdiction — health care, labor, higher education — is separately governed at government level with little or no interaction among the key decision makers.	The future calls for a high-ranking inter-ministerial office that can engage the ministry of finance for fiscal matters. This office comprises, in equal partnership, representation from government, higher-education institutions, professional bodies and health care organizations.
Transparency and information	Critical decision making requires access to accurate and timely information. Information and data now are infrequently up to date or even available.	Government establishes data reservoirs staffed by highly qualified statisticians, epidemiologists, geospatial and urban modelers, and financial scenario planners. These individuals do not have to be government employees. Rather, synergy between the public, education, and private sectors also would serve to develop and maintain capacity in this vital area.
Supervision and regulation	Many government agencies have excessive controls and influence over education and health care, making appointments to boards and senior academic posts.	Government will develop appropriate oversight regulations and promote increasing autonomy for institutions of higher education and health care delivery, both public and private. Funding will increasingly take the form of block funding.
Stakeholder participation	Governmental decision making is overly centralized. Yet there is no central strategy for health care and health professional education. In terms of global health governance, Fidler (2007) refers to this as open source anarchy. Governments negotiate with donors and	Government establishes an arms-length council on higher education charged with recommending higher education policy, curriculum standards, and quality assurance mechanisms. Considering the plethora of actors engaged in the health care delivery and health professional fields, it is essential that their input and their efforts be utilized for maximum benefit. The council comprises membership from all universities, colleges, and vocational institutions. Within the

	donor agencies for issues related to health human resources but do not consider the importance of long-term capacity building and may not include the institutions that are expressly mandated to educate new health professionals.	council are sectoral sub-tables, such as health. This particular sectoral table includes representation from the professional bodies that have specific mandates for education, (e.g. medicine, nursing and midwifery, dentistry, pharmacy, allied health professionals). Room also is provided for representatives of the health care system and community. While funding is provided in significant measure by the government (institutions also pay a share to ensure buy-in), the council is free of political interference.
Accountability	Specific accountabilities are required at every level of governance: financial benchmarks, outcomes measured against targets, quality, etc. This accountability principle is equally valid at the level of government, its bureaucracy and finally in each higher education institution.	Quality assurance procedures are well in place and governed by national policies. For smaller jurisdictions, consideration should be given to developing partnerships, regional quality assurance bodies, or both. Since quality assurance can take various forms, it may be wise to build toward accreditation bodies (whether national or regional) in incremental steps beginning with institutional self-study programs.
Stability and consistency		The pursuit of good governance does not yield success in a day, or even in a year. Rather, inculcation of good governance practices requires sustained and systematic leadership and practice. Stability and consistency therefore are required, both directional and financial. Application of the principles of good governance to areas and domains where the practices are not yet systemic requires a culture shift. Exhorting quality performance may at first appear threatening and elicit defensive rather than constructive behavior. Strongly supported leadership is essential.

the fact that in many developing countries, education of physicians, dentists, and pharmacists is controlled by the ministry of [higher] education and provided by universities. Nursing, on the other hand, is controlled by the ministry of health and provided by colleges. Well-structured programs and additional resources are needed to be able to bring the undergraduates and graduate students in communities.

In SSA, there is a trend for Anglophone universities to engage in the education of other health professionals, especially nursing, dentistry, and pharmacy, more frequently than universities from other linguistic jurisdictions (Table 5.6). This tends to occur in the form of Colleges of Health Sciences. Francophone universities rarely include nursing.

The advantages of the development of system-wide approaches to and integration of health professional education are evident. Governance at all levels — government, institutions, professional bodies, and sectors — are a critical and permissive component. Whether this takes the form of inclusive colleges of health sciences or other forms of collaboration will depend on jurisdictional involvement. For optimal benefit, however, the implementation would have to be at least national; a patchwork approach by individual organizations would not be desirable as quality would be much more difficult to achieve and measure without a nationwide baseline.

Additionally, the development of national, regional, and international consortium approaches involving higher education and the health sectors

Table 5.6   Number of Institutions, By Language of Jurisdiction, That Educate Other Health Professionals

Language	Number of institutions[a]	Public health[b]	Nursing[b]	Other[c]
Anglophone	59 (46)	12 (20)	32 (54)	29 (49)
Francophone	40 (32)	6 (15)	1 (2)	10 (25)
Lusophone	6 (5)	0	2 (33)	1 (17)
Arabic	22 (17)	3 (14)	4 (18)	9 (41)

Notes: [a]Number in parentheses represents percent of all institutions.
[b]Number in parentheses represents the percent of institutions per language jurisdiction that have programs of education.
[c]Represents schools of pharmacy, dentistry, and allied health professions.

together with civil societies, government, and business will significantly expand the opportunities for new education design, and implementation. This approach will obligate the different participants, with their different governance systems and structures, to seek common purpose and ground. Leadership of a very different nature will be required.

Finally, the involvement of the private sector in the future development of the higher education system presents opportunities and risks. Without strong national governance and oversight, dilution of quality is possible. With strong national governance and engagement of all actors in higher education for health professionals, there is a very real opportunity for significant capacity building in the pursuit of quality.

Strong national governance and oversight translates into the development of stringent quality assurance structures and processes, including accreditation. In SSA, for example, using the African Union and the Association of African Universities as implementation vehicles in sub-Saharan Africa, the opportunity is promising for aligning the development of national quality assurance exercises along continent-wide principles. National and regional quality assurance bodies, developed as a function of these principles, would allow sub-Saharan Africa to make enormous strides in meeting the peoples' health needs and contributing to international efforts in standardization and excellence in health professional education and health care delivery.

Advances in technology has been transforming the educational process in the medical education process. Although, these innovative tools in communication are not designed to replace conventional teaching and learning practices, they will receive universal acceptance among this generation of technologically savvy students and in future generations that will follow. In order to help guide medical educators on how to implement these innovative future advancements in technology into the medical education curriculum, a working group of educators have provided several suggestions. Firstly, they recommended that educators use the existing technology to support the learning experiences for students while adhering to the fundamental principles of teaching and learning. Secondly, insure that the institution's governing body allocates the necessary financial resources for faculty to implemen ideas.

Some opine that the historical practice of "hands-on" training in the health professions — students providing care to real patients under direct faculty supervision in accredited degree programs — may not be sustainable as the predominant model for preparing health professionals. The reasoning spans from the capability of the schools to provide such resources as well as it relates to the self-education model and the role of technology in connecting and educating students.

Distance is no longer a problem when people discuss and work together. Thus, the development of distance-learning technology that recognizes the lessons learned from students and teachers during this last decade coupled with sensitive simulation modules from studying anatomy to performing invasive procedures and/or operations (i.e. neurosurgery) will help students learn and practice in the medical field. Two challenges are currently on the plate of developing countries' medical institutions: a change in mindset reflected in the current national education plans, and the capacity to advocate and raise resources that will provide the needed infrastructure. Medical technology can partly substitute for the lack of teachers in many developing countries and increase the performance of medical students but, at least for now, the cost is not meager. Solutions at the national and regional levels are needed for efficient, effective, and less costly solutions. The industry can also play a role in supporting and tailoring their products for low-resource environments. All these can be factored into the national strategies to provide for the legitimacy and the vision of a new system.

Endnotes

1. Although Salmi (2009) deals with the development of world-class research-intensive universities, he recognizes the need for the development of "alternate institutions to meet the wide range of education and training needs that the tertiary education system is expected to satisfy". He goes on to say that "excellence ... ought, perhaps, to be also measured in terms of how much added value is given by institutions in addressing the specific learning needs of an increasingly diverse student population ... Focusing efforts on the local community and economy ... could lead to more effective and sustainable development than broader world-class aspirations". Success in these endeavors also calls for robust national and institutional governance systems.

2. Mikkelson-Lopez, I., C. Baez-Carmago, K. Wyss, and D. de Savigny, "Towards a new approach for assessing health systems governance", Geneva Health Forum, 2010, April 19, accessed at http://www/ghf10.org/ghf10/files/presentations/ps24 mikkelsen-lopez Inez.pdf.
3. Frenk, J., L. Chen, Z. A. Bhutta, J. Cohen, N. Crisp, T. Evans, H. Fineberg, P. Garcia, Y. Ke, P. Kelley, B. Kistnasamy, A. Meleis, D. Naylor, A. Pablos-Mendez, S. Reddy, S. Scrimshaw, J. Sepulveda, and D. Serwadda, "Health professionals for a new century: Transforming education to strengthen health systems in an interdependent world", *Lancet*, doi:10.1016/S0140-6736(10) 61854-5.
4. Mullan, F., S. Frehywat, F. Omaswa, E. Buch, C. Chen, S. R. Greyson, T. Wasserman, D. E. D. E. G. Abubakr, M. Awases, C. Boelen *et al.*, "Medical schools in sub-saharan Africa", *Lancet*, doi:10.1016/S0140-6736(10)-61961-7.
5. Zoellick, R. B., "Securing development", Speech at the United States Institute of Peace, Washington, DC, 2009, available at: http://http://siteresources.worldbank.org/NEWS/Resources/RBZUSIPSpeech010809.pdf.
6. Kaufman *et al.*, "Reforming public institutions and strengthening governance: A world bank strategy — implementation update", Unpublished Working Paper, 2002, accessed at http://web.worldbank.org/WBSITE/EXTERNAL/COUNTRIES/MENAEXT/EXTMNAREGTOPGOVERNAN CE/0,,contentMDK:20513159~pagePK:34004173~piPK:34003707~theSit ePK:497024,00.html.
7. UNDP (United Nations Development Programme), "Governance for sustainable human development", Policy Paper, New York, NY, 1997, accessed at (http://magnet.undp.org/policy/chapter1.htm#b).
8. Leadership Foundation for Higher Education, "What is Governance?", accessed at http://www.lfhe.ac.uk/en/audiences/governance-old/about-governance/what-is-governance.cfm.
9. A critical link is seen in the tight positive correlation between the corruption perception index (CPI) and per capita incomes. As corruption decreases, incomes increase. This vital observation underscores the important contributions of higher education to skills' development in the economy. The CPI of sub-Saharan African countries ranges from 5.8 (Botswana) to 1.0 (Somalia) and a mean of.... see Lambsdorff (2009).
10. Cited in Watson (2000).
11. Boggs, A. M. (2010). "Understanding the origins, evolution and state of play in UK University Governance", The New Collection Vol. 5 (2010), Oxford: New College, 1–8. ISSN 1757–2541.

12. Governance, Council Secretariat University Administration and Services, University of Oxford, accessed at http://www.admin.ox.ac.uk/councilsec/governance/

13. The UK Inter-professional group (UKIPG), The educational role of professional regulatory bodies A Position Statement by UKPIG, 2000, accessed at http://www.ukipg.org.uk/publications/Educ_Position_Statement.pdf.

14. The Times Higher Education, accessed at http://www.timeshighereducation.co.uk/world-university-rankings/2012/reputation-ranking.

15. Loi No 2007-1197 du 10 août 2007 relative aux libertés et responsabilités des universités, accessed at http://www.legifrance.gouv.fr/affichTexte.do?cidTexte=JORFTEXT000000824315&dateTexte=vig#LEGISCTA000006118024.

16. Agence d'évaluation de la recherché et de l'enseignement supérieur, accessed at http://www.aeres-evaluation.fr/Agence/Savoir-faire/Demarche-qualite.

17. Mohamedbhai, G., "Views on Bologna process", 3rd EUA Convention of European Higher Education, Glasgow, March 31–April 2, 2005.

18. International Conference on Accreditation, Quality Assurance and Recognition of Qualifications in Higher Education in Africa, Communique, Nairobi, Kenya, February 6–8, 2006, accessed at http://www.unesco-nairobi.org/documents/highereducation.pdf.

19. UNDP (United Nations Development Programme), "Democratic "Governance", www.undp.org/governance/about_us.shtml.

20. University graduates in African countries demonstrate increased critical thinking skills and are more likely to form considered opinions about national economic and political performance, to criticize government and state institutions and to prefer democracy as the preferable form of government, they are no more likely to actively participate in democratic citizenship (Mattes and Mughogho, 2010).

21. "Survey: Higher education, a world of opportunity", Economist, September 8, 2005.

22. See Endnote 3.

23. Avicenna Directories. Copenhagen University and WHO, accessed at http://avicenna.ku.dk/database/medicine/.

24. Database of Medical Schools. 2005. Institute for International Medical Education, accessed at www.iime.org/database/index.htm.

25. FAIMER (Federation for Advancement of International Medical Education and Research), International Medical Education Directory (IMED), accessed at www.faimer.org/resources/imed.html.

26. UNIBEN, "Igbinedion medical schools lose accreditation", The World from African Perspective, 2010, accessed at http://newafricanpress.com/2010/12/07/uniben-igbinedion-medical-schools-lose-accreditation/.

27. Association of African Universities, accessed at www.aau.org/.

28. South African Regional Universities Association, accessed at www.sarua.org/.

29. Inter-University Council for Eastern Africa, accessed at www.iucea.org/.

30. Conférence internationale des doyens et des Facultés de médecine d'expression française, accessed at www.cidmef.u-bordeaux2.fr/.

31. Agence universitaire de la francophonie, accessed at www.auf.org/.

32. International Colleges & Universities, accessed at www.4icu.org/.

33. Africa south of the Sahara, accessed at http://library.stanford.edu/depts/ssrg/africa/africaneducation/african-universities.html.

34. Association of African Universities, "The quality assurance situation and capacity building needs of higher education in Africa", 2007, accessed at http://afriqan.aau.org/userfiles/file/The_Quality_Assurance_Situation_and_Capacity_Building_Needs_of_Higher_Education_in_Africa.pdf.

35. Conseil Africain et Malgasche pour l'Enseignement Supérieur, accessed at www.lecames.org.

36. Inter-university council for East Africa, accessed at www.iucea.org.

37. South African regional universities association, accessed at www.sarua.org.

38. Vision 2030, "Joint inspection of medical and dental schools in EAC", Kenya Medical and Dental Practitioners Board, accessed at http://www.medical-board.co.ke/index.php?option=com_content&view=article&id=2:vision-2030&catid=3:activities&Itemid=29.

References

Achebe, C. (2011). "Nigeria's Promise, Africa's Hope", *New York Times,* January 15, 2011.

ACPE (Accreditation Council for Pharmacy Education), "Accreditation standards and guidelines: professional degree program", Chicago, IL, 2007.

Aghion, P., M. Dewatripont, C. Hoxby, A. Mas-Colell, and A. Sapir, *Higher Aspirations: An Agenda for Reforming European Universities,* Breugel Blueprint Series V. Brussels: Breugel, 2008.

ADA (American Dental Association), "Accreditation standards for dental education programs", Chicago, IL: CODA (Commission on Dental Accreditation), 2010.

ANA (American Nurses Association), "Standards for accreditation of baccalaureate and graduate nursing programs", Washington, DC: Commission on Collegiate Nursing Education, 2010.

Anand, S. and T. Barnighausen, "Health workers and vaccination coverage in developing countries: An econometric study", *Lancet*, **369**, 1277–1285, 2007.

Anand, S. and T. Barnighausen, "Human resources and health outcomes: Cross-country econometric study", *Lancet*, **364**, 1603–1609, 2004.

Bloom, D., D. Canning, and K. Chan, "Higher education and economic development in Africa", World Bank, Washington, DC, 2005.

Brinkerhoff, D. W., "Accountability and health systems: Toward conceptual clarity and policy relevance", *Health Policy Planning*, **19**, 371–379, 2004.

Burns, T. and F. Köster (eds.). *Governing Education in a Complex World, Educational Research and Innovation*, OECD Publishing, Paris, 2016.

Capaldi, N., A. Das Gupta, S. O. Idowu, and L. Zu, *Encyclopedia of Corporate Social Responsibility*, Berlin; New York: Springer, 2013.

Committee on the Governance and Financing of Graduate Medical Education; Board of Health Care Services; Institute of Medicine; J. Eden, D. Berwick, G. Wilensky, (eds.). *Graduate Medical Education that Meets the Nation's Health Needs*. Washington (DC): National Academies Press (US), 2014, **3**, GME Financing.

Conference Board of Canada, "Governance gone global: The principles behind good governance practices", Briefing by D. L. Brown and D. A. H. Brown, Ottawa: Conference Board of Canada, 1999.

Driessen E., Jan Van Tartwijk, Cees Van Der Vleuten, and V. Wass, "Portfolios in medical education: Why do they meet with mixed success? A systematic review", Blackwell Publishing Ltd, *Medical Education* **41**, 1224–1233, 2007.

Harcleroad F., "Council for higher education accreditation, quality assurance in higher education in the twenty first century and role of the council for higher education accreditation", Institute for Research and Study of Accreditation and Quality Assurance, Washington DC, 2011.

Popescu, C., Despre viață și economie, Editura ASE, 2011, București.

Popescu, C., Modul ecolonomic de gandire- Perespective Holistica, Edictura EcoPrint, 2017, Satu Mare.

Dieleman, M., D. M. P. Shaw, and P. Zwanikken, "Improving the implementation of health workforce policies: A review of case studies", *Human Resources for Health*, **9**, 10–20, 2011.

Eckel, P. D. and J. E. King, "An overview of higher education in the United States: diversity, access and the role of the marketplace", Washington, DC: American Council on Education, 2004.

EU (European Union), "European Governance", A white paper. Brussels: Commission of the European Communities, 2001.

Eurydice, "Higher education governance in Europe: Policies, structures, funding and academic staff", European Unit, Eurydice, Brussels, 2008.

Fernandes, A. M. and A. Mattoo, "Professional services and development: A study of Mozambique", Working Paper, World Bank, Washington, DC, 2009.

Ferrhino, P., I. Fronteira, M. Sidat, F. da Sousa, and G. Dussault, "Profile and professional expectations of medical students in mozambique: a longitudinal study", *Human Resources for Health*, **8**: 21–24, 2010.

Fidler, D. P., "Architecture amidst anarchy: Global health's quest for governance", *Global Health Governance,* **1**, 1–17, 2007.

Fielden, J., "Global trends in university governance", World Bank, Washington, DC, 2008.

General Medical Council, "Promoting excellence: Standards for medical education and training", 2015, at website: www.gmc-uk.org/education/standards.asp.

Gostin, L. O., E. A. Friedman, G. Ooms, T. Gebauer, N. Gupta, D. Sridhar, W. Chenguang, J.-A. Rottingen, and D. Sanders, "Joint action and learning initiative: Toward a global agreement on national and global responsibilities for health", *PLoS Med*, 1.8:e1001031, 2011.

Gottret, P. and G. Scheiber, *Health Financing Revisited: A Practitioners Guide,* Washington, DC: World Bank, 2006.

HEFCE (Higher Education Funding Council for England), "Higher education in the UK", Bristol: HEFCE.

Independent Commission on Good Governance in Public Services, 2004, *The Good Governance Standard for Public Services*. London: Office for Public Management Ltd and The Chartered Institute of Public Finance and Accountancy.

Institute of Medicine, "Graduate Medical Education That Meets the Nation's Health Needs", (Eds.)., Jill Eden, Donald Berwick, and Gail Wilensky, 2014.

Lambsdorff, J. G., "Macro-perspective and micro-insights into the scale of corruption: Focus on business", Chapter 7 in *Global Corruption Report* 2009: *Corruption and the Private Sector"*, New York, NY and Cambridge, UK University of Cambridge for Transparency International, 2009.

LCME (Liaison Committee on Medical Education), *Accreditation Standards*, Washington, DC: LCME, 2010.

Lemieux,V., "Government roles in governance processes", Canadian Center for Management and Development, Ottawa, 2000.

JLI (Joint Learning Initiative), *Human Resources for Health*: *Overcoming the Crisis*, Cambridge, MA: Harvard University Press, 2004.

Lewis, M. and G. Pettersson, "Governance in health care delivery: raising performance", Policy Research Working Paper 5074, World Bank, Washington, DC, 2009.

Materu, P., "Higher education quality assurance in sub-Saharan Africa: Status, challenges, opportunities, and promising practices", Working Paper 124, World Bank, Washington, DC, 2007.

Mattes, R. and D. Mughogho, "The limited impact of formal education on democratic citizenship in Africa", Paper prepared for the Higher Education Research and Advocacy Network in Africa (HERANA). Wynberg, South Africa: Centre for Higher Education Transformation, 2010.

McKechnie, A., "Drawing on experience: Transforming fragile states into effective ones", *Development Outreach*, World Bank Institute, Washington, DC, 2009.

Mohamedbhai, G., "The effects of massification on higher education in Africa", World Bank, Washington, DC, 2008.

Ng'ethe, N., G. Sibotzky, and G. Afeti, "Differentiation and articulation in tertiary education systems: A study of twelve African countries", Washington, DC: World Bank, 2008.

O'Brien, P. and L. O. Gostin, "Health worker shortages and inequalities: The reform of United States policy", *Global Health Governance*, **2**, 1–29, 2008.

OECD (Organisation for Economic Co-operation and Development), *OECD Principles of Corporate Governance*, Paris: OECD, 2004.

OECD (Organisation for Economic Co-operation and Development), "Changing patterns of governance in higher education", *Education Policy Analysis*, **63**, 70–71, 2003 (ed.), Paris: OECD.

Pierre, J. and B. G. Peters, Governing Complex Societies: Trajectories and Scenarios, London/New York: Palgrave Macmillan, 2005.

Porter, M. E. and M. R. Kramer, "Strategy and society: The link between competitive advantage and corporate social responsibility", *Harvard Business Review*, **84**, 78–91, 2006.

Renders, A., A. Gaeremynck, and P. Sercu, "Corporate-governance ratings and company performance: A cross-European study", *An International Review*, **18**(2), 87–106, 2010.

Robin, B. R., McNeil, S. G., Cook, D. A., Agarwal, K. L., Singhal, G. R., "Preparing for the changing role of instructional technologies in medical education", Academic Medicine: Journal of the Association of American Medical Colleges, **86**(4), 435–439, 2011.

Saint, W., C. Lao, and P. Materu, "Legal frameworks for tertiary education in sub-Saharan Africa: The quest for institutional responsiveness", World Bank, Washington, DC, 2009.

Salmi, J., "The challenge of establishing world-class universities", World Bank, Washington, DC, 2009.

Salmi, J., "The tertiary education imperative: knowledge and skills for development", Sense Publishers Rotterdam, Netherlands, 2017, Springer.

Savedoff, W. D., "Governance in the health sector: A strategy for measuring determinants and performance", Washington, DC: World Bank, 2009.

Savedoff, W. D. and P. Gottret, (eds.). *"Governing Mandatory Health Insurance*: *Learning from Experience"* Washington, DC: World Bank, 2008.

The Economist, How Europe fails its young, 2005, p. 4.

The EU and the Bologna Process, Working together for change, 2015 at http://ec.europa.eu/education/policy/higher education/bologna-process_en.htm.

Theisens, H., E. Hooge, and S. Waslander, "How exceptional are the dutch? Identifying general and country specific characteristic of governance in multi-layered polycentric education systems", Paper #2 for the Symposium 'Steering Dynamics in Focus' presented at the 2017 AERA Conference, 27 April — 1 May, San Antonio, Texas.

Transparency International, *Global Corruption Report 2009*: *Corruption and the Private Sector*, Cambridge, UK: University of Cambridge, 2009.

UNDP (United Nations Development Programme) *Governance for the Future: Democracy and Development in the Least Developed Countries*, (eds.). by G. Welch and Z. Nuru, New York, NY: UNDP, 2006.

UNDP (United Nations Development Programme), "Governance for sustainable human development", Policy Paper, New York, NY, 1997.

UNECE (United Nations Economic Commission for Europe), *Guidebook on Promoting Good Governance in Public–Private Partnerships,* New York and Geneva: United Nations, 2008.

UNESCO (United Nations Educational, Social, and Cultural Organization), "Arusha convention on the recognition of qualifications in higher education in Africa", UNESCO, Paris, 2002.

UNESCO Institute for Statistics, Higher education in Asia: Expanding out, expanding up, the rise of graduate education and university research", UNESCO, Montreal, Quebec, Canada, 2014.

University of Oxford, "White paper on university governance", *Oxford University Gazette*, p. 136, 2006, Supp. 5.

Watson, D., *Managing Strategy,* London: Open University Press, 2000.

Verger, A. and M. Moschetti, Public–private partnerships as and education policy approach: Multiple meanings, risks and challenges, education, research and foresight series, No 19, Paris, UNESCO, 2016, accessed at htts://en.unesco.org/node268820.

Ramalingaswami V., "Medical education: How is change to come about", *Medical Education*, **23**, 328–332, 1989.

WHO (World Health Organization), *The World Health Report: Working Together for Health*, Geneva: World Health Organization, 2008a.

WHO (World Health Organization), *World Health Report 2000: Health Systems: Improving Performance*, Geneva: WHO, 2000b.

World Bank, "Reform and regional integration of professional services in East Africa: Time for action", Washington, DC: World Bank, 2010.

"Accelerating development outcomes in Africa: Progress and change in the Africa Action Plan", Paper prepared by World Bank Africa Region Staff, for consideration at the April 15, 2007, Development Committee Meeting, Washington, DC.

WHO, *World Development Report 2004: Making Services Work for Poor People.* Washington, DC: World Bank, 2004.

WHO, "Higher education in developing countries: Peril and promise", Prepared by the Task Force on Higher Education and Society. Washington, DC: World Bank, 2000.

World Bank, "Benchmarking the governance of tertiary education systems", paper prepared under the overall guidance of Ariel Fiszbein and Dena Ringold, Washington, DC: World Bank, 2010.

Chapter 6

Fiscal Constraints to Investing in Health Education

Alexander S. Preker, Marko Vujicic, Yohana Dukhan,
Caroline Ly, Hortenzia Beciu, Peter Nicolas Materu,
and Khama Rogo

All countries face fiscal constraints in scaling up the education of health workers. The economics of scaling up education for health workers are reviewed in this chapter in the context of the Africa region. The resources likely to be available to the health and education sectors by 2015 are assessed using different assumptions about political commitment to economic growth, spending on health care, and institutional development. The number of additional staff that countries could hire under the different resource envelope scenarios, and the cost of scaling up health worker education in terms of recurrent and capital costs are estimated, country-by-country. Regional estimates are based on the sum of this detailed country-level analysis. Scaling up health education has significant implications for both the health and the education sectors. The cost of employing new staff falls on the health sector while the cost of educating health workers falls mainly on the education sector.

The research presented in this chapter was carried out under the auspices of the Task Force on Scaling up Health Education (TFSHE), established in 2006 under the Global Health Workforce Alliance (GHWA). The data and analysis was based on time series available at the time of the work undertaking for the Task Force on Scaling up Health Education (TFSHE). Although the country rankings and values would be different today, the overall story of the fiscal challenge of financing a significant scaling up of human resources and training in Africa remains a major constraint in achieving heath goals in the Africa region, as it does elsewhere in the world.

The review used a combination of cross-sectional and longitudinal analysis to explore the various dimensions of the economics of scaling up health education in the Africa region. Several economic models were built and tested based on available data on the countries' macroeconomic contexts, sources of financing for the health sector, health expenditure trends, cost of both health education and higher education, and evidence on investment cost of health and higher education today. For details, see Appendix 6A.

Focus is on four important and interlinked issues:

- From where — and how much — additional money might be expected?
- How much would it cost to train more health workers?
- Can better value for money be obtained?
- What would be the contribution to overall growth and development?

From Where — and How Much — Additional Money Might Be Expected?

The total resource envelope for training, hiring, and paying health workers can come from both domestic and foreign sources. The funding from domestic sources depends on

- GDP level
- Share of GDP channeled through the public sector (central and local governments), the share of those resources allocated to health care, and the portion of public health care resources allocated to training and paying health workers
- Share of GDP channeled through the private sector (directly used by households), household spending on health care, and the share of private expenditure on health care devoted to health workers.

Shifts in any one of these variables affect the resource envelope available to pay for health workers. In practice, the range of freedom to make such changes is significantly reduced and often not directly affected by public policy. In the Africa region, three policy trends predominate:

- All countries in the Africa region are striving to achieve economic growth.
- All countries in the Africa region have made a commitment to increasing public spending on health up to 15 percent of total government expenditure (Abuja target for health care spending).
- Many countries are trying to introduce health insurance as an attempt to channel some out-of-pocket household spending and some public subsidies through risk-sharing mechanisms such as health insurance.

Other factors that need to be considered include efficiency and effectiveness in the deployment of human resources in the health sector (including geographic distribution), productivity, and public–private mix.

Table 6.1 illustrates the impact on the total resource envelope that can be used to train and hire health workers through changes in three factors: GDP growth rates, share of government spending devoted to health care, and the introduction of health insurance (insurance effect).

The best-case scenario in terms of the total resource envelope available for hiring staff would occur if GDP grew at a steady rate of

Table 6.1   Health Expenditure Scenarios

Scenario	Annual economic growth (%)	Public health spending as percent of government spending by 2015	Insurance effect as percent of out-of-pocket spending
Worst case	–5	–5% change	0
Intermediate 1	–5	15	0
Intermediate 2	5	–5% change	30
Best case	5	15	60
Projection of 10 past years' trend	Average growth, 1996–2005	Average health expenditure, 1996–2005	0

five percent, political commitment to government spending on health care increased so that total public spending reached the 15 percent Abuja target, and a 25 percent insurance effect resulted from channeling 60 percent of out-of-pocket expenditures through health insurance rather than direct payments to providers. The worst-case scenario would occur if GDP dropped by five percent annually, political commitment eroded so that public spending on health dropped by five percentage points in absolute terms, and no insurance effect came about. The two intermediate scenarios allow offsetting achievements under growth and government commitment (i.e. improvements in government spending but economic recession or economic growth with lack of political commitment). Finally, the linear projection of past trends makes a forecast based on past performance in the variables examined.

The implications in terms of the total resource envelope available to the health sector are major. If all the countries in the Africa region achieved the best-case scenarios, health care resources would double between 2005 and 2015 (Table 6.2). A worst-case scenario reflecting a slowdown in economic growth and lack of political commitment could lead to a 50 percent drop in overall resources, indicating the importance of these variables. Even significant changes in aid flows do not have nearly as big an impact on the future resource envelope available to the health sector.

Table 6.2   **Projected Expenditure Trends in the Africa Region, 2015**

Item	Total health expenditure (US$ billion)	Total health expenditure per capita (population weighted)
Baseline, 2005	27.0	367
Worst case	15.8	17.4
Intermediate 1	20.7	22.7
Intermediate 2	45.1	49.5
Best case	57.5	63.1
Projection of past trends	42.4	46.5
Aid decrease of 50%	41.3	45.3
Aid increase of 100%	46.7	51.3

Memorandum item:
Total estimated population 2005, 736 million; 2015, 912 million

Some countries have already surpassed the best-case scenario targets. For example, in 2005 Ghana, Sierra Leone, Liberia, and Mozambique had economic rates of growth that surpassed the 5 percent target. And spending on health care exceeded 15 percent of government revenues in Burkina Faso, Rwanda, Liberia, and Malawi. Others are however progressing more slowly. For example, only six countries exceeded the 5 percent growth target from 2000 to 2005. GDP in most countries is growing but more slowly than the desired 5 percent, and about a dozen countries have recently experienced negative growth. Likewise, since the heads of state made a political commitment to spend 15 percent of government resources on the health sector, about 50 percent of the countries in the region have been moving toward that target while the rest have experienced erosion in political commitment to public spending on health care. Many of the countries that are performing well in this respect have enjoyed political and social stability. Those that have gone through social turmoil and civil war are among the poor performers. Finally, only a few countries have so far succeeded in introducing health insurance. Among those that have pursued this path such as Ghana and Rwanda, financial resources to the health sector from those sources has increased.

Other factors that would also have an impact on the total domestic resource envelope available for training and hiring health workers include: (a) the share of GDP channeled through the public sector (central and local governments), (b) the share of health expenditure used to pay for health workers; and (c) flow of funds through the private sector. Changing these factors often depends on a complex arbitrage among strongly vested stakeholders with competing economic motives. Since there are no clear-cut regional trends in this respect, these variables were held constant for the purpose of the above illustration. They should be included in detailed follow-up studies because they could have a major impact on the country-level resource envelope made available to scale-up health worker education.

The role of the International Monetary Fund (IMF), the World Bank, and regional banks in contributing to or constraining the overall resource envelope available to health and other parts of the social sector has been intensely debated since the structural adjustment era of the 1980s. Today, achieving the Millennium Development Goals (MDGs) is a central mission of the Bank and many of the other international finance institutions. All are firmly committed to ensuring that fiscal policies contribute to both growth and poverty alleviation. Although these policies are usually consistent with the reality on the ground, health and other parts of the social sector comprise a large and increasing share of the public budget. They are therefore particularly vulnerable to changes in fiscal policy.

Considering the importance of overall economic growth to the total resource envelope available to the health sector, any sectoral policy that increases the size of the labor force or the wage bill in the public sector must be closely coordinated to ensure consistency with the overall fiscal policy. Uncontrolled public spending that might lead to inflation or a slowdown in economic growth would have a serious negative impact on the overall future resource envelope available to the health sector and, more specifically, the health labor force. Policy makers therefore must be careful that short-term policy objectives do not hurt medium- to long-term development objectives.

How Much Would it Cost to Train More Health Workers?

In estimating the cost of scaling up the education of health workers, the following factors must be considered: (a) the recurrent operating cost of training a higher number of students; (b) the number of students to be trained; (c) the associated investment cost of strengthening the capacity of the existing education system to scale up the production of health care workers; and (d) the cost of absorbing the additional graduates into the workforce once they complete their training program.

The total cost of scaling up health worker education can be broken down into two major categories, each dependent on several major factors:

- Total recurrent operating costs: average cost of training current students, marginal cost of training additional students
- Total number of students to be trained
- Capital cost: initial investment cost, depreciation over time; and cost of upgrading the existing capital stock over time

Training Costs

Estimating recurrent operating cost for educating health workers is complicated by several factors. Fixed overhead and other operating costs are shared with the institutions that provide tertiary education during the pre-clinical phase of the training. And they are shared with health care service delivery institutions during the in-service phase of their training. The resulting costs are spread across the Ministry of Education (MOE) and Ministry of Health (MOH), with additional support from non-governmental organizations (NGOs) and the private sector (Table 6.3).

For example, students in the pre-clinical stage of their medical education may benefit indirectly from subsidies received from the MOE, which allow the training institutions to lower their tuition and fees. These subsidized costs are therefore not a good indicator of the total cost of this stage of medical education. Following their pre-clinical education, the students continue to receive undergraduate clinical and post-graduate in-service training in a teaching hospital that receives MOE funding for providing training and the MOH for providing care.

Where possible, detailed country-level analysis was used to estimate the costs of scaling up health worker education. Such analysis indicates that the unit cost for training each type of health worker varies greatly from country to country and between developed and low-income countries (Table 6.4).

Table 6.3   Where Health Worker Training Monies Go

Education sector	Health sector
• Pre-service training	• In-service training
• Shared infrastructure and staff with tertiary education institutions	• Shared infrastructure and staff with hospitals and clinics

Table 6.4   Annual Costs of Physician Training, by Location (US dollars)

Location	Costs
United States/United Kingdom	US$70,000 to US$100,000
Ghana	US$8,000 to US$12,000

Table 6.5   Recurrent and Capital Costs

Item	Education	Health
Recurrent expenditures	• Teacher salaries • Administration of tertiary level institutions • Infrastructure maintenance costs and materials	• Cost share of salaries of professors who provide clinical training, work in service delivery, conduct medical R&D • Administration of teaching hospitals • Maintenance and materials at teaching hospitals
Capital investment	• Classroom construction • Purchases of educational materials • Student housing	• Construction of teaching hospitals and clinics • Purchases medical equipment and teaching materials • Student housing

These variations are often due to differences in the methodology of the estimation rather than true differences in the cost structure of the training program. Some of the key factors that need to be considered in the future to standardize such work are summarized in Table 6.5.

The estimates of the recurrent costs of training in this chapter were based on available data on public expenditures on tertiary education and health professional education. It has been observed that there is an inverse nonlinear relationship between GDP per capita and public expenditures on tertiary education across all countries and within the Africa region, ranging from 0.4 to 12.1 times GDP per capita. This may be an indicator of the variable quality, inefficiency of tertiary education at lower-income levels, fixed overhead, and economies with increasing numbers of students.

Analysis of existing training programs indicates that average annual costs of training a doctor is about five times the costs of a tertiary-level student. The average annual costs of a nurse were about twice the costs of a tertiary-level student.

The expenditures on health professional, general tertiary, and other non-tertiary education for 2015 were forecasted by applying the GDP growth rates used in the corresponding resource envelope scenarios. It was assumed that the existing political commitment to education, represented by the portion of GDP spent on education would remain the same.

Table 6.6   Cost of Medical Study Abroad

Language	Costs applied (US dollars)	Training country
Anglophone	14,100	South Africa
Francophone	10,700	Senegal
Lusophone	8,500	Mozambique

For countries that had a medical school but no medical training cost data, these multiples were applied to estimate the costs of training a doctor and a nurse. The annual costs of training a community health worker was assumed to cost the same as a tertiary-level student. For countries that did not have a medical school, it was assumed that the countries would have to send their students abroad to study. These countries without medical schools faced the costs of sending their students to a country within the same language cluster. For example, Anglophone African countries without a medical school were assumed to train their medical workers in South Africa (Table 6.6).

A combination of these methods was used to undertake a bottom up estimate of the overall training cost for the region.

Number of Workers that Could Be Trained at Current Costs with Additional Money

Setting targets for the number of students that should be trained in a country requires complex trade-offs between normative targets, expressed needs, competing priorities, and economic affordability. Factors that have to be considered include productivity, equity, and efficiency (wage levels, skill mix, deployment, and quality of care). Such analysis was beyond the scope of this report.

Instead, for illustrative purposes, examples are given based on the existing wage bill and a rigid labor market cost structure (i.e. assuming that the ratio of the wage bill to total health care costs remains fixed). Allowances were made for population growth which would affect per capita ratios over time.

Changes in labor cost ratio to total health expenditure, salary levels, and skill mix would have a significant impact on the total staffing levels and additional staff under each of the six scenarios (Table 6.7). Increase in the cost structure within the health sector, with a greater share of the total health expenditure allocated to the wage bill, means that more resources would be spent on labor costs. Wage increases and shifts to a higher skill mix (more expensive workers) would reduce the number of health workers that could be hired with the additional resources. The opposite would be true if real wages were to decrease over time and there was a shift to lower skill mix (less-expensive workers). Precise estimates were not made of these trade-offs.

Total Operating Cost of Training

Table 6.8 illustrates scaling up health worker education to the level that would be affordable under different future resource envelopes. These estimates are derived by multiplying different scenarios of the future number of staff by the estimated unit cost of additional health workers to the workforce. Once again, these estimates are based on an assumption of a fixed labor-cost ratio of total health expenditure, no wage change, and no skill-mix shift. Costs for increasing productivity, equity, and efficiency (skill mix, deployment, and quality of care) factors were not included in the estimates. Such changes could have a significant impact on the estimated cost of scaling up education.

Table 6.7 Projected Staffing Levels in 2015 Using Different Resource Envelope Levels

Item	Total staff (millions)	Additional staff (millions)
Baseline 2015	1.6	0
Worst case	0.8	−0.8
Intermediate 1	1.2	−0.4
Intermediate 2	2.3	0.7
Best case	3.3	1.7
Projection of past trends	2.2	0.6

Assumptions
Fixed labor cost ratio, no wage change, and no skill mix shift

Table 6.8   Total Training Costs, 2008–2015 (2006 US dollars, billions)

Scenario	All countries in Africa region	IDA countries	Non-IDA countries
Baseline 2015	—	—	—
Worst case	—	—	—
Intermediate 1	0.3	0.3	0.0
Intermediate 2	14.2	5.3	8.9
Best case	30.0	15.8	14.2
Projection of past trends	14.7	8.0	6.7
Aid decrease	13.9	7.4	6.5
Aid increase	19.3	11.2	8.1

Note: — = not available.

The average dropout rate of students in the health profession is 30 percent. The brain drain rate of health profession graduates in Africa is 28 percent for highly skilled workers such as doctors and pharmacists and 11 percent for nurses and public health workers. Most countries therefore have to train a significantly higher number of students than the end target for scaling up health education.

As seen earlier, only the best-case scenario would allow the health sector to meet the one million additional health care worker target set by the WHO for the Africa region. It is notable that in this case, the cost of scaling up the education of health workers would consume more than 50 percent of public expenditures on tertiary education.

Investment Costs

Scaling up health education also has significant implications in terms of the costs of strengthening existing education facilities and building new ones. Although information on investment costs are not readily available, recent pre-investment studies in Liberia, Sierra Leone, Ghana, Nigeria, and Rwanda indicate that the cost could easily range from US$10 million to US$50 million, and even higher in some large countries such as Nigeria. Costs vary depending on the state of existing infrastructure and staffing levels, the number of schools, and the desired capacity of the training program.

In post-conflict countries like Liberia and Sierra Leone, destroyed infrastructure has to be rebuilt at a significant investment cost even when the population is relatively small. In more stable but larger countries like Ghana or larger federalist states like Nigeria, the needed investment costs may be much greater. Proper analyses of investment costs would be country-specific and not only examine costs of infrastructure development or rehabilitation but also review of the necessary investment to meet minimum standards of quality and efficiency for the education provided. Most major capital investments will lead to associated increases in recurrent costs.

Is it Possible to Get Better Value for Money?

This section looks at some possible ways of getting better value for money both in mobilizing additional resources and investing in the education of health workers so that the precious additional money devoted to scaling up the education of health workers will be well spent.

At the international level, the aid flow to the health sector has increased significantly. Many previously neglected priority vertical programs have already benefited but now, due to human resource constraints, they are at risk of failing, and thus wasting huge sums of money.

Two negative effects are at the root of this problem. First, although many of the vertically funded programs devote significant resources to short-term training of human resources and other capacity-building activities, few support the basic education of health workers. At the same time, they compete for funding with such basic education. A continuation of this trend will damage the priority programs that the international community has put so much emphasis on during recent years.

Second, due to an ability and willingness to pay significantly higher salaries, these programs have caused wage inflation and competition for staff that are impairing the ability of other core programs such as maternal and child health programs. Many of the latter programs now face a severe shortage in staff because of the distortion caused by a disproportionate amount of donor money flowing into a few programs.

At the national level, health worker education systems are often plagued by significant inefficiency. There is considerable scope for improving the unit cost of training by some of the following actions:

- Reducing the dropout rate of students;
- Reducing the rate of brain drain;
- Increasing collaboration among schools and countries;
- Sharing of staff and teaching facilities across different schools and among countries;
- Sharing some of the cost and delivery of pre-clinical training with the basic science programs of associated universities;
- Adapting the teaching curriculum to the appropriate skills level needed by individual countries.

Discussion of Main Findings

Some of the main findings are described in this section in terms of the existing and future resource envelope, number of staff that could be trained using these resources, and the cost of training them (both recurrent and capital costs).

Resource Envelope

Much progress has been made in recent years in terms of spending on health care in the Africa region, partially due to economic growth, increased government spending, and greater donor commitment. Currently the region spends US$24.4 billion (three percent of the current regional GDP). Despite such progress, the current analysis indicates that significant challenges lie ahead in terms of securing the resources needed to achieve the MDGs for health.

The Role of Economic Growth

Nearly half of the countries in Africa are now enjoying growth rates of five percent or more (Figure 6.1). This economic growth has been the major driver of health expenditures during the past few years, translating

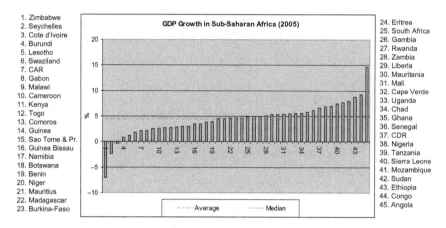

Figure 6.1   GDP Growth

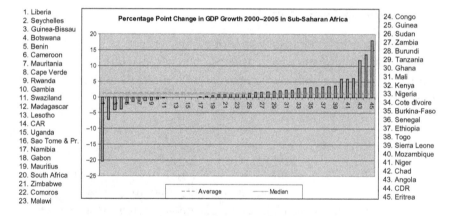

Figure 6.2   Changes in GDP Growth

into significant increases in total health expenditures (public and private). Although many countries have succeeded in sustaining growth over the past five years, only a few have done so at current high growth rates, and a significant number have actually experienced negative growth (Figure 6.2). Contracting economic performance has a very negative impact on both total and public expenditures on health. Poor economic management and civil war have been major causes of such poor economic performance.

Government Commitment

There is currently a great variation in public spending on health care across the Africa region both in absolute and relative terms. The regional mean is around nine percent of total government spending. Most countries have not reached the Abuja target of 15 percent government spending on health care agreed in 2001 by the African heads of state. Although many countries have increased the public sector commitment to health in terms of the share of government expenditures allocated to health, commitment in a number of countries has eroded (Figure 6.3). Many of the countries that are performing well in this respect have enjoyed political and social stability. Those that have gone through social turmoil and civil war are among the poor performers (Figure 6.4).

Insurance Effect

There is a well-known strong correlation between the level of GDP and total health care expenditures. In the medium term, countries going through rapid economic growth reach a higher level of spending on health care over time than countries that are growing more slowly. In the short

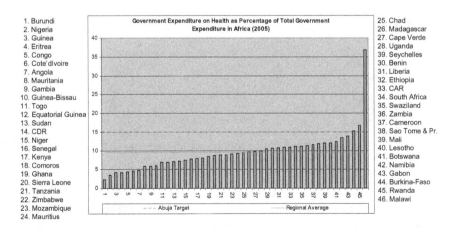

Figure 6.3 Share of Government Spending on Health

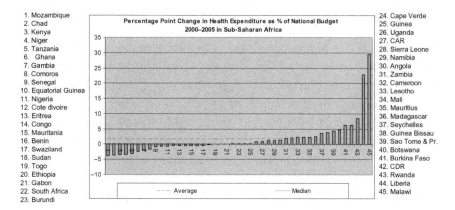

Figure 6.4   Changes in Government Spending on Health Care

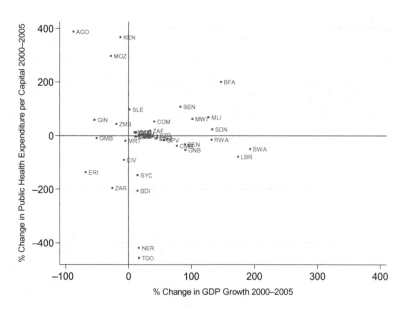

Figure 6.5   Change in Public Spending and Changes in GDP Growth

term, however, changes in GDP growth are only weakly correlated with changes in public spending on health care (Figure 6.5). This indicates that economic growth does not automatically translate into greater public commitment to spending on health care.

Instead, as countries get richer, many begin looking at health insurance as an alternative to core government subsidies in funding the health sector. Among the Anglophone group of countries, significant reforms have recently been introduced in Ghana, Rwanda, and Nigeria, while Kenya, Namibia, Zimbabwe, Botswana, and South Africa have a longer history of using health insurance. Others like Uganda and Tanzania are considering a similar shift toward health insurance. Among the Francophone/Lusophone countries, there is a long tradition of community financing and health insurance mutual organizations but coverage rates and total resources mobilized through such mechanisms have remained of marginal significance.

Total Resources Generated under Different Scenarios

If all the countries in the Africa region achieved the best-case scenarios, health care resources would double between 2005 and 2015 (Table 6.9). Projection of past trends without any major policy change would also give a significant boost to health expenditure in the Africa region.

The best-case scenario is, however, very unlikely because many countries are struggling to achieve a five percent economic growth target and only a few countries have achieved the Abuja public spending target of 15 percent of total government spending on health care. Only a few

Table 6.9   Total Health Expenditure

Baseline	Worst case	Intermediate 1	Intermediate 2	Best case	Projection of past trends
2005	2015	2015	2015	2015	2015
Total Health Expenditure $US billions (constant)					
27.0	15.8	20.7	45.1	57.5	42.4
Public Health Expenditure $US (constant)					
11.5	6.6	11.4	17.9	31.1	19.6

countries have embraced health insurance, a major new source of funding for the health sector.

If a significant number of countries experience both a lack of political commitment to the current health agenda in the Africa region and a significant deterioration in economic performance, overall resources would go down compared with current spending levels. Since many countries in the region are heavily dependent on donors for core budget support to the health sector, donor fatigue could lead to such a situation, threatening the current resource envelope allocated to the health sector.

Total Number of Health Workers

The total health workforce levels (per capita and absolute) that are economically sustainable for the Africa region under the different health expenditure and labor market scenarios are summarized in Tables 6.10 and 6.11. The results require careful interpretation in order to take population growth into account.

Under the best-case expenditure scenario, the economically sustainable level of the health workforce ranges from just over four million health workers (when wages do not change and hiring is focused on the lower-skilled cadres) to 2.1 million health workers (when wages increase and hiring is focused on higher-skilled cadres).

It is clear from the results that wage changes and skill-mix changes have a significant impact on the economically sustainable staffing levels. Wage increases and shifts to higher-skill mixes reduce the number of health workers that can be hired with additional resources. Of course, such policies also result in higher skill mixes which may be desirable. The model was not designed to address these tradeoffs, simply to outline the implications of alternative skill mix and wage policies on aggregate staffing levels.

Under the best case for health expenditure, an additional 1.7 million health workers can be absorbed. However, with even a relatively modest wage increase of 25 percent, the additional training needs to fall considerably to 1.1 million health workers.

Table 6.10 Total Economically Sustainable Staffing Levels (per 1,000 population)

Scenario	No wage change, no skill mix change	25% wage increase, no skill mix change	No wage change, skill mix shifts to high skill	No wage change, skill mix shifts to low skill	25% wage increase, skill mix shifts to high skill	25% wage increase, skill mix shifts to low skill
Baseline	1.8	1.8	1.8	1.8	1.8	1.8
Worst case	0.9	0.7	1.2	0.5	1.0	0.4
Intermediate 1	1.3	1.0	1.5	1.1	1.2	0.9
Intermediate 2	2.5	2.0	2.2	2.9	1.8	2.3
Best case	3.6	2.9	2.9	4.4	2.3	3.5
Projection of past trends	2.4	1.9	2.2	2.7	1.7	2.2

Table 6.11   Total Economically Sustainable Staffing Level (million)

Scenario	No wage change, no skill mix change	25% wage increase, no skill mix change	No wage change, skill mix shifts to high skill	No wage change, skill mix shifts to low skill	25% wage increase, skill mix shifts to high skill	25% wage increase, skill mix shifts to low skill
Baseline 2015	1.6	1.6	1.6	1.6	1.6	1.6
Worst case	0.8	0.6	1.1	0.4	0.9	0.4
Intermediate 1	1.2	0.9	1.3	1.0	1.1	0.8
Intermediate 2	2.3	1.8	2.0	2.6	1.6	2.1
Best case	3.3	2.6	2.6	4.0	2.1	3.2
Projection of past trends	2.2	1.8	2.0	2.5	1.6	2.0

Cost of Training

Estimating the cost of educating health workers is difficult for several reasons. Costs are spread across the Ministry of Education, Ministry of Health, NGOs, and the private sector (Table 6.12).

The cost of educating health workers and needed investment cost vary considerably across countries (Table 6.13).

As described earlier, at the regional level, only the best-case scenario would allow the health sector to absorb a significant increase in health workers numbers (a little over the one million target set by WHO).

Figure 6.6 compares the total cost of scaling up the education of health workers in a projection of past trends economic context in each of the six staffing scenarios to the aggregate projection of public expenditures on tertiary education made by the African countries modeled. As expected, the costs of training doctors, as seen in the no skill mix and high skill mix scenarios are a considerable portion of the total costs.

Table 6.12   Allocation of Government Responsibilities

Ministries of education	Ministries of health
• Pre-service training.	• In-service training.
• Shared infrastructure with tertiary education institutions.	• Only two percent of THE in OECD is spent on medical training.

Note: THE = total health expenditure.

Table 6.13   Cost of Educating Health Workers and Cost of Needed Investments

Country	Annual costs of training a doctor (US dollars)	Total costs based on WHO estimates (US dollars)
United States	70,000–100,000	1.6 million
United Kingdom	50,000 pounds (88,000 USD)	1.4 million
Ghana	8,100	24,000

Note: The WHO estimated training costs by applying a multiple of 37× and 18× GDP per capita to estimate the costs of training a physician and nurse, respectively. This multiple does not account for the pattern found in higher education costs that suggest that it is relatively more expensive to pursue higher education in lower-income countries.
Sources: AAMC, GHS, UK Medical Schools Council.

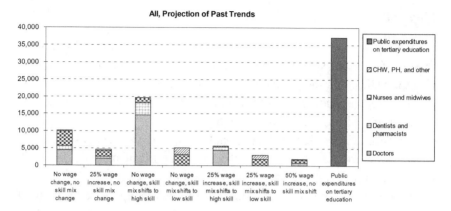

Figure 6.6   Cost of Training per Category of Health Worker and Total Expenditures on Tertiary Education in the Projection of Past Trends Scenario (2006 US dollars million)

Note: Public expenditure on tertiary education are based on government estimates which may not always include the expenditures for training low-skilled health care workers such as midwives, some categories of nurses and community health care workers. Often, these activities are carried out by the MOH, donors, and the private sector and may not be fully captured in this figure.

Figure 6.7 compares the total cost of scaling up the education of health workers in a projection of past trends economic context in each of the six staffing scenarios to the aggregate projection of public expenditures on tertiary education made by the African countries modeled. As expected, the costs of training doctors, as seen in the no skill mix and high skill mix scenarios, are a considerable portion of the total costs.

Figure 6.8 shows the costs in a best-case scenario, which comes closest to achieving the normative recommendation of having 2.3 health workers per 1,000 populations. It is notable that in the case of a no wage change but shift to low-skilled workers (a scenario which would allow training of a maximum number of staff), the cost of scaling up health education exceeds by a large margin the total cost of public expenditure on tertiary education. Under this scenario even keeping skills and wages constant, scaling up health education has significant financial implications for both the health and education sectors. Scaling up the labor force by an

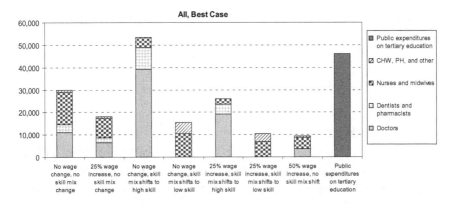

Figure 6.7   Training Costs for Best-Case Scenario (2006 US dollars, million)
Note: Public expenditures on tertiary education are based on government estimates that may not always include the expenditures for training low-skilled health care workers such as midwives, some categories of nurses, and community health care workers. Often, these activities are carried out by the Ministry of Health, donors, and the private sector and may not be fully captured in this figure.

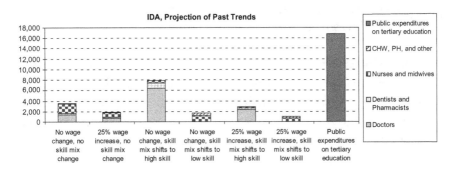

Figure 6.8   Total Training Cost for IDA Countries under the Projection of Past Trends (2006 US dollars, millions)

additional one million health worker would require significant external assistance to both sectors.

Figure 6.8 provides a similar comparison for the scenario that projects current trends into the future. Detailed country-by-country analysis is also available for all the countries in the Africa region. A summary of all the various staffing scenarios applied to each of the six economic models is provided in Appendix 6A.

Investment Costs

Scaling up health education also has significant implications in terms of the cost of strengthening existing education facilities and building new ones. Although information on investment costs are not readily available, recent pre-investment studies in Liberia, Sierra Leone, Ghana, and Nigeria indicate that the cost could easily range from US$10 million to US$50 million, and in some cases, like Nigeria, as high as US$100 million, depending on the size of the country and the state of existing institutions. In post-conflict countries like Liberia and Sierra Leone, the destroyed infrastructure has to be rebuilt. This requires a significant investment even when the population size is relatively small. In more stable but larger countries like Ghana or larger federalist states like Nigeria, the needed investment costs may be much greater. Proper analyses of investment costs would be country-specific and not only examine costs of infrastructure development or rehabilitation but also review the necessary investment to meet minimum standards of quality and efficiency for the education to be provided. In addition, any additional capital investments will be met with increasing recurrent costs, which are a significant component of total costs in health professional education.

Conclusions

The main conclusions from this review follow:

- Past reviews have indicated that human resource shortages in the Africa region have become a binding constraint in implementing many priority health programs in the region.
- Scaling up health education has major implications for financial sustainability in both the health and the education sectors.

- The resource envelope available to scale up human resources is a major binding constraint that needs to be considered on country-by-country.
- Other factors to consider include efficiency and effectiveness in the deployment of human resources in the health sector (including geographic distribution), productivity, and public/private mix.

Countries trying to scale up health education may also want to consider parallel measures to improve the earmarking of some Official Development Assistance for this purpose, especially in the case of some of the larger international funds devoted to addressing major public health priorities.

An effort is needed in many countries to ensure that the secondary education system produces a sufficient supply of graduates to feed a scaling up of health education.

Recommendations

Detailed country-level analysis is needed before specific recommendation can be made on the best policies for scaling up the education of health workers in specific countries.

Different countries have different circumstances with, for example, different levels of growth and different dependencies on aid. Moreover, it is the priority which countries give to tackling the health worker crisis and the decisions countries themselves make that will be crucial. Individual countries will make their own decisions on the difficult trade-offs they believe are appropriate to determine how many workers of what type they will support — and on what they agree are the priorities for aid expenditures with their development partners and the international financial institutions.

For example, on the revenue side, many countries are not on track in progressing toward the best-case scenario in terms of the overall expenditure envelope due to weak growth, lack of political commitment, and the significant out-of-pocket share of total health expenditures. Strong macroeconomic policies, coupled with political stability and strong trade policies, are among the most important factors that would lead to improved growth in the countries that lag in this area. The associated economic growth would also allow those countries to meet past political commitments to increase public expenditure on health care.

In countries that have a weak taxation capacity, finding other mechanisms for mobilizing resources could also be considered. The populations in many counties have a much greater willingness and ability to pay for health care than what governments have been able to mobilize through formal taxation instruments. Channeling some of these resources through a pre-paid risk-pooling arrangement or health insurance program would be another way of mobilizing more resources.

In countries spending a very small part of total health expenditures on the wage bill, some shift in the relative allocation of human resources could also be considered. But institutional rigidity often makes such shifts difficult.

Donor funding could be increased, but a very significant increases in donor funding would be needed to address the current funding gap. Even then it would not have as great an impact as strong economic growth, public commitment to spending on health, and a strong insurance effect of channeling out-of-pocket expenditure through a pre-payment or insurance mechanism.

On the expenditure side, a major priority should be to address some of the inefficiencies in the education of health care workers described in this chapter. This would include significant decreases in the student dropout rate and in the brain drain. Much greater efforts should also be made to increase coordination among countries and among health education programs to achieve efficiency in the education of health workers (such as shared faculty and facilities among programs and some integration in the pre-clinical training between health education programs and general science training at the undergraduate university level). Donor agencies should better coordinate their activities so as to avoid labor market distortions arising out of differential pay for staff working on some of the priority vertical programs. Some funds from these programs should be earmarked for general support in scaling up the education of health workers at the country level.

Acknowledgments

The authors are grateful for the contributions and direct inputs provided by many people. In particular, valuable guidance was provided by Ruth Kagia, Yaw Ansu, Ok Pannenburg, Eva Jarawan, and William Experton.

Others who contributed to this report through broader work on health labor markets and higher education reform include Agnes L. B. Soucat, Peter Darvis, Laura Rose, Christopher H. Herbst, Katherine Anne Tulenko, Christophe Lemière, Mathieu Brossard, Chloe Fevré, Jean J. de St. Antoine, and Bina Valaydon. The team also collaborated with Tessa Tan-Torres at WHO (Geneva), Richard Scheffler at Berkeley University, and Eliot Sorel at George Washington University.

Appendix 6A. Methodology for Estimating Number of Health Workers

The Model

The following identity summarizes that relationship between health expenditure (*HEXP*) and staffing levels for different cadres of health workers (n_i) in a particular country:

$$HEXP \times S_w = \Sigma_i w_i n_i$$

where S_w is the share of health spending devoted to the wage bill and w_i is the wage level for cadre i. The overall staffing level (Σn_i) can be changed by (i) altering health expenditure, (ii) altering the share of health spending on the wage bill, (iii) altering the skill mix, and (iv) altering the wage level of the health worker cadre.

For each of the health expenditure scenarios developed, it is possible to model the overall staffing levels (and skill mix) that are affordable under different assumptions on the share of health spending on the wage bill, skill mix of staff, and wages.

Data

The inputs to the model are the health expenditure scenarios and the current staffing levels by cadre. The current staffing levels and selection of cadres were taken from the WHO human resources for health database.

The analysis is carried out in two ways. The first is by doing a country-by-country analysis and then aggregating across countries to reach a total for Africa. The second is by treating the Africa region as a single data point.

Table 6A.1   Relative Wage Assumptions

Skill level	Wage level relative to doctor
Doctor	1.00
Nurse	0.50
Midwife	0.33
Dentist	1.00
Pharmacist	0.50
Pub/Env	0.40
Community health worker	0.30
Lab	0.40
Other	0.30

As accurate wage data are not readily available for countries in the Africa region, wages were imputed for each cadre from expenditure and staffing data. To do this, however, requires an assumption on the relative wages of one cadre to another. Using available data from a few country studies in the Africa region, the following assumption on relative wages was used in the analysis (Table 6A.1).

Methodology of Training Costs

The total number of additional medical graduate output, *t* required as a result of the brain drain is as follows:

$$t = \sum_{i=1}^{47} d_i (1 + b_i)$$

where b_i = The country-specific estimate for the brain drain rate of doctors and nurses, based on the Center for Global Development's database on stock of doctors and nurses from African countries that are practicing outside of Africa relative to the number of doctors and nurses that are practicing inside of Africa. For all of sub-Saharan Africa, the brain drain rate is approximately 27 percent for physicians and 12 percent for nurses. d_i = The number of health professionals that can be absorbed into the health care system for each country.

Therefore, if for all the 47 African countries modeled, the brain drain rate were 50 percent and the number of health workers that could be absorbed into the system were 100, then the total number of graduates that were needed, t would have 150. If this number were to be reduced by α, 25 percent and 50 percent, t would fall to

$$\sum_{i=1}^{47} d_i(1+(1-\alpha)b_i), 138 \text{ and } 125 \text{ graduates, respectively.}$$

The annual cost of training all the graduates, U if they went to school in one cohort is as follows:

$$U_i = f(g_i, s_i, x_i, y_i, l_i) \text{ and } U = \Sigma \, U_i$$

where U_i is a function of:

g = country's GDP/Capita;
x = relative cost of higher education measured by the public expenditures on higher education per student as a multiple of GDP/capita;
s = dummy variable representing whether or not there is an in-country medical school;
l = dummy variable representing the country's national language which determines the cost of training if a country does not have a medical school. For example, Botswana which does not have a medical school but is an Anglophone country will be applied with the costs of South Africa's medical schools for its graduates.
y = the unit costs of medical and nursing education which is estimated for countries where this data does not exist.

To account for the drop-out rate, r which is the percentage of students who drop-out halfway through the program, the drop-out rate is applied as follows to get the total costs of training doctors by 2015, w:

$$w = (t * u + 0.5 * t * u * (r/(1 - r))) * y$$

y = # of years to train a health worker. For a doctor, it is six years; four years for dentists and pharmacists; three years for nurses and mid-wives; two years for public health specialists; one year for community health and other health workers.

If the drop-out rate is decreased by λ, then the resulting costs would be

$$(t * u + 0.5 * t * u * (\lambda \ r/(1 - \lambda \ r))) * y$$

Key Issues

Though shouldering more than 24 percent of the global burden of disease, the Africa region receives less than one percent of global health spending and has less than three percent of total health workers (Figure 6A.1). Similarly, the lower the density of health workers, the higher are the mortality rates (Figure 6A.2). Recent research has shown strong links between income, health spending, number of health workers, and health outcomes.

The Joint Learning Initiative (JLI) commission suggested that on average, countries with less than 2.5 health care professionals (counting only doctors, nurses, and midwives) per 1,000 population will fail to achieve a minimum of 80 percent coverage rate for deliveries by skilled birth attendants and measles immunization. At in 2007, when the research findings were released, 57 countries that fell short of this threshold; 36 of them were in the sub-Saharan Africa region. Although the number of health

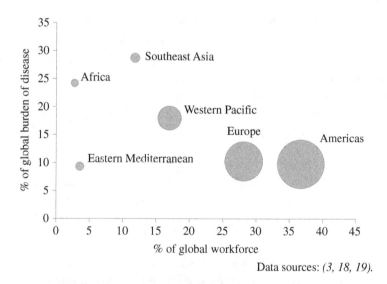

Data sources: *(3, 18, 19)*.

Figure 6A.1   Distribution of Health Workers
Source: WHO 2006 Report, Working Together for Health.

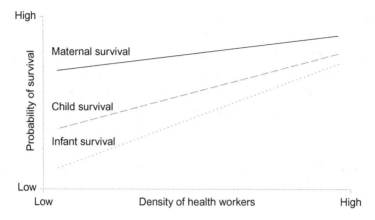

Figure 6A.2 Health Workers Save Lives
Source: WHO 2006 Report, Working Together for Health.

workers (physicians, nurses, and midwives) has increased globally, as reported in 2006, sub-Saharan Africa still lags behind all other regions, with a density of 1.3 health workers per 1,000 population.

The global number and the regional disparities in enrollment and graduation in medical schools are further examples of how far behind the rest of the world sub-Saharan Africa is in health. Securing an adequate mix of training and skills is also important (Gali and Gertler, 2007). Increasing the availability of the medical care is not enough. The skills of health workers have to be raised so that they provide quality care.

Based on this and other analyses, Africa needs 817,992 doctors, nurses, and midwives to meet the critical minimum threshold of 2.5 health care professionals per 1,000 population according to estimates by the World Health Organization (WHO).

Objectives

In its review, the Task Force on Scaling Up Health Education sought specifically to estimate:

- The resources that could be made available for health and education over the next few years in different countries in the Africa region under different assumptions about economic growth, public and private spending, and donor assistance.

- The number of additional staff that different countries could hire by using the resulting resources under different assumptions about total number of staff, skill mix, and wage structure of the workforce.
- The cost of scaling up education in different countries based on the above in terms of (a) the additional capital investment needed to strengthen the training institutions to handle the increased student volume; and (b) the additional expenditures needed to run the expanded capacity of the health education system.

Methodology

The review used a combination of cross-sectional and longitudinal analysis to explore the various dimensions of the economics of scaling up health education in the Africa region. Several economic models were built and tested based on available data on the countries' macroeconomic contexts, sources of financing for the health sector, health expenditure trends, cost of both health education and higher education, and evidence on investment cost of health and higher education today. For details, see Appendix 6A.

The analysis built upon ongoing work in the areas of: (a) fiscal space and public expenditure reviews; (b) national health accounts and marginal budgeting for bottlenecks; (c) financing and expenditure analysis in higher education; and (d) selected country-level reviews on the cost of investing in health education and financing such education.

Estimating the Resource Envelope

A critical constraint to scaling up human resources in the health sector is the funding envelope available to: (a) employ staff once they have been trained (the cost of which falls mainly on the health sector); and (b) educate the staff (both cost of health education and cost of expanding training capacity). This section describes an approach for estimating this resource envelope and projecting future scenarios for 2015 in the Africa region. Regional estimates are based on the aggregates of country-level analysis.

Main Variables

The total resource envelope that can be used to pay for staff depends on several factors:

- Overall level of GDP
- Share of GDP channeled through the public sector
  - o Share of public sector resources allocated to health care
    - Share of health expenditure in public sector used to pay for health workers
- Share of GDP channeled directly through households
  - o Household spending of health care
    - Share of private expenditure on health care devoted to health workers

In theory, shifts in any of these variables will affect the total resource envelope available to pay for health workers. In practice, the range of freedom to make changes is significantly reduced and often not directly affected by public policy.

In the Africa region, three trends predominate:

- All countries are striving to achieve economic growth.
- All have made a commitment to spend 15 percent of total government budgets on health care (Abuja target for health care spending).
- Many countries are trying to introduce health insurance in an attempt to channel some out-of-pocket household spending and some public subsidies through risk-sharing mechanisms such as health insurance, health maintenance organizations, and other pre-payment schemes.

For these reasons, the three main variables modeled under different scenarios include GDP growth, percent of government spending on health care, and the additional resources mobilized through the introduction of health insurance (insurance effect).

Assumptions

Several assumptions were made that would affect the overall resource envelope that could be used to pay for health workers. Assumptions were made based on current trends in the Africa region to model scenarios described in the next section. In the case of GDP growth, several countries in the Africa region are growing at an annual rate of five percent or more, while a few have contracted at a similar or greater rate. The range for the growth in GDP was therefore set between an annual growth rate of five percent (best-case scenario) and annual contraction of five percent (worst-case scenario).

In the case of shifts in the share of public expenditure on health, many countries have moved toward the Abuja target of allocating 15 percent of the public budget on the health sector agreed by the African heads of state in 2001. Some countries have moved more quickly, and others have lost ground, spending less now than they did at the time of the agreement. The range for public spending for health was therefore set between a maximum of 15 percent of total government expenditure (best-case scenario) and a drop in absolute terms of five percentage points (worst-case scenario) by 2015.

In the case of the insurance effect, it has been observed that total spending on health increases when health insurance is introduced as a resource-mobilization mechanism. Populations that can and will contribute to insurance often continue to pay some money out-of-pocket for health care not covered through the insurance system. This is more pronounced at low-income levels where the services covered under insurance are often restricted. Current experiences in Ghana, Rwanda, Namibia, and elsewhere indicate that countries can reach a coverage rate of 30–60 percent or higher even at low-income levels. The range of insurance coverage was, therefore, set at zero percent (worst-case scenario) to 60 percent of out-of-pocket spending with an insurance effect of 25 percent additional resources mobilized through the introduction of health insurance (best-case scenario).

The share of GDP channeled through the public sector was held constant. It was assumed that any increase in GDP channeled through the public sector would be associated with an offsetting decrease in private consumption and might have a negative effect on GDP. Likewise any decrease in GDP channeled through the public sector would be associated with an offsetting increase in private consumption and might have a positive impact on GDP growth.

Finally, the share of the health budget used to pay for health staff was assumed to be constant. It was assumed that any increase in relative spending on the wage bill would negatively affect other spending in the health sector, thereby offsetting the benefits of increasing the number or income level of staff. Likewise any decrease in relative spending on the wage bill would have an offsetting impact on other sources of increased health expenditure.

Scenarios

Several scenarios were modeled (see Table 6A.2), including a best case, a worst case, two intermediate cases, and a projection of past trends. In each case, the scenarios and projections were made for each country in the Africa region using the current available data for health expenditure (public and private) and country-level macroeconomic data. Regional estimates were based on the aggregate of such country-level assessments.

The best-case scenario in terms of the total resource envelope available for hiring staff would occur under steady five percent growth in GDP,

Table 6A.2   Health Expenditure Scenarios

Scenario	Annual economic growth (%)	Public health expenditures as percent of gov. expenditures by 2015	Insurance effect (as percent of out-of-pocket spending)
Worst case	−5	−5% change	0
Intermediate 1	−5	15	0
Intermediate 2	5	−5% change	30
Best case	5	15	60
Projection of past trends	Average growth from 1996–2005	Average HE from 1996–2005	0

an increase in political commitment to government spending on health care so that total public spending reaches the 15 percent Abuja target, and a 25 percent insurance effect from channeling 60 percent of out-of-pocket expenditures through health insurance rather than direct payments to providers. The worst-case scenario would occur if GDP dropped by five percent annually, political commitment eroded so that public spending on health dropped by five percentage points in absolute terms, and there was no insurance effect.

Estimating Affordable Workforce Levels

With health expenditure scenarios modeled, a second model was developed to estimate the level and composition of the health workforce that is economically sustainable in 2015 for each of the health expenditure scenarios (see the section "Methodology" under Appendix 6A). Comparing the economically sustainable health workforce levels in 2015 to current health workforce levels identifies the number of additional health workers that can be absorbed into the labor market by 2015. This estimate — the health workforce gap — is then used to model additional training needs and training costs.

Main Variables

The main variables used to model the economically sustainable staffing levels under a given resource envelope included: (a) the skill mix of newly hired staff; and (b) health worker wages.

Assumptions

Assumptions were made about the share of health spending devoted to the wage bill, efficiency, and effectiveness in the deployment of staff (including geographic distribution), productivity, and public/private mix.

Different scenarios were defined by making assumptions on the skill mix of newly hired staff and wages. The assumptions were based on current trends in the Africa region and elsewhere, subject to data availability. In the case of skill mix, it is assumed that policy makers may want to shift the mix of the future workforce toward highly skilled workers (doctors and nurses) or toward lower skilled workers (mainly community workers) or to maintain the current skill mix. Given that the overall skill mix of staff can change only so rapidly — i.e. the staff cannot be fired all at once and a new mix created in one swoop — the scenarios for altering the skill mix are applied to newly hired staff only. In other words, the distribution of newly hired staff across cadres is either the same as the existing workforce, disproportionately concentrated on higher-skilled cadres, or disproportionately concentrated on lower-skilled cadres.

In the case of wages, many countries are introducing performance bonuses and other financial incentives to encourage workers to move to rural areas and to prevent them from leaving the country for better-paid employment elsewhere. The range for altering wage changes was set at no change at one extreme and a 25 percent wage increase at the other.

Scenarios

Three scenarios were modeled for altering the skill mix:

- Skill mix of staff does not change
- Skill mix of staff shifts toward the higher-skilled cadres (doctors and nurses)
- Skill mix of staff shifts toward the lower-skilled cadres (community health workers).

Two scenarios were modeled for altering wages:

- Real wages do not change
- Real wages increase by 25 percent by 2015 for all cadres.

This leads to six distinct labor market scenarios for each health expenditure level (Table 6A.3).

The best-case scenario in terms of total staffing levels would occur if without any increase in wages and with a shift in skill mix toward lower-skilled (i.e. less-expensive staff). The worst-case scenario in terms of total number of staff would occur under a 25 percent wage increase and a shift in skill mix to higher-skilled (i.e. more expensive) staff.

Table 6A.3   Shift in Skill Mix and Wage Level

Scenario	Shift to low-skill mix	No skill-mix change	Shift to high skill mix
No wage change	Least expensive Largest number of staff	In between	In between
25% wage increase	In between	In between	Most expensive Smallest number of staff

Estimating Future Training Costs and Investments in Health Education

Identifying the actual costs of providing health worker training is complicated because the infrastructure for medical training is shared with institutions that provide tertiary education and health care service delivery. As a consequence, the costs of training health workers are shared by multiple entities. For example, students who are in the pre-clinical stage of their medical education may be based in a large public university that receives public funding from the Ministry of Education and private revenues from tuition and fees. Following their pre-clinical education, medical students may continue on to receive under-graduate clinical and post-graduate in-service training in a teaching hospital that receives public funding from the Ministry of Health and revenues for providing services. For these reasons, the detailed costs of educating health workers are not readily available (Table 6A.4).

Assumptions

The assumptions for estimating the costs of training were as follows:

- The costs of training the additional number of health workers that can be absorbed into the health system are considered outside of the resource envelope allocated for health because it is largely financed by the education sector and other non-health expenditures. In reality, the resource envelope allocated for health must include some of the costs for training health workers.

Table 6A.4   Recurrent and Capital Costs

Item	Education	Health
Recurrent expenditures	• Teacher salaries • Administration of tertiary-level institutions • Infrastructure maintenance costs and materials	• Cost share of salaries of professors who provide clinical training, work in service delivery, conduct medical R&D • Administration of teaching hospitals • Maintenance and materials at teaching hospitals
Capital investment	• Cost of building classrooms, buying educational equipment	• Cost of building teaching hospitals, buying medical equipment

- The drop-out rate of students in the health profession is 30 percent. The graduation rates of medical students varied from 10 percent in Mozambique to 56 percent in Namibia (World Bank 2003). An estimate of drop-out rates in higher education in Africa based on Ethiopia, Nigeria, and South Africa, however, found that drop-out rates were approximately 30 percent. To apply this attrition rate, it was assumed that 30 percent of the students who begin their health training studies will drop-out half way through the program.
- The brain drain rate of graduates of the health profession in Africa is 28 percent for high-skill workers such as doctors and pharmacists and 11 percent for nurses and public health workers. Country-specific data on the "brain drain" based on the Center for Global Development's database of health professional emigration from Africa were applied to each African country (Clemens and Pettersson, 2006).

Scenarios

In the Africa region, the cost of tertiary education varies significantly across sub-Saharan Africa, ranging from 0.4 to 12.1 times GDP per capita. In addition, there is an inverse nonlinear relationship between GDP per capita and public expenditures on tertiary education across all countries and within the Africa region (Figure 6A.3). This suggests that applying a

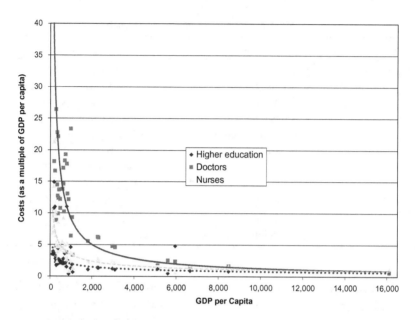

Figure 6A.3   Relationship between Education Spending and GDP

general factor to GDP per capita to estimate the costs of medical education would not appropriately capture the costs for countries in the lower- and higher-income quartiles.

This may be an indicator of the variable quality and efficiency of tertiary education and subsequently, the education of health workers in Africa. In scaling up the number of health workers, the current level of quality of the medical education offered in Africa is not identified in this chapter, and no attempt is made to define the cost of improving quality. Instead, to generalize about the existing differences in costs and quality of medical education, the authors used the specific costs (from the limited, reliable data) from training programs for health workers which were available to estimate the country-specific costs of training health workers relative to the per student public expenditures on tertiary education. The average annual costs of training a doctor were about five times the costs of a tertiary-level student. The average annual costs of a nurse were about twice the costs of a tertiary-level student.

Table 6A.5   Cost of Medical Study Abroad

Language	Costs applied (US dollars)	Training country
Anglophone	14,100	South Africa
Francophone	10,700	Senegal
Lusophone	8,510	Mozambique

For countries that had *a medical school but no medical training cost data*, these multiples were applied to figure out the costs of training a doctor and a nurse. Training a community health worker was assumed to cost the same as a tertiary-level student. However, it was assumed that countries that did not have a medical school would have to send their students abroad to study. These countries without medical schools faced the costs of sending their students to a country within the same language cluster. For example, Anglophone African countries without a medical school were assumed to train their medical workers in South Africa (Table 6A.5).

The expenditures on medical, tertiary, and other non-tertiary education for 2015 were forecasted by applying the GDP growth rates used in the corresponding resource envelope scenarios. It was assumed that the existing political commitment to education, represented by the portion of GDP spent on education, would remain the same.

References

Clemens, M. and G. Pettersson, "A New Database of Health Professional Emigration from Africa", CGD Working Paper No. 95, Center for Global Development, Washington, DC, 2006.

Gali, J. and M. Gertler, "Macroeconomic modeling for monetary policy evaluation", *Journal of Economic Perspectives*, **21**(4), 25–46, 2007.

Preker, A. S., M. Vujicic, Y. Dukhan, C. Ly, C. Beciu, and P. N. Materu, Fiscal constraints to scaling up the education of health workers in Africa. World Bank Submission to Task force on Saving Lives. Chaired by Nigel Crisp. World Bank: Washington. DC, 2008.

WHO, *Scaling Up Saving Lives*. Task force on Saving Lives. Chaired by Nigel Crisp. WHO: Geneva, 2008.

WHO Report, *Working Together for Health*, WHO: Geneva, 2006.

World Bank, "Cost and financing of education: opportunities and obstacles for expanding and improving education in Mozambique", Working Paper No. 26699, Washington, DC: World Bank, 2003.

Chapter 7

Investment and Financing in Health Education

Eric L. Keuffel, Alexander S. Preker, and Caroline Ly

Background

As will be detailed in this section, the critical shortage of physicians, nurses, and health workers (human resources for health, HRH) has been a central policy issue inhibiting developing countries from improving health outcomes for several decades. While substantial resources and efforts have ameliorated and addressed shortages in some contexts, the recently developed United Nations Sustainable Development Goals underscore the continued support which HRH will require to deliver many of the health outcomes anticipated by 2030.

In the past, one of the reasons for limited support of tertiary and health sector specific educational institutions received were the expected higher financial rates of social return across other competing investments for developing countries. For example, with respect to Africa over the past three decades, internal and external investments in the education systems have been targeted to the primary and secondary levels of the education sector (Tilak, 2000). Historically, the focus on the lower levels of education was supported by research indicating that the social rate of financial return for investment in primary and secondary education were higher than returns anticipated from higher education (Kapur and Crowley,

2008; Psacharopoulos *et al.*, 1986). A comprehensive analysis examining 98 countries over 37 year (1960–1997) estimated socials rate of return from primary schooling at 18.9 percent and tertiary education 10.8 percent (Psacharopoulos, 2002).

However, there is an increasing recognition that the methodologies for evaluating rates of return likely did not capture the full benefit of tertiary education (as usually just wage effects for the individual were evaluated as the benefit) and that, as "knowledge workers" become more important in developing the institutional capacity of countries, the benefits to a strong tertiary education system will likely grow even larger (Kapur and Crowley, 2008; Birdsall, 1996).

The number of qualified secondary school graduates has increased, leading to a larger pool of potential higher education students. The expansion of education at lower levels has increased the value of tertiary education investments, including health education (Salmi and Hauptman 2006a). Table 7.1 reflects the growth in secondary education in sub-Saharan Africa (one of the critical geographic areas for health workers) and suggests the growth in the demand for tertiary education — including health education will be robust (UNESCO, 2010).

As recent developing country, economic growth has typically been between 3 and 6 percent per annum, continued growth in this range will offer new opportunities to harness gains in human resource development, especially the production of health workers via increased volume and efficiency of investments in tertiary level health training.

A number of strategies to address the health worker shortage, as outlined in the WHO 2006 World Health Report, focus on three areas: *entry* through better planning, education and recruitment; *workforce* through better management of existing health workers; and *exit* by improving health worker retention (WHO, 2006, 2008). This chapter focuses on financing issues related to *entry*.

While there are numerous policy options available to promote expansion of health education, this chapter will not necessarily advocate for a particular approach, but rather focus on two goals: (1) identify historical financing patterns in education and health education, and (2) relate how finance theory (capital structure, risk) applies to policy and financing with respect to health education institutions in developing countries.

Table 7.1 Growth in Secondary School Enrollment, Selected sub-Sahara African Nations (gross enrollment ratio)

Country	1985[a]	1995	2009–2012[b]		1985[a]	1995	2009–2012[b]
Benin	18.6	13.2	51.4	Malawi	5.9	11.8	34.2
Botswana	28.2	57.1	81.7	Mali	7.6	11.7	39.5
Burkina Faso	3.7	—	22.6	Mauritania	14.3	16.2	27.0
Burundi	3.3	6.4	28.0	Mauritius	48.6	61.7	90.9
Cameroon	21.3	25.0	51.3	Mozambique	7.1	7.3	26.4
Cape Verde	11.8	—	89.7	Namibia	37.4	57.7	—
Chad	6.0	7.9	25.4	Niger	5.2	6.5	14.4
Comoros	28.5	20.0	—	Nigeria	33.0	—	44.0
Congo, DR	22.0	24.7	39.8	Rwanda	6.5	—	35.8
Congo, Rep.	62.6	48.5	—	São Tome and Principe	—	—	69.2
Cote d'Ivoire	18.9	21.7	—	Senegal	12.2	14.9	42.1
Eritrea	—	13.7	32.6	Sierra Leone	19.3	—	—
Ethiopia	11.0	9.9	37.6	South Africa	52.0	82.9	93.8
Gabon	38.5	43.3	—	Sudan	17.9	19.1	39.0
Gambia, The	17.8	23.2	54.1	Swaziland	36.5	46.9	60.0
Ghana	38.8	33.4	59.2	Tanzania	3.3	5.3	35.1
Guinea	13.7	12.1	41.7	Togo	18.3	21.4	56.5
Kenya	—	39.9	60.2	Uganda	9.8	11.1	28.1
Lesotho	21.5	30.4	49.2	Zambia	18.1	24.5	—
Madagascar	30.0	14.2	31.1	Zimbabwe	41.5	40.6	—

Notes: Gross enrollment ratio is the number of pupils enrolled in a given level of education regardless of age expressed as a percentage of the population in the theoretical age group for that level of education.

— = not available.

[a]Comoros, Namibia, and South Africa figures from 1986.

[b]Most recent report from 2009–2012.

Source: World Development Indicators, 2013, June 15, accessed at http://data.worldbank.org/data-catalog/world-development-indicators. Washington, DC: World Bank.

Tertiary Education Finance

As is the case generally, financing options for tertiary education institutions depend on organizational form. Private for-profit models allow for both debt and traditional equity (via the sale of shares of ownership) as sources of finance, while non-profits and state institutions are more so constrained to debt when seeking external funding although retained earnings (if the surpluses exist) and charitable donations serve as other potential forms of equity for non-profits and/or government entities. There is a long tradition of private non-profit and state provision of tertiary education in both developing and developed countries. Typically these forms are reliant on taxes, bonds, individual fees/tuition, and endowments to fund operations. However, for-profit models are emerging in both developed and developing countries in tertiary education, even in health education sectors (such as entry level nursing degrees via online/for-profit institutions). As such, capital structure (balance between debt and equity) and equity risk may increasingly gain relevance if for-profit models continue to emerge.

Given that financing structure depends on organizational form, part of the discussion surrounding financing should include not only the nature of revenues and costs for educational institutions, but also the degree to which the private sector could play a role in the financing and provision of medical education (see Chapter 7 for more on private sector role in health finance).

A History of Public or External Subsidization

Generally, the cost structure for tertiary education favors either a public or "private subsidized" model for the provision of education (although financing frequently taps both public and private sources). Unlike standard private sector business models ("For profit" in Figure 7.1), the "sticker price" to the individual for tertiary education often is a fraction of the school's cost of providing it (even without any individual regional grants or scholarships) ("Not-for-profit" in Figure 7.1). This explains why private institutions in tertiary education markets typically are in the form of not-for-profit institutions and are heavily reliant on endowments or other

For-Profit Firm   Not-for-Profit Educational Institution

Revenues = Costs + Profit   Costs =Tuition revenues + Subsidy

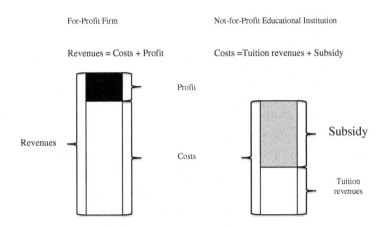

Figure 7.1   Cost Structure in Education Markets
Source: Authors' characterization adapted from Winston *et al*. (1998).

private support (e.g. charities, limited state funding) (Winston *et al*., 1998; Winston, 1999). The nature and timing of labor and capital costs for educational institutions is discussed in more detail below.

For US medical schools, teaching is not the primary source of revenues. In allopathic schools, the revenues from student tuition and fees are a minor fraction of the total revenues. Estimates suggest that tuition contributes just 10 percent of revenues in private freestanding medical schools. Instead, the bulk of revenues stem from health care service delivery and research activities. Osteopathic schools, which rely on voluntary clinical faculty, can cover their lower costs with a greater share of tuition revenues, representing 40 percent of the total (Korn, 1996).

Health Education Costs: What Financing Covers

In Africa, comparative studies on unit costs in higher education have shown that education in Africa tends to be relatively expensive highlighting African universities' low internal efficiencies. Costs components for medical institutions can be classified across various typologies such as the frequency of expenditure (one-time/initial versus recurrent), the type of input (labor versus capital), and the degree of variability (fixed versus variable). While the capital expenditure is an important component of finance, typically capital costs are highest during initial development of the school's physical plant and represent a fixed/initial cost. After the initial costs, capital maintenance costs generally are estimated in the range between 10 and 25 percent of total costs. Figure 7.2 summarizes the sources of finance which support the development of health workers at health education institutions.

Health professional education is more labor intensive than other types of higher education. There is a degree of socialization that necessitates lower student-to-teacher ratios and interaction as a pre-requisite to developing proper health professional-to-patient relationships. Therefore, the recurrent costs are even larger than other types of higher education recurrent costs. Labor, the salaries for highly qualified knowledge workers, constitute the majority of educational costs. Universities employ a high number of expatriates, with international market salaries, taking between 25 and 50 percent of teaching positions and non-teaching staff who outnumber teaching staff in some cases at a ratio of 2:1 (Banya and Elu, 2001). A 2010 survey of African Medical Schools indicates the relative scale of labor and recurrent capital costs in annual budgets (Table 7.2) (Mullan *et al.*, 2011).

Given the centrality of labor in the cost equation, cost estimation methodologies ideally identify the work hours, wages, and activities of these knowledge workers and attribute their activities (often impacting both education and health delivery) appropriately. Figure 7.3 summarizes some of the specific categories of costs for both recurrent (mainly labor) and capital-focused (mainly fixed) costs.

Because medical education straddles both the education and health sectors, identifying the recurrent and capital costs specific to medical education becomes complex. Health education institutions often create joint outputs which include research and health service production. In pre-service settings, the infrastructure used for training health workers is typically shared with the training of other university students. During the in-service phase, the infrastructure for training is shared with that of service delivery. As a result, it is difficult to separate out the actual costs of training health workers from the costs of training other university students, providing health care services or conducting R&D. Some theorists argue that the appropriate economic cost extends to the resources required for research and health service provision as these components

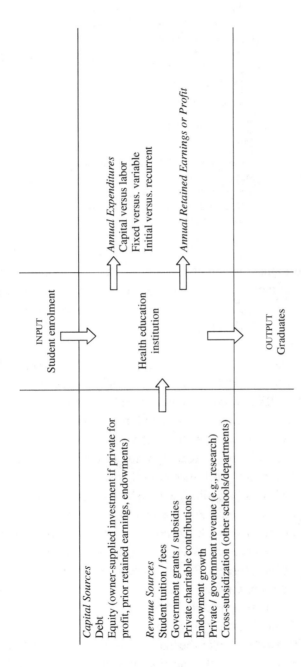

Figure 7.2 Revenues, Expenditures, and Output at Health Education Institutions

Table 7.2 Annual Expenditure Shares in African Medical Schools (mean percentages)

Professional personnel	45.4
Goods and services	19.0
Capital equipment	17.8
Non-professional personnel	14.3
Other	3.5

Source: SAMSS (Sub-Saharan African Medical School Survey) 2013, June 10, accessed at http://www.samss.org/samss.upload/wysiwyg/SAMSS%20Report_FinalV2_120110b.pdf.

also contribute to the educational mission of these institutions. Naturally cost estimates for these "total resource" cost estimates typically are larger than estimates which calculate either the "proportional share" or "marginal cost" of medical education.

Cost studies in Table 7.3 shows how expensive medical education is (Beciu and Haddad, 2009a, 2009b; Bicknell *et al.*, 2001; Franzini *et al.*, 1997; Goodwin *et al.*, 1997; Rein *et al.*, 1997; Valberg *et al.*, 1994; Vimolket *et al.*, 2003). Training a medical student in the United States has been estimated to cost more than $100,000 per year (2013 US dollars). If the business of teaching medical students were profitable, schools would be able to rely on tuition as a greater portion of their revenues, and there would be many more for-profit medical schools. However, that is not the case in the United States. Medical schools are all not-for-profit or public institutions. This may be due to US accreditation standards recommending that medical schools should be not-for-profit institutions, but this is typically the case in most developed and developing nations (at least with respect to physician training). Reputable schools that produce most of a country's graduates are typically public or not-for-profit institutions with long traditions of mission-oriented objectives.

Educational provision for lower cadre health workers (from nurses to public health workers) may be more feasible given the lower costs associated with these forms of education may allow for private for-profit

a. Sources of Finance

Individual / family	Private (for-profit)	Private (Not-for-Profit)	Public
• Student/family wages, income, wealth • Alumni gifts • Donations	• Bonds or equity • Student loans (banks) • Microfinance initiatives (for profit, including mobile applications for lower health cadres) • Research partnerships (private firms) • Corporate contributions	• Bonds • Foundation grants (or loans) • Endowments • Social microfinance (e.g. Grameen Bank) • North–South academic partnerships • NGO finance	• Bonds • Taxes (general taxation, VAT, industry/individual specific taxes) • Vouchers, scholarships and student loans • External government or multilateral aid/loans • Contracting out (to private organizations)

b. Provision: by Type of Tertiary Educational Institution

Private (for-profit)	Private (not-for-profit)	Public
• For-profit organizations (generally more focused on vocational/lower health cadre education)	• Ecumenical organizations (esp. for education of lower cadre/rural cases) • Regular universities • Institutions run by non-governmental organizations	• Public education at health institutions

c. Capital and Recurrent Expenditures

Recurrent expenditures	Capital expenses / investments
Labor: salaries for teachers, researchers, staff Non-labor: Education commodities (books, materials, supplies), Maintenance, depreciation (related to prior capital investments)	Infrastructure / Physical plant property and equipment Can include teaching, research and health delivery facilities (e.g. labs, hospital space), student/faculty housing, equipment, furnishings, municipal service (e.g. water)

Figure 7.3   Finance and Spending of Different Types of Educational Institutions

Note: Costs may capture either the resources devoted solely to teaching (marginal cost of education approach) or all of the elements that affect the quality of education including research and health service delivery costs (total resource cost approach).

Source: Patrinos and Sosale (2007).

Table 7.3   Selected Medical Education Cost Studies across Countries (Physicians)

Country	Study	Metric	Study year	Study cost estimate	Inflation adjustment	Convert to US$ (2014)	Standardize Metric to Cost Per Graduate and Convert to US$ (2013)
Canada	Valberg *et al.*	Annual cost per student	1994	C$48,330	C$70,720	$63,936	$350,421
Ghana	Beciu and Jacob	Annual cost per student	2009	$8,975	$15,201	$6,589	$56,935
Thailand	Vimolket *et al.*	Cost per graduate	2003	฿2,174,091	฿3,004,615	$92,507	$95,969
US	Rein *et al.*	Cost per graduate	1994–1995	$357,000	$572,838	$572,838	$732,802
US	Goodwin *et al.*	Annual cost per student	1994–1995	$69,992	$112,308	$112,308	$574,681
US	Franzini *et al.*	Annual cost per student	1994–1995	$57,370	$92,055	$92,055	$471,046
US	AMA	Annual cost per student	2002	$80,000–$105,000	$107,420–$140,988	$107,420–$140,988	$635,550 (mean)
US	Jones and Korn	Annual cost per student	1996	$72,000–$93,000	$110,891–$143,234	$110,891–$143,234	$650,197 (mean)
UK	UK, PSSRU	Cost per graduate	2014	£175,332	£175,332	$288,503	$305,397

Note: Although reported in 2009 dollars, the Ghanaian estimate declines due to the shift in exchange rates (devaluation of Ghanaian Cedi) after 2009.

entry — particularly if regulation is favorable. However, the capacity to rely on individual financing for these lower cadre positions may be muted as the long run earnings for graduates naturally is less than that of physicians.

Finance Implications of New Education Models

The potential for new organizational forms in health education institutions (Chapter 10) may have important implications for finance and policy for educational institutions and governments. These include:

(1) In situations when for-profit educational firms enter the market, the modes of finance increase — debt remains a source of finance but options for accessing equity (via sale of ownership shares in the organization) increase.
(2) To the extent that new organizational forms reduce initial fixed costs or limit expenditures on salaries, the resources required decrease and potential for positive return on investment (or retained earnings for non-profits) increases.[1] This process would naturally help promote entry of new institutions.
(3) Investors or financing institutions will increasingly evaluate market risk to justify investment in education institutions that may compete in potentially monopolistic or monopsonistic markets (for example, when policies favor state provision of education).
(4) Regulators seeking to prompt entry by for-profit (or not-for-profit) private educational institutions should examine current financing policies (particular state subsidization restrictions for loans).

Financial Structure for Private For-Profits (Debt versus Equity)

The mechanisms for financing operations and investments are a significant but often overlooked part of health care and health education delivery. Health care and education capital investments are made by both public and private sources and the instruments used can broadly be categorized into two forms: debt and equity (equity can be interpreted to include grants and charitable contribution in the case of non-profits). Capital structure refers to the relative amount of debt and equity which finance the organization. Capital structure is important as it affects the cost of capital or the effective return that programs and projects must generate to remain financially viable. While non-profits are not beholden to equity investors, they still should generate sufficient positive economic returns in order to remain financially viable and sustain their mission.

Cost of Capital

In both for-profit and not-for-profit private institutions — the use of debt and equity comes with a cost. The annual cost of debt typically is the interest rate required to service the debt. As this is a contractually obligated amount, the cost of debt to the organization is transparent. The cost of equity, particularly forms which are common among non-profits such as grants or charitable contributions, is somewhat more opaque to estimate For-profits may infer the implicit expected returns required to justify an equity investment (or cost of equity) on the basis of tools such as the capital asset pricing model (CAPM, discussed later) and other methods which help estimate the relative risk and return required to justify investment from equity holders for organizations which are small or privately held or both. The cost of equity typically exceeds the cost of debt, particularly in the case of for-profits, given that debt obligations are paid off before equity holders access any additional earnings in the form of dividends or profit shares. Given this "residual claimant" status, equity investors are at greater risk than debt holders and, as such, demand a higher expected return on investment in order to justify the assumption of additional risk. Even in the case of non-profits which receive a large grants, donor aid or charitable contributions, there is an expectation for some positive return on investment for equity, but the percent return is somewhat more uncertain and depends, in part, on the mission of the organization and the degree to which it is willing to sacrifice financial return for mission-oriented programs (some of which may not be financially viable). Often, it is assumed that the return on equity for a non-profit (or "cost of equity") should be positive, but likely less (in percentage terms) than the cost of equity for a for-profit. In either the for-profit or non-profit case, the total cost of capital depends of the relative shares of debt and equity that finance the organization and the cost associated with either form of capital (less any tax advantage associated with debt and interest payments which may reduce tax burden) as depicted in Equation (7.1), the cost of capital,

$$\text{Cost of capital} = [W_D {}^* R_D {}^* (1 - T_C)] + [W_E {}^* R_E] \qquad (7.1)$$

where

R_D = Cost of debt
R_E = Cost of equity
T_C = Corporate tax rate (if applicable)
W_D = Share of capital in form of debt (= Debt/Value)
W_E = Share of capital in form of equity (= Equity/Value)
Value = Amount of capital (Debt + Equity).

Generally firms seek to balance their capital structure between debt and equity in order to minimize their cost of capital (relative to their operational constraints). A lower cost of capital results in a greater ability to invest in financially marginal projects. Under conditions when equity costs exceed debt cost (often the case in the for-profit sector), capital costs are minimized under limited debt (in part since interest payments reduce taxable income and in part since debt usually is less risky than equity since lenders are contractually obligated to make their interest payments first). Table 7.4, a hypothetical scenario, demonstrates that the cost of capital may be minimized, in some cases, when a limited amount of debt is adopted.

However, in the case of private non-profits, the effective cost of equity can, in principle, be less than the cost of debt, particularly if the initial start-up equity is effectively provided by donors or NGOs (which do not seek out a return) and lenders of debt (banks or potential bond purchasers) perceive the financial risks of providing health education services in developing countries as a particularly risky endeavor (lowering the likelihood of successful payment of interest and eventual retirement of debt). In this case, cost of capital is likely minimized by avoiding debt.

Table 7.4   Hypothetical Cost of Capital Estimates as Debt Share Increases

Percent debt	Cost of equity	Cost of debt[a]	Cost of capital[b]
0	0.25	0.10	0.250
10	0.26	0.12	0.246
20	0.27	0.14	0.244
30	0.28	0.16	0.244
40	0.29	0.18	0.246
50	0.30	0.20	0.250
60	0.31	0.22	0.256
70	0.32	0.24	0.264
80	0.33	0.26	0.274
90	0.34	0.28	0.286
100	0.35	0.30	0.30

Notes: [a] After tax cost of debt.
[b] Shaded regions represent the level of debt which minimizes cost of capital in this hypothetical organization.

Investment Decisions and the Cost of Capital

The cost of capital serves as a "hurdle rate" which organizations use to assess whether investments in projects, goods or service lines (such as educational services) are financially viable. Whether projects are subsidized by public programs/financing (such as direct educational grants or public tuition loan programs) or private payments for tuition, organizations should optimally meet or exceed the cost of capital "hurdle rate" on any project they pursue in order to remain financially viable. Part of the challenge for policy makers interested in spurring interest in the private provision of health education is to assess the cost of capital for various organization types (for-profit, not-for-profit) and then examine whether it is realistic for such organizations to participate sustainably in health education markets.

Another important concept with respect to cost of capital is the notion of risk. In theory, relatively risky projects (for example, if tuition payments are uncertain) may justify a "risk premium" which will raise the cost of capital associated with these riskier projects. As such, stability in revenues (and costs) will help increase the likelihood of adopting projects in health education. Policies that improve stability promote entry even if the expected returns remain constant. As such policy makers interested in promoting a favorable investment climate should not only examine the expected returns but also the likely level of consistency and stability in these returns (lower risk will prompt greater entry, naturally).

Forms of Debt and Equity in For-Profit and Not-For-Profit Private Organizations

Equity (For-Profit)

The concept of equity is more defined in the case of for-profit organizations. Typically for-profit organizations raise equity capital via an offering of ownership shares in the organization. Retained earnings (those profits not distributed to owners in the form of dividend payments) are another form of equity on the balance sheet of private organizations. In the case of publicly traded for-profit firms (rarely the case in education, but occasionally relevant), the expected return that equity-holders demand from their investment serves as the effective "cost of equity" or the annual return (typically stated in percentage terms) that the organization should realize for their investors. This estimated return is frequently estimated for publicly traded for-profits via the Capital Asset Pricing Model (or CAPM) or a similar variant such as the Fama–French Three Factor Model (2002), which estimates the relative risk of the business with respect to the historic returns of the organization and the market (CAPM is discussed later in this chapter). The funds with which the public purchases the ownership shares act as equity that the organization can spend to improve operations and undertake new service (or product) initiatives. But these investments or service lines should generate net returns equal or in excess of the "expected" return generated in the CAPM model (after accounting for the share of capital from debt and the cost of debt). In privately owned for-profits, more common in health education within particular geographies (Asia) and cadre types (nurses, medical assistants), the cost of equity expected from private investors is typically larger than the publicly traded case as these organizations are smaller (size premium), less diversified, and generally riskier. Hence, one approach to estimating what the cost of equity is for privately held for-profits is to take the expected cost of equity for a similar publicly traded for-profit and then add additional premiums for size or risk.

Equity (Not-For-Profit)

In the case of non-profits, the sources of equity are somewhat different. Frequently the initial start-up equity capital for a not-for-profit stems from an initial charitable contribution or subsidy from a sponsoring institution (or even government or donor programs supporting non-profit private sector development). As there are no legal owners in the not-for-profit structure, the use of market data to infer an expected returns for equity is not feasible (as one might infer from the CAPM model) and it is unclear what type of "return" should be achieved to maintain financial stability and incentives. Some argue that there should be no expectation of return as the funds were intended for community development (in this case, development of the health workforce) and, so long as that goal is met, no returns are necessary. However, given the reality of depreciation of assets (buildings, labs, facilities) and the common expectation that non-profit will expand their operations over time — a strong argument can be made for having a positive return on investment. As there is no investor (or residual claimant) in the non-profit scenario, these retained earnings are captured by the organization entirely and can be reinvested in the existing operations of the business or new initiatives which also serve the mission. Typically, even with this expectation of a return, the magnitude of the return on equity is often lower than the return required to service debt (particularly for financially risky investments relative to expected returns) — as is often the case health-related non-profits which seek return on equity at levels less than 10 percent per annum on their initial equity investment. One of the benefits of establishing an appropriate return on equity benchmark for health education institutions is the financial discipline it imparts on decision-making for the organization going forward. It focuses effort on those services and initiatives that are both financially feasible and mission-driven. Moreover, this discipline helps ensure that the organization will be financially viable to serve its mission in the future. Selecting the appropriate benchmark is a balancing act. If the benchmark is too low the future financing of the organization is at risk, but if it is too high then fewer beneficial projects and services will be undertaken.

Debt

While non-profits are constrained in their access to equity given the restriction on sale of ownership share, no such constraint exists in the debt market. Both for-profits and non-profits use similar tools to increase capital via debt through (a) loans from small investors, (b) a line of credit with a bank, (c) bank loans, and (d) bond offerings. Unlike equity, in which equity investors receive rewards when profits are generated, bond investors, banks and other lending entities are, by contract, required to receive interest payments. Among for-profit private organizations, this typically means that there is less risk (and hence typically lower returns) for debt investors than equity investors. The cost of debt, typically measured by the effective interest rate on the debt (less the value of reduced taxes from reduction of taxable income from interest payments), frequently is less than the cost of equity in for-profits (Table 7.5). However, in the non-profit private sector, the cost of debt may be more than the cost of equity in some instances. In many scenarios, particularly for health educations institutions in developing country markets with a limited financial track record, the cost of equity (as discussed above) may well be less than the cost of debt. In these scenarios, the use of equity as a capital source is preferred although typically equity contributions are constrained and some debt may be required to fully fund operations or start-up costs. Given risks, however, early-stage non-profits may find debt to be prohibitively expensive to issue, but over time after establishment of a financial track record debt may be more feasible (and less expensive) to access.

Table 7.5   Cost of Capital Debt and Equity Components across Organization Type

Organization type[a]	Potential sources of equity	Cost of equity	Potential sources of debt	Cost of debt
For profit (publicly traded) e.g. University of Phoenix (Apollo Group — US/Intl)	Sale of shares to public (ownership)/initial public offering, Retained earnings	Cost of equity reflects the expected returns that private investors demand given the risk level of the organization. The Capital Asset Pricing Model (CAPM) and three-factor Fama and French CAPM are examples of methods used to estimate the cost of equity for publically traded for-profit firms. Typically, the cost of equity is higher than the cost of debt since debt holders bear less risk (debt gets paid out before equity holders receive returns).	Bond issue Bank loan Line of credit Institutional loan	Interest rate (variable or fixed) on debt. Typically, the cost of debt is less than the cost of equity for for-profits.
For profit (privately held) e.g. Manipal Education and Medical Group (India/Intl)	Sale of shares to private investors (venture capital, angel investors), Retained earnings	The reduced size (usually) and illiquidity likely lead to a higher cost of equity for privately held for-profits relative to publicly traded for-profits.	Same as above	Same as above
Not-for-profit (mature) e.g. Aga Khan Foundation (Health Education, Kenya)	Charitable or government contributions (especially for recurrent expenditures) Grants, Retained earnings	As not-for-profits do not have owners (by law), the concept and sources of equity are somewhat different. Initial charitable contributions (either private or public) and grants may serve as initial "seed" funding for capital development. Organizations may also fund new ventures with existing revenue sources	Same as above	Cost of debt may exceed the cost of equity, especially when equity is in the form of charitable contributions.

			(cross-subsidization models). In either case, the cost that is ascribed to equity typically is lower than in the for-profit scenario, but the "correct" amount is not well specified.	
Not-for-profit (early stage) e.g. Catholic University of Mozambique (Medical School)	Charitable or government contributions (especially. for capital expenditures), Grants Retained earnings	Early stage private health education non-profits usually have very limited resources to establish facilities and operations. Reliance on existing revenue sources (e.g. hospital or other revenue-generating portions of the university) may provide some of the initial capital and also serve to help minimize the absolute costs required to establish operations (e.g. if the university engineering department assists with construction, refurbishment of the facilities instead of an external firm). As the organization matures and establishes a financial track record, new forms and sources of capital may become available to expand operations (e.g. more banks willing to offer loans). Also the organization should review capital policy periodically as it grows to determine to optimal level of debt relative to equity.	Same as above	Cost of debt may exceed the cost of equity, especially when equity is in the form of charitable contributions. Debt may not be an option, given the high potential borrowing rates for risky enterprises.

Note: [a] In developing-country health education markets, private contribution is more likely to emerge from not-for-profit entities although some for-profit initiatives may enter specific niche areas.

An Economic Framework for Assessing Capital Structure

Capital structure theory[2] helps explain the mix of debt and equity firms use to finance their investments. It is most relevant in the for-profit context, but there are implications for private non-profits and even government supported health education institutions. The starting point for a *for-profit firm* is Modigliani–Miller's capital structure theory, which holds as one of its propositions that under perfect market conditions (i.e. no taxes, no transaction costs, and the costs of borrowing are the same for corporations and individuals), a firm's value is unaffected by its choice of capital structure (Brealey and Myers, 2003; Modigliani and Miller, 1958). Further work on capital structure has sought to highlight the conditions in which capital structure *does* matter. A number of factors may influence the capital structure decisions of a firm such as the tax deductibility of interest (relevant for for-profits), costs of financial distress, agency costs, informational asymmetries, etc. (see Box 7.1). There are still unresolved differences between the competing theories on capital structure. The goal is not to provide supporting evidence for any one capital structure theory, but to offer insight for capital and financing decisions for health worker education. The existing theories provide a framework in which we can model our understanding of the appropriate financing that should be made available to health care education institutions in developing countries.

Funding Initial Capital/Physical Plant Costs

While health education is generally a labor-intensive undertaking, the efficiency and effectiveness of the labor depends on the quality and appropriateness of the physical capital that it is combined with. Although building and equipment expenses account for a minority share of health-related expenditures and health education expenditures, the "footprint" with respect to health capital projects determines how and where health resources will be spent in the future and how efficient and equitable the health system can be over time (Rechel *et al.*, 2009). Moreover, the upfront, fixed costs of establishing new educational institutions (a necessity to both retain quality and increase production simultaneously) will require institutions to address capital start-up fixed costs as an initial

Box 7.1 Theories and Determinants of Capital Structure

Modigliani–Miller theory forms the basis for theories on capital structure. The theorem provides two propositions:

Proposition I: Under perfect market conditions (and without taxes), a firm's value is unaffected by its choice of capital structure.

Proposition II: The expected yield on common stock relates linearly to the firm's debt-to-equity ratio.

The key assumptions that underlie these propositions are no taxes, no transaction costs, and the same lending rates for individuals and corporations. The implications of this theory provide insight into how reality deviates from these assumptions and propositions (Brealey and Myers, 2003; Modigliani and Miller, 1958). Potential determinants of capital structure that would cause a firm's value to be affected by its financing decisions are as follows:

1. *The Static Trade-off Model* states that firms determine their optimal capital structure on the basis of the costs and benefits of raising additional capital. Trade-offs are made between the costs and benefits of taxes, bankruptcy costs, and agency costs of debt and equity:

   a. An important benefit of debt finance is the tax deductions for interest payments which serves as an incentive to finance with more leverage. But increasing debt share of finance also increases the effective tax rate relative to a fixed equity investment which may temper the incentive to use debt from the perspective of the equity holders. In general, the tax implications (typically only relevant for for-profits) are an important consideration in determining optimal capital structure.

   b. The demand for debt may also be affected by the potential costs of bankruptcy (which favors using less debt) and agency conflicts between stockholders and bondholders (Fama and French, 1993, 2002). The threat of bankruptcy costs should be higher for firms with volatile earnings and low profitability. Hence, firms that are smaller, less-diversified, or not very profitable may use less debt. In the

(Continued)

Box 7.1   (*Continued*)

education market, policies with respect to transferability of government loans toward private institutions and other policies that affect distribution of students across schools will naturally affect the extent (and volatility) of earnings for private institutions.

2. *Agency costs* are the costs due to the conflict of interests and incentives of those groups that have a claim to the firm's resources. The types of conflicts that can arise are as follows (Harris and Raviv, 1991; Jensen and Meckling, 1976):

   a. *Shareholders versus managers [Favors More Debt]*. When managers have less than full claim to the firm's profits, they have an incentive to divert resources away from profit-maximizing activities and toward their own personal benefit (e.g. excessive salaries, perks). This problem is minimized, as managers increase their share of the firm's equity. The use of debt to raise capital also minimizes this conflict of interest since debt commits the firm's cash flows to finance interest expense and therefore limits the size of the cash flows controlled by managers. Debt-holders can threaten liquidation when cash flows are poor and if management's absolute stake in the firm held constant, then the use of debt also increases management's share of firm equity.

   b. *Shareholders versus debt holders — the "asset substitution effect" [Favors More Debt — from equity holders perspective]*. With cofinancing from debt, equity holders have incentives to take on higher risk investments. In a successful investment, equity holders capture all the gain above the costs of debt, whereas debt holders receive only their fixed interest and principle. Equity holders have an incentive to undertake a higher risk and return investment opportunity, whereas debt holders do not.

   c. *Shareholders versus debt holders — the "debt-overhang effect"[Favors Less Debt]*. If a firm has excessive debt relative to equity, raising new investment financing will be difficult. This is because existing debt holders tend to hold more senior claims to the firm's resources. Therefore, in cases of liquidation, holders of

(*Continued*)

Box 7.1 *(Continued)*

newer issues of debt and equity will be less likely to get their money back.

3. *Asymmetric information.* When managers or other insiders hold private information about the firm's characteristics or investment opportunities, asymmetric information results *vis-à-vis* investors. This may have implications for the cost of the financing decisions.

   a. *Pecking order hypothesis.* If investors are less informed than insiders about the value of the firm's assets, value of equity finance raised in the market may be underpriced. As a result, the pecking order framework states that the firm does not set a defined debt-to-value ratio target but in making financing decisions it prefers internal to external financing and debt to equity if it issues securities (Myers, 1983). The cost of issuing new securities may outweigh the other costs and benefits of dividends and debt. As a result, firms prefer financing new investments in the following order: retained earnings, safe debt, risky debt, and then equity, when under duress.

   b. *Debt signaling.* Since managers may have better knowledge of the firm's value, they will issue debt as a signal to investors of firm value. High debt signals a high-quality firm. Low-quality firms will not issue more debt, even if to imitate high-quality firms, because they have a higher cost of bankruptcy. Consequently, firm value is directly correlated with debt–equity values. Variations of this concept explore the consequences of low-quality firms that issue debt.

4. *Corporate control decisions* are affected by the capital structure of a firm. This focuses on the equity component of capital structure and ways equity consequently controls the firm's decision-making power. The relationship between equity held by managers and equity held by outsiders influences the firm's value. Specifically, the capital structure determines how much equity ownership a manager has in a firm, and consequently how easily the firm and the decision-making power of the firm can be taken over.

barrier to entry. Estimates range for full costs of start-up to establish capital and are naturally dependent on the type of institutions (MD versus nurse versus public health), but estimates peg to cost of a medical school start up in sub-Saharan Africa, an important geography for health worker generation, between US$2 million and US$20 million.

Capital investments in medical education traditionally have two components: an undergraduate training institution and a teaching hospital. Greenfield investment or rehabilitation involves building or fixing an undergraduate training institution that is vertically integrated with a teaching hospital; or some combination of an undergraduate training institution that is standalone or associated with an tertiary-level institution; and a separate teaching hospital.

The degree of needed rehabilitation or Greenfield infrastructure investment varies within each country context. Post-conflict countries like Sierra Leone and Liberia have medical schools that are in dire need of massive rehabilitation and new equipment. Other public medical schools that have been better established may be more focused on investing in technology to modernize their medical education. The costs of these investments would vary widely, depending on the specific state of the country's medical education infrastructure and strategy for expanding it.

Last, while capital finance is an important first step, salaries for highly qualified staff are the most significant long-run recurrent cost for most medical education institutions. Shortages in the availability of instructors and clinical educators are a crucial barrier to increasing output of quality health workers. Perhaps novel forms of education (e.g. internet teaching) could help leverage the capacity of current faculty to effectively instruct a larger number of students without sacrificing quality, but addressing the educator supply issue is of central importance (see Chapter 10 for more on innovative educational approaches).

Evaluation of Risk

As the financing models shifts from a donation or subsidy mechanism to an investment mechanism (with both social or market rates of return expected), techniques and approaches to evaluate investment risk become increasingly relevant as a finance prerequisite.

Table 7.6 Select Financial Strategies across the Life Cycle for Private Health Education Institutions

Stage	Minimizing cost of capital	Limiting costs	Maximizing revenues
Start up (years 0–5)	• Access necessary capital using the least costly forms first (possibly equity in the case of not-for-profit charitable contributions)	• "Renting" part-time faculty • Using resources from other departments/schools within the university (or health system) to reduce initial start-up expenses (e.g. engineering faculty assist with redesign of medical school) • Rehabilitating existing facilities versus new construction	• Consider front-loaded tuition payments (multiple years of tuition paid in bulk up front) to assist with initial facility development or labor costs • Examine feasibility of differential tuition (out-of-country versus in-country; non-merit versus merit) • Cross-subsidies from other tuition sources in profitable components of the university and/or health system
Emerging (years 5–10)	• After establishing financial history, reassess forms of capital. Cost of debt and cost of equity may have changed	• Focus on limiting recurrent costs now that initial capital costs have been incurred • Depreciate existing assets (plan for future replacement)	• Develop partnerships with NGOs non-governmental organizations, other academic medical centers, donors, and industry sources to supplement and complement existing educational services with revenue-generating research or clinical services/programs
Mature (years 10+)	• Develop a long-run optimal capital allocation between debt and equity • Selectively refinance debt and/or equity if possible to achieve target debt-to-equity ratio	• Consider whether additional expansion of educational services may lead to economies of scale	• Demonstrating quality and improving reputation over time may increase access to sources of student financial aid and potentially increase tuition revenue

The capital asset pricing model is a general framework for evaluating the relationship between risk and return. It is a general financial model which is easily applied to numerous investment types, including a portfolio of capital finance projects.[3] Equation (7.2), the basic formula for the capital asset pricing model, stipulates that the expected return on a particular investment R_I should equal the risk free rate of return (R_F) plus a risk premium which is related to the risk of the investment *relative* to all other investments in the portfolio of projects (beta, β) and the difference between the expected return across the portfolio and the risk free rate (R_M–R_F).(Ross, 1993).[4]

$$R_I = R_F + \beta*(R_M - R_F) \tag{7.2}$$

The model has three major implications with respect to investment decisions, including decisions for health education finance projects (Table 7.6). First, as with many financial models, investments with greater risk (after adjusting for covariance with other investments) will generally have to yield a "risk premium" to justify investment — if risk is higher, expected returns should be larger. Second, the risk of any individual investment from the perspective of the investor depends on all of the other investments in the portfolio. A high risk individual investment which has countercyclical returns with respect to the rest of the firm's basket may be less risky (and not require as large a risk premium) with respect to the investor than a lower risk investment which is strongly correlated with the other investments in the market bundle. Third, as a consequence, governments seeking to partner with private investors to build capital projects may find that those with well-diversified portfolios (typically with multiple projects across a range of geographies) may have a greater capacity to invest in individually risky projects if the anticipated returns from the projects are countercyclical to the other investments in the investor's portfolio.

The model has implications for motivating private finance in health education. First, from the perspective of a regulator in a developing country, a country must be careful to account for the risk associated with private capital investment before penalizing industries for "excessive" profits or adjusting reimbursements downward — otherwise investors will exit. In the past regulatory restrictions of private sector health insurers has led to exits. Given the high risk profile associated with setting up plans due to poor information on patients, adverse selection and moral hazard in these environments, larger returns may have to occur in order to justify entry from private sector organizations (Preker *et al.*, 2007a,b). A similar situation may exist in the health education realm as uncertainty about regulation risk (willingness to allow new private institutions to compete against existing schools and requirements for ensuring quality of education) may limit investment appetite. Institutional capacity to provide credentialing of private institutions is another important factor that may affect market risk. Unless new entrants can attain accreditation from a reliable government or quasi-government source, uncertainty about the quality of the education in novel institutions may limit the attractiveness of these institutions to potential students, threaten revenue streams, and undermine the validity of the educational enterprise. There are concerns about the capacity of the Ministry of Education (MOE) or other government regulators to effectively certify the quality of education given the resource constraints in most ministries.

Second, to the extent possible, attracting a private investors with well diversified portfolios may likely increase entry or competition in these markets (but private investors will seek out attractive country environments with sufficiently strong market potential and favorable investment climates for their voluntary investments).

Policy Support for Private Sector Development (and Access to Additional Sources of Finance)

In developing and developed countries alike, regulation has been a central feature in determining the output of medical education (while ensuring quality of graduates). In many OECD countries, governments undergo a process of centralized planning; in most cases, they forecast the need for health workers in order to determine the necessary number of health professional schools, student intake, and graduate output. Here, public financing follows centralized plans, limiting or expanding the resources available to universities and to alter student capacity. In the OECD, countries such as Australia, Belgium, Canada, France, Greece, Ireland, the Netherlands, New Zealand, Norway, Spain, Sweden, and the UK follow some form of centralized process to determine the number of slots available to medical students (Simoens and Hurst, 2006). Even if governments do not directly control the intake in medical schools, medical schools are still highly regulated by governmental or independent self-regulating bodies. These regulatory bodies can influence the supply of medical schools and health worker output through either directly limiting the number of slots available in medical schools or requiring a minimum standard for accreditation which increases the costs of producing medical graduates.

These constraints on supply distort the link found between spending on higher education and number of graduates. There is a strong correlation between spending in tertiary education and output of graduates. But because of the influential role of governing bodies over the supply of health professionals, this correlation is not as strong in the case of medical education. Unlike the relationship between higher education financing and graduate output, the financing of medical schools is not necessarily linked to physician output (Box 7.2).

Box 7.2   The Effects of Self-Regulation, Regulation, and Financing on Medical Education: US Physician Supply in the Twentieth Century

In the United States, the supply of physicians is controlled through both physician licensure requirements and medical school accreditation. Medical schools must be accredited by the Liaison Committee on Medical Education (LCME) which is empowered jointly by two non-governmental bodies, the American Medical Association (AMA), and the American Association of Medical Colleges (AAMC). At a minimum, accreditation by the LCME is required before a medical school is allowed to receive federal grants or partake in a federal loan program.

From 1930 to 1965, the growth in physician supply held pace with population growth rates of about one percent a year but could not keep up with the rising demand for health care due to technological improvements and increases in prepaid group practice plans. During this time, the

(Continued)

Box 7.2 *(Continued)*

self-regulating controls on physician supply led to a series of government interventions. In 1941, the U.S. Department of Justice found the Washington D.C. Medical Society and the AMA guilty of conspiring to monopolize trade in physician services. Then, the U.S. Congress passed the Health Professions Educational Assistance Act of 1963, requiring medical schools to increase their capacity and allow foreign doctors to practice. Through this, states built more medical schools, and existing schools received increased government funding under the condition that medical student enrollment increase by at least five percent a year (Getzen, 1997). As a result, two decades after the legislation was passed, the number of medical school graduates more than doubled.

Thus, the increase in physician supply has been predominantly influenced by legislation. The flow of public funds has served only as a political tool. In the United States, the medical student output has not matched medical school revenues. The 1963 legislation had the biggest effect on medical student output. Graduate output increased rapidly while medical school revenues grew modestly. Subsequently, medical school revenues grew the fastest from 1980 to 1995, while the number of medical students remained fairly constant.

The high degree of regulation in medical education may provide one reason for why most medical schools worldwide are publicly funded or faith-based institutions even in more market-oriented environments. The high degree of supply regulation increases the costs of production due to accreditation requirements to meet a minimum standard of education quality, limiting the profitability of medical schools — however, as noted earlier, the beneficial market signal that credentialing can confer countervails the negative costs associated with administration and regulation (which may fall upon the school or taxpayers).

With respect to finance, three policy options are proposed to countries that wish to encourage new forms of health education institutions.

(1) "Level the Playing Field" for financial resources to support both public and private high-quality institutions. If private institutions cannot

compete for government funding for education, the appeal of the market is naturally reduced. It is best to have a policy that all are welcome to apply and to use evaluative mechanisms in which the money "follows the student" or tracks results (e.g. financing according to number of students enrolled or even outcome measures such as graduates passing qualifying exams). Competition in this context can have desirable side effects.

(2) Evaluate the degree to which individuals can finance their own education. The state is heavily involved in financing higher education for health on the basis that health is an important public good. However, in many cases (not just high cadre jobs), the individual gains a substantial return on the training. Finding the appropriate level of subsidy is not easy but the student should bear at least some of the cost in relation to the expected future private income benefits.

(3) Seek novel financing sources for both fixed capital costs and recurrent expenditures. Both private and non-profit organization should consider leveraging their capabilities to extract revenue from firms or organization in the health business that can help subsidize research, health delivery and education at institutions which engage in training health workers. These may include developed country institutions (U.S. National Institutes of Health) and private firms (pharmaceuticals) seeking to conduct research and development in Africa.

Conclusions

There is an increasing recognition of the acute shortages of medical personnel and limited capacity of current health education institutions to train sufficient numbers of students to address the health demands in lower income countries.

The nature of the primary cost drivers related to capital and recurrent costs for health education institutions are discussed in this chapter. Both traditional and novel approaches to finance these costs are also discussed:

(1) Current modes of financing and delivering health education (an expensive endeavor) are unlikely to allow the significant scale-up of

health worker production that is required to meet the UN SDGs and improve other health outcomes dramatically.

(2) Novel organizational forms for health education may help reduce fixed capital expenditures and high recurrent costs (mainly for faculty), or at least serve as another stream of revenue to assist financing health education (even if the magnitude of costs remains constant/increases).

(3) Financing options increase with new organizational forms — specifically equity in for-profit private institutions. However, investment will naturally focus on potentially profitable segments of the education market. Nevertheless, these resources may free up government resources to focus on those areas needing subsidization. Investors will be attuned to risk and will evaluate the expected value of revenues relative to these risks.

(4) Government policy with respect to restrictions on loans, subsidies for schools, and accreditation can help to increase the viable market size for new entrants and reduce uncertainty among investors. There are, however, trade-offs given the transaction (monitoring) costs associated with accreditation.

There is no standard "ideal" policy with respect to health education, but governments in developing countries that seek to expand the resources available for health education should carefully examine the variety of means by which health education can be financed.

Endnotes

1. This cost reduction may be more relevant for lower cadre health worker — training institutions. Fixed costs may be reduced if the educational process becomes less reliant on physical structures (e.g. virtual education) or costs can be more easily shared across multiple institutions (as with subsidized models or twinning models).

2. The term "capital" is used both with reference to financing (debt and equity), but also with reference to physical capital (such as hospitals, clinics, production facilities). *Capital structure* refers to the mix of debt and equity to finance a firm or organization. *Health capital*, as discussed earlier, refers to physical capital.

3. In theory, there should be no difference between long-run capital investments and other forms of investment (such as shorter-run stocks or bonds). In practice, however, information on volatility, correlation, and covariance across investment options may be more readily available in equity or bond investments without a long-run capital component.

4. Technically, beta measures the covariance of the market portfolio return and the return of the individual investment, $Cov(R_I, R_M)$, divided by the variance of the market return, $Var(R_M)$. A beta measure of 0 suggests that there is no risk associated with the individual investment and the expected return for the investment equals the risk-free rate of return, R_F. A beta of 1 occurs when the volatility of the individual investment equals the volatility of the market basket and the expected return for the individual investment equals the expected return for the market bundle. When beta exceeds one, the risk of the individual investment exceeds the market bundle and the expected return for the individual investment should exceed the return on the market bundle of investments.

References

Banya, K. and J. Elu, "The World Bank and financing higher education in sub-Saharan Africa", *Higher Education*, **42**, 1–34, 2001.

Beciu, H. and D. Haddad, *Human Resources for Health: Costing Ghana's Pre-Service HRH Scale Up Plans*, Washington, DC: World Bank, 2009a.

Beciu, H. and D. Haddad, *Scaling Up Education of Health Workers in Ghana: A Country Assessment*, Washington, DC: World Bank, 2009b.

Beciu, H. and R. P. Jacob, *Global Trends in Tertiary Medical Education: Policy Recommendations for Sub-Saharan Africa*, Washington, DC: World Bank, 2009.

Bicknell, W. J., A. C. Beggs and P. V. Tham, "Determining the full costs of medical education in Thai Binh, Vietnam: A generalizable model", *Health Policy and Planning*, **16**(4), 412, 2001.

Birdsall, N., "Public spending on higher education in developing countries: Too much or too little?" *Economics of Education Review*, **15**(4), 407–419, 1996.

Brealey, R. A. and S. C. Myers. *Principles of Corporate Finance*, New York, NY: McGraw-Hill Higher Education, 2003.

Bruns, B., A. Mingat, and R. Rakotomalala, *Achieving Universal Primary Education by 2015: A Chance for Every Child*, Washington, DC: World Bank, 2003.

Chen, L. and T. Evans, "Human resources for health: Overcoming the crisis (Joint learning initiative)", Harvard University: Cambridge, MA, accessed at http://www.who.int/hrh/documents/JLi_hrh_report.pdf.

Fama, E. F. and K. R. French, "Common risk factors in the returns on stocks and bonds", *Journal of Financial Economics*, **33**(1), 3–56, 1993.

Fama, E. F. and K. R. French, "Testing trade-off and pecking order predictions about dividends and debt", *Review of Financial Studies*, **15**(1), 1–33, 2002.

Fielden, J. and N. LaRocque, "The evolving regulatory context for private education in emerging economies", Education Working Paper No. 14, International Finance Corporation (IFC), Washington, DC, 2008, 2013, July 15, accessed at http://www.ifc.org/wps/wcm/connect/7db3ed804970bff99a01da336b93d 75f/Discussion%2BPaper%2BFinal.pdf?MOD=AJPERES.

Franzini, L., M. D. Low, and M. A. Proll, "Using a cost-construction model to assess the cost of educating undergraduate medical students at the University of Texas-Houston Medical School", *Academic Medicine*, **72**(3), 228, 1997.

Getzen, T., *Health Economics*: *Fundamentals and Flow of Funds*, New York: Wiley, 1997.

Glewwe, P., M. Kremer, E. Hanushek, and F. Welch, "Schools, teachers, and education outcomes in developing countries", In *Handbook of the Economics of Education*, (eds.). by K. J. Arrow and M. D. Intriligator, pp. 945–1018, Oxford: Elsevier, 2006.

Goodwin, M. C., W. M. Gleason, and H. A. Kontos, "A pilot study of the cost of educating undergraduate medical students at Virginia Commonwealth University", *Academic Medicine*, **72**(3), 211–217, 1997.

Harris, M. and A. Raviv, "The theory of capital structure", *Journal of Finance*, **46**(1), 297–355, 1991.

IFC (International Finance Corporation), *The Business of Health in Africa*: *Partnering with the Private Sector to Improve People's Lives*, Washington, DC: International Finance Corporation, 2007.

Jensen, M. and W. Meckling, "Theory of the firm: Managerial behavior, agency costs, and capital structure", *Journal of Financial Economics*, **3**(4), 305–360, 1976.

Jones R. F. and D. Korn, "On the cost of educating a medical student", *Academic Medicine*, **72**(3), 200, 1997.

Kapur, D. and M. Crowley, "Beyond the ABCs: Higher education and developing countries", CGD Working Paper No. 139, Center for Global Development, Washington, DC, 2008.

Korn, D., *The Financing of Medical Schools: A Report of the AAMC Task Force on Medical School Financing*, Association of American Medical Colleges, Washington, DC, 1996.

MacDonagh, R., M. Jiddawi, and V. Parry, "Twinning: The future for sustainable collaboration", *BJU International*, **89**(s1), 13–17, 2002.

Modigliani, F. and M. H. Miller, "The cost of capital, corporation finance and the theory of investment", *The American Economic Review*, **48**(3), 261–297, 1958.

Mullan, F., S. Frehywot, F. Omaswa, E. Buch, C. Chen, S. R. Greysen, T. Wassermann *et al.*, "Medical schools in sub-Saharan Africa", *The Lancet*, **377**(9771), 1113–1121, 2011.

OBHE (Observatory on Borderless Higher Education). 2009. *Higher Education by Distance: Opportunities and Challenges at National and International Levels*, by B.D. Denman. Consultant report, London: OBHE. 2013, July 15, accessed at http://www.obhe.ac.uk/documents/view_details?id=730.

Patrinos, H. A., P. Barrera-Osorio, and J. Guaqueta, *The Role and Impact of Public–Private Partnerships in Education*, Washington, DC: World Bank, 2009.

Patrinos, H. A. and S. Sosale, *Mobilizing the Private Sector for Public Education: A View from the Trenches*, Washington, DC: World Bank, 2007.

Preker, A. S., M.Vujicic, Y. Dukhan, C. Ly, H. Beciu, and P. N. Materu, "Scaling up health professional education: Opportunities and challenges for Africa", Paper prepared for the Task Force for Scaling Up Education and Training for Health Workers, Global Health Workforce Alliance. World Bank, Washington, DC, 2007a.

Preker, A. S., R. M. Scheffler, and M. C. Bassett, (eds.). *Private Voluntary Health Insurance in Development: Friend or Foe?* Washington, DC: World Bank, 2007b.

Psacharopoulos, G. and H. Patrinos, "Returns to investment in education: A further update", Policy Research Working Paper 2881, Washington, DC: World Bank, 2002.

Psacharopoulos, G., J. P. Tan, and E. Jimenez, *Financing Education in Developing Countries: Exploration of Policy Options*, Washington, DC: World Bank, 1986.

PSSRU-UK. *Unit Costs of Health and Social Care 2014*. University of Kent (UK): Personal Social Services Research Unit (PSSRU) 2015.

Rechel, B., J. Erskine, B. Dowdeswell, S. Wright, and M. McKee, "Capital investment for health: Case studies from Europe", Observatory Studies

Series No. 18. European Observatory on Health Systems and Policies, Copenhagen, 2009.

Rein, M. F., W. J. Randolph, J. G. Short, K. G. Coolidge, M. L. Coates, and R. M. Carey, "Defining the cost of educating undergraduate medical students at the University of Virginia", *Academic Medicine*, **72**(3), 218–227, 1997.

Ross, S. A., R. W. Westerfield, and J. F. Jaffe, *Corporate Finance*, Boston: Irwin, 1993.

Salmi, J. and A. M. Hauptman, *Innovations in Tertiary Education Financing: A Comparative Evaluation of Allocation Mechanisms*, Washington, DC: World Bank, 2006.

Scheffler, R. M., J. X. Liu, Y. Kinfu, and M. R. Dal Poz, "Forecasting the global shortage of physicians: An economic- and needs-based approach", *Bulletin of the World Health Organization*, **86**, 516–523B, 2008.

Simoens, S. and J. Hurst, "The supply of physician services in OECD countries", OECD Health Working Paper 231, Organisation for Economic Cooperation and Development, Paris, 2006.

Sosale, S., "Trends in private sector development in World Bank education projects", Policy Research Working Paper 2452, World Bank, Washington, DC, 2000.

Tilak, J. B. G., "Higher education in developing countries", *Minerva*, **38**(2), 233–240, 2000.

UNESCO (United Nations Educational, Scientific and Cultural Organization), "Trends in tertiary education: Sub-Saharan Africa", *UNESCO Institute for Statistics (UIS) Fact Sheet*, No. 10, 2010, December, accessed at http://www.uis.unesco.org/FactSheets/Documents/fs10-2010-en.pdf.

Valberg, L. S., M. A. Gonyea, D. G. Sinclair, and J. Wade, "Planning the future academic medical centre", *Canadian Medical Association Journal*, **151**(11), 1581, 1994.

Vimolket, T., P. Kamol-Ratanakul, and K. Indaratna, "Cost of producing a medical doctor at Chulalongkorn University", *Journal of the Medical Association of Thailand Chotmaihet Thangphaet*, **86**(1), 82, 2003.

WHO (World Health Organization), *Working Together for Health: 2006 World Health Report*, Geneva, Switzerland: WHO, 2006.

WHO, *Scaling Up, Saving Lives: Task Force for Scaling Up Education and Training for Health Workers*, Geneva. Switzerland: WHO, 2008.

Winston, G. C., "For-profit higher education: Godzilla or chicken little?" *Change: The Magazine of Higher Learning*, **31**(1), 12–19, 1999.

Winston, G. C., J. C. Carbone, and E. G. Lewis, "What's been happening to higher education? A reference manual", Williams Project on the Economics of Higher Education, 1998, accessed at http://siher.stanford.edu/documents/pdfs/DP-47.pdf.

World Bank, *Accelerating Catch Up: Tertiary Education for Growth and Competitiveness in Sub-Saharan Africa*, Washington, DC: World Bank, 2009.

World Bank, *Higher Education in Developing Countries: Peril and Promise.* Washington, DC: World Bank, 2000.

Chapter 8

Role of the Private Sector in the Financing of Health Education

Eric L. Keuffel and Alexander S. Preker

Introduction

The public sector has typically played an extensive role in health personnel training through its provision of institutional support for a wide variety
of programs, colleges, and universities in developing countries. In their
current form across numerous countries, the sole use of public finance
cannot keep pace with the growing demand for higher education and the
scale up required of health workforce to meet health outcome goals, particularly in Africa and Asia. Augmentation of public finance of health
institutions with innovative private sector sources, novel public finance
approaches, and unique mechanisms of finance for health institutions may
help bridge the gap between the demand for health workers in developing
countries and the current capacity of the state to fund the production of
human capital for health. This chapter highlights key issues related to
private or public sector finance for tertiary health education institutions,
examines potential novel sources of funding from various sectors (public,
private for-profit, private not-for-profit) and evaluates the costs, benefits,
and feasibility of these potential financing solutions. While the lessons in
this chapter are broadly relevant across many developing country locales,
we will focus particular attention in Africa as the dearth of health workers

and resources are particularly acute there. Our analyses are relevant for researchers, students' private sector investors, policy makers, and donors. We aspire to move these actors toward concrete actions to adopt useful financial practices and innovative mechanisms from the public and private sectors in order to address the human resources in health crisis.

Background

The human resources crisis is a key constraint in many developing country health systems. The critical nature of the crisis in human resources in health (HRH) has been brought to the forefront of the health debate in the last 15 years (WHO, 2006; Chen and Evans, 2004; Dovlo, 2006; World Bank, 2004). Even prior to the adoption of the United Nations Sustainable Development Goals (SDGs) in 2015, studies had highlighted the extent of human resource shortages in the health sector. According to needs-based estimates by the World Health Organization (WHO), an additional 1.5 million health workers are required to meet basic health care needs in Africa and reach the Millennium Development Goals (MDGs) for health, at a training cost of $2.6 billion per year. Demand-based estimates indicated a lower but still acute shortage of 800,000 health care workers in 31 African countries by 2015 (WHO, 2008; Scheffler *et al.*, 2008) More recent demand based estimates developed for the UN SDGs indicate that by 2030 (in a subset of 165 countries with sufficient data) demand will support 80 million health workers globally (while 2013 estimates peg the number of health workers at 43.5 million health workers which is 10 percent lower than the 2013 estimated demand-based optimal number of health workers) (WHO, 2016). In the context of the private sector in particular, *The Business of Health in Africa* report emphasized the human resources crisis as one of the five principle constraints affecting the private sector (IFC, 2007).

Financing the production of skilled health workers is a vital ingredient in the strengthening of health systems. But it takes a considerable investment of time and resources to train them. Preliminary studies indicate that changing the skill mix of health workers is an important first step toward improving the supply of health workers given a fixed resource envelope. Nevertheless, expanding financing and improving the efficiency of existing financial inputs are crucial for meeting the urgent need to increase the

Table 8.1   Health Worker Density in WHO "Critical Shortage" Countries

Country	MD/1000	RN/1000	Country	MD/1000	RN/1000
Afghanistan	0.3	0.1	Madagascar	0.2	—
Angola	0.2	1.7	Malawi	<0.1	0.3
Bangladesh	0.4	0.2	Mali	0.1	0.4
Benin	0.1	0.8	Mauritania	—	—
Bhutan	0.3	1.0	Morocco	0.6	0.9
Burkina Faso	<0.1	0.6	Mozambique	<0.1	0.4
Cambodia	0.2	0.8	Myanmar	0.6	1.0
Cameroon	0.1	0.4	Nicaragua	0.9	1.4
Central African Republic	<0.1	0.3	Niger	<0.1	0.1
Congo, Rep.	0.1	0.8	Nigeria	0.4	1.6
Côte d'Ivoire	0.1	0.5	Pakistan	0.8	0.6
Djibouti	0.2	0.8	Papua New Guinea	0.1	0.6
El Salvador	1.6	0.4	Peru	1.1	1.5
Ethiopia	<0.1	0.2	Rwanda	0.1	0.7
Gambia, The	<0.1	0.6	Senegal	0.1	0.4
Ghana	0.1	0.9	Sierra Leone	<0.1	0.2
Guinea	0.1	—	Somalia	<0.1	0.1
Guinea-Bissau	<0.1	0.6	Tanzania	<0.1	0.4
India	0.7	1.7	Togo	0.1	0.3
Indonesia	0.2	1.4	Uganda	0.1	1.3
Iraq	0.6	1.4	Yemen, Rep.	0.2	0.7
Kenya	0.2	0.9	Zambia	0.2	0.8
Lao PDR	0.2	0.9	Zimbabwe	0.1	1.3
Liberia	<0.1	0.3	**World**	**1.5**	**3.3**

Notes: Estimate year range spans from 2008–2014. Burundi, Chad, Comoros, Congo DR, Equatorial Guinea, Eritrea, Honduras, Mauritius, Lesotho, and Nepal did not report physician or nurse/midwife densities between 2008 and 2014, but were considered critical shortage countries in the 2006 WHO World Health Report.
— = not available.
Sources: WHO (2006); World Development Indicators, 2017, April 6, accessed at http://wdi. worldbank.org/table/2.15#, Washington, DC: World Bank.

number of medical, nursing, and allied health workers, and train them to have relevant skills.

There is potential to expand the health workforce in developing countries given improved uptake of primary and secondary education (Tables 8.1 and 8.1a). For example, Africa has a large number of potential health workers. For the past three decades, internal and external investments in African education systems have been targeted to the primary and secondary levels of the education sector. As a result, the number of qualified secondary school graduates has increased, enlarging the pool of potential higher education students. The expansion of education at lower levels has increased the marginal value of tertiary education, including health education (Salmi and Hauptman, 2006). As low-income country economies grow at approximately 3–6 percent per year, new opportunities arise to harness potential gains in human resource development, especially the production of health workers. One way to accomplish this is to invest in and improve tertiary-level health training.

Recent examinations of the role of the private sector and private finance in tertiary educational institutions across a range of

Table 8.1a   2013 and 2030 Health Worker Estimates and Shortages (WHO)

WHO region	Estimated stock of health workers (millions)		Estimated health workers needs based shortage[a] (millions)		Estimated health worker demand (millions)[b]	
	2013	2030	2013	2030	2013[a]	2030[a]
Africa	1.9	3.1	4.2	6.1	1.1	2.4
Americas	9.4	14.0	0.8	0.6	8.8	15.3
Eastern Mediterranean	3.1	5.3	1.7	1.7	3.1	6.2
Europe	12.7	16.8	0.1	0.1	14.2	18.2
Southeast Asia	6.2	10.9	6.9	4.7	6.0	12.2
Western Pacific	10.3	17.3	3.7	1.4	15.1	25.9
World	**43.5**	**67.3**	**17.4**	**14.5**	**48.3**	**80.2**

Notes: [a]Needs-based shortage only includes countries identified by WHO as having a minimum capacity to provide services across 12 key health indicators (SDG Index).
[b]Estimates based on 165 countries due to data constraints in remaining geographies.
Source: Global strategy on human resources for health: Workforce 2030 (WHO, 2016 accessed at https://pps.who.int/iris/bitstream/handle/10665/250368/?sequence=1.

developing-country settings inform some of the opportunities and challenges associated with engaging private sector finance mechanisms to support expansion of health education (Beciu and Jacob, 2009, Beciu, 2009; Patrinos *et al.*, 2009; Preker *et al.*, 2008; UNESCO, 2009) In addition, some unique characteristics associated with health institutions may allow these schools to access specific sources of finance (such as health research funds from industry- or government-sponsored research). In this chapter, we address both more general private and public funding sources (e.g. banks) and health-specific sources (e.g. R&D in clinical research).

Objective

The overarching goal of this chapter is to examine how innovative finance approaches, particularly those which incorporate the private sector, could bolster lower income countries' capacity to scale up and strengthen the production of quality health workers.

Current Situation

This chapter examines the literature to compare models and innovations in education finance (especially tertiary education), developing-country finance, and health finance (especially private health finance) and, to the extent possible, examine sources that focus on intersections of these three areas (Figure 8.1). To the extent that only a limited amount specifically addresses tertiary education finance within health for developing countries, it will be covered, but the review of these related streams of research yields useful insights regarding the financing options for tertiary health education in lower income settings (such as Africa) and the role the private sector may play. Specific country examples provide context for key issues in this chapter.

Develop and Evaluate Options

Based on the characterizations and issues identified in the literature review, key gaps and shortcomings in existing financing mechanisms and

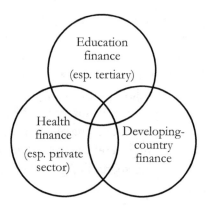

Figure 8.1   Financial Innovation Focus Areas

recommendation for new innovative financing mechanisms for tertiary health education projects will be identified. The potential role for the private sector to participate in either the finance or investment process is highlighted for public, private, or mixed (public–private partnership, PPP) modes. The chapter also evaluates options with respect to efficiency, equity, and feasibility of implementation. We provide detailed recommendations on the prerequisites, including any policy changes required to make the proposed improvements and innovative financing mechanisms a success. Ideally, this framework will allow policy makers and investors to select the approaches they deem most suitable. We primarily focus on Africa as a case study in the chapter as it highlights many of the central issues involved related to improving finance and the role of the private sector for health workers.

Current Situation

There is a wide range of health training institutions in lower income countries with regard to output (MDs, nurses, midwives, community health workers), experience, capabilities, and financial resources. For example, many African countries initially established public tertiary education facilities upon (or in some case prior to) independence and continue to rely on public sector as the dominant form of provision. Medical schools in Africa (the form of health education in which data on schools are most robust) appear to follow a similar bias toward public provision of education prior to and during independence. Undoubtedly, the predilection toward public provision was (and continues to be) at least partially motivated on the basis that health is a "public good" and it is necessary to develop human resources to address health-related needs of society. As indicated by a recent survey conducted among 100 African medical schools in 2010, of the 100 medical schools that responded to the survey,[1] just seven were established prior to 1960, and 35 were founded between 1960 and 1990 (Table 8.2). None of the medical schools founded prior to 1990 in the survey were private. Since 1990, however, private entry has increased substantially. Twenty-two of 58 new entrants with full information in the survey were private (seven for-profits and 15 not-for-profits). Some of the non-responders or recently identified schools are most likely private institutions.

The approach to financing has mirrored the public-focused approach to provision in African tertiary education (Table 8.3). Before and during independence, financing for students was usually generous and state-supported in order to promote equity and to encourage talented students to attain tertiary education. As sustainable funding became less viable during budget crises (particularly through the 1970s and 1980s), states restructured their tertiary care education programs by reducing funding and incorporating user fees — leaving students (or their families) responsible for at least some of the direct and indirect educational costs. Concomitant loan programs were usually established to address equity concerns, although the amount of the loan and terms of payment varied considerably. In many cases, the loan programs relied on means-testing or restricted access to individuals that met a minimum level on entrance exams (merit-based loans) or invoked both strategies to limit their funding exposure. Several loan schemes, usually organized by the state, have become insolvent due to the high default rate and have been restructured (or bailed out) by the governments. In short, outside some pockets in Anglophone Africa, government resources for supporting tertiary health education are usually limited. As a result, more attention has been devoted to expanding the private sector's role (in tertiary education generally) for both provision and financing of education.

Current evidence from medical schools in Africa suggests a bifurcation in finance sources for public and private medical schools.

Table 8.2   Sub-Saharan Medical Schools, by Type and Date of Establishment

School type	Year established				
	Pre-1960	1960–1989	1990–1999	2000–2009	Total
Public	7	35	17	19	78
Private (not-for-profit)	0	0	7	8	15
Private (for-profit)	0	0	1	6	7

Note: 169 Medical Schools received surveys, but only 100 completed the survey.
Source: SAMSS (Sub-Saharan African Medical School Survey) 2013, June 10, accessed at http://www.samss.org/samss.upload/wysiwyg/SAMSS%20Report_FinalV2_120110b.pdf.

Table 8.3   Sub-Saharan Medical School Funding Sources, by School Type

Funding source	School type	
	Public ($n = 78$)(%)	Private ($n = 22$)(%)
Government	73	13
Student tuition and fees	15	74
Donors, international and local	5	5
Grants	5	1
Other[a]	2	7

Note: Percentages are approximate (± 1 percent) category.
[a] Includes investment income, capital supplied by medical school owners (private) and bank loans.
Source: SAMSS (Sub-Saharan African Medical School Survey 2013, June 10, accessed at http://www.samss.org/samss.upload/wysiwyg/SAMSS%20Report_FinalV2_120110b.pdf.

Approximately three quarters of all funding for public institutions comes from the government (e.g. Ministry of Education) while private institutions rely on tuition and fees to finance almost three quarters of their institutional expenditures.

As a result of private institutions' reliance on tuition, tuition and fees naturally are generally higher among private medical institutions in Sub-Saharan Africa (Table 8.4).

Currently, most health education institutions in the region typically operate on very limited budgets and struggle to finance recurrent costs

Table 8.4   Sub-Saharan Medical School Tuition, by School Type

Tuition range (US$)	Public (number)	Private (number)	Total (number)	Private (%)
0	9	0	9	0.0
1–100	15	0	15	0.0
100–500	23	1	24	4.2
501–1,000	8	0	8	0.0
1,001–2,000	8	3	11	27.3
2,001–3,000	3	6	9	66.7
3,000–4,000	4	2	6	33.3
4,001–5,000	3	6	9	66.7
5,001–6,000	3	1	4	25.0
6,001–7,000	1	1	2	50.0
7,001–10,000	0	1	1	100.0
10,000+	1	1	2	50.0
Total	78	22	100	

Source: SAMSS (Sub-Saharan African Medical School Survey) 2013, June 10, accessed at http://www.samss.org/samss.upload/wysiwyg/SAMSS%20Report_FinalV2_120110b.pdf.

such as faculty salaries and capital expenditures for facilities and infra-structure development (Preker *et al.*, 2008; World Bank, 2000). The SAMSS survey confirms that labor costs absorb almost two thirds of expenditures.[3] In some cases (e.g. Ghana), the limited resources are con-centrated on salaries and short-run variable costs with little funding for long-term capital improvement or maintenance[4] (Beciu and Haddad, 2009a). A broader study of 55 low-income countries indicates that, on average, 74 percent of these recurrent expenditures are directed toward teacher salaries and benefits at the basic education level (Glewwe and Kremer, 2006; Bruns *et al.*, 2003). Existing physical structures and infra-structure for health education is under strain as a result of poor upkeep and swelling student-demand for tertiary education (including health).

The paucity of public funding is further complicated by principle–agent issues since often the Ministry of Education (MOE) or Ministry of Finance (MOF) may serve as the primary finance contributor while the

Ministry of Health (MOH) sets goals and expectations for their output but plays a minority role in financing tertiary health education. For example, in Ghana circa 2010, the MOH covered a third of expenditures for health schools (primarily medical schools) but drove the agenda for expectations regarding the output of all health workers. There was a wide chasm between MOH short-run goals for health worker production and the feasible output from medical and nursing schools given resource constraints (Beciu and Haddad, 2009a). This is a central issue. Although this review did not attempt to identify countries that coordinate health policy objectives, targets, training, and budgets; this issue deserves further attention in future qualitative and quantitative work to identify mechanisms that improve coordination across these objectives.

To make up for the limited resources in the public sector, the private sector may contribute in three basic ways.

- *Finance.* First, the private sector can serve as a source of finance.[5] One example of private financing is student loans from private banks (in some cases state guaranteed or subsidized) to assist students with tuition or user fees (at either public or private schools). Innovative mechanisms to involve private finance either via direct support of tertiary education institutions or indirect support via student focused financing mechanisms expand available resources while developing important capabilities for continued future growth (Salmi and Hauptman, 2006). Financing may cover either recurrent or capital expenditures.
- *Provision.* Second, the private sector may also be involved in provision of education. Schools may be built, owned, operated, and managed by private organizations (or may focus on a subset of these services). In the general tertiary education sector, many private schools (of varying quality) have recently been established in low-income settings.
- *Expansion of health systems.* Investment by the private sector in hospitals, clinics, and other health service organizations that employ physicians, nurses, and health workers improves the labor market for health workers. A more robust health labor market indirectly can help influence the finance and provision of health education because it assures potential students that health work is a viable, well-paying post-graduation employment option. Moreover, the improved financial

viability increases the private sector's willingness to provide (or finance) educational services.

Table 8.5 summarizes the public and private roles in finance and provision.[6] Although this matrix was designed for primary and secondary education projects, it applies as well to tertiary health education in low-income settings (Sosale, 2000).

Important determinants of the extent of private sector finance or provision in education markets include the regulatory controls related to education and finance and the attractiveness of the market for private sector organizations, both for-profit and not-for-profit models. While not-for-profits may have a lower implicit cost of capital and may be more likely to enter market niches that are less attractive profit centers (e.g. ecumenical organizations providing health worker education in rural

Table 8.5   Public and Private Roles in Finance and Provision

Source	Public financing	Private financing
Public institution	Traditional public school typically with state financing (usually via taxes distributed to Ministry of Health or Ministry of Education) User fees at public institutions may also be covered via state-supported scholarships, grants, and loans (often subsidized)	Public schools that charge students tuition or user fees to help fund recurrent or capital expenditures. Students and families borrow from private organizations (banks) or pay out of pocket or sometimes receive government scholarships or grants Public school with financing from other private sources (foundations, private firms, non-governmental organizations)
Private institution	Public financing or vouchers (with individual choice) for use with privately delivered education Contracting out of management operational, facility, professional, or education services	Pure private schools with tuition Non-governmental organization or non-profit institutions (especially. in rural areas for lower cadre health workers)

Source: Sosale (2000).

environments in Africa to improve the human resources available for public health) — these organizations also are more likely to emerge and remain viable in environments in which they do not suffer persistent financial losses.

Regulation can serve as a critical enabler for emergent private sector provision models. The frequent perception of private institutions in the health education tertiary market positions them as low-quality "credentialing shops" servicing residual demand for lower quality students with resources to pay for further education (Kapur, 2008). There are exceptions to this perception, but future entrants will benefit from regulation, particularly accreditation and quality assurance mechanisms that certify the quality of the institution to the public. This type of credentialing is already beginning to occur in the developing world among health service organizations by accreditation institutions such as Joint Commission International.

Another important organizational form which have emerged to address education objectives are PPPs (Patrinos *et al.*, 2009). There is an emerging body of evidence from the general education literature in developing countries (both primary and secondary education) to indicate that these organizational forms can effectively address financial, quality, and access goals more effectively than the public sector alone. The applicability of these results to the health sector is discussed later.

The spectrum for the degree of private entry in both provision and finance is very broad. The government, in some cases, plays a dominant role in both the provision and financing of education. While a completely private solution to education is unlikely, increasingly government organizations are partnering with private entities in PPPs or encouraging independent efforts by private organizations in the provision and delivery sectors. Figure 8.2 summarizes the range of approaches for educational policy.

Figure 8.3, an adaptation from a prior World Bank analysis (Patrinos *et al.*, 2009), summarizes the potential finance, provision, and spending options across tertiary health education institutions. Incentives and programs to encourage private participation may focus on addressing particular needs with respect finance, provision, and spending. For example, as

Provision	Gov	Gov	Gov	Mix[a]	Mix[a]	Mix[a]	Private	Private	Private
Financing	Gov	Mix[a]	Private	Gov	Mix[a]	Private	Gov	Mix[a]	Private

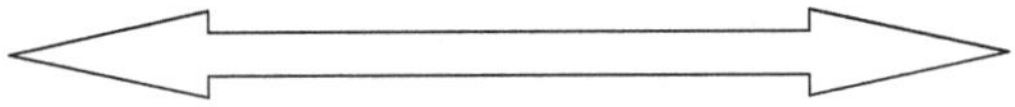

Pure public ⟵ ⟶ Pure private

Figure 8.2   Public–Private Education Spectrum

Note: [a] "Mix" refers to either (1) independent participation by both government and private organizations or (2) coordinated involvement in programs using some government and some private participation (PPPs).

tertiary health schools in Africa struggle with capital expenditure, then if one assumes that the public sector is less efficient in undertaking capital projects and transaction costs are not prohibitive, then contracting out facility development, in which the government partners with the private sector to improve efficiency of capital expenditures may be warranted (Patrinos and Sosale, 2007). Such is an example of public finance with private provision for a specific spending category (capital). PPPs in education come in a myriad of forms, but they generally address at least one element from each category (finance, provision, spending) listed in Figure 8.3.

The public sector has traditionally played a dominant role in financing tertiary education, and public financing decisions affect the supply and demand for private finance and involvement in tertiary education markets. This chapter, therefore, first examines characteristics and innovations of public sector financing innovations and ways the organization of public finance influences or motivates private investment.

Rationale for Public Sector Finance and Provision of Education

Public economic theory contends that public sector investment in services such as education is justified when the magnitude of the social benefit exceeds the private benefit (Chapman, 2006, Jimenez, 1986) Absent this condition (if social benefit equals or is less than private benefit), individuals rationally invest in education (assuming credit

a. Finance: Potential Funding Sources

Individual/family	Private (for-profit)	Private (not-for-profit)	Public
• Alumni gifts • Donations • Tuition	• Student loans (banks) • Bonds • Microfinance initiatives (for-profit, including mobile applications for lower health cadres) • Research partnerships (private firms) • Corporate contributions	• Foundation grants (or loans) • Endowments • Social microfinance (e.g. Grameen Bank) • Charity bonds for health education (akin to IFFIm role with GAVI vaccines) • North–South academic partnerships • Non-governmental organizations	• Taxes (general taxation, VAT, industry-specific taxes [pharma], individual specific taxes [health emigration]) • Vouchers, scholarships, and student loans • External government aid/loans • Multilateral aid/loans • Government support for health education bonds • Contracting out (to private organizations)

b. Provision: Types of Tertiary Educational Institutions

Private (for profit)	Private (not for profit)	Public
• For-profit organizations (generally more focused on vocational/lower cadre education)	• Ecumenical organizations (especially for education of lower cadre/rural cases) • Traditional non-profit universities/colleges • Non-governmental organizations	• Public education at traditional universities and health-specific colleges

c. Expenditures: Capital and Recurrent

Recurrent expenditures	Capital expenses/investments
• Education commodities (books, materials, supplies) • Salaries • Maintenance/depreciation expense	• Infrastructure expansion/improvement • Endowment formation

Figure 8.3 Sources of Finance in Education, Provision, and Major Expenditures

Note: VAT = value-added tax, IFFIm = International Financing Facility for Immunization, GAVI = Global Alliance for Vaccines and Immunization, pharma = pharmaceuticals.

Source: Adapted from Patrinos and Sosale (2007).

Table 8.6   Non-market and External Benefits of Education

Benefit type	Findings
Child education	Parental education affects child's educational level and achievement
Child health	Child's health positively related to parental education
Fertility	Mother's education lowers daughter's births
Own health	More education increases life expectancy
Spouse's health	More schooling improves spouse's health and lowers mortality
Job search efficiency	More schooling reduces cost of search, increases mobility
Desired family size	More schooling improves contraceptive efficiency
Technological change	Schooling helps R&D, diffusion
Social cohesion	Schooling may increase voting and reduces alienation
Crime	Education may reduce criminal activity

Sources: Patrinos *et al.* (2009); Wolfe and Zuvekas (1997).

availability) up to the point where the marginal private costs equal the marginal private benefits. Although the externalities associated with education may differ across the different educational strata (primary, secondary, tertiary), the social externalities include additional health, education, social, and labor benefits. Table 8.6 summarizes some of the benefits aside from direct labor market effects (e.g. salary) that accrue to the individual (Wolfe and Zuvekas, 1997; Patrinos *et al.*, 2009; Jamison *et al.*, 2007).

While it is likely that several of the proposed benefits to primary and secondary education are not applicable to tertiary education, particularly health tertiary education — there are likely significant social benefits to training additional health workers which are not recognized or accounted for by the individual while making the decision to seek additional tertiary health education. These may include the social and economic benefits of improved health and productivity of future patients (particularly those in the workforce or who contribute to home production). These externalities support the subsidization of tertiary health education (either by finance or provision), but the degree of subsidy should, in theory, depend on the magnitude of the externality relative to overall social benefit.

Rationale for Private Sector Financing or Provision of Tertiary Education

The existence of at least some private benefit suggests that there is a role for private sector provision and financing in tertiary health education. The major internalized benefit is future wages (often quite high relative to educational costs among the upper cadres). Approximately 28 percent of sub-Saharan physicians and 11 percent of nurses emigrate to large developed economies to practice (Clemens and Pettersson, 2006). In these cases, the realized individual gains can increase by an order of magnitude (10 times or more) relative to origination country wage levels. In addition, independent of emigration, the internalized benefits relative to externalities are likely to differ across cadre and even within profession (e.g. high-skill versus low-skill nurses).

Naturally, the mix of internalized and external net benefits (benefit less cost) is a strong motivation behind finance and delivery models in health education. Another logical argument for emphasizing a private solution for health education markets is the nature of credentialing in the labor market for these professions. Educational status is measurable (e.g. MD, RN) and contestability from substitutes (say, from a traditional medicine healer) is limited in the market — particularly given advancements in technology and the informational advantages that health workers maintain relative to patients and payers (Preker *et al.*, 2000). These characteristics argue for a more private-oriented solution for the provision of education. Figure 8.4 offers a *conceptual* characterization of how the relative net internalized and external benefits (relative to the costs of education) may shift as cadre level increases. In reality, the ideal educational provision and financing models (public versus private) should depend on the internalized versus external net benefits relative to educational costs (e.g. a private solution could, in theory, be appropriate for certain community health workers).

In practice, it is not uncommon to see greater public resources concentrated for medical schools relative to nurse/other health worker

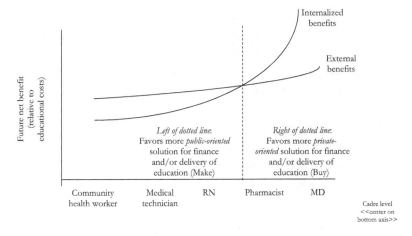

Figure 8.4   Internalized and External Net Benefits, by Cadre: Implications for Education Delivery and Finance

training institutions despite that significantly higher private wages garnered by doctors. Some of the benefits of private provision and financing, as described by Fielden (2008), include:

- Supplementing the limited capacity of government institutions to absorb growth in higher education enrollments. Private resources can be (and often are) focused on providing additional inputs (e.g. textbooks, infrastructure, IT, training, and development) aimed at improving the quality of education delivered in government institutions.
- Opportunities for governments to support publicly funded students in private higher education institutions — often at a lower per student cost than in the public sector.
- A mechanism to raise both the efficiency and quality of education delivery since studies indicate that private delivery of education can be more efficient than public delivery, when measured on a per-student basis (IFC, 2001).
- New skills and knowledge — pedagogic, technical, and management — to all levels of education. The greater management flexibility enjoyed by the private sector means that it is much better placed than public

schools to introduce curricular and program innovations, improved assessment methods, and modern teaching techniques. Private organizations can also circumvent unnecessarily restrictive employment laws and outdated pay scales that limit the ability of public schools to hire appropriate staff and organize delivery in a more efficient and effective manner.

- The competition from increased private delivery of education can generate improved performance among both public and private schools.
- A wider set of financing options, frequently less restricted by government bureaucracy.

The Extent of Private Financing and Provision in Tertiary Education in the Developing World and Africa

There has been a recent expansion in the provision of private education, both within and outside the health sector, across various education levels. Enrollment in private primary education grew by 58 percent between 1991 and 2004 — increasing absolute enrollment from 39 million to 62 million.[7] Moreover, much of the growth occurred in sub-Saharan Africa, the Middle East and South Asia (Patrinos *et al.*, 2009). In some cases, these for-profit or not-for-profit schools are formally recognized and licensed by the state, but in some cases these are relatively small, unlicensed operators that fulfill a specific market niche (usually within a particular geographic areas such as rural regions). These schools respond more to market demand than to an explicit national policy effort to expand the private provision of schooling. The composition of tertiary education markets in lower income settings typically includes a few large, public institutions (often with high quality faculty and a significant history) and numerous, smaller private institutions that fill specific market geographic or worker-type segments. For example, private tertiary education institutions outnumber public institutions in sub-Saharan Africa, but account for only approximately 20 percent of student enrollment (World Bank, 2009).

Despite data limitations with respect to public and private financing shares, UNESCO data for a subset of African countries suggest that public finance plays the dominant role in tertiary education (and education expenditure generally) — an unsurprising result given the historical

Table 8.7   Private Expenditure Share in Tertiary Education, Select African Countries

Country	Tertiary education public expenditure (percent of GDP)	Tertiary education private expenditure (percent of GDP)	Private sector share of tertiary education expenditures	Year
Benin	0.52	0.27	34.1	2007
Burkina Faso	0.44	0.14	24.4	2007
Cape Verde	0.24	0.11	30.8	2007
Guinea	0.40	0.04	9.0	2008
Kenya	0.79	0.48	37.6	2003
Niger	0.21	0.22	51.1	2006
Rwanda	1.03	0.00	0.0	2008

Notes: In the case of Guinea, Niger, and Rwanda, private share was calculated by subtracting total expenditure from public expenditure within the database for the relevant statistics (these figures are italicized).
Source: UNESCO (United Nations Educational, Scientific and Cultural Organization) Institute for Statistics Database, UNESCO, Paris 2013, July 1, accessed at http://stats.uis.unesco.org.

support of public tertiary institutions on the theoretical justification of large social externalities associated with education (which are also relevant for health education). Table 8.7 shows that the share of private expenditures in tertiary education markets is below 50 percent and, more commonly, roughly one third of total expenditures. Evidence from international comparisons and country-specific analyses also suggests the limited role for private sector provision in the health sector in Africa (Beciu and Jacob, 2009; World Bank, 2000).

The expansion of primary and secondary education has resulted in a larger pool of individuals seeking to further their education with tertiary skills.[8] In developed and developing countries, private provision tends to be more common at the tertiary level than at primary or secondary levels, but still is generally a minority share of overall expenditure and enrollment (Fielden, 2008). Table 8.8 reflects enrollment growth for tertiary education over a five-year period (across both public and private institutions). Based on country-level reports, similar growth patterns are present within the health tertiary education sector, too.

Table 8.8   Enrollment in Tertiary Education (Full and Part Time)

Country	2005	2015	Annualized growth, 2005–2015 (%)
Burkina Faso	27,942	74,276[a]	13.0
Burundi	16,915	44,887[a]	13.0
Cameroon	99,864	389,974	14.6
Cape Verde	3,910	12,538	12.4
Ethiopia	191,212	757,175	16.5
Ghana	119,559	417,534	13.3
Madagascar	44,948	113,025[b]	10.8
Malawi	5,810	12,203[d]	13.1
Mali	22,632	97,278[c]	15.7
Mauritania	8,758	20,800	9.0
Niger	10,799	21,764	10.5
Senegal	59,127	144,827	11.6

Notes: [a] = 2014 data, [b] = 2013 data, [c] = 2012 data, [d] = 2011 data. Start date for Mali is 2002.

Source: UNESCO (United Nations Educational, Scientific and Cultural Organization) Institute for Statistics Database, UNESCO, Paris 2017, April 10, accessed at http://stats.uis.unesco.org.

Schools and other educational institutions have struggled to keep pace with the significant growth in demand. In many cases, countries have simply increased class size and enrollment without increasing teacher recruitment and development or upgrading capital equipment and facilities to accommodate the increase in students. For example, in Cameroon, the tertiary student population almost quadrupled between 2005 and 2015, but the number of instructors at the tertiary level increased only doubled. Given the high technical knowledge in health and medical fields, the trend is most likely even more pronounced with respect to health tertiary education, especially for training of higher-cadre health workers. Country-level analysis of Ghanaian health education has borne this out (Beciu and Haddad, 2009a; Beciu and Haddad, 2009b; Beciu and Jacob, 2009).

Table 8.9   Tertiary Gross Enrollment Ratios, by Region, 1970–2008 (percent)

Region	1980	1990	2000	2014
North America and Western Europe	37.0	49.0	64.0	86.2
Central and Eastern Europe	—	—	41.0	69.7
Latin America and the Caribbean	13.0	17.0	23.0	73.0
Central Asia	—	—	23.0	34.6
East Asia and the Pacific	5.0	7.0	15.0	76.1
Arab States	—	—	20.0	27.0
South and West Asia	4.0	6.0	9.0	18.5
Sub-Saharan Africa	2.0	3.0	4.0	21.6
World	12.0	13.0	19.0	44.0

Note: — = not available.
Source: UNESCO (2010).

The growth in tertiary participation (as a share of eligible entrants) is faster in sub-Saharan Africa than all other regions, but Africa still lags well behind most regions in terms of absolute share of enrollment. Table 8.9 reflects global trends in tertiary enrollment (UNESCO, 2010, 2017).

While UNESCO does not report enrollment in the private sector at the tertiary level in the UNESCO online database, enrollment in primary and secondary levels, generally ranges from 0 to 30 percent — with a few outliers exceeding one third of enrollment.[9] However, examination of enrollment rates over a range of years, as exhibited in Table 8.10, indicates that the enrollment shares in higher private education within Africa generally lag behind those in other developing economies in Asia and Latin America (PROPHE, 2010). The institutional share is frequently quite large for nations in sub-Saharan Africa. Combined with the relatively low enrollment shares, this finding reflects the fact that most private institutions participate on a much smaller scale than their public tertiary higher education counterparts.

Across all sectors (not just tertiary), some of the increase in private sector enrollments over time reflects, in part, entry by low-cost private schools

Table 8.10   Private Shares of Higher Education Enrollment and Institution Number

Region	Country	Private share of higher education enrolment (percent)	Private share of higher education institutions (percent)	Year[a]
Sub-Saharan Africa	Botswana	28.6	86.0	2007
	Ethiopia	24.0	60.0	2003
	Kenya	17.9	13.1	2008/4
	Mozambique	32.1	50.0	2004
	Nigeria	4.0	36.0	2006
	Senegal	11.0	96.0	2003
	Uganda	15.0	85.0	2004
	Zimbabwe	4.5	41.0	2004
Latin America	Argentina	23.9	53.5	2003/5
	Bolivia	27.8	75.9	2004
	Brazil	74.6	89.1	2007
	Chile	77.6	92.8	2007/5
	Colombia	49.6	70.6	2005/7
	Costa Rica	54.6	47.1	2004
	Dominican Republic	49.7	88.4	2005
	Ecuador	28.7	58.7	2004
	Guatemala	48.1	90.0	2003/4
	Honduras	19.7	60.0	2002
	Mexico	33.4	72.7	2007
	Nicaragua	47.5	58.5	2005/3
	Panama	18.3	83.1	2003/4
	Uruguay	11.7	22.2	2007/3
	Venezuela, RB	41.6	56.8	2004/5
Asia	China	8.9	39.1	2002
	Japan	77.1	86.3	2000
	Malaysia	39.1	92.2	2000
	Mongolia	26.0	64.2	2003
	Pakistan	64.0	17.8	2004/0
	Philippines	75.0	81.0	1999
	Taiwan, China	71.9	65.8	2004
	Thailand	33.0	46.3	2003

Note: [a]First year is date for percentage enrollment record; second year is date for percentage institutions record.
Source: PROPHE (2010).

which target students who do not qualify (by either their ability or by means-testing) for tuition subsidization in high-quality government (or private) schools or who cannot afford tuition at high-cost private schools.

Public Funding Mechanisms: Implications for the Private Sector

A characterization of the basic options and mechanisms for public funding of public (or private) sector education demonstrate how public sector decisions may improve efficiency (and in some cases, equity and access) and potentially motivate greater investment by the private sector in either provision or finance. Many of these mechanisms and country examples are discussed in detail by Salmi and Hauptman (2006). They can broadly be divided into two primary strategies — funding to assist institutions directly, or supply-side funding, and funding for the demand-side participants in the education market (students and their families).

Institutional (Supply-Side) Funding Options

The traditional approach to funding public tertiary institutions operational/ teaching or research capacity (including health education institutions) generally consists of a yearly budget renewal (perhaps with an inflation adjustment), but more innovative mechanisms explicitly base funding on inputs, outputs, performance, or combinations of the above. In principle, public finances can be distributed to either public or private institutions (e.g. charter schools which rely on private management and public funding), but using mechanisms such as performance criteria or priority targets may more appropriately allow private schools to compete (especially if private institutions have greater flexibility in organizing their institution to reach key targets).

One important characteristic of funding mechanisms is the degree to which the university versus government administrators decide how funding is allocated within public (or sometime private) schools. Annual budget renewals may have very different effects depending on the incentives and governance characteristics of the funding process. If governments issue very discrete line-item budgets and have limited knowledge about how funding affects incentives or functioning of educational institutions with respect to output or efficiency, then specific line-item budgets with limited latitude for university-level allocation decisions may result in inefficient use of funding. However, if school management has weak incentives to innovate or improve schools and enjoys excessive freedom with respect to their budget allocation, say via a block grant, then "too much" freedom may result in poor use of funding. The choice over how budgets are spent should account for the information available to both regulators and administrators and the types of incentives that each group faces. For example, Ecuador shifted to a less-regulated approach emphasizing the use of block grants while Australian education policy migrated to a more stringent "line-item" budget in which the regulators restrict the ways schools can use that funding (Salmi and Hauptman, 2006). In the low and middle country health education context, the control of the budget and its effects on efficiency are also likely to depend on the relative strengths of the school management, regulator knowledge, and the incentives/capacity to innovate at the school level.

Central to generating incentives at the school level are the mechanisms for deciding upon the magnitude (and conditions) of funding for specific educational institutions. Funding formulas or mechanisms that incorporate priority-based funding, performance "set asides", and base payments on measurable results may more effectively engage the private sector's participation for several reasons. First, if public education institutions can increase their share of funding simply by increasing student population (e.g. if budgets are input-based), the public sector may monopolize funding simply by expanding the student body — with little incentive to improve quality or, perhaps, even increase the number of graduates. Usurpation of resources by public institutions via traditional funding formulas may inhibit private entry or participation.

Second, private institutions' flexibility with respect to their inputs and management structure (e.g. limited extent of unions) may allow for greater capacity to meet goals of outcome-oriented payment mechanisms. The applicability of this differential flexibility between public and private institutions may vary with level of education or nature of the input mix. In the case of tertiary health education in Africa, the number of qualified professors that can teach in medical schools is likely limited (and many of them may be tied to state institutions). Faculty for nursing schools and/or community health work may be in greater supply or more easily shifted between public and private sectors. Under this condition, performance-based funding may better invoke competition between public and private schools for faculty and students.

Nevertheless, even if public medical institutions dominate enrollment share (e.g. medical schools for physicians), performance-based incentives may still effectively encourage institutions to seek more private research funding if matching incentives are instituted. At the research level, competition for initial public funding to encourage future private sector funding for research (particularly in medical schools) may be motivated by project-based funding and innovation funds (Saint, 2006). Supporting institutions that conduct research (perhaps more relevant for nursing or physician-training institutions rather than health technicians or lower-cadre health workers) can serve as a mechanism to benefit private schools — particularly if the organization that disperses the grants does not favor public affiliation over merit and private institutions have strengths in these areas relative to public education facilities (not always the case).

To augment state or student revenue sources, public (and private) tertiary education institutions in developing countries have sought funding from non-traditional sources (Table 8.11). These include partnerships with private organizations for research, use of facilities/faculty for additional private education or instruction from which revenues assist with public sector financing (especially during night or weekend hours), alternative taxes, endowments, gifts, and international aid. For example, in Nigeria, public tertiary education is almost entirely financed by the government — in part these funds are generated by a two percent tax on profits of limited liability corporations (LLCs). These are complemented by private financing and donation supporting for professorships and prizes (Ajayi and Alani, 1996). Kenya has historically aimed to cover approximately 15 percent of overhead expenditures via external research partnerships. In South Africa, sale of auxiliary services, contracts, and private gifts help fund the 15 percent of the institutional budget for which each institutions (rather than the state) is responsible.[10]

Table 8.11   Finance Allocation Mechanisms in Tertiary Education

General type of funding	Funding target	Funding mechanism(s)	Mechanism options
Direct institutional support (supply-side funding)	Instruction, operations and investment components of institution	Line item Block Grant	Formulas based on: (1) Historical level of funding (2) Costs per input: Student or Staff (average, actual or normative cost per student or staff) (3) Organizational development (4) Performance based formula • Performance set asides • Performance contracts • Competitive funds • Payment for results
	Research within institutions	Line item Block Grant	Matching or Non-Matching Institutional demonstrated capacity (Block Grant) Centers of Excellence (Block Grant)
Indirect institutional support (demand-side funding)	Students/families[a]	Demand-side vouchers	Government reimburses schools after school collects vouchers from students/families
		Government grants and scholarships	Means-tested/Merit Based/Both Administrative institution: MOF, MOE, MOH, other Scope: Tuition/Living Expenses/Both Use of tax system: Credits and Deductions

Student loans

Repayment plans
- Mortgage-type loans (Term Loans)
- Graduated/extended repayment plans
  o Income contingent repayments
    □ Mandatory/optional
  o Fees initially paid by students
  o Fees initially paid by government
- Graduate tax
- Human capital contracts

Source of funds
- Private sources
- Public sources
- Internally financed loans
  o Deferred payments plans
  o Privately financed and serviced
- Creative finance
  o Secondary markets
  o Securitization

Eligibility and Coverage
- Means-tested/Merit based/Both
- Course load/level of study
- Tuition/living expenses/both

Source: Salmi and Hauptman (2006).

Non-institutional (Demand-Side) Funding: Implications for the Private Sector

Perhaps the most robust mechanisms to motivate entry and promote competition between public and private institutions in Africa are the demand-side (non-institutional) funding mechanisms that the state supports: student loans, scholarships, and voucher schemes. These programs may allow students greater flexibility to choose the school that most appropriately meets their needs. If students are able to choose their institution, schools should respond to their demands or risk obsolescence.[11]

In response to the increasing demand for tertiary education, public and private institutions have imposed increased cost sharing as discussed by Johnstone (2004) and the International Comparative Higher Education and Finance Project Database.[12] Public institutions have increased (or adopted) tuition and additional fees or restricted the subsidies and stipends for living expenses. One key concerns associated with these fee increases is the degree to which they dissuade lower income (or even middle-income) individuals from pursuing additional desired education — particularly in an environment of constrained credit availability common in developing country settings. The primary check to prevent income- or asset-based educational sorting has been the adoption of student loans, grants, or scholarships from both public and private sector organizations (Salmi, 2003). User fees and tuition increases have engaged private sector financing both at an individual level (demanding greater fees from students/families) and corporate level (as the public sector has encouraged banks to issue loans to individuals for tuition and fees by subsidizing or guaranteeing loans). To encourage entry by private banks (both in developing and developed countries), governments have subsidized or guaranteed loans to individuals to offset default risks — which has traditionally been high in crossnational studies of education finance. This option focuses on increasing access to education by involving the private sector for finance, but not necessarily encouraging private provision of education. Table 8.12 summarizes ways in which various tertiary education institutions (generally in the public sector) proceeded with imposition of user fees and cost-sharing in four African countries.

Table 8.12   Recent Cost Sharing Mechanisms for Tertiary Education in Africa

Ethiopia   In 2003, a cost sharing graduate tax required students to cover their full costs
of food and lodging plus a minimum of 15 percent of the total
instructional costs of their university program. All enrolled students had
the option of contracting with the government to plan their repayment
schedule. Borrowers began repayment after a one-year grace period (after
higher education completion) and were required to complete repayment
within 15 years. Students may also could pay the calculated amount
up-front at a 5 percent discount rate (Yizengaw, 2007).

Ghana   In 1997, the adoption of the "Akosombo Accord" divided responsibility for
university funding between the government (70 percent) and three sources
(30 percent) including university internal revenue-generation, private
donations, and student tuition fees. Student academic and residential
facility user fees were introduced in 1998. Students living in university
housing pay both; students living off campus pay the non-residential
academic facility user fee and a small non-residential facility user fee.

Kenya   In theory, cost sharing in tertiary institutions started in the early 1970s, but
obligations were usually covered by grants from the Higher Education
Loans Fund (HELF) until the 1990s when cost sharing began in earnest
due to declining state budget, increased intake of students, and a high
default rate (81 percent in 1987) on student loans (Sanyal and Martin,
1998). In 1995, the loan scheme was renamed the Higher Education Loan
Board (HELB) and began using means testing to identify needy students,
including those from "disadvantaged regions" (including Samburu,
Turkana, West Pokot, and other districts in Eastern and North Eastern
provinces) and AIDS orphans. The interest rate was low (about
four percent a year), and loans covered 75 percent of annual higher
education costs that students and their family bore (This aid was limited,
however, to students in particular programs and in private universities). In
1995, the maximum amount was K sh 42,000 but increased to K sh 55,000
(US$733) in 2005–206 (with a minimum of K sh 35,000). HELB paid
KES 8,000 directly to the university toward the student's tuition costs. The
remaining loan funds were paid directly to the student (for food, lodging,
and other living expenses). In addition to the loans, needy students in
public institutions receive bursaries or additional grants via means testing,
although these are capped at K sh 8,000 (US$107) (Ngolovoi, 2006).
Other functions of the Loans Board included loan recovery, establishing a
revolving fund, and seeking additional funds from the private sector and
donors (Otieno, 2004).

(Continued)

Table 8.12   (*Continued*)

Uganda	In 1992, the government report (Education Strategic Investment Plan — ESIP) recommended cost sharing, private sponsorship, evening and weekend programs, and entrepreneurship ventures to offset declining governmental funding (Musini, 2003). More recently, the basic approach toward finance segmented students into three populations — high achievers who receive full scholarships to public university (with exception of some living expenses and books, approximately 6,000 students per annum), merit-based scholarships for top performers (aside of the public university entrants) and students who pay for their education to private universities.

Source: International Comparative Higher Education and Finance Project (Database). "Higher Education Financing and Cost Sharing Profiles by Country". University of Buffalo 2010, March 5, accessed at http://gse.buffalo.edu/org/intHigherEdFinance/project_profiles.html.

An important precondition for effective engagement of the private sector is the inclusion of private institutions as valid organizations for voucher redemption, government scholarships, or student loans. If voucher programs are too restrictive and institutions are not able to reimburse the vouchers with government payers, the incentive to participate in education markets is diminished among private organizations. Similarly, if education grants or scholarships are applicable only in public sector institutions (e.g. when high achievers receive education solely in the public system), the capacity of private institutions to compete for students is naturally limited. Many governments in sub-Saharan Africa require students who qualify for maximum merit-based subsidies or grants to attend public programs. Given the traditional strength of the public sector institutions, historic presence, and uncertainty about quality of private schools (particularly if there is a regulatory vacuum with respect to public information), the expansion of vouchers, grants, and loans will not necessarily motivate more entry or result in greater market share for private educational providers. Nonetheless, it is an important mechanism for demand-side finance which private institutions rely upon to justify entry.

Extending the types of organizations that grants, vouchers, and scholarship and student loans can target is an important step in attracting private involvement in tertiary health education provision, but the future financial viability of these programs is also important. As indicated earlier, the default rates on student loans for tertiary education have typically been high, for example, 81 percent in Kenya in the 1980s. As a result, the types of students that receive assistance have been increasingly restricted. These limitations on demand-side finance may have some beneficial effects for private sector institutions. Private institutions that compete on price with those in the public sector (which now charge increasingly large fees) may become more attractive schooling options. On balance, limitations in financing for students reduce the viable market size, although certain segments (particularly lower-cadre tertiary health schooling which is less expensive) could, in theory, see an increase in demand as government support dwindles, but the demand for some tertiary education remains (albeit at a lower quality or level of training).

Reductions in finance from public sources for students may also represent an opportunity for private banks to participate in the financing of education, although they naturally will want to ensure that loans have a strong likelihood of repayment (perhaps via government guarantee). In the case of private finance, the viability of financing mechanisms presumably depends on the expected earnings that the education confers (or family assets) and willingness to pay for the education. If individuals do not have access to credit or grants, the ability to pay tuition or other costs (e.g. room and board) associated with education is restricted. The public sector may also wish to provide education for equity reasons as private sector finance may first focus on the most lucrative (high-income) market segments and, as a result, leave lower income groups (which are often credit constrained as well) outside the educational system, particularly at higher levels (Chapman, 2006).[13]

Options and Evaluation

To improve financing and involve the private sector in tertiary health education in the developing world context, countries may pursue four general options. These are:

- Expand public finance with additional taxes or bond revenues (and use the marginal revenue to, in part, contract out to the private sector);
- Augment public finance with novel private sources of revenue;

- Rely on private sector institutions such as banks to directly finance demand-side or supply-side educational funding;
- Rely on or partner with the private sector to finance and/or provide education.

Expansion of Public Finance Resources

If the government wishes to retain a dominant role in financing care to ensure equity or guarantee subsidization of health education (either via public or private provision), novel mechanisms to expand the resources available for education are important to consider. Because capital financing and updating are frequently a concern due to the expansion of the student population and a lack of facility expansion or improvement — new mechanisms that can inject funding for maintenance and capital construction while existing funding covers recurrent costs (mainly teacher salaries) are an attractive option. In other areas of global health, notably vaccine purchasing, the use of bonds, guaranteed by future payments from international donors, has effectively enabled countries and regions to fund vaccine purchases today that will have long run health benefits. The International Financing Facility for Immunization (IFFIm) relied on future donations by developed countries to serve as the underlying asset for future bond coupon payments.

Considering the international community's recognition that it is important to support health systems, not just high priority diseases, in order to address health disparities and meet international objectives (e.g. UN SDGs), donors might possibly fund a similar bond for health education. However, alternative sources to finance the coupon payments are important to consider — particularly in view of the level of donor fatigue and the recent global financial crisis. One option discussed more broadly in development is the notion of *diaspora bonds,* bonds funded by contributions from emigrants (Ketkar, 2009). While countries such as India and the Philippines have a large bases of ex-country workers to fund the bond, other developing countries could theoretically introduce a bond as well. Considering transaction costs, however, it may be more viable to implement the bond on a regional basis rather than nationally (which may help subsidize financing costs for smaller countries). One of the key issues with this mechanism is the voluntary nature of the funding source. In principle, "mandated remittances" from emigrants in developed countries with high earnings power via an additional tax (administered by the developed country) could ensure a higher level of funding. However, governments may have to guarantee the level of funds to lock in a strong bond market rating. In the case of Africa, preliminary analyses of a small (3 percent) additional income tax on physician and nurse emigrants during the first 10 years of (non-residency) medical service in developed countries suggest that the bond offering could raise between US$1 billion and US$2 billion equivalent at Pan-African level in light of the widespread emigration by nurses and physicians (authors' estimate, Clemens and Pettersson, 2006). This is just one potential mechanism for funding a bond issuance — a myriad of others are possible and may be more suitable depending on country characteristics and current financing for health education.

New taxes levied within each country on either individuals and businesses (such as Nigeria's tax on profits of limited liability companies) are another potential option. However, these are administratively difficult to implement and are likely to result in unfavorable economic distortions.

Augment Public Funding with Private Sources of Revenue

As indicated earlier, several countries have tapped private funding sources as a means of supporting public provision of education by renting facilities out to private institutions or conducting industry research in return for funding (or effectively taxing professors who receive private grants). Within the field of health, the latter may be useful as industry relationships could increasingly offer opportunity for profitable research collaboration. Partners may include for-profit pharmaceutical firms or contract research organizations, not-for-profit academic institutions in other countries, and government institutions (such as U.S. National Institutes for Health) which are increasingly active in developing therapies for "developing-country" diseases such as AIDS, tuberculosis, and malaria.

The expansion of funding for "developing-country" diseases via the Global Fund, GAVI, and other multinational organizations and foundations has motivated an increase in concomitant R&D activity. Recent policy such as the Food and Drug Administration priority review vouchers for approval of "neglected disease" approvals (United States) and separate approval mechanisms for therapies aimed at developing-country markets (European Union) will likely motivate additional clinical work going forward (Grabowski *et al.*, 2009). Africa is still a relatively small segment of the overall pharmaceutical market, but one that will grow fast. As several of these trials move into clinical phases which require patient populations, partnerships in developing-country markets become increasingly valuable. Currently, a limited number of trials are ongoing in Africa ($n = 5,856$ in Africa, about two percent of the Global Total as of April 2017), and 40 percent of those trials occur in the relatively developed infrastructure of South Africa ($n = 2,296$).[14] But the faculty capabilities for medical research are improving across Africa, and institutions such as the European and Developing Country Clinical Trial Partnership (EDCTP) are increasing the potential for collaboration (Matee *et al.*, 2009).

It is unlikely, however, that all health institutions would benefit from these relationships. The technical capacity requirements are high and most likely are available within medical schools with strong hospital and clinical linkages. Nevertheless, motivating institutions to develop the capacity to house clinical research via challenge grants might generate a viable steam of additional income for schools to augment operational or capital expenses in the long run.

Additional Private Sector Finance for Demand-Side or Supply-Side Funding

Many developing countries, as indicated earlier, rely on private banks to fund education via student loans. In principle, the scope of the private sector could expand (and perhaps include loans directly to educational institutions) but some important considerations affect the viability of these markets. These include:

- What is the likely default rate on loans?
- Is there a mechanism to ensure payment on bad loans (government assurance)?

- What segment of the market will these loans cover (low- versus high-cadre health workers, rural versus urban, risk level, type/characteristics of students)?
- Is the bank "at risk" or simply a loan administrator?
- Are there regulatory restrictions such as repayment schedules or limits on repackaging/securitization of loans?

As the government typically plays a dominant role in the financing of tertiary and health education, the "residual" market available to the private sector may have very different risk features. For example, if governments heavily subsidize physicians in training, then perhaps only the nurse or health worker market is a viable segment — and within that group the government may offer stipends or financing to high achievers (often the case in tertiary care). The remaining group has, perhaps, a different capacity to pay back their loans and effectively are part of a different market. For example, health workers may require only limited finance as the duration of education is shorter, and the costs are lower, but so, too, is the income potential of graduates. To prompt private entry into risky markets, governments have historically guaranteed loans (to an extent). This guarantee, though limited, has the benefit of injecting private capital but the potential cost of moral hazard is high for the banks if the terms of the guarantee are too generous.

Private banks may also simply serve as an administrator of loans, leaving financial risk with the government, but leveraging banks' ability to monitor and process payments in a manner that may exceed the government's capacity. Government policy also must balance the risk between the student and private banks so as to ensure reasonable repayment schedules and rates. Last, the ability of banks to package loans as securities may allow greater investment in "risky" student populations, but the bundling risk may not be viable, inasmuch as future incomes in the health sector may be strongly correlated across health workers (perhaps due to the influence of government in reimbursement for the health system). It is also not clear to what extent banks in developing countries package these types of loans for resale (as organizations such as Fannie Mae does for real estate in the United States).

Private Sector Finance and Provision

An alternative to simply engaging the private sector to offer finance for health workers is a "bundled" approach in which the government encourages private participation in finance and provision of educational services. Within this option, the government can either try to motivate the private sector to compete with public institutions directly or perhaps involve the private sector to focus on particular types of education, such as nurse or technician training, which have different entry requirements and which may be less likely to warrant government subsidy. Last, the government may wish to involve private provision for particular functions (e.g. capital development or management services) while retaining control of other core functions in a PPP.

PPPs can take myriad forms within tertiary education — many of them applicable to the health education context in lower income countries. The scope of services and responsibilities for private participants can vary

Table 8.13   Types of Contract in Education for Inputs, Outputs, and Processes

Level of production	General type of government contracts	What governments purchase
Input	Management, professionals, support services	• School management (financial and human resources management) • Support services (meals and transportation) • Professional services (teacher training, curriculum design, textbook delivery, quality assurance, and supplemental services)
	Facility availability	• Infrastructure and building maintenance
Process	Operational services	• The education of students, financial and human resources management, professional services, and building maintenance
Output	Education services (outputs)	• Student places in private schools (by contracting with schools to enroll specific students)
Input and output	Facility availability and education services	• Infrastructure combined with services (operational and educational outputs)

Source: Adapted from Patrinos *et al.* (2009).

Table 8.14   The Range of Options for PPPs in Infrastructure

Type of partnership	Features
Traditional design and build	The government contracts with a private partner to design and build a facility to specific requirements.
Operations and maintenance	The government contracts with a private partner to operate a publicly owned facility.
Turnkey operation	The government provides financing, the private partner designs, constructs and operates facility for a specified time period, while the public partner retains ownership of facility.
Lease–purchase	The private partner leases a facility to the government for a specified time period, after which ownership is vested with government.
Lease or own–develop–operate	The private partner leases or buys a facility from the government and develops and operates the facility under contact to the government for a specified time period.
Build–operate–transfer	The private partner obtains an exclusive contract to finance, build, operate, maintain, manage, and collect user fees for a facility for a fixed period to amortize its investment, and at the end of the franchise, the title reverts to the government.
Build–own–operate	The government either transfers ownership and responsibility for an existing facility or contracts with a private partner to build, own, and operate new facility in perpetuity.

Source: Adapted from Patrinos *et al.* (2009).

widely across inputs (human and physical capital), output (actual graduates), or processes (critical and auxiliary functions such as maintenance, etc.).

With respect to inputs, one of the key constraints currently burdening the system is the lack of physical capital infrastructure for health education. These restrictions are likely more acute at institutions which have high physical capital and infrastructure requirements — namely medical schools. Tables 8.13 and 8.14 summarize some of the options for involving private development of new infrastructure.

Just as the viability of private finance likely differs for medical versus nurse versus other health worker institutions, the degree to which the private sector can and will provide these services (and the policy justification for their involvement) is variable. As the private sector becomes more involved in both finance and operation of schools — the capacity of the state to manage risk and oversee contracts efficiently becomes more important. Interestingly, evidence from the primary and secondary education segment in developing countries suggests that the infrastructure projects which are turned over to state providers for operation in the future are somewhat difficult to manage effectively since the development risk (e.g. cost over runs in construction) require a large finance premium from government payers to offset the developer risk (particularly as the developer has no/limited ability to recoup any losses with operational revenue downstream) (Patrinos *et al.*, 2009).

Criteria for Entry (Education Providers)

New private sector education providers evaluating entry into a market are likely to consider a variety of regulatory and market criteria.

Regulatory Criteria

Whether as a partner in a PPP or an independent organization, providing education independent from the public sector, the regulatory foundation that the government establishes for private organizations are critical in developing a viable private industry. A recent work on regulatory practices in developing-country education cites the following eight tenets as central to enabling an efficient and well-performing private education sector (Fielden, 2008). These include:

1) Provide a sound policy framework for the operation of the private education sector
2) Introduce clear, objective, and streamlined criteria and processes for establishing and regulating private education institutions
3) Allow for-profit schools to operate

4) Allow private schools to set their own tuition fees
5) Provide incentives and support for private schools
6) Provide parents and students with information to help them select quality private education
7) Establish quality assurance/monitoring processes
8) Develop government's capacity to implement policy and manage private providers.

These criteria underscore that regulation is a mechanism that can ensure quality via credentialing, an important benefit given the uncertainty about quality and asymmetric information that consumers (students) may have with respect to the quality of the education. Students and families sacrifice current time, income and assets to purchase education — but with excessive uncertainty are less likely to do so. Of course, extreme bureaucratic barriers increase the cost of entry and limit competition across institutions to provide good quality relative to price. The private sector may operate in a limited way, even in countries with strong preferences for delivery via public institutions, and there are clearly numerous unregistered or non-licensed tertiary education institutions which have emerged to meet perceived market demand. But these schools, usually small in size with limitations in faculty quality, are less likely to operate efficiently in a regulatory vacuum.

In order to construct appropriate regulation for a particular country context, policy makers should identify the degree to which they wish to promote the private sector (Figure 8.3), the types of functions or markets that the private sector will participate in, and the nature of the interaction with public sector entities (competitors versus partners). This determination depends on the goals that the state has with respect to quality and number of health workers produced.

Market Criteria

The decision to enter markets and market competitiveness for health educational provision depends on the relative current and future costs and revenues associated with entry. These may differ quite dramatically across market segments in health education (as suggested in Table 8.15).

Table 8.15   Relative Input Costs and Output Revenue Potential across Health Education Institutions

Institution type	Physical capital requirements/ costs	Human resource requirements/ faculty costs	Graduate earnings (Reflective of revenue potential)
Medical school (MDs)	High	High	High
Nursing school	High/medium	High/medium	Medium
Medical technician school	High/medium	Medium	Medium
Community health worker	Medium/low	Medium	Medium/low

Health Education Type and Market Entry

The costs of entering the medical school market are high due to human resource and capital requirements (and the need for heavy market regulation and credentialing). The capacity of individuals (or the state) to support these institutions hinges, in part, on graduates' future income and government's willingness to subsidize education (also in the private sector) in return for the future social benefits of physician care. While physician incomes are high and private medical schools do exist, it is unlikely that entry for stand-alone schools will occur to a large extent if state-run institutions have already captured the best students (and subsidize their tuition more generously), and the finite high-quality faculty are already employed in public institutions. More likely to improve quality and outcomes are private financing initiatives that outsource components of education (perhaps even management) to independent for-profit or not-for-profit entities.

Nursing schools may vary in quality and type of nurse production and thus differ on input requirements and costs. The reduced revenue potential due to lower nurse salaries (relative to physicians), however, may be offset by the larger number of graduates that schools can produce per faculty member or capital overhead. Regulatory hurdles may also be less stringent and the requirements for faculty, at least for some courses, may be reduced relative to the case with medicine. Although tuition and graduate revenues are lower in lower cadre institutions, the input costs may be significantly lower (with the exception of capital equipment that medical technicians may use in training), and the duration of study is a fraction of higher-level health workers.

Summary

This chapter examined the literature to gauge the extent of public and private finance and provision in tertiary education (generally and in health) and identified key options and issues that both public and private education providers and financial institutions will face as the health education markets evolve to meet the increased demand for education and requirements of health systems in lower income countries. Key insights include:

1) The justifications for the roles of both public and private finance and provision of education are theoretical as well as practical. In many cases, the public good aspects of health education supported state-based financing and provision of health education. The recent shift toward implementing user fees has shifted the balance in select cases, but few countries have a clear and deliberate policy and related financing arrangements to maximize production of health workers by strategically taking advantage of both public and private sector possibilities.

2) Training health workers offers substantial private benefit for students: (incomes are good, if not high, for all cadres relative to alternatives). The subsidy to health-related training need not be 100 percent and might be a much lower percentage of total cost to account for the social benefit, which exceeds the private benefit. Government policies and practices that hinder or obstruct private provision of training (such as subsidizing the best students, subsidizing the costs of government schools) do not have to be taken as immutable and could be changed to save on scarce government resources and to alleviate constraints on private provision.

3) An enabled regulatory environment (for both private finance and provision models) that addresses school quality and promotes entry/

competition is central to a robust private sector. As stressed in the related market study on provision (Chapter 11), privately provided training looks to be more dynamic, flexible, and innovative than publicly provided training, but private provision must be regulated to ensure quality.

4) Capital costs and recurrent expenditures differ significantly across different cadres in the health sector. The role that the private sector should ideally play (in both finance and provision) accounts for differences in educational costs relative to the public or private benefits conferred by the education.

5) Examination of PPPs in health education is warranted. Because the health sector traditionally is highly regulated, health education is frequently publicly provided. The extent of variation with respect to how public sector and private sector providers and financial institutions can interact (both competitive and collaborative models) and the specific functions/markets should be further explored. Specifically, how do lessons from primary, secondary, or non-health tertiary PPPs inform how to develop these organizational forms in the tertiary health sector?

6) Both public and private financial resources can be expanded by exploring alternative sources of finance. Industry research collaborations, microcredit models, and hospital affiliations are examples of potential means of extending the budgets of educational institutions.

7) The demand side (students) and supply side (tertiary health-sector educational institutions) are both viable targets for novel finance models.

These and other issues are important to examine in detailed country, market and institutional level analyses.

Endnotes

1. The study identified and queried 169 schools; 100 of them fully responded to the survey.
2. Data in this section are from SAMSS (Sub-Saharan African Medical School Survey) 2013, June 10, accessed at http://www.samss.org/samss.upload/wysiwyg/SAMSS%20ReportFinalV2_120110b.pdf.

3. Professional personnel and non-professional personnel account, respectively, for 45.6 percent and 14.3 percent of expenditures. Goods and services account for 19 percent and capital equipment 17.6 percent of expenditures.

4. Less than three percent in some Ghanaian Medical Schools.

5. Private provision of education may also be enhanced by allowing public funding sources for individuals, such as public merit-based scholarships and needs-based grants to be directed toward private institutions. In most of francophone Sub-Saharan Africa, this practice is uncommon (exception, perhaps, in Côte d'Ivoire).

6. Provision may encompass ownership of the school, management of the school, or both.

7. During the same period, public enrollment also increased, but at a 10 percent rate.

8. From a theoretical standpoint, the relative private rate of return between tertiary education and primary or secondary education increases as the supply of primary and secondary graduates increases. Competition is greater for wages and increased value associated with seeking additional education to differentiate one's skills within a larger pool of job applicants with primary or secondary education.

9. Data in this section are from International Comparative Higher Education and Finance Project (Database), "Higher education financing and cost sharing profiles by country", University of Buffalo, 2010, March 5, accessed at http://gse.buffalo.edu/org/intHigherEdFinance/project_profiles.html.

10. See Endnote 9.

11. Some observers contend that demand-side strategies such as vouchers have not always promoted improved academic performance across the distributions of students. Some evidence suggests that the strongest effects are concentrated on top students and that parents do not always sort on the basis of school academic performance (Patrinos *et al.*, 2009).

12. See Endnote 9.

13. However, the numerous public–private partnerships that engage the private sector to provide management, operational, educational, and facility services have frequently been implemented with specific contract targets to increase access to low-income or difficult-to-access (rural) groups. Many of these programs have been quite successful in fulfilling these goals (Patrinos *et al.*, 2009).

14. Clinical trial data are from ClinicalTrials.gov. US National Institutes of Health, Washington, DC 2017, April 10, accessed at available at: http://clinicaltrials.gov.

References

Ajayi, T. and R. A. Alani, *A Study on Cost Recovery in Nigerian University Education: Issues of Quality, Access, and Equity*, Accra: Association of African Universities, 1996.

Beciu, H. and D. Haddad, "Human resources for health: Costing Ghana's pre-service HRH scale up plans", (Africa Regional Human Development), Washington, DC: World Bank, 2009a.

Beciu, H. and D. Haddad, "Scaling up education of health workers in Ghana: A country assessment", Washington, DC: World Bank, 2009b.

Beciu, H. and R. P. Jacob, "Global trends in tertiary medical education: Policy recommendations for sub-Saharan Africa", Washington, DC: World Bank, 2009.

Bruns, B., A. Mingat, and R. Rakotomalala, *Achieving Universal Primary Education By 2015: A Chance For Every Child*, Washington, DC: World Bank, 2003.

Chapman, B., "Income contingent loans for higher education: International reforms", In *Handbook of the Economics of Education*, (eds.). by E. Hanushek and F. Welch, pp. 1435–1503, Amsterdam: Elsevier, 2006.

Chen, L. and T. Evans, "Human resources for health: Overcoming the crisis (joint learning initiative)", Harvard University, Cambridge, MA, 2013, July 15, accessed at http://www.who.int/hrh/documents/JLi_hrh_report.pdf, 2004.

Clemens, M. and G. Pettersson, "Medical leave: A new database of health professional emigration from Africa", Center for Global Development, Washington, DC, 2006.

Dovlo, D., "The health workforce in Africa: challenges and prospects", Africa Working Group of Joint Learning Initiative, New York, NY, 2013, July 15, accessed at http://www.who.int/hrh/documents/HRH_Africa_JLIreport.pdf, 2006.

Fielden, J. and N. LaRocque, "The evolving regulatory context for private education in emerging economies", Education Working Paper Series 14, International Finance Corporation, Washington, DC: World Bank, 2008.

Glewwe, P. and M. Kremer, "Schools, teachers, and education outcomes in developing countries", In *Handbook of the Economics of Education*, (eds.). by E. Hanushek and F. Welch, pp. 945–1017, Amsterdam: Elsevier, 2006.

Grabowski, H. G., D. B. Ridley, and J. L. Moe, "Encouraging innovative treatment for neglected diseases through priority review vouchers", In *Prescribing Cultures and Pharmaceutical Policy in the Asia-Pacific*, (ed.). by K. Eggleston, pp. 347–366, Washington, DC: Brookings Institution Press, 2009.

IFC (International Finance Corporation), *The Business of Health in Africa: Partnering with the Private Sector to Improve People's Lives*, Washington, DC: International Finance Corporation, 2007.

IFC, *Investing in Private Education: IFC Strategic Directions*, Washington, DC: IFC, 2001.

Jamison, E. A., D. T. Jamison, and E. A. Hanushek, "The effects of education quality on income growth and mortality decline", *Economics of Education Review*, **26**(6), 771–788, 2007.

Jimenez, E., "The public subsidization of education and health in developing countries: A review of equity and efficiency", *World Bank Research Observer*, **1**(1), 111–129, 1986.

Johnstone, D. B., "The economics and politics of cost sharing in higher education: Comparative perspectives", *Economics of Education Review*, **23**(4), 403–410, 2004.

Kapur, D. and M. Crowley, "Beyond the ABCs: Higher education and developing countries", CGD Working Paper 139, Center for Global Development, Washington, DC, 2008.

Ketkar, S. and D. Ratha, "New paths to funding", *Finance & Development*, **46**(2), 43–45, 2009.

Matee, M. I., C. Manyando, P. M. Ndumbe, T. Corrah, W. G. Jaoko, A. Y. Kitua, H. P. A. Ambene, M. Ndounga, L. Zijenah, D. Ofori-Adjei, S. Agwale, S. Shongwe, T. Nyirenda, and M. Makanga, "European and developing countries clinical trials partnership (EDCTP): The path towards a true partnership", *BMC Public Health*, **9**(1), 249–255, 2009.

McPherson, M. S. and M. O. Schapiro, "U.S. higher education finance", In *Handbook of the Economics of Education*, (eds.). by E. Hanushek and F. Welch, pp. 1403–1434, Amsterdam: Elsevier, 2006.

Mullan, F., S. Frehywot, F. Omaswa, E. Buch, C. Chen, S. R. Greysen, T. Wassermann *et al.*, "Medical schools in sub-Saharan Africa", *The Lancet*, **377**(9771), 1113–1121, 2011

Musini, M., "Uganda", In *African Higher Education: An International Reference Handbook*, (ed.). by D. Teferra and P. G. Altbach, pp. 611–623, Bloomington, IN: Indiana University Press, 2003.

Ngolovoi, M., "Means testing of student loans in Kenya", Paper presented at Comparative and International Higher Education Policy: Issues and Analysis Workshop, Albany, NY, 2006.

Otieno, W., "Student loans in Kenya: Past experiences, current hurdles and opportunities for the future", *Journal of Higher Education in Africa*, **2**(2), 75–100, 2004.

Patrinos, H. A., F. Barrera-Osorio, and J. Guaqueta, *The Role and Impact of Public–Private Partnerships in Education*, Washington, DC: World Bank, 2009.

Patrinos, H. A. and S. Sosale, *Mobilizing the Private Sector for Public Education: A View from the Trenches*, Washington DC: World Bank, 2007.

Preker, A. S., A. Harding, and P. Travis, "'Make or Buy' decisions in the production of health care goods and services: New insights from institutional economics and organizational theory", *Bulletin of the World Health Organization*, **78**, 779–790, 2000.

Preker, A. S., M. Vujicic, Y. Durkan, C. Ly, H. Beciu, and P. N. Materu, "Scaling up health professional education", Washington DC: World Bank, 2008.

PROPHE (Program for Research on Private Higher Education International Dataset), "Sub-Saharan Africa's private and public higher education shares (2002–2009)", University of Albany Program for Research on Private Higher Education, Albany, NY, 2010, accessed at http://www.albany.edu/dept/eaps/prophe/international_databases.html.

Saint, W., "Innovation funds for higher education: A users' guide for World Bank funded projects", Education Working Paper Series 1, International Finance Corporation, Washington, DC, 2006.

Salmi, J., "Student loans in an international perspective: The World Bank Experience", 2013, October 25, accessed at http://siteresources.worldbank.org/INTLL/Resources/student_loans.pdf, Washington DC: World Bank, 2003.

Salmi, J. and A. M. Hauptman, "Innovations in tertiary education financing: A comparative evaluation of allocation mechanisms", Education Working Paper Series 4, International Finance Corporation, Washington DC: World Bank, 2006.

Sanyal, B. and M. Martin, "Management of higher education with special reference to financial management in African countries", International Institute for Educational Planning Contributions No. 28, UNESCO, Paris, 1997.

Scheffler, R. M., J. X. Liu, Y. Kinfu, and M. R. Dal Poz, "Forecasting the global shortage of physicians: An economic and needs-based approach", *Bulletin of the World Health Organization*, **86**, 516–523B, 2008.

Sosale, S., "Trends in private sector development in World Bank education projects", World Bank Policy Research Working Paper No. 2452, Washington DC: World Bank, 2000.

UNESCO (United Nations Education, Scientific and Cultural Organization), "Trends in tertiary education: Sub-Saharan Africa", UNESCO Institute for Statistics (UIS) Fact Sheet, December (No. 10), 2010, accessed at http://www.uis.unesco.org/FactSheets/Documents/fs10-2010-en.pdf.

UNESCO (United Nations Education, Scientific and Cultural Organization). "Financing tertiary education in Africa", 2013, October 25, accessed at http://www.unesco.org/education/WCHE2009/synthese170609.pdf UNESCO, Paris, 2009.

WHO (World Health Organization), *Global Strategy on Human Resources for Health*: *Workforce 2030*, Geneva, Switzerland: WHO, 2016.

WHO (World Health Organization), *Scaling Up, Saving Lives*: *Task Force for Scaling Up Education and Training for Health Workers*, Geneva. Switzerland: WHO, 2008.

WHO (World Health Organization), *Working Together for Health*: *2006 World Health Report*, Geneva, Switzerland: WHO, 2006.

Wolfe, B. and S. Zuvekas, "Nonmarket outcomes of schooling", *International Journal of Educational Research*, **27**, 491–502, 1997.

World Bank, *Accelerating Catch Up*: *Tertiary Education for Growth and Competitiveness in Sub-Saharan Africa*, Washington, DC: World Bank, 2009.

World Bank, "The state of the health workforce in sub-Saharan Africa: Evidence of crisis and analysis of contributing factors", accessed at http://info.worldbank.org/etools/docs/library/206769/The%20State%20of%20Health%20Workforce%20in%20SubSaharan%20Africa.pdf Washington, DC: World Bank, 2009.

World Bank, *Higher Education in Developing Countries*: *Peril and Promise*, Washington, DC: World Bank, 2000.

Yizengaw, T., "Implementation of cost sharing in the ethiopian higher education landscape: Critical assessment and the way forward", *Higher Education Quarterly*, **61**(2), 171–196, 2007.

Chapter 9

Public–Private Partnerships in Financing Health Education

Taara Chandani and Ilana Ron Levey

Introduction

Private sector participation in tertiary medical education is gaining prominence in developing countries as a complement to public sector provision and a way to accelerate the production of health workers. Private actors are increasingly entering the health education marketplace, an area that has traditionally fallen under the purview of governments. The explicit partnerships between the public and private sectors that are emerging carry enormous potential to scale up the health workforce, improve efficiencies and quality, and spur innovation.

Definition and Framework

The term "public–private partnerships" (PPP) carries a range of interpretations according to geographic context, and as donors, governments, and the private sector commonly adopt different definitions. Fundamentally, PPPs are founded on the premise that governments can meet — and potentially enhance — their policy objectives by using service delivery models that go beyond the traditional publicly financed and delivered ones. The World Bank describes a PPP as a partnership between the public and private sector for the purpose of delivering a project or a service that may come in a variety of different legal or contractual forms. Adding more specificity, this chapter defines a PPP as a formal collaboration between government at any level (federal, state, district, city) and the private sector (commercial or non-profit actors) to jointly regulate, finance, or implement the delivery of medical education. While the scope and formality of PPPs may differ substantially in practice, the literature identifies certain common elements that frame these partnerships (Patrinos, 2007):

- Involve public and private sectors
- Entail a formal arrangement with contractual basis
- Involve sharing of risks and rewards
- Maintain a focus on outcomes
- Recognize complementary role of public and private sectors.

This chapter focuses on PPPs in the tertiary medical education sector. It considers the full range of post-secondary certification and degree programs for medicine, public health, midwifery, nursing, pharmacy, and allied health professions. Institutions that offer these programs are diverse in terms of ownership (public, private, or hybrid), formality, and teaching philosophy, among other factors. For instance, public training institutions may experience varying degrees of autonomy from central ministries, and in some cases, are privately managed. Private institutions may be for-profit or not-for profit in their operating status, or aligned with faith-based movements (Frenk *et al.*, 2010, 22). Beyond these core educational establishments, other actors involved in the supply of medical education include regulatory bodies, professional councils, associations, and research organizations. Figure 9.1 is an illustrative list of public and private actors involved in the supply of tertiary medical education.

Formal partnership arrangements that have a contractual basis at their core are discussed at length in this chapter. However, other, more informal or *ad hoc* types of partnerships are also useful for expanding high-quality medical education. For instance, in the United States, private, philanthropic funds may be used to fund a research initiative or facilities upgrade in a public university. This discrete act of private philanthropy involves

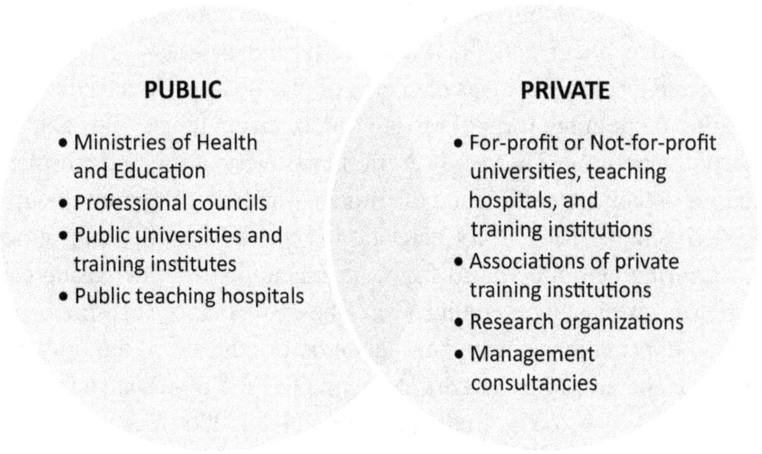

PUBLIC	PRIVATE
• Ministries of Health and Education • Professional councils • Public universities and training institutes • Public teaching hospitals	• For-profit or Not-for-profit universities, teaching hospitals, and training institutions • Associations of private training institutions • Research organizations • Management consultancies

Figure 9.1   Public and Private Actors in Medical Education

considerable public–private intersection and interaction while falling short of the components of a more formal PPP. This chapter investigates formal PPPs in medical education but recognizes that an increasing number of less formal public–private interactions are emerging in the education landscape, particularly in the developed world.

Public and Private Dynamics in Tertiary Education

Throughout the developing world, private participation in education has dramatically increased over the last 20 years for citizens at all wealth quintiles (Patrinos *et al.*, 2009). Governments typically have three core policy objectives with regard to the delivery of education, which are also relevant to health worker education. These include governance (who decides?), ownership/delivery (who provides?), and financing (who pays?) (Patrinos, 2007; Enders and Jongbloed, 2007). The "publicness" of higher education — in the form of provision, legal authority, and funding — is being transformed in many ways, as private features of higher education grow in incidence and importance (Enders and Jongbloed, 2007). Increasingly, the boundaries between private and public are blurred: public policy is delegated to semi-autonomous agencies and independent networks, and public universities are outsourcing research and teaching, even as elements of private are also introduced into the public realm in the form of private funding from households and state-induced competition. There are several key drivers of this transformation, including a lack of sufficient government funding to accommodate an expanded demand for tertiary education (and traditionally, with governments prioritizing public funds for basic education), the increasing use of market or quasi-market policies in the governance of universities, increased expectations for higher standards of education, the emergence of distance and cross-border education, and the rise of private educational institutions (Bollag, 2004; Enders and Jongbloed, 2007).

Public–private dynamics in tertiary medical education largely follows this trajectory, resulting in mixed public and private patterns of governance, management, and financing (Frenk *et al.*, 2010). Tertiary medical education produces important positive externalities for society in the form of an expanded health workforce and improved health systems, and thus falls under the close purview and responsibility of governments. At the same time, tertiary medical education (compared with basic or secondary education) ensures a private return on investment by giving individuals the professional credentials to obtain employment or access higher wages. This private benefit translates into a willingness to make private contributions — relative to the expected pay-off. On the supply side, private medical educational institutions are increasingly entering the market and are well positioned to respond to increased aggregate demand for medical training and labor market needs, producing more and differentiated cadres of health workers. For example, non-governmental faith-based organizations train as much as 70 percent of the nurses and midwives in Uganda and Malawi and between 30 percent and 55 percent in Zambia and Tanzania, respectively (Pearl *et al.*, 2009). Private medical educational institutions have also demonstrated impressive growth in India and Brazil. In India, more than 75 percent of the medical schools established in the last three decades are private for-profit institutions. The emergence of private medical establishments presents a welcome source of funding, but also raises questions about their regulation and quality (Frenk *et al.*, 2010, p. 28).

Other drivers in the emergence of PPPs for medical education include a conducive national regulatory framework and legal environment that allow both public and private stakeholders to openly and systematically meet, share information, and form contractual arrangements. The greater the private sector role in contributing to national health and education policies and debates, the more plentiful are the opportunities to discuss PPPs as a potential option for raising funds to expand medical education. At the global sociopolitical level, globalization and corresponding patterns of cultural and information exchange may broaden knowledge and awareness of PPPs for education and therefore increase their use in neighboring countries.

The well-known medical schools of the Caribbean region illustrate some of the complex dynamics resulting from globalization in contemporary medical education. While these schools have not entered into formal, transnational partnerships with the United States, close interaction between these private schools and medical licensure body in the United States exists. For instance, the St. James School of Medicine designs its curriculum to prepare students for the United States Medical Licensing Examination (USMLE) and produces graduates that are eligible to practice as a medical doctor in the United States or Canada. The St. James School of Medicine is also accredited by the Caribbean Authority for Education in Medicine, the Israeli Ministry of Health and, provisionally, by the United Kingdom.[1] Likewise, the Ross University of Medicine in Dominica has graduated over 7,700 physicians over the last 30 years and views its mission as "providing students with rigorous curricula that mirror the education of our U.S. peers".[2] While not formal partnerships in the traditional PPP sense, there are high levels of trans-border public–private interaction and engagement in these Caribbean examples.

Determinants of Private Sector Involvement in Medical Education

Key determinants of private sector involvement in financing and delivery of tertiary education include regulatory controls and incentives and the attractiveness of the market for private actors (IFC, 2010, p. 6). In practical terms, involvement by the private sector in medical education depends

Table 9.1   Input Costs and Output Potential Across Health Cadres

Type of institution	Capital requirements	Human resource/faculty costs	Graduate earnings
Medical school	High	High	High
Nursing school	High/medium	High/medium	Medium
Medical technician school	High/medium	Medium	Medium
Community health worker	Medium/low	Medium	Medium/low

on the opportunity and the costs, both current and future. These opportunities and costs are a function of the particular context and labor market dynamics as well as the type of health cadre enrolled. Table 9.1 summarizes the relative input costs and output revenue potential across health cadres (IFC, 2010, p. 30). For example, medical schools require relatively higher capital investments and human resources than nurse training schools, but offer a higher payoff for students and can potentially leverage greater private contributions.

Table 9.2 classifies public and private roles in education according to financing and ownership/ delivery. While the regulatory and certification functions of tertiary medical education are largely housed — as they should be — in the public domain, its financing and delivery take on a variety of configurations. The public–private interplay manifests itself in the introduction of user fees at public institutions (left column, bottom row), and through various types of government support to private educational institutions (right column, top row).

A governance function overlays this entire matrix, and the governance of private medical education is discussed extensively in this book. Even privately owned and financed institutions experience political interference from governments and require high levels of support and interaction from national and state governments. For instance, in India, privately owned and financed medical schools are required to have a government-determined proportion of "merit seats" that allow qualified students to pay a lower tuition rate for the first four years of medical school (Beciu and Jacob, 2009, p. 102).

However, there are few truly "public" or "private" tertiary medical education institutions in either developed or developing countries due to

Table 9.2   Public and Private Roles in Education, by Financing and Ownership/Delivery

		Ownership/Delivery	
		Public	**Private**
Financing	**Public**	Traditional public institutions — Subsidized or no user fees	Private institutions that receive government support — Contracting out — Targeted vouchers — Tax incentives — Transfer payments or subsidized loans
	Private	Public institutions with private cost-sharing — User fees — Student loans — Private contributions	Independent private institutions (for-profit and not-for-profit) — User fees — Student loans — Private contributions, equity or debt

Source: Adapted from IFC (2007, 2009, 2010).

the many permutations of public–private interactions that occur distinct from formal PPPs. In sub-Saharan Africa, for example, boards of directors in public medical universities may perform private governance functions and the same public university may contract out cleaning services to a private maintenance company. Likewise, in the Netherlands, all schools are publically funded but most are administered by private school boards (Patrinos *et al.*, 2009). Many public medical universities utilize textbooks delivered by or curriculum designed by private sources. These examples suggest that a broad spectrum of public–private interactions and small-scale contracting arrangements exist side-by-side with larger, more formal PPPs in medical education. As explicit forms of engagement, PPPs can enhance the inherent interconnectedness between the public and private sectors to achieve greater performance, efficiency, and innovation in tertiary medical education.

Types of Public–Private Partnerships

Considered in this chapter are public and private partnerships that are bound by varying degrees of formality, geographies, and types of

Table 9.3   Public–Private Partnerships in Medical Education

Type	How it works
Contractual	Governments contract with private operators to manage public training institutions.
Legal requirements or tax incentives	Governments require private educational institutions to provide scholarships to low-income students or provide tax breaks to encourage greater public benefit.
Supply-side subsidies	Governments subsidize the establishment or operations of private educational institutions.
Demand-side subsidies	Governments finance vouchers, scholarships, or loans for students to enroll in private institutions.
Sale of public assets	Governments allow the private sector to purchase part or all of a public university's assets and manage its operations.
Voluntary or philanthropic partnerships	The private sector makes financial, intellectual or in-kind contributions to build capacity and support operations of public medical training institutions.

voluntary and legal arrangements. It does not consider government regulation and oversight of private institutions as a PPP, since this is a core public function. Table 9.3 lists illustrative PPPs in medical education; specific examples of each type are discussed in the penultimate section of this chapter.

Why Medical Education PPPs, and Why Not?

While there is little empirical evidence about the effectiveness of PPPs in tertiary medical education, there is ample guidance from the health and education sectors more broadly about the value proposition in structuring PPPs. Following is a discussion of the key benefits that can result from PPPs in tertiary medical education:

1) *Expand the health workforce by accessing new sources of financing, knowledge, and skills.* Governments can leverage the private sector to increase the overall supply of medical education — in the form of physical infrastructure, financial resources, human capital or teaching faculty, and management skills or information technology.

2) *Align public and private incentives and improve coordination and planning.* PPPs offer a pathway for governments to strategically engage and align incentives with the emerging private sector (PwC, 2010). Explicit partnerships can also preempt governments to improve their coordination, data collection, and planning functions across public and private sectors. Over time, improved quality and use of information between the relevant ministries and public and private sectors can harmonize the demand for and supply of medical professionals to meet health system needs and priorities.

3) *Encourage public and private partners to focus on their core capabilities.* Partnerships can enable different actors to focus on their comparative advantages, leading to higher efficiency, scale, and quality of medical education. Given their specialized skills, private players can potentially introduce new advances in research, curriculum design, and technologies. Meanwhile, by transferring a portion of their responsibility in supplying and financing medical training to the private sector, governments can focus on their stewardship role and strengthen regulatory frameworks that are coordinated across public and private institutions.

4) *Ensure greater responsiveness to the labor market and increase access to underserved groups.* Private institutions can help to meet the expanded and differentiated demand for medical education. Traditionally, it is argued that public higher education universities serve the elite and do not meet their purported goals to ensure open, fair access that is based on merit (Enders and Jongbloed, 2007, p. 22). Private institutions are often formed in response to a real, local need for higher education and "give voice to the communities that they reach";[3] private institutions typically need to attract more students and thus have incentives to introduce cost-effective and innovative channels that increase access, such as distance learning programs.

5) *Pilot innovation and foster transformative learning.* Partnerships with the private sector have potential to transform modalities of learning, whether they entail the introduction of new technologies such as e-learning platforms, or innovative curricula that focus on competency based, individualized learning (Frenk *et al.*, 2010, p. 38). Private actors, including networks of accredited training institutions, IT specialists, or research consultancies can spur innovation and take on higher risk with regards to innovation.

Against these potential benefits are also costs to structuring PPPs in medical education. Designing and negotiating a partnership between the public and private sectors can require considerable time and money, so developers or "brokers" should be able to make the case that the investment will pay off in terms of improved efficiencies or health outcomes.

Why There Are Traditionally Few PPPs in Tertiary Medical Education

There are fewer PPPs in tertiary medical education than in the wider health care system or higher education in other sectors. Starting in the 1990s, PPPs in the health sector were dominated by infrastructure projects, typified by the National Health Service hospitals in the United Kingdom where the government outsourced construction and maintenance of nearly 100 hospital facilities to the private sector. By 2010, the footprint of PPPs expanded in scale and scope, reaching many parts of Africa and Asia, and extending well into the delivery of clinical care and information technology (PwC, 2010).

Governments have traditionally maintained strong, centralized control over tertiary medical education — with regards to defining standards of education, curriculum and teaching pedagogy, as well as financing and managing these services. Education at all levels is seen as crucial to nation-building and typically considered a public good; this also holds true in tertiary medical education where governments across different geographies maintain relatively high control of supply. Against this backdrop, private medical institutions face barriers to entry with unfair competition, complex accreditation protocols, costly teaching infrastructure, and limited ability to attract credentialed faculty. This is especially the case for universities that confer medical degrees and less so for training institutes that produce lower level health cadres, where fixed costs and entry requirements are relatively lower (IFC, 2009, p. 20). Besides high entry barriers, regulatory frameworks may not be suitable for private sector participation. In some cases, for example, governments do not appropriately credential students who graduate from private schools to work, constraining these institutions' ability to attract students (IFC, 2009, p. 23).

Finally, limited public sector capacity to establish partnerships is also a factor contributing to the relative dearth of PPPs in tertiary medical education. Developing country governments commonly lack the capacity and experience to structure partnerships, manage risk and measure the performance of a given PPP.

Examples of PPPs in Medical Education

This section details examples of PPPs in tertiary medical education world-wide. They are organized under specific types of partnerships to highlight a particular angle, though many examples represent more than one type of partnership. These examples were derived from a thorough desk review of published, peer-reviewed literature, as well as gray materials and self-reported studies by specific schools.

Contractual PPPs

There is growing evidence of government contracting with the private sector to take over management and teaching functions of tertiary medical training institutions. While historically much of the experience with contracting has involved non-academic or management services (such as the University of Dar es Salaam (USDM) in Tanzania), the landscape is shifting to models in which the public sector outsources the delivery of core clinical or teaching functions. The theoretical literature regarding education PPPs suggests that contracting arrangements with the private sector for education allows more flexibility than public sector arrangements, particularly around the hiring and firing of instructors (Patrinos *et al.*, 2009, p. 4).

Various forms of contracting to the private sector are used in education, including management services, operational services, education services, and facility availability (Patrinos, 2006). In the United States, United Kingdom, and Latin America, private actors have been contracted to run or "take-over" low-performing public schools or to run schools for remote or hard-to-reach populations. This contracting of operational services for medical education has rarely occurred in sub-Saharan Africa, even with large percentages of remote or hard-to-reach populations and underperforming medical education institutions.

In Tanzania, the University of Dar es Salaam, a public institution, underwent a long phase of reform involving cost-cutting and quality improvements — at the heels of two decades of severe funding cuts. USDM for both adapted its curriculum to meet changing labor market needs and prepare a new cadre of entrepreneurs and managers, including introducing a degree in public health. As one of its cost-cutting measures, USDM for both outsourced its non-academic services such as catering and security. It utilized an open, competitive bidding process to select contractors, resulting in significant cost savings and, in some cases, improved quality of services. Factors that were critical to the success of this transformation included strong, sustained leadership to drive the process, introduction of formal mechanisms to structure and monitor the transformation, and a broad consultative process to include staff, students, and the community in the planning (Bollag, 2004).

In Brazil, the Professional Qualification Program for Health Professionals (PROFAPS, 2005–2009) has established itself as an important national effort to scale up health worker education through extensive collaboration and partnership. Similar in design to Brazil's predecessor Program for Training Auxiliary Nurses (PROFAE), the PROFAPS initiative was built on a foundation of public engagement between health and education ministries, a vast network of stakeholders and involvement of private medical training institutions (GHWA 2008a, pp. 20–21). Under the initial effort, over 300 technical schools were accredited and contracted to train a specialized cadre of nurse auxiliaries; a vast majority of these institutions were private and went through a competitive bidding process to participate. As a result, over 320,000 health attendants and auxiliary nurses went through the program and upgraded their clinical skills (IDB, 2006). The PROFAE program also introduced innovative distance-learning methodologies which allowed it to train more than 13,000 new health workers since 2000 (GHWA, 2008a, p. 54).

The Christian Health Association of Malawi (CHAM), a not-for-profit organization, is responsible for a large portion of health service delivery and health worker training in Malawi. The association owns 10 nurse training hospitals that produce over 70 percent of trained nurses. CHAM is a key partner with the government in implementing the Emergency Human Resources Program (EHRP) that was introduced in 2004. As a comprehensive health workforce scale up plan, the EHRP was driven by the government of Malawi, the UK Department for International Development (DFID), the Global Fund, and various local stakeholders. The government contracted CHAM to expand its health worker training capacity and implement the EHRP widely. According to the Global Health Workforce Alliance, as a result of the sectorwide approach and coordination with non-governmental organizations (GHWA, 2008a, p. 22), between 2003 and 2007, the government was able to increase pre-service training capacity of health workers by 165 percent and increase fourfold the number of medical training places (GHWA, 2008b). As of 2009, CHAM-affiliated training institutions provided as much as 70 percent of pre-service training for nursing and midwifery, and 40 percent of health worker training overall (Pearl *et al.*, 2009).

In India, there are numerous efforts to utilize PPPs to expand medical education. For instance, the Directorate of Health Services in the Andaman and Nicobar Administration is at an early stage of contracting a private provider to develop and manage a medical college, and construct or upgrade several additional hospitals. The private contractor is expected to invest 50 percent of the total capital outlay needed, retain revenues and operate the institute under a 30-year contract on a "no-profit, no-loss" basis. The contractor will also oversee the core teaching and general management functions of the college.[4]

In Uttar Pradesh, the state government is establishing five medical colleges and two paramedical colleges and is in the process of bidding and contracting to the private sector to finish building the schools and manage the institution. Originally, the Uttar Pradesh government had planned to build and manage these seven institutions on its own, but abandoned these plans in favor of a contracting approach.[5] To encourage private investment, the Uttar Pradesh government will give an additional 100 acres of land to selected private bidders.

Demand-side Subsidies

Demand-side subsidies may be one of the most robust mechanisms for encouraging entry of private institutions and increasing competition between public and private institutions. There is evidence worldwide of governments' providing full or partial financial aid to students who enroll at private medical institutions. The exact terms of the assistance range from grant scholarships to subsidized student loans, and vary in their design and sustainability. Experience from across the world shows consistently high default rates (due to moral hazard) when governments directly manage and sponsor student loan schemes (IFC, 2010, p. 21). Governments also fund scholarships and vouchers for students studying in the private sector, though in some cases (such as in Uganda), only not-for-profit institutions can benefit from such subsidies.

The Kenyan government's Higher Education Loan Board (HELB), established in 1995, offers students, in both public and private institutions, access to subsidized loans. Loans are structured at four percent annual compounded interest and have a one-year grace period following graduation from a program. Where possible, repayments are automatically deducted by the employer and are structured to not exceed 25 percent of a graduate's monthly salary. The maximum loan amount offered is approximately $2,000. In 2006–2007, the HELB administered nearly 29,000 loans. According to HELB, the volume of loans recovered has steadily increased between 1995 and 2005; however, the rate of default in the 1990s was known to be greater than 80 percent (World Bank 2010, p. 79).

The *Government of Tanzania* has expressly supported the financing of medical students, leading to greater demand and access to education and an increase in the number of medical schools in the country. Through the Higher Education Student Loan Board, the government sponsors means-tested and interest-free student loans for full-time university students (SAMSS, 2009). In 2007, more than 55,000 students accessed loans through this facility that is worth over US$250 million.[6] This volume of lending is significant and validates data from other sources that as much as 80 percent of students in higher education access a government loan in Tanzania (SAMSS, 2009). The government also offers means-tested grants to students in public or private medical training institutions, and recipients have a five-year service requirement in either the public or private health sector.

The *Government of Uganda* has initiated a partnership with the DANIDA, the Danish Foreign Ministry's development cooperation agency and other development partners to offer scholarships for students enrolled in private not-for-profit faith-based institutions. The scheme is targeted to students from hard-to-reach districts who agree to serve in an underserved area for the same duration as the length of the course. Students can choose to enroll in any institute within the Catholic, Protestant, or Muslim Medical Bureaus. The scheme was launched in May 2009 and thus far has supported 200 students to enroll in nursing, midwifery, and allied health training programs. The scholarship is set at roughly $2,500 for the average course, covering tuition, room, and board. DANIDA is committed to funding this program for three years, with the expectation of reaching 600 more students. The Ugandan government is contributing 25 percent of the total fund in the first year and will increase this to 100 percent by the fourth year.[1] (Uganda Protestant Medical Bureau, 2010).

More broadly across education in both the developing and developed worlds, vouchers are an important and controversial demand-side tool to finance enrollment in private schools and potentially increase the number of students utilizing the private education sector. For instance, beginning in 1981, Chile began financing both public and most private schools with vouchers. The data on the impact of vouchers on education outcomes are mixed due to selection bias but in the case of Chile, findings suggest the enrollment in private school franchises conveys a larger academic advantage than enrollment in public or private independent schools. Franchises may benefit from the scale of education professional and administrators, as well as bulk purchasing of supplies and equipment (Elacqua, Contreras, and Salazar, 2007). Although few examples exist, exploring the role of vouchers, as well as medical school franchises, for medical education in countries with a developed enough private education market, could be useful.

Supply-side Subsidies Including Public Investment

Though limited in number, there is important evidence of supply-side subsidies to the private education sector in developing countries. These include up-front public investment in private universities or ongoing subsidies to fund operating costs of private training institutions. Given the cost structure of private medical education and the need for public or charitable support (IFC, 2009), these examples of effective supply-side subsidies are extremely relevant and instructive.

An innovative and ambitious public–private partnership, the Public Health Foundation of India, was established in 2006 to scale up access to public health education and help address the growing disparities in access to health care in the country. The foundation is structured as an independent body and receives a mix of public and private funding. Specifically, it leveraged seed funding from Indian philanthropists (more than $20 million), the Indian government, and the Bill and Melinda Gates Foundation ($15 million each). Besides the up-front investment by the federal government, the foundation will continue to partner with local and state governments and engage in new cost-sharing arrangements. In the short term, the foundation is partnering with four state governments to create eight training institutes of public health, building much needed capacity in health policy, management, epidemiology, and other related fields. Ultimately it aims to achieve national scale and create a new cadre of health leaders to respond to emerging needs in the private and public health sectors (Chen, 2006).

The Herbert Kairuki Memorial University (HKMU) in Tanzania is a private for-profit medical institution that presents various elements of a public–private partnership. It was founded in 1997 as the first accredited private medical institution in Tanzania. HKMU raised start-up capital from internal savings and was donated land from its affiliate hospital. A critical ingredient in its growth was access to a soft loan from the government of Tanzania that helped fund capital expansions; the government also supported professional development and donated a computer laboratory. On the demand side, the government offers scholarships and loans to help students cover the cost of tuition; these scholarships and loans are extremely important to maintain ongoing operations, given that nearly half the students have difficulty paying their tuition (SAMSS, 2009; Rugarabamu, 2010). Beyond financial support, HKMU partners with public district hospitals to give students the hands-on, practical learning experience they need and expose them to health care working conditions across the country (Mullan *et al.*, 2011).

In India, the Directorate of Medical Education under the state government of Uttar Pradesh is transferring public assets to private developers to establish five medical colleges and two paramedical institutions to scale up the production of much-needed health professionals. The state government stalled after partially laying the infrastructure for the institutions and decided to outsource the initiative to the private sector. The state government donated the partially completed buildings and 100 acres of land to private developers. During start up, the government outsourced several private management companies to assist with the competitive selection and negotiation process. Ultimately, the developer will be responsible for managing and operating the medical training institutions although the exact ownership and revenue model is not decided.

Voluntary and Philanthropic Partnerships

Voluntary, professional relationships between academic and research institutions, commonly in the form of South–South or North–South exchanges, are prevalent and a valuable source of support for private and public training institutions. Typically, such relationships are centered on improving the quality of education and research rather than scaling-up the production of workers (IFC, 2009, p. 29). Additionally, individual philanthropic efforts through endowments or private philanthropy can establish research chairs, improve facilities, and launch teaching initiatives. In many South African universities like the University of Cape Town and the University of the Witwatersrand, alumni serve as an important source of philanthropic commitments. "Twinning" is a common type of partnership that takes a variety of forms including student and faculty exchanges, secondment of consultants, technical exchanges, and staff capacity building. According to the SAMSS, these types of partnerships are present in virtually all medical training institutions; for instance, all 10 medical schools (public and private) that were visited during the SAMSS have partnerships with universities and funding institutions in other countries (Mullan *et al.*, 2011, p. 55). Many twinning relationships are funded with donor resources, primarily from the United States Government and the Bill and Melinda Gates Foundation.

Makerere University in Uganda, a renowned public institution, has a handful of partnerships with private international and local organizations. For example, Johns Hopkins University, Walter Reed Hospital, Baylor

College of Medicine, and Yale University have an ongoing presence on its campus, collaborating with research as well as teaching. The Makere has also been able to draw on support from some of these partners to contribute housing and transport allowances for students and to cover the cost of their placement in community-based health sites (Mullan *et al.*, 2011, p. 56).

Another public institution, the College of Medicine (COM), in Malawi, has an extensive network of collaborating partners in Africa (South–South) and outside the continent. One such partnership is with the non-governmental Southern Africa Human Capacity Development (SAHCD) Coalition that represents a network of colleges in the region. Under this framework, an innovative and ambitious public–private partnership, COM graduates work in other countries and return to complete their service in Malawi. The network of participating colleges receives assistance with accreditation and quality assurance, thus ensuring standardized education across the region. Besides this collaboration, COM has various partnerships with donors (e.g. the World Health Organization and the Norwegian Agency for Development Cooperation, and private universities in the United States, including Johns Hopkins University. Research initiatives funded under these partnerships provide supplemental income for faculty — in addition to supporting the cost of carrying out research — and is a key factor in ensuring staff retention (Mullan *et al.*, 2011, p. 56).

In Kenya, a non-governmental institution, the African Medical Research Foundation (AMREF) is working to upgrade the professional skills of certified nurses in partnership with the Nursing Council of Kenya (NCK), the Kenyan Ministry of Health, and Accenture (a global management consulting and technology services company). The consortium of partners has developed an innovative distance-learning model, the AMREF Virtual Nursing School, with the aim to register as many as 20,000 nurses. Partners bring complementary expertise and resources to the table: Accenture provided financial and technical support in setting up the digital infrastructure for the Virtual Nursing School, NCK worked closely with AMREF to develop the curriculum and manage the training efforts, while the Ministry of Health approved the curriculum and allows nurses graduating from AVNS to register for clinical placements at accredited public and private institutions (Nguku, 2009).

Through the support of the US government, the Medical and Nursing Education Partnership Initiative (MEPI and NEPI) is in the process of investing over $100 million to strengthen approximately 30 African medical and nursing schools, as well as national ministries of health and education.[7] Specific award activities are determined in collaboration with national government agencies and institutional stakeholders but broadly have the mandate to increase the number of graduates of medical and nursing institutions. MEPI and NEPI are two of the largest twinning efforts ever attempted.

Legal Provision PPPs

Partnerships established through legal mandates can take various forms, adapted to a country's legal and regulatory, economic, and educational environment. In one type of legally driven partnership, the government establishes legal requirements that private universities provide scholarships to low-income or otherwise disadvantaged students. Two components are essential to this modality: a desire to promote the public good as well as generate private expenditures triggered by a legislative requirement. Alternatively, a country's legislation can include provisions in which universities receive tax exemptions by providing scholarships to poor or marginalized students. Another mode of partnership through legal provision requires the inclusion of civil society or business community members on the boards of directors of higher education institutions.

In Malaysia, private educational institutions accounted for 52.5 percent of student enrollment as of 2009. Despite the private sector's already large contribution to higher education, the government maintains tax policies to further promote its expansion. Schools providing technical, vocational, or scientific courses (including medical and health sciences) benefit from tax incentives administered by multiple government agencies, including the Malaysian Industrial Development Authority, the Multimedia Development Corporation, and the Inland Revenue Board of Malaysia. These tax incentives include investment tax allowances, tax exemptions (sometimes up to 100 percent), duty-free importation of multimedia equipment, industrial building allowances, and accelerated capital allowances, to name a few.

Due, in part, to this type of partnership, the private sector's high level of participation in higher education has increased access not only for Malaysian citizens, but for international students as well, many of whom come from developing countries (Tham, 2011).

Sale of Public Assets Provision

Selling public assets to a private buyer is a seemingly straightforward tactic to increase private sector participation in higher education but can be politically contentious. Under this type of PPP, the government permits a private entity to purchase all or part of a public university's assets, often resulting in greater autonomy for the institution. While such PPPs would seem common, few completed transactions have been formally documented.

Since Mongolia's democratic transition in 1990, the country has taken steps to increase private sector engagement in its system of higher education through contracting arrangements for management services and the sale of assets. In the case of the University of the Humanities, the government used both approaches. In 2001, the Mongolian government entered into a management contract with the school administration. In 2003, after a two-year pilot, the government evaluated the contract performance and decided to sell the university (property and other assets) to the management team. The team then established a plan to further develop the school, which it shared with the government. Since the sale of the university, enrollment has increased, and the school has enjoyed greater freedom to modify curricula and programs of study (such as adding two new majors) and increased access to information technology by installing an 80-computer laboratory. There have been some complaints, however, about the shift in ownership and about strains of market pressures. Additionally, as a private institution, the university no longer offers its professors the same benefits received by professors under the public system. For some, this shift has raised concerns over retention and educational quality as professors seek out positions at public universities. Others, in contrast, are optimistic about the private education system and believe the new ownership will encourage staff to work harder (Holzhacker *et al.*, 2009).

Education Franchising

There has been a growth in social and commercial franchises in Africa over the last 10 years, particularly for health care. These franchises offer standardized health care procedures and quality assurance procedures, as well as the benefits of centralized branding, marketing plans, and training for personnel. Many American and British universities like New York University and the University of Bolton have built satellite campuses in different countries, often in partnership with local governments. The new campuses benefit from association with an education "brand name", access to high-quality curricula and teaching methods, and utilization of academic staff association with the home institution.

The Johns Hopkins School of Medicine initiated a new institute dedicated to international medical education in May 2011, in collaboration with the government of Malaysia. The Johns Hopkins Dr. Mohan Swami Institute for International Medical Education will use its *Genes to Society* curriculum for instruction at all partner institutions globally. The institute will develop Malaysia's first fully integrated, private, four-year graduate medical school and teaching hospital through a PPP with the government of Malaysia and has plans to replicate this model globally (Johns Hopkins Medicine, 2011).

Lessons from PPPs in Medical Education Worldwide

Public–private partnerships in medical education are nascent in much of the developing world and present an opportunity to apply best practices from sectors where PPPs are more common. Though there is little documentation or evaluative evidence of the impact of PPPs in medical education in developing countries (GHWA, 2008a, p. 46, 60), they have the potential to leverage much-needed resources, competencies, and technologies to scale up health worker education.

The emergence of private medical training institutions in many parts of Asia, Latin America, and Africa is an important precursor to the formation of PPPs. Market dynamics and regulatory frameworks that are conducive to the entry of private institutions can facilitate opportunities for explicit partnerships between the public and private sectors; however, greater private sector participation also calls for stronger oversight and supervision of medical education systems.

Voluntary forms of collaboration between institutions, across and within national borders, can greatly enhance educational quality and productivity. Such partnerships are widely prevalent across geographies and represent an important short-to-medium term strategy to scale up the production of health workers (GHWA, 2008a, p. 12). Faculty exchanges, sharing of curricula, and collaborative research can directly improve key institutional functions in education, research, and service. Collaborations between academic and non-academic institutions (such as information technology or business consulting firms) can also lead to important advances in innovation, quality, and productivity (Frenk *et al.*, 2010, p. 33).

PPPs that address systemic gaps in the demand and supply of medical training may require a longer-term horizon. If a medical education market is dominated by a subsidized public sector, governments may need to incentivize entry of new private institutions through financial subsidies or tax breaks — instruments that take time to have an impact. Governments may thus have to consider a longer-term horizon before realizing cost-savings or performance gains from certain types of PPPs.

Government-led demand-side subsidies for students (vouchers, loans, or scholarships) should follow the student rather than the institute. This approach will help ensure a level playing field between public and private training institutions and develop a differentiated market for medical training. In general, government support in the form of grants and vouchers should be means-tested to ensure the optimal use of subsidies for the poor.

Effective student loan initiatives require the sharing of risk between public and private stakeholders and can benefit from innovative PPPs. Experience shows that purely government-sponsored student loan schemes are unlikely to succeed or be sustained, and the commercial banking sector on its own will not offer high-value loan products for students. There is a compelling case for the introduction of subsidies by government (such as partial risk guarantees) that can incentivize private actors to respond to the growing demand for education loans.

In addition, governments should ensure that adequate information is available to students and other stakeholders about the private education market. Many prospective students in the developing world may not be aware of the private medical education market in their countries. Thus, standardized data on key indicators such as graduation rates, job placement rates, and class sizes of private (and public) medical training institutions should be made easily accessible. An independent accreditation agency that measures and disseminates both public and private school performance data is an important step in building an informed consumer base.

Conditions for Success in PPPs in Medical Education

1) Assess the need and feasibility of a PPP in the context of the broader health system — ensuring the availability of qualified teaching staff, access to clinical training sites, adequate employment opportunities and remuneration, and governance of the education and health system.
2) When structuring a PPP, ensure that a strong and conducive regulatory framework is in place that coordinates between the education and health systems and is supportive of public and private involvement in medical education.
3) Identify a champion within the public sector to drive the formation of PPPs in medical education, review their effectiveness and advocate for relevant models.
4) Invest in improving health management information systems to match training capacity with demand for health workers across public and private sectors.
5) Revitalize the associations of medical schools to advocate for better harmonization of public and private sectors and serve as a clearinghouse for data and dialogue.
6) Base all decisions on the type of partnership to structure — contracting out services or introducing demand-side financing at private institutions — on a careful analysis of the gaps in the health system and labor market, and ensure that it is aligned with the government's short- and long-term goals.

7) Build consensus among partners in defining the scope, structure, and expected outcomes of a given partnership. Successful PPPs are based on identifying a solution that is mutually beneficial to all partners, where the risks and rewards are appropriately balanced.

8) Voluntary, twinning partnerships between academic institutions should be based on a clear identification of need at a given institution, definition of a common and long-term vision between both partners and strong inter-institutional trust.

9) As far as possible, ensure that partnerships have clear performance-based goals in place and measurable results.

Endnotes

1. Uganda Protestant Medical Bureau, interview, 2010.
2. For more information, visit http://bonaire.sjsm.org and http://anguilla.sjsm.org.
3. For more information about the Ross University of Medicine, visit www.rossu.edu.
4. For more information, visit the webpage, "Public–Private Partnerships and Giving Voice to Communities for Improving Health and Education", on the World Bank website at http://web.worldbank.org/WBSITE/EXTERNAL/TOPICS/EXTEDUCATION/0,contentMDK:21550596~menuPK:2448393~pagePK:210058~piPK:210062~theSitePK:282386~isCURL:Y,00.html.
5. For more information about this public–private partnership, visit http://healthmarketinnovations.org/program/medical-college-ppp-andaman-and-nicobar-islands.
6. To learn more about this contracting arrangement, visit http://www.financial-express.com/news/up-allows-pvt-sector-entry-into-medical-education/650449.
7. See an international comparison of government student loan programs at http://gse.buffalo.edu/org/inthigheredfinance/files/Student_Loan_Matrix.pdf.
8. For more information, visit http://www.pepfar.gov/about/2010/150649.htm.

References

Beciu, H. and R. P. Jacob, *Global Trends in Tertiary Medical Education: Policy Recommendations for Sub-Saharan Africa*, Washington, DC: World Bank, 2009.

Bollag, B., *Improving Tertiary Education in Africa*: *Things that Work*, Washington, DC: World Bank, 2004, accessed at: http://siteresources.worldbank.org/ AFRICAEXT/Resources/no_66.pdf.

Chen, L. C., "Philanthropic partnership for public health in India?" *The Lancet*, **367**(9525), 1800–1801, 2006.

Elacqua, G., D. Contreras, and F. Salazar, *The Effectiveness of Franchises and Independent Private Schools in Chile's National Voucher Program*, 2007.

Enders, J. and B. Jongbloed, (eds.). *Public–Private Dynamics in Higher Education: Expectations, Developments and Outcomes*, Bielefeld, Germany: Verlag, 2007.

Frenk, J., L. Chen, Z. A. Bhutta, J. Cohen, N. Crisp, T. Evans, H. Fineberg, P. Garcia, Y. Ke, P. Kelley, and B. Kistnasamy, "Health professionals for a new century: transforming education to strengthen health systems in an interdependent world", *The Lancet*, **376**(9756), 1923–1958, 2010.

GHWA (Global Health Workforce Alliance), *Scaling Up, Saving Lives. Task force for Scaling Up Education and Training for Health Workers*, 2008.

GHWA (Global Health Workforce Alliance), *Malawi's Emergency Human Resources Programme*, Country Case Study. Geneva: World Health Organization, 2008b.

Holzhacker, D. O., O. Chornoivan, D. Yazilitas, and K. Dayan-Ochir, *Privatization in Higher Education*: *Cross-Country Analysis of Trends, Policies, Problems, and Solutions*, Washington, DC: Institute for Higher Education Policy, 2009.

IDB (Inter-American Development Bank), "National training program revamps the nursing profession in Brazil", 2006, accessed at: http://www.iadb.org/en/ news/webstories/2006-04-13/national-training-program-revamps-the-nursing-profession-in-brazil,3009.html.

IFC (International Finance Corporation), *The Private Sector and Tertiary Medical Education*, Investing in People Series, Paper 4, Washington, DC: World Bank, 2009.

IFC (International Finance Corporation). *Role of the Private Sector in Health Education in Africa*, Investing in People Series, Paper 5, Washington, DC: World Bank, 2010.

Johns Hopkins Medicine, "Hopkins to house new international medical education project", Press Release, 2011, accessed at: http://www.hopkinsmedicine.org/ news/media/releases/hopkins_to_house_new_international_medical_ education_project.

Mullan, F., S. Frehywot, C. Chen, R. Greysen, T. Wassermann, H. Ross, H. Ayas, S. B. Chale, S. Cyprien, J. Cohen, and T. Haile-Mariam, *The Sub-Saharan African Medical Schools Study*: *Data, Observation and Opportunity*, Washington, DC: The George Washington University Medical Center, 2011.

Nguku, A., *Nursing the Future*: *e-Learning and Clinical Care, in Kenya*, London, UK: Africa Research Institute, 2009.

Patrinos, H. A., *Public–Private Partnerships*: *Contracting Education in Latin America*, Preliminary Draft, 2006.

Patrinos, H. A., *International Evidence on Public–Private Partnerships to Improve Access and Quality in Education*, Washington, DC: World Bank, 2007.

Patrinos, H. A., F. Barrera-Osorio, and J. Guáqueta, *The Role and Impact of Public–Private Partnerships in Education*, Washington, DC: World Bank, 2009.

Pearl, E., S. Chand, and C. Hafner, *Training Health Workers in Africa: Documenting Faith Based Organization's Contributions*, Technical Brief 17. Chapel Hill, NC: The Capacity Project, IntraHealth International, Inc, 2009.

PwC (PriceWaterhouse Coopers), *Build and Beyond*: *The (R)evolution of Health Care PPPs*, 2010.

Rugarabamu, P., "Herbert Kairuki Memorial University", presentation, African Medical Education Symposium, Dar es Salaam, Tanzania, 2010.

Tham, S. Y., *Exploring Access and Equity in Malaysia's Private Higher Education*, ADBI Working Paper 280. Tokyo: Asian Development Bank Institute, 2011, accessed at: http://www.adbi.org/working-paper/2011/04/19/4513.access.equity.malaysia.higher.educ.

SAMSS (Sub-Saharan African Medical Schools Study), *SAMSS Site Visit Report: Hubert Kairuki Memorial University*, 2009.

World Bank, *Financing Higher Education in Africa*, Washington DC: World Bank, 2010.

Chapter 10

The Market for Health Education

Howard Tuckman, Alexander S. Preker, and Eric L. Keuffel

Introduction

As has been documented in earlier chapters, the human resources crisis is a key constraint in growing LMIC health systems to meet systemic needs. The critical nature of the lack of human resources in health (HRH) has been brought to the forefront of the health debate in the last few years (Scheffler *et al.*, 2008, IFC, 2007).[1] Donors thus far have focused on public interventions to address the HRH crisis. Numerous forums and initiatives have been set up to address the issue of the HRH crisis.[2] While many of these have examined the economy as a whole, both tradition and history have caused the focus of these to be interventions by donors and governments. As a consequence, there has not been a vision as to how best to tap the private sector's potential. For current purposes, this sector is defined to include both small and large private businesses, non-governmental organizations (NGOs), financial institutions that create markets and participate in medical institutions, foreign entities interested in establishing a presence in LMIC countries, and the community of international investors. These entities have been largely untapped and poorly integrated into the framework of the discussion and the strategies for scaling up the resources devoted to the sector. Given the severity of the crisis, it is essential that novel strategies recognize the depth and breadth of private resources available in LMICs.

There is a paucity of data on the private sector in medical education within LMICs and a lack of rigorous analysis of its role. In part, this is a reflection of the attention paid in the past to public solutions. In part, too, it reflects the limited reliable data and systematic analytical work on the private sector in general in developing countries. Since systematic data collection does not occur, researchers and policy makers must rely on survey data collected episodically. This data vacuum restrains the ability of policy makers, donors, and private investors to generate evidence-based policies and investments.

The policy community lacks an analytical framework for thinking about the potential contribution of the private sector. Given the lack of data and in-depth analytical work in the area, the dialogue around the private sector in HRH still too often reverts to stereotyped interactions between private–public in medical education in developing countries. This traditional view purports that the private sector absorbs workers from the public sector. At best, the private sector is said to take up the excess demand for medical education primarily at the lower end of the quality spectrum (in terms of students and program strength). There is a clear need to understand the system more holistically, and understand both the potential contribution and the risks of the private sector. At a minimum, the relevant private players in the provision of medical education need to be identified and the markets in which they provide resources. Systematic identification and clarification of their role is an important prerequisite for developing strategies that lead to the expansion of the resources devoted to medical education by the private sector.

There are untapped opportunities in knowledge transfer from other sectors. Numerous models for funding medical education exist within the world's health community. These emerge as a result of differences in resources available, in training methods, availability of skill sets within a country or region, the infrastructure base, different cultures and mores, and types of illness treated. There is a lack of transfer of knowledge and innovative models to the human resources crisis in LMICs from private non-medical education and private medical education outside LMICs. This chapter aims to demonstrate the potential applicability of these model to private medical education is LMICs.

In considering which business models may work within the context of health education sector in LMICs, a deductive approach is used in this chapter. Starting with a general characterization of the potential market, discussion proceeds to specific business or organizational models that may contribute to improving production of human resources for health. As such, the review has five sections (each with a goal):

- In "Market Frameworks", market frameworks and the private sector's role are identified. The conceptual approaches are broadly summarized to first define and then assess markets and the role the private sector plays as a participant within the marketplace.
- In "Characterization", select health education market(s) are described based on the available data and literature.
- In "Present Models and Issues", select business models are identified and described and we propose important policy issues for health education markets.
- In "Organizational Assessment", the managerial, financial, operational, and strategic criteria for evaluation of specific health education institutions are highlighted. This section is a preview of the case studies in the second half of the volume.
- In "Recommendations and Conclusions", recommendations are discussed, and the ability of policy makers to inhibit or promote the entry or emergence of private health education is assessed.

Market Frameworks

Economists agree that a market exists whenever buyers and sellers come together to engage in trade. This simple but robust definition can accommodate a wide range of market situations from the sale of fish in the Thai floating markets to the types of Internet trading that exist on Amazon, to the large global markets for currency.

Market Types

Numerous theoretical and empirical studies contribute to the way in which researchers and practitioners define the boundaries for a market, and explore how homogeneous a market will be. Indeed, there are many different ways to do business within the confines of a market (high-quality versus low-cost product), and this can create disagreements among those who examine the market for health education services. Key to marketplace analysis is the realization that people trade only when it is to their benefit to do so, that trades give rise to valuable information on how both price and quantity are decided by sellers and responded to, and that markets exist at many levels (e.g. local, regional), that the market for labor interacts with the market for goods and services, and that differences among markets in price and quantity will equalize when markets are allowed to operate freely (e.g. the market for the Swedish krona in Bogota will adjust to changes in the exchange rate for the krona in Iceland). While this analysis primarily relies on the framework provided by economics, it is recognized that other important contributions stem from the sociological and even biological realms. These are not relevant in the current discussion, but they do have a bearing on the recommendations that are proposed.

Variation exists in how efficiently markets operate and the role of private sector participants may differ depending on several key variables. Classic microeconomics, which is concerned with the study of the theory of the firm, broadly characterizes markets as "perfect competition", "monopolistic competition", "oligopoly", and "monopoly" (as well as other variants) on the basis of the number of firms (and buyers), the level of differentiation of products or services across firms, the degree to which market actors are fully informed, and the barriers to entry (such as large fixed costs). Table 10.1 summarizes these market types (Katz and Rosen, 1994). As a first step in assessing the market for private tertiary health education institutions in Africa, the type market that applies most appropriately is characterized (and the reasons explained). It is likely that different markets exist within the LMIC tertiary health education market (e.g. nursing, lab technician, community worker), and these may reflect

Table 10.1 Market Types and Characteristics

Market characteristics	Market type			
	Perfect competition	Monopolistic competition	Oligopoly	Monopoly
Number of firms/ buyers	Many firms Many buyers	Many firms (but price makers), many buyers	Few firms selling to many buyers	One firm Many buyers
Product/service differentiation	Identical products	Differentiated products (limited distinctiveness of product/ service)	Product may be identical or differentiated	No substitutes
Information	Perfect information for buyer and seller	Usually well informed	Either well informed or poorly informed	Perfect information
Barriers to entry	No entry barriers	No entry barriers	Usually barriers restrict entry	Very high barriers, No entry possible
Strategic behavior	No	No	Yes (across sellers, according to price or production)	Yes (by seller)
Role of private sector	Private firms enter and leave easily. Service provided at lowest average cost. Competition determines price.	Potential for either "too much" or "too little". Firms use resources to differentiate their product. Number of firms is less than in perfect competition. Price higher	Potential for private firms to either compete on price (Bertrand equilibrium: 0 profit) or collude to segment market volume (Cournot equilibrium)	Private monopolist has no competition in its market. Has strong control over price unless regulated Sets price and quantity produced
Marginal incentive for private entry	Earns a market return if enters	Earns a normal return but may be able to extract modest extra return	Usually earns a return that involves excess profit Persistence depends on competition	High but strong barriers to entry Monopolists may be subject to regulation

Source: Katz and Rosen (1994), authors' analysis.

different market conditions (e.g. ease of entry and exit), creating diverse roles for the private sector.

Market Characterizations: Accounting for Supply and Demand

In addition to the classic microeconomics characterization of markets, several business disciplines integrate the core disciplines and examine markets and/or the role of firms, organizations, or actors within markets (Figure 10.1). Within the field of business, these disciplines include marketing, management, and industrial organization. Each of these subdisciplines has its own set of theoretical and/or applied constructs that characterize markets and/or the environment in which firms or organizations operate. For example, in the management literature that examines theory explaining firm or organizational success within a market, key constructs include the "Structure–Conduct–Performance" approach (Porter, 1980), the Resource-Based View (Barney, 1991; Rumelt, 1984), and "Dynamic Capabilities" (Dierickx and Cool, 1989; Levinthal, 1997; Teece *et al.*, 1997).[3] By its nature, the management literature tends to more explicitly examine characteristics of firms and organizations on the supply side of the market (although the effects of demand are more implicit, they are still recognized as vital). In contrast, the marketing literature has generally focused more on the demand-side considerations when conceptualizing the market (Kotler *et al.*, 2008; Adcock *et al.*, 2001). The industrial organization literature concentrates on market structure and how changes in information, homogeneity of product, ease of entry and exit, and number of players affect both the output and price of a good or service (Schmalensee *et al.*, 2007). This area of economics provides unique insights into monopoly, oligopoly, game theory, and how the effects of regulation and the market conditions listed above create a framework for analyzing how effectively markets operate as compared to a perfectly competitive marketplace.

There are myriad applications within each of these disciplines (and wide variability in how each of these may be implemented across industry). For example, within the marketing field, the "Four Ps" (price, product, placement, and promotion) create a popular customer-oriented

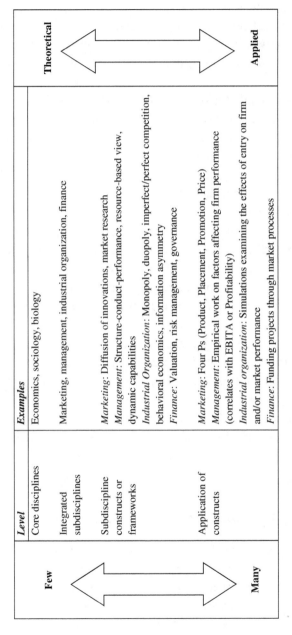

	Level	Examples
	Core disciplines	Economics, sociology, biology
	Integrated subdisciplines	Marketing, management, industrial organization, finance
	Subdiscipline constructs or frameworks	*Marketing*: Diffusion of innovations, market research *Management*: Structure-conduct-performance, resource-based view, dynamic capabilities *Industrial Organization*: Monopoly, duopoly, imperfect/perfect competition, behavioral economics, information asymmetry *Finance*: Valuation, risk management, governance
	Application of constructs	*Marketing*: Four Ps (Product, Placement, Promotion, Price) *Management*: Empirical work on factors affecting firm performance (correlates with EBITA or Profitability) *Industrial organization*: Simulations examining the effects of entry on firm and/or market performance *Finance*: Funding projects through market processes

Figure 10.1 Academic and Empirical Approaches to Market Assessment

framework that some researchers adopt to assess a market and determine how to optimally position an existing product/service or develop a new product/service. Instead of arguing for a particular mechanism to describe a market, the argument suggests that, at their crux, these mechanisms should optimally attempt to evaluate some type of supply and demand determinants.

As such, this market assessment (Table 10.2) identifies the potential role for private sector involvement via an examination of the elements that affect both supply and demand for goods. Looking across other health-related markets (e.g. pharmaceuticals, health insurance, health training, provider services) helps demonstrate the type of role the private sector can play as well as the attendant policy environment that may affect private decisions (e.g. patents).

Market-based approaches also provide guidance to what causes market failure. Imperfect and /or asymmetric markets, inadequate demand, continuously falling average costs, large externalities and other barriers to the production of goods and services affect the operations of markets, as can expectations. Applications of market-based approaches should take these into account in the planning process. Table 10.2 characterizes the key features (entry barriers, information environment, potential for strategic behavior, and product/service differentiation) on affecting supply and demand within particular health markets (Dranove and Satterthwaite, 2000; Scherer *et al.*, 2000; Sloan, 2000; Gaynor, 1994; Pauly, 2000; Zweifel and Manning, 2000). It also identifies the overall market characterization and the role of the private sector. This exercise helps motivate the characterization of the health education market(s) in the second section.

Market Characterization: Health Education

Extending the market analysis framework to health education markets helps elucidate where private sector firms are most likely to sustainably participate in the market and to increase social welfare (Figure 10.2). Information on the tertiary private health education market is very limited,

Table 10.2 Market Characteristics in Select Health-Related Markets

Health market	Supply-side market characteristics	Demand side market characteristics
Pharmaceuticals Overall characterization: Monopolistic competition/oligopoly	*Entry (supply)* • Low marginal cost of production(usually), high fixed costs of development (low cost of generic development) • Intellectual property protection (Patents) are barrier to entry *Information* • Transparency/disclosure knowledge available (FDA, EMEA etc.) aims to ensure accurate public information regarding efficacy/safety/effectiveness of products • Regulators regulate merger and acquisition *Product differentiation* • Therapeutic-level competition between manufacturers (branded, generic) • Access to distribution networks (esp. in developing countries) • Competition at both research and development (R&D) and marketing (product, price, placement, position) level • Patents limit molecular-level competition	*Entry (demand)* • Many buyers, but various levels of customer (individual, employer, health plan; typically individual-level demand in developing country settings) • Demographic/epidemiologic level demand (upper bound) • Economic demand (influenced by income, extent of insurance, and subsidies) • Individual or insurer demand/reimbursement (based on efficacy, price, safety) *Information* • Physician/pharmacist serves as "informed intermediary" for individuals *Product differentiation* • Generic versus brand market share • Price differentiation mechanisms (different prices across different groups/willingness to pay) *Strategic behavior* • In some countries, government wields monopsony power

(Continued)

Table 10.2   (*Continued*)

Health market	Supply-side market characteristics	Demand side market characteristics
	Strategic behavior	*Private sector's role*
	• Potential for monopoly pricing due to patents	• Private individuals pay copays or total cost (if uninsured)
	Private sector's role	• Health plans/employers (for profit/not-for-profit) negotiate prices for private insured populations
	• Generally private manufacturing (both generic and branded products)	• Governments purchase for public insured population
	• Revenue potential; clinical trials, job creation, subsidies for training	• Attract skilled workers
Health insurance	*Entry (supply)*	*Entry (demand)*
Overall characterization:	• Government systems: Dominant public insurer (e.g. United Kingdom)	• Individual and/or collective (employer-based, government, sickness fund) purchasing
Monopoly (government) oligopoly	• Social insurance systems: Multiple "sickness funds" (e.g. Germany)	• Adequacy of coverage/substitutes
	• Mixed systems: Bifurcated insurance with multiple private (for-profit/not-for-profit) insurance providers and dominant government provider in some segments (e.g. Medicare, Medicaid in United States)	*Information*
		• Individuals may have poor information on quality of physician in network.
	• Relatively high fixed costs to enter private market	• Moral hazard results in increased utilization due to insurance coverage (individuals use more covered services than they otherwise would given the reduced marginal price to the consumer resulting from insurance coverage).
	Information	*Product differentiation*
	• Heavy regulation of private market to prevent abuses	• In competitive markets, differentiation via extent of services and price (quality versus price trade-off) sorts market in competitive markets→Adverse selection (e.g. cream-skimming) possible
	• Firms may have poor information on individual and/or group level risks	

Product differentiation

- In competitive markets, differentiation via extent of services and price (quality versus premium price trade-off) sorts market in competitive markets→adverse selection possible (e.g. cream-skimming)
- Quality differentiation dependent on human resources (physician and provider networks), but providers serve multiple insurers (usually)

Strategic behavior

- Sole government provision may mandate enrolment and financing (via taxes) and limit product differentiation, but addresses equity, access, and cost

Private sector's role

- Variation in degree of government provision and financing across countries
- Usually at least some private provision (for-profit/not-for profit) in most systems/market for private insurance

- Pooling and separating equilibrium across different segments (some markets require government action/mandates to ensure cross-subsidization)
- In some markets, government is oligopolist
- Quality differentiation dependent on human resources (physician and provider networks)

Strategic behavior

- In competitive local private markets, large purchasers (employers or large groups) may control significant market share

Private sector's role

- Private purchasers of health insurance include individuals, employers or other groups (for non-government systems or components)

(Continued)

Table 10.2   (*Continued*)

Health market	Supply-side market characteristics	Demand side market characteristics
Hospitals Overall characterization: Oligopoly	*Entry (supply)* • High fixed costs limit entry • Market is usually defined at regional or local level. • Certificate of Need (United States) or similar policies aim to reduce excess investment across hospitals for specific health products (e.g. MRIs), but potentially constrain entry. • Developing country typically characterized by large, government urban hospital with limited competition and limited supply of beds relative to total demand. • Presence of religious order hospitals alters marketplace. *Information* • Heavy regulation for both government and private hospitals to ensure quality and limit expenditures. *Product differentiation* • Can accomplish by multiple provider networks one stop shopping. • Access and location differentiate. • Quality is important when known.	*Entry (demand)* Inelastic demand for emergent care, surgery. Rationing or queues (via willingness to pay and/or insurance) for some services (e.g. Hip/knee replacement in UK). *Information* • Consumers have difficulty distinguishing high-quality from, low-quality hospitals, given the complexity of input (physicians, nurses, staff, facilities). • Referring physicians select physician (e.g. surgeon) rather than hospital in some instances • Some evidence of volume-outcomes relationship (more procedures, better outcomes for individual physicians and institutions). • Limited use of private hospital chains. *Product differentiation* • Consumers may choose hospitals based on the sub-specialty strengths of the hospital as well as insurers contracts with hospital (for non-emergent care).

Strategic behavior

- May be affiliated with insurance product (Kaiser Permanente in United States) or government insurance (e.g. hospitals in United Kingdom).
- Physicians (key input) may be employees (e.g. US academic medical centers) or may have privileges at multiple hospitals.
- May mix profit and non-profit markets (e.g. drug provision and health education).

Private sector's role

- Government and private hospitals coexist in some instances (depending on a country's health system).
- For-profit and not-for-profit private hospitals (tax treatment differs in United States — but behaviors may be similar).
- Developing country: Typically major public hospital with limited private competition, some non-governmental organizations, and cross-subsidy models (Aravind Eye Institute in India).

Strategic behavior

- In market system with health insurance, sufficiently large insurers/groups may garner lower pricing for procedures ect.

Private sector's role

- Private (private for-profit/not–for-profit) insurers may represent individuals collectively.
- Limited competition from private outpatient clinics.

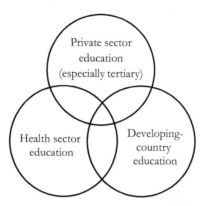

Figure 10.2   Markets Related to the LMIC Health Education Market

but lessons from private education markets, developing-country education trends, and health education in both developing- and developed-country settings help inform the understanding of important issues likely to affect health education private markets in LMICs.

The following sections examine important supply and demand issues across these market types.

Traditional Public Supply in Tertiary Education and Private Entry

Government subsidization and provision of education, even tertiary education, is justified by the externalities (social benefits not captured by the individual) which education produces (Poterba, 1995). This feature of education has long been recognized and health is no exception. However, given the large potential payoff for some individuals (particularly in high-skill cadres), it is important to consider the degree to which individuals should harbor financial burden for financing (while retaining some measure of equity). Presumably private sector models become more realistic to implement if the private benefits are large in comparison to the cost of the education and there is less reliance on the state for both financing and provision.

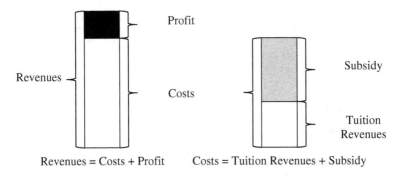

Revenues = Costs + Profit   Costs = Tuition Revenues + Subsidy

Figure 10.3   Select Components of Cost Structure in Education Markets
Source: Adapted from Winston *et al.* (1998).

Even in developed country education markets such as the United States, the cost structure for education favors either a public or "private subsidized" model. The "sticker price" to the individual for tertiary education often is a fraction of the school's cost of providing it (even without any individual regional grants or scholarships) (Figure 10.3). This explains why private institutions in the US tertiary market typically are in the form of not-for-profit institutions and are heavily reliant on endowments or other public and private support (e.g. charities, limited state funding) (Winston, 1999).

Despite this cost structure, a for-profit tertiary education sector has emerged rapidly across a range of markets. Between 1979 and 2009 in the United States, the for-profit tertiary education market grew at over nine percent per annum relative to 1.5 percent across all institutions (Wilson, 2010). The absolute share is still relatively small (seven percent), but for-profits account for more than one million students and are financially successful (Table 10.3). The US for-profit market share is anticipated to grow at a robust pace, although the relatively high failure rates of students, many of them subsidized via government financial programs, have recently drawn increased attention to the industry. In addition, the type of education, traditionally very trade-oriented in the early years, has shifted. More than 90 percent of the students enrolled in for-profits are associates, bachelors, masters, and doctoral candidates spread across a variety of disciplines (including health-related ones such as nursing). The average

Table 10.3   Select US For-Profit Tertiary Education Firms

Institution	Students (1,000s)	Revenue ($ millions)	EBITDA ($ millions)	Students in Bachelor's or Masters (%)	Students over 30 (%)
Apollo Group (Univ. Phoenix)	443	3,141	829	57	52
Capella Education	29	272	52	99	78
Devry	101	1,091	206	89	67
Grand Canyon Education	34	161	13	100	92
ITT Education Services	79	1,015	315	7	22
Strayer Education	54	396	157	83	61

Note: EBITDA = Earnings before Interest, Taxes, Depreciation and Amortization.
Sources: Fielden (2010). Higher Education Almanac 2009–2010.

tuition "sticker price" for these for-profits is higher than traditional education in public institutions (in-state) in the United States ($14,174–$7,020 per year), but the virtual (online) and in-person courses are designed to allow customers (students) the ability to continue to work while attending and also avoid costs associated with room and board (which can be extensive) (Higher Education Almanac, 2010). Costs are limited by eliminating institutions such as tenure for faculty (instructors are usually hired and paid per course taught) and relying on the Internet (though not solely) for instruction. These institutions qualify for government educational grants, and firms have demonstrated significant profitability despite the higher default rates among students relative to traditional education (where students do not need to borrow as much given lower pricing). The largest firm, Apollo Group (University of Phoenix), has 200 campuses across the United States, Canada, Mexico, Netherlands, and Puerto Rico (OBHE, 2009b).

These "borderless higher education" organizations are expanding internationally into other developed, emerging, and even developing-country settings. Naturally, entry occurs in the segments in which profits are anticipated.

An important factor that may affect the viability of these models (in the health-related professions or otherwise) is the extent to which the degrees issued by a school/country are accredited in other markets, particularly internationally. Regulation at the national, bilateral, and international levels likely affects the portability of a student's degree and its quality. For example, in a recent report Fielden notes (2010, p. 40):

> The General Agreement on Trade-in Services (GATS) administered by the World Trade Organization (WTO) has introduced a new set of rules and principles to govern the import and export of any service, including education, with the aim of further liberalizing trade-in services. This framework is relevant to all aspects of provision — and providers (both for-profit and not-for-profit) — which operate commercially and could in the longer term have far-reaching consequences for other forms of regulation that have traditionally been applied to higher education. In the medium term, GATS negotiations are likely to affect the portability of professional qualifications.

In fact, the GATS pertains to multiple "modes of supply" for education that affect the viability of several of the private sector models discussed in subsequent sections. These include "cross-border supply" (distance and virtual education models), "consumption abroad" (transnational student models), "commercial presence" within a country (branch campuses, twinning arrangements between universities, franchising), and "movement of natural persons" (faculty exchanges or travel).

Opening up the educational market to borderless institutions is not, however, a simple issue for LMICs that wish to ensure that their control over the quality and equity dimensions of the private sector. One concern posits that unfettered entry by these institutions hampers state control with respect to national policy and could result in low-quality "credentialing shops" for relatively wealthy clientele, adding little real productive value while potentially straying from merit-based systems for educational and professional advancement. For example, with reference to the prospect of increased educational trade, the South African Minister of Education noted "[South Africa must] remain vigilant to ensure that increased trade of education does not undermine national efforts to transform higher education … [and] erode the public-good agenda for higher education"(Kapur, 2008). Of course, appropriate entry of novel institutions that can absorb additional students using low-cost methods and produce effective graduates in important areas (such as health) would be very attractive. The goal is both to build a country's educational infrastructure and to contribute toward improvement of its institutional capacity in the health and other key commercial and government sectors.

Novel sources of supply and new forms of production are important (discussed in the next section). The important feature to capture here is the recognition that private (both not-for-profit and for-profit) institutions have played a significant role in the development of the educational market in the developed world. If conditions allow, they may play a growing and important role in the future in developing countries. At the moment, medical education appears to be offered primarily by the state, although some newly emerged semi-elite or lower-level institutions admit less-qualified, but typically wealthier, students. According to the International Medical Education Directory, most African countries (an important share of the LMICs) have a few accredited medical schools for physician training spread across the entire country. Census data on nursing and allied health schools are not as well documented.

Demand Growth

Over the past 25 years, much effort has focused on improving education and expanding access at the primary and secondary levels in developing-world settings, including Africa and LMICs (Ilak, 2000). Historically, the focus on the lower levels of education was supported by research indicating that the social rate of return for investments at primary and secondary levels was higher than the returns from higher education (Kapur, 2008; Psacharopoulos *et al.*, 1986). A recent analysis examining 98 countries over 37 years (1960–1997) estimated social rates of return from primary schooling at 18.9 percent and tertiary education at 10.8 percent (Psacharopoulos, 2002). However, there is increasing recognition that the methodologies for evaluating rates of return likely did not capture the full benefit of tertiary education (as usually just wage effects for the individual were evaluated as the benefit) and that, as "knowledge workers" become more important in developing the institutional capacity of countries, the benefits to a strong tertiary education system will likely grow even larger (Kapur, 2008; Birdsall, 1996).

Table 10.4   Growth in Secondary Education Participation, Selected Sub-Saharan African Nations (Percent of Secondary School Enrollment)

	1985[a]	1995	2009–2012[b]		1985[a]	1995	2009–2012[b]
Benin	18.6	13.2	51.4	Malawi	5.9	11.8	34.2
Botswana	28.2	57.1	81.7	Mali	7.6	11.7	39.5
Burkina Faso	3.7	—	22.6	Mauritania	14.3	16.2	27.0
Burundi	3.3	6.4	28.0	Mauritius	48.6	61.7	90.9
Cameroon	21.3	25.0	51.3	Mozambique	7.1	7.3	26.4
Cape Verde	11.8	—	89.7	Namibia	37.4	57.7	—
Chad	6.0	7.9	25.4	Niger	5.2	6.5	14.4
Comoros	28.5	20.0	—	Nigeria	33.0	—	44.0
Congo, DR	22.0	24.7	39.8	Rwanda	6.5	—	35.8
Congo, Rep.	62.6	48.5	—	Sao Tome and Principe	—	—	69.2
Cote d'Ivoire	18.9	21.7	—	Senegal	12.2	14.9	42.1
Eritrea	—	13.7	32.6	Sierra Leone	19.3	—	—
Ethiopia	11.0	9.9	37.6	South Africa	52.0	82.9	93.8
Gabon	38.5	43.3	—	Sudan	17.9	19.1	39.0
Gambia, The	17.8	23.2	54.1	Swaziland	36.5	46.9	60.0
Ghana	38.8	33.4	59.2	Tanzania	3.3	5.3	35.1
Guinea	13.7	12.1	41.7	Togo	18.3	21.4	56.5
Kenya	—	39.9	60.2	Uganda	9.8	11.1	28.1
Lesotho	21.5	30.4	49.2	Zambia	18.1	24.5	—
Madagascar	30.0	14.2	31.1	Zimbabwe	41.5	40.6	—

Notes: [a] Comoros, Namibia and South Africa, 1986 data.
[b] Most recent report, 2009–2012.
Source: UNESCO (2013).

The success of basic education initiatives has resulted in strengthened demand by an increasingly large share of the population for tertiary education — including health education — as reflected in Tables 10.4 and 10.5 (UNESCO, 2013). But the market's capacity to

Table 10.5   Tertiary Gross Enrollment by Region 1970–2008 (Gross Enrollment Ratios)

Region	1970	1980	1990	2000	2008
North America and Western Europe	30.0	37.0	49.0	64.0	70.0
Central and Eastern Europe	—	—	—	41.0	64.0
Latin America and the Caribbean	6.0	13.0	17.0	23.0	38.0
Central Asia	—	—	—	23.0	25.0
East Asia and the Pacific	3.0	5.0	7.0	15.0	26.0
Arab States	—	—	—	20.0	21.0
South and West Asia	4.0	4.0	6.0	9.0	13.0
Sub-Saharan Africa	1.0	2.0	3.0	4.0	6.0
World	9.0	12.0	13.0	19.0	26.0

Note: — = not available.
Source: UNESCO Trends in Tertiary Education: Sub-Saharan Africa (2010).

service demand is limited by government budgets and the traditional role of government-financed and -operated institutions as the primary source for funding and provision of education, particularly in health institutions.

Supply Responses to Demand Expansion

Considering the increased demand for tertiary and health education in developing countries, the question becomes "How does the educational system respond?" Numerous options exist, but at a basic level an increase in size among existing institutions or entry by new institutions might be expected. During the expansion in demand for tertiary education in the United States from 1955 to 1997, higher education supply grew both in the number of schools (suggesting more competition for students and expenditure on fixed costs) and in the average number of students per institution (Kwoka and Snyder, 2004). Entry among new schools was most robust by public and two-year institutions and was strongest during periods of strong macroeconomic growth.

Public Sector Expansion

One of the ways in which developing countries have responded to demand expansion for tertiary education is by increasing the size of existing institutions, for example, in Mexico, Argentina, and India. Public institutions such as National University of Mexico have over 200,000 students (Kapur, 2008). Nevertheless, there is a natural upper bound for capacity. The public university in Kenya has 9,000 spots, although over 40,000 qualify for university admission (Oketch, 2003). According to anecdotal reports, faculty now work multiple shifts in universities to try to accommodate current demand (Beciu and Haddad, 2009; Beciu and Jacob, 2009). Further expansion of the public sector schools is likely to require creative new ways of delivering tertiary education. Greater use of the Internet might provide further expansion using redeployment of resources.

Private Sector Entry

While macroeconomic growth has been relatively strong in Africa and LMICs, public expansion of education capacity is unlikely. To the degree that policy makers wish to engage private participation, improvements in regulation and use of lower-cost educational models may promote entry — perhaps even at higher cadre levels (Sosale, 2000). In the context of the African tertiary health education scenario, entrant institutional size has tended to occur in the form of small institutions that are still dwarfed by existing public providers. Entry of tertiary institutions is most robust at the lower cadre levels where fixed-costs and faculty scarcity may be less constraining (Johnstone, 2004, 2009).

Private Sector Provision in African and Asian Health Education Institutions

Where public resources are constrained, the private sector has started to fill the void and created opportunities to contribute to scaling up education in some countries that face shortages. For example, the number of medical and nursing graduates doubled from 2001–2003 in the Democratic Republic of the Congo largely due to the private sector-led increase in the training of health workers (WHO, 2006). The expansion mimics similar growth in private sector health education (even among for profits) in other developing countries such as India (Box 10.1).

Box 10.1   The Experience with Private Medical Education in India

India is an example of a country where the private sector is a major part of the medical education landscape. Over the last five decades, the number of undergraduate medical institutions grew eight-fold, and the number of student slots grew five-fold due mostly to the private sector. Private medical colleges had a small share in the 1950s, but now account for over 45 percent of all medical institutions.

Admissions to public medical schools are determined by merit-based entrance exams. Private medical schools also offer subsidized "merit seats" based on exams. The rest of the slots for medical students are determined through a "management" quota, which also considers merit but have substantial student fees. Despite laws that require transparent merit-based admissions and minimum infrastructure and faculty standards for private institutions, there are still anecdotal cases of compromised student quality, high tuition fees as well as inadequate staff and infrastructure (Table B10.1).

Moreover, private allopathic medical schools are set up predominantly in wealthier states. This locational preference is linked with increasing inequality of enrollment as the share of medical students with wealthy backgrounds rises. This is significant because physicians tend to practice near wherever they studied. So, not surprisingly the distribution of new physicians in India has disproportionately been located in richer states, while many of the better graduates from higher ranked public institutions migrate to western countries. Thus, despite the significant private sector-led scale up of physician output in India, equity disparities persist in access to health care (Mahal and Mohanan, 2006).

According to IFC estimates, given the public sector's resource constraints, there is a private investment opportunity of $1.7 billion in medical

(Continued)

Box 10.1 (*Continued*)

Table B10.1   Inequality in Access: Distribution of Seats for Bachelors of Medicine and Surgery

Income bracket	Public		Private	
	Seats	Share (%)	Seats	Share (%)
Lowest 50 percent	4,712	30	520	7.8
Top 50 percent	8,008	63	6,115	92.2

Source: Mahal and Mohanan (2006).

education in Africa (IFC, 2007). More important, it provided case examples in Senegal and Tanzania where the private sector offers sustainable models of nursing and medical education while innovating to solve resource constraints.

There are still a number of limitations that the private sector faces in developing countries. Many of the same constraints that are applicable to promoting private sector industry are also relevant to medical education. Having the appropriate legal and financial infrastructure to increase access to investment finance for private sector firms and for individuals making personal investments in their education are crucial but lacking. Health worker education is also a sensitive area because it traditionally falls within the public sector's jurisdiction. There are general concerns that the private sector's involvement will compromise quality and access to education. However, this does not necessarily need to be the case. Investment in the private sector must go hand-in-hand with regulatory oversight to ensure minimum standards are met and appropriate targeting of education opportunities to ensure equitable access to low-income students. This is important to ensure that more quality health workers in high-need areas are produced.

Some expansion and entry by private education institutions has occurred (within or outside health), but most LMICs do not have substantial enrollment in private tertiary institutions. After several African nations passed legislation during the 1990s to allow private tertiary education, increased entry occurred: now about one third of the 300 universities in sub-Saharan Africa are private (Kapur, 2008; Materu, 2006). There is

Table 10.6   Private Sector Enrollment Share of Tertiary Education

Private share of enrolment (percent)	Countries (sample number)	African countries in sample
>50	n = 30	Botswana, Cape Verde
25 – 50	n = 23	Angola, Burundi, Côte d'Ivoire, Kenya, Rwanda
10 – 25	n = 25	Senegal
<10	n = 32	Cameroon, Chad, Ghana, Tanzania, Uganda

Source: Kapur (2008).

room for building the market for tertiary private education either through collaboration with non-profits or through social entrepreneurship in this area. Moreover, the barriers to entry for this type of education are low, although appropriate certification procedures could slow demand. To date, much of the entry has been in inexpensive, high-demand fields — rather than, say, engineering or medicine where graduates have a much more important potential influence on country institutions. A UNESCO Institute for Statistics survey from 2005 across 110 countries (13 from sub-Saharan Africa) found the tertiary private share of enrollment was still generally low in most countries (Table 10.6).

Overall, the private sector's role in tertiary education is likely to remain low without additional incentives to encourage delivery of health care education. Enrollment shares do not reflect the quality of the educational experience across different institutions. Generally, the public universities have greater prestige (and funding) than private institutions and are more likely to attract higher-quality faculty (although, in some cases, private institutions rent both facilities and faculty). There is a market for private higher education in health within Africa, but it is likely certain market segments will be easier for different types of private institutions (for-profit versus not-for-profit) to enter.

Health Education Industry Structure

Given the characteristics of supply and demand, the education markets can be broadly characterized, but with the caveat that characteristics vary from country to country (Table 10.7). With their strict regulation (at least

Table 10.7 Tertiary Health Education in Africa: Market Characteristics

Health market	Supply- side market characteristics	Demand-side market characteristics
Education Overall characterization: Ranges from regulated / government oligopoly or monopoly to monopolistic competition	*Entry (supply)* • Fixed costs for entry (capital expenditures) vary depending on the type of school. These range from high (physician, some nursing , pharmacy or technician training programs) to low (community health workers). • Government provision and heavy regulation limit entry (e.g. graduates from some private schools may not be appropriately credentialed to work). • Shortages in labor supply (qualified faculty) restrict entry into markets, particularly in rural areas. • Many students may be priced out of the market. *Information* • Accreditation certifies the program quality, but threat of type I error (poor quality with accreditation) or type II errors (high quality without accreditation). The ranking of schools relative to each other is usually not formally conducted.	*Entry (demand)* • Larger pool of individuals with secondary education–demand for tertiary and health education likely exceeds supply • Acceptance into school may, in part, depend on merit (e.g. national exams), income (user fees/tuition), and demographics (slots for minority/female etc.). *Information* • Lack of transparency about the quality of schools or the effects on individual productivity influences decisions to attend and/or select schools. • Information is lacking on returns to scale if private providers service multiple locations (e.g. University of Phoenix).

(Continued)

Table 10.7   *(Continued)*

Health market	Supply-side market characteristics	Demand-side market characteristics
	Product differentiation	*Product differentiation*
	• Wide variation in the quality of institutions ranging from internationally recognized institutions to "credentialing shops" focused on volume rather than quality of graduates.	• Individuals likely evaluate different institutions (or types of institutions) on the basis of expected private return relative to opportunity cost.
	• Student learning is difficult to measure and compare across institutions.	• Word of mouth may serve to differentiate markets.
	• Location: Most schools concentrated in urban centers.	• Religious providers may be differentiated in the marketplace.
	Strategic behavior	*Strategic behavior*
	• Government role as primary education provider may restrict competition between schools.	• People typically seek (or do not seek) higher education on their own, but politically entitled/ wealthy may account for at least some slots (esp. in public institutions).
	Private sector role	• Suppliers do not seem to have an incentive to offer top quality tertiary education.
	• For profit entry more likely in lower-cost program types, programs with higher private returns.	*Private sector role*
	• Entrepreneurship is needed to ferret out and exploit markets where cost-effective training is feasible.	• Private finance mechanisms (loans) are important to allow for access for low income individuals (esp. if user fees and tuition are weakly subsidized) when state funding is poor.
	• Private organizations (for-profit and NFP), relatively young entrants, will likely be dependent on certification/accreditation if they are to compete with entrenched public institutions in a credible manner.	• We lack good examples of health education collaborations between institutions in the public and private sector.

for the production of higher-level cadre workers) and heavy public provision, health education provision markets might best be described as regulated monopolies (in the case of single institutions) or oligopolies (which distribute supply rather than compete on price). In light of the easier entry requirements (lower fixed costs and faculty inputs), the education markets for less technical health professions, particularly those whose graduates that can command high wages, are more akin to "monopolistic competition" (particularly because quality varies from school to school). Here we focus on Africa, but other LMICs share similar market characterizations.

Private Sector Models and Key Policy Issues

Criteria for Successful Entry

Private sector models, either for-profit or not-for-profit, are sustainable only if they are financially viable and politically accepted. For financial viability, any novel model has to generate sufficient revenue and constrain costs (though to varying degrees depending on organizational form and external support). As such, crucial revenue and cost-related criteria include:

1) Which educational market niches will most likely yield sufficient revenues to attract students demanding education in the current market structure? How would government and other active financiers participate under the assumptions of the business model?
2) Expansion requires both adequate funding and a viable business model. How will entry and recurrent costs (capital costs, operating costs) be financed for for-profit or not-for-profit private entities? Will tertiary private organizations rely only on full-funding student fees and tuition, government grants, endowments, charitable contributions, or on other funding mechanisms as well?
3) What kind of marketing plan models are available to education institutions to use to market successfully to students or other groups that may provide auxiliary sources of funding (e.g. corporations interested in research collaborations)?

390   Financing the Education of Health Workers: Gaining A Competitive Edge

4) What alternative business models are available for reducing cost while preserving quality? Can institutions collaborate or merge to achieve economies of scale, higher-quality teaching and other resources, and access to potential donors?

5) Can Internet delivery reduce costs without lowering quality? What business models exist for online delivery of health services?

6) What models of successful regulation exist to guide countries that need to upgrade the quality of their training?

Market Selection

With regard to the first criteria, variation exists in the degree of competition, government intervention, and entry barriers across various market segments. These segments may be characterized by type of graduate (physician, nurse, technician, pharmacist, community health worker); service type (provision of education, financing of education, support services for educational institutions), and geographic location (rural, urban). Organizational form may also play a role in the likelihood of success within each of these niches. For example, ecumenical NGOs have a history of serving rural populations where government or for-profits do not have funding or do not desire to provide service.

Finance

Financing, discussed in detail in Chapter 7, this volume, is central to educational models since, as discussed earlier, the economics of higher education often require some form of auxiliary finance to contribute to the costs of the education. In the African context, the student tuition is also often covered by government programs. The degree to which individuals cover (either via out-of-pocket payments or loans) their expenses should depend on the anticipated private benefit associated with each degree type. Generally, there is a sense that, especially for high-skill professions, the state's contributions should be reduced (especially if individual income in subsequent years is taxable by the state to repay loans).

Marketing

Addressing uncertainty regarding the quality of new educational institutions via accreditation would help resolve information asymmetries and improve new entrants' ability to market their services to potential customers. The political will to institute these accreditation programs may be limited within governments if entrenched schools (typically public organizations) perceive the expansion of the education market to new suppliers as a threat to their long-standing dominant position. Given the potential for international organizations to enter the education market — regulatory and accreditation efforts are likely required at the local, national, bilateral, and international levels. Developing the administrative capacity to develop and enforce accreditation is a major institutional hurdle, but one that should be addressed if countries wish to seriously encourage private entry to both absorb additional demand and improve educational quality. With accreditation, the potential student pool will have better information on the quality of the institution — this is a case in which regulation benefits private organizations by addressing the information asymmetries of consumers.

Private institutions (as well as public) may improve their financing and quality via partnerships with industry. Leading institutions have already adopted this approach. For example, at Makerere University in Uganda, approximately one third of funding is from industry research collaborations. These relationships may be particularly fruitful in the health sector in light of the extensive (and increasing) clinical and medical health research that private and public partners may undertake in African settings.

Inputs

On the cost side, a key constraint is the finite availability of faculty — a rare resource. Local scarcity may favor adoption of innovative models, such as international schools or franchise schools, which either import faculty into the country or virtually connect students to faculty in other locales. Higher-end schools require physical spaces such as labs, which further inhibits entry.

Internet

Education over the Internet can bring scarce teachers into rural communities, provide the latest material and teaching methods, promote interaction, and reduce travel and teaching costs. It can also require stable electric supply, purchase of equipment, teacher training costs, website maintenance, and a resident specialist. Over time, Internet education will grow in importance, but the literature is not yet available on the effectiveness of this delivery model in the developing-country health context.

Regulation

As discussed in the credentialing section, regulation can have a salubrious effect on the functioning of the private market by reducing uncertainty, standardizing the educational product, and improving information among consumers.

Innovative Education Models (Provision)

Several of the recent innovations in the delivery of education (typically, though not always, implemented in the private sector) attempt to address some of the barriers that previously precluded educational entry. These include lowering fixed costs, achieving greater customer focus, and improving quality. One of the important overarching trends is that of internationalization or, broadly defined, the movement of faculty, students, or curricula from one country to another (Harden. 2006). While many novel forms of education are growing rapidly in developed economies, the prospect for increased adoption in developing countries is strong. Many of the models may have an international component, but certainly localized variants exist as well. While African countries and select other LMICs have relatively few cross-border and international initiatives, there are numerous examples and cases to learn from and significant potential for program expansion.

Virtual / Distance Learning

Virtual or distance educational models are evolving rapidly in both developed and developing world. According to the Observatory on Borderless

Table 10.8 International Distribution of Distance Education (percent)

North America	16
Western Europe	8
Latin America and Caribbean	12
Sub-Saharan Africa	8
Middle East and North Africa	2
South Asia and Indian Ocean	14
East Asia and Pacific Ocean	4
Australia and New Zealand	1
Eastern Europe and Central Asia	35

Source: OBHE (2009b).

Higher Education (OBHE), "[Distance education is] generally defined as a form of education in which the location of teacher and student are not in proximity. Higher education by distance has evolved from the contexts of lifelong learning, professional and continuing education to one that now includes operational elements such as multi-campuses, interinstitutional partnerships, and dedicated, international online networks"(OBHE, 2009a,b) (Table 10.8). The predominant mode of learning typically relies on information technology such as the Internet and/or DVDs/CDs, but often these modules are coupled with face-to-face sessions. Although high-cadre forms of health education typically require at least some standard instruction, mixed models may allow reductions in capital and recurrent costs while maintaining quality and improving access (especially for hard to reach rural areas). As indicated earlier, several for-profit models in the United States, including health-related degrees (such as nursing), have effectively trained medical personnel.

Regional Model: African Virtual University (Kenya, Senegal)

The African Virtual University was established by the World Bank in 1997, but has subsequently transferred operation to Kenya (with a regional office in Dakar). It is the largest network of Open Distance and e-Learning institutions in Africa with more than 50 partner institutions in 27 African countries. While the revenue model still relies on multilateral funding, the network seeks to rely increasingly on private sector sources by generating revenue via short courses, workshops, and consulting engagements; developing a subscription and contribution model; and charging project-management fees.[4] Although it focuses on language and computer science instruction, the novel contribution of this model is the regional level implementation focus. Small countries in the region may benefit from these models given the potential to limit initial fixed costs and support higher quality by encouraging learning from across the region (not just in one institution). A regional network of institutions for instruction may also build the capacity for research activities in the health sector. A multi-institutional collaborative network across a region may more readily be able to serve demand from potential private funding sources such as pharmaceutical firms or institutions seeking to conduct multicenter clinical trials for vaccines or pharmaceuticals.

AMREF (Kenya)

AMREF is an NGO that promotes health in Africa in part by providing distance education to nurses through 127 schools and e-centers (as of 2007). Graduates earn a registered nurse (RN) certificates by completing a combination of computer and clinic sessions (IFC, 2007). The e-learning component grew rapidly in 2005–2007 from 145 students (four sites) to 4,500 students (20 percent of Kenya's nursing student population). Scale-up occurred both in rural (70 percent) and urban settings (30 percent) with an annual operating budget of $0.5 million (about $110 per student).

The success of the program stemmed from effective partnerships with public and private institutions. The Nursing Council of Kenya offered support and certification for the program, and Accenture, a business consulting firm, assisted with development of the e-curriculum. AMREF extensive history in medical provision in the region added credibility to the effort as well.

Branch Campuses/Franchise Models

Institutions with established reputations in either developed or developing countries may expand locally, regionally, or internationally with additional (sometimes modest) campuses that expand the educational and research options for faculty and students in the original campus or service educational markets in host countries/regions. A variant model, the franchise, seeks to establish multiple sites and expand into new markets where possible. Franchises are more likely to exist as for-profit models. In each case, both expect that the name recognition associated with the institution transmits credibility and addresses student/customer uncertainty with respect to the quality of the educational experience.

Aga Khan University (Kenya)

Pakistan's Aga Khan University, part of the Aga Khan Development Network (AKDN) opened a campus to provide nursing education in East Africa in 2002 (Altbach and Knight, 2007). The Kenya program is tied to the Aga Khan hospital in Nairobi, founded in 1958 and now with a well-established record in health. Technically the Kenyan institution is a separate campus and health facility from the others in Asia and Africa operated by AKDN and may be somewhat different from a branch campus. Nonetheless, this hospital does benefit from name recognition, an important marketing factor that improves credibility of the newer institution. Anecdotal evidence from early interviews, however, stresses that the capacity to recruit local faculty for training is limited and poses a significant challenge to scaling-up operations. Another example of a branch campus, outside of health, is Monash University (with six campuses in Australia, one in Malaysia, and one in South Africa).

Country-Level Response and Branch Campus

Additional entry from branch campuses can help alleviate the scarcity of human resources, but organizations must be responsive to country policy with respect to external institutions. For example, South Africa's stricter regulatory and accreditation approach resulted in several educational institutions' pulling out of the country due to accreditation issues (Altbach and Knight, 2007). As indicated earlier, the political sensitivities surrounding issues of access and quality may trump desire to maximize output.

Twinning Arrangements and Exchanges

Twinning arrangements are formal institutional affiliations between developing-country educational/service organizations and developed-world counterparts (Table 10.9). Typically, the models allow for faculty exchange, research collaborations, or other mutually beneficial linkages,

Table 10.9   Twinning Arrangements in Africa, Selected Institutions

Developing country	Institution(s)	Developed country(-ies)	Institution(s)
Côte d'Ivoire	Cocody University	United States France	University of California University of Marseille UMVF
Ethiopia	Addis Ababa University Jimma University	United States United States Denmark Belgium Germany	Emory University Columbia University Johns Hopkins University Copenhagen University Belgian Universities Ludwig Maximilian University
Eritrea	Orotta School of Medicine	United States	George Washington University
Ghana	Kwame Nkrumah University of Science and Technology	United States	University of Michigan
Kenya	Moi University University of Kenya	United States United States	Indiana University University of Washington
Mali	Université de Bamako, Faculté de Médecine, de Pharmacie et d'Odonto- Stomatologie	United States United Kingdom France	University of Maryland Tulane University Liverpool School of Tropical Medicine University of Aix Marseilles University of Angers University of Paris

(Continued)

Table 10.9　(*Continued*)

Developing country	Institution(s)	Developed country(-ies)	Institution(s)
Mozambique	Catholic University, Faculty of Medicine	United States	University of Pittsburgh West Virginia University
		Italy	CUAMM
		United Kingdom	University of Ipswich
		Holland	Maastricht University
Nigeria	University of Ibadan (Medicine)	United States	University of Illinois University of Pennsylvania University of Chicago
Rwanda	University of Rwanda	United States	Duke University
Tanzania	Hubert Kairuki Memorial University	United States	University of Utah Duke University Yale University University of Connecticut
	Muhimbili University of Health and Allied Sciences	Australia United States	Darwin University University of California (SF)
Uganda	Makerere University College of Health Sciences	United States	Johns Hopkins University Baylor College of Medicine Yale University

Note: CUAMM = Collegio Universitario Aspiranti Medici; UMVF = L'Université Médicale Virtuelle Francophone.
Source: SAMSS (2010).

but they may also include direct support for operations in developing countries (MacDonagh *et al.*, 2002; SAMSS, 2010). Twinning and exchange programs are more focused on improving the quality of medicine and research across universities rather than directly on increasing the supply of physicians, nurses, or other medical workers. A large share of affiliations in these types of twinning or exchange programs occur in private institutions. Even elite institutions are participating aggressively in these arrangements as evinced by the Yale University/National University of Singapore (NUS) collaboration.

Stand-Alone or Cross-Subsidization Models

Private universities start up without some of the advantages of existing organizations in franchise, branch, twinning or distance/virtual models. Higher fixed costs of entry likely result in participation only if the local demand for the education services provided to individuals appears sufficiently strong. To cover a breadth of programs, some universities may offset losses in specific programs with revenues from other departments (e.g. business school revenue covering health or science programs).

Central University, Ghana

Central University (Accra) has used a cross-subsidization model in which the business school (in operation for 10 years) assists with the funding of the School of Applied Sciences (medical assistant, pharmacist, and nursing school). The capital costs of a health-related school are estimated at between US$0.3 million and US$2.0 million for a modest size program.

Hubert Kairuki Memorial University, Tanzania

Multidisciplinary training institutions such as medical schools likely have set up costs ranging between US$2 million and US$10 million. Hubert Kairuki was established in Tanzania as a private institution with degree programs across a range of disciplines in medicine and nursing (MD, Master of Medicine, Bachelor of Nursing). Student tuition covers 90 percent of recurrent costs, but enrollment is growing well — increasing the probability that the school will be profitable in the future. The justification for start-up, in part, was based on the strong demand for medical professionals. The school is accredited and has a strong reputation. According to the list of priorities developed by the institution, many of the current top priorities are focused on marketing, finance and operations, with research and infrastructure less important (Table 10.10).

Table 10.10   Priorities at Hubert Kairuki Memorial University

Priority rank	Priorities
1	*Legal and accreditation* Improved legal framework (organization and governance) *Marketing* Expansion of enrolment Improved marketing, public relations, and linkages *Operations* Enhanced scope and quality assurance of teaching and learning Improved information and communication technology capacity and application Improved human resources management Improved handling of students affairs Improved HIV / AIDS prevention, care, and support for staff and students *Finance* Improved Financial Resource Mobilization and Management
2	*Research* Enhanced research and publications capacity Improved library capacity and services *Equity* Improved gender balance
3	*Public–Private services* Improved consultancy and services to the public *Facilities* Improved infrastructure and facilities

Source: Hubert Kairuki Memorial University, accessed at http://www.hkmu.ac.tz.

International Health Sciences University (Uganda)

International Health Sciences University (IHSU) is a not-for-profit company established in 2008 to offer certificate, diploma, degree, and post-graduate health programs (currently it primarily focuses on nursing and health management programs as of 2013) but it is located on the top floor of International Hospital of Kampala (IHK), the flagship hospital of the

International Medical Group (IMG) a for-profit health care entity in Uganda. In addition to IHK and IHSU, the operations of IMG, a health care conglomerate with both for-profit and not-for-profit components, includes a pharmaceutical group (IMG Pharmaceutical), a diagnostic center (International Diagnostics Center), a specialist network (International Medical Center), a captive health maintenance organization (IAA Healthcare), and a non-profit NGO (International Medical Foundation). In addition to the physical space and capital provided by the IHK, IHSU can also tap its labor pool of IMG staff (as well as affiliated clinicians) and IMG financing to support its educational mission.

Assessment of Health Education Models

Because these educational models are a novelty in the developing world (and health sectors specifically), there is little current anecdotal or statistical evidence with regard to the strengths and weaknesses of the organizational models. Nevertheless, there are clear distinguishing features and likely trade-offs with choice of organizational form. Moreover, depending on the market characterization within a particular country (monopoly, oligopoly, degree of government control), adopting particular forms may make more sense to adopt than others, especially in resource-constrained environments such as sub-Saharan Africa.

Table 10.11 summarizes some of the likely relative benefits and drawbacks of distance/virtual, branch, twinning, and traditional models with respect to cost, quality, and access (similar to finance, marketing, and regulatory success factors identified in the beginning of the section). These should be viewed as provisional assessments, but the evidence base will likely expand over time to improve understanding of the benefits and costs of each model.

Policy Issues and Institutional Considerations

As this work is aimed at both policy makers and private organizations (current or future), in this sub-section some policy issues are considered that government bodies should address and the strategic considerations

Table 10.11   Comparison of Educational Models

Model	Characteristics
Traditional private start-up	*Cost.* High initial fixed capital costs (esp. for high-cadre health workers) limit entry. Funding from NGO, donor or government loan is often necessary unless sponsored by a social entrepreneur. Ongoing operational/recurrent costs also are significant.
	Access. Market acceptance likely depends on prior reputation of affiliated organization. Fixed location limits the degree to which individuals can have access (especially in rural areas).
	Quality. Quality is variable. A big question is the degree to which an entrant can compete with entrenched state schools for faculty. Collaborative models do exist in which private institutions "rent" faculty.
Virtual/distance learning	*Cost.* Lower costs for operation and reduced initial fixed costs for infrastructure are large benefits, particularly in resource constrained environments.
	Access. Access depends on the prevalence and quality of the technology medium, but low-tech solutions exist (e.g. correspondence programs). Considering the lack of historical record in providing viable health education and producing good employment/productivity outcomes, individuals (and regulators) may be wary of new models.
	Quality. Quality of the modality, especially for high-cadre health professionals may be legitimately questioned and, as a result, accreditation will hinge on proving the model. Most likely a "mixed" model will be more effective (and favorably viewed). States likely have limited regulatory capacity to evaluate some of these potentially new health education forms.
Branch	*Cost.* High fixed costs for new campus (but perhaps less than pure new start-up).
	Access. Improves access to new populations. Reception by public may also be better than a traditional start-up or virtual approach if the reputation of the educational institution is already established on the basis of the main campus
	Quality. Interaction with other faculty from separate branches may aid quality of teaching and research.

(*Continued*)

Table 10.11   (*Continued*)

Model	Characteristics
Twinning	*Cost.* A low-cost (but also low-yield) strategy. These relationships may improve the skills of current students but might not have an appreciable effect on the total output of physicians, nurses, or health workers. *Access.* Improves access of students to other settings (and different skills). *Quality.* Main effect is to improve quality rather than quantity of graduates.

that private educational organizations (both novel and traditional) may wish to examine.

Role of Regulation as an Enabler

Regulation can enable the private market. In considering the degree to which the government wishes to invoke the private market to contribute to production of health workers, government policy can influence the entry, recognition, accreditation, and quality assurance of existing private institutions and new entrants (either in traditional or novel forms). Regulation is a key enabling mechanism for the private market considering the power that accreditation and formal recognition can have on consumer decisions to seek further education using private modalities — particularly in scenarios in which the public, state-run health education institutions have dominated the production of health workers. The caveat is that some governments will go beyond accreditation and actively limit behavior, try to control content, or deliberately reduce expenditures.

Differential recognition, accreditation, and quality assurance mechanism may be warranted for different education markets. The viability of the private sector to "self-regulate" and produce effective physicians, nurses, and other health workers may vary depending on type of worker and availability. In competitive markets with high potential for entry, clear information and low entry barriers, and a relatively unfettered private market may "cull" weak organizations. In less competitive market, the private sector may be more carefully managed and entry restricted. These markets will likely continue to behave in a manner more consistent with regulated oligopoly — producing fewer but better prepared health workers. Accreditation and quality assurance can strike a balance between quality and quantity of health workers.

Government Regulatory Capacity in Flux

Government's regulatory capacity (especially for new private models) is in flux and may require modification. For example, with regard to branch campuses, the foreign ownership of the branch campus may result in more regulatory burdens, restrictions on the fees and tuition that can be charged, greater taxes, and export/import limitations of hard currency (OBHE, 2009b). Changing these regulations may more readily invite institutions with broader experience to contribute to the market. Of course, some countries may wish to enforce these industrial policies. In some cases, international branch campuses are legally recognized and registered in the host and home countries. But some host countries do not evaluate the quality of foreign branches due to lack of capacity or political considerations (OBHE, 2009b).

Transferability of Degrees

Policy makers should establish a position with regard to the transferability of the degrees conferred by private institutions (or public for that matter) to other countries. A large share of physicians and nurses in Africa emigrate from host countries in sub-Saharan Africa — 28 percent of physicians and 11 percent of nurses, according to Center for Global Development (Clemens, 2006). On one hand, if efforts and funding to train health works only produce "brain drain" and deplete human resources, this can have negative consequences on the productivity of the education system (Gaynor, 1994). On the other, these inducements also motivate some individuals who will remain in the country to enter these professions. Novel initiatives such as the Brain Gain initiative linking Arab and African universities or programs that encourage temporary cross-border exchange of health workers are reshaping the debate on the value of transferability (Kapur, 2008; UNESCO, 2009).

Entry Influenced by Public Finance Decisions

Public finance decisions can also influence the extent of private entry into a market. Because the state is frequently involved in both finance (grants/loans/loan guarantees) and provision of education, the ease with which these sources of finance can be applied to private health education institutions likely has an important affect on the viability of the market. High-cost education programs (physicians), all else equal, will be more influenced by more open forms of public finance.

Organizational Assessment

The prior sections in this chapter offer perspective on identifying the *market-level* characterization of the health education market in developing country settings as well as some institutional specific responses. In order to evaluate organizations at a micro level, the following tools and criteria in Table 10.12 can be applied. The characterizations of the strategic/managerial, operational, and financial business model of the organization and the resultant outcomes are both important dimensions to evaluate.

Business Model

Four important parts of the strategy and management approach of health education institutions include defining the target market, developing competititve advantage, providing clear value propositions for key stakeholders, and aligning organizational structures to ensure the institution can deliver on value proposition (value configuration) (Osterwalder and Pigneur, 2010). The target market for health education institutions refers to the cadre or student type. However, some institutions may focus on recruitment of students from specific subgroups either on the basis of income,

Table 10.12   Institutional Business Model and Outcomes Rubric

Business model	Outcomes
Strategy/Management	*Production of Health Workers*
— Target market	— Graduation rates
— Competitive advantage	— Health worker retention rates
— Value proposition	*Quality/Reputation*
— Value configuration	— Graduate employment rates
Operations	— Reputation among peers and employers
— Instructional design	*Financial Performance*
— Faculty	— Risk (liquidity and capital structure)
— Collaborations/affiliations	— Return (profitability)
— Efficient use of resources	— Efficiency (turnover ratios)
Finances	*Stakeholder Satisfaction*
— Revenue sources	
— Cost minimization approaches	

Source: Adapted from Osterwalder and Pigneur (2010).

merit, or other determinants. Moreover, the targets may shift or expand over time as organizational resources improve or the mission of the institution changes. Realistically, some newer private entrants will more likely focus on the residual demand after publicly funded institutions have filled.

Sources of competitive advantage may include human resources, physical capital, superior financing, managerial dexterity, geographic location, or a range of other potentially significant points of differentiation. Even if new private entrants are not able to match the capabilities of existing schools, determining the areas of comparative advantage (those capabilities in which they are at least *relatively* strong in) will help to differentiate the institution.

The value proposition for customers (students) naturally may reflect the degree to which the costs of the education (generally time and tuition) are exceeded by the current and future benefits of the education. New private entrants also seek to demonstrate value to other stakeholders central to the mission (external funders, potential faculty, government regulators, etc.) in order to thrive. Lastly, the institution must be organized to develop and execute the capabilities, routines and activities required to deliver the value proposition to customers and stakeholders.

With respect to operations, the choice of curriculum (to the extent that choice exists within regulated programs) and mode of delivery is a central decision that should be reviewed frequently. How to optimally hire and retain faculty to deliver the curriculum affects both the costs and quality of the instruction. In many developing-country contexts, the lack of available faculty is a central concern of education institutions (especially newer ones) — as such collaborations and affiliations with external institutions in health, medicine, and health education within and outside the country/region can help fill voids in faculty, capabilities, or finance. Examples include the aforementioned twinning programs.

With regard to the business model and finance, organizations must map out the primary sources and amounts of revenue over time. Understanding the organization's cost structure (fixed versus variable costs) and timing/extent of costs in conjunction with revenue expectations can help the organization understand whether it is financially viable and if economies of scale exist. Although private health education institutions, especially for higher cadres, may be more likely to be non-profit, they still are "not for loss" and must be financially viable to deliver on their mission. In addition to profit (or for non-profits) the degree of risk, as evinced by the extent of debt, and capital structure (debt versus equity) are also important financial characteristics of the institution.

Outcomes

The central outcome of higher education institutions is the production of graduates. Metrics include the annual absolute number of graduates, graduation rate (graduates divided by number of first year students, by cohort), and employed graduate share (share of graduates with employment upon or soon after graduation). In addition to sheer quantity of graduates, the quality of graduates and, in turn, the reputation of the program are important outcomes — particularly for new educational institutions aiming to establish credentials with stakeholders including potential future students. Survey results among stakeholders may serve as another useful source of quantitative and qualitative feedback for institutional assessment.

Financial outcomes and ratios for education institutions can be applied to health education schools in developing countries, but care should be applied in interpretation of the ratios given the context, particularly for relatively new organizations. One commonly applied set of tools for education are the ratios included in the Composite Financial Index (CFI) as specified by Prager, McCarthy & Co. (2005). These aggregate various metrics reflective of the return, risk, liquidity, and efficiency of the organization.

The CFI is a single indicator of overall institutional financial health based on performance in four principal domains of finance: sufficiency and flexibility of financial resources, management of debt, performance of assets, and results from operations. Each domain is measured by a core financial ratio: (1) primary reserve ratio, (2) return on net assets ratio, (3) net operating revenues ratio, and (4) viability ratio. The CFI is widely accepted as a valid and reliable mechanism with which to measure and interpret the financial position of college and universities *in the United States*. The definitions of each of these ratios as well as the methodology of computing the CFI are provided in Appendix 10A.3 of this chapter.

The CFI score falls on a scale of 1 to 10. A score of 1 represents very little financial health; 3, the threshold value represents a relatively stronger financial position; and 10, the top score. Some institutions will exceed the top score; however, for purposes of measuring financial health, there is no reason for the scale to be extended beyond a score of 10. Only select case studies in the second half of this volume yielded sufficient financial information to evaluate CFI and other metrics reflective of risk, efficiency, and return.

Conclusions and Recommendations

Considering the limited body of literature on private sector models in most LMIC markets, this review and analysis expands understanding of market structure and potential new forms of private organizations that may bolster the region's capacity to produce health workers. With some justification, private entrants in health education markets are now generally (but not exclusively) viewed as second-rate institutions aiming to enter high-profit areas (in the case of for-profits) for a "quick return" as a "credentialing shop". But new entrants with different business models are not restricted to competing as low-quality, small-scale entrants. However, while novel forms of private education are rapidly emerging in the developed world market for higher education (including some health professions such as nursing or public health), there is proportionally less activity in LMICs and only a share of that naturally occurs in health education markets. The potential of some models to reduce cost and increase output of health workers exists, although the level of technology adoption within country markets (say, Internet access) may have important infrastructure effects on the viability and quality of the several modes for educating health workers. Nevertheless, government and institution decisions will play a crucial role in the extent of development of these models. Based on this initial literature review, recommendations are proposed in four areas: regulation, inputs, models, and finance.

Regulation

1) Improve regulatory capacity to develop accreditation and credible quality assurance mechanisms. This may take the form of public or private regulators. The informational value to consumers/students will encourage greater adoption of potentially lower-cost training programs. The mechanisms should be periodically reviewed.

2) Characterize education markets at the health worker/country level and develop regulations accordingly. The regulatory requirements for lower-cadre programs may differ from high-cadre sectors. Over-regulating a competitive market will reduce production and efficiency. It also wastes government resources. Not ensuring quality in more restricted markets may invite poor-quality production and entry. Modern accreditation and certification organizations can play

a critical role in aligning personal, professional, and countrywide needs.

3) Strongly consider adopting measures that allow recognition of qualifications either regionally or internationally. Each country must consider (A) the capacity for programs to train workers at international or regional standards and (B) the degree to which the costs (potential for emigration) compare to benefits (more incentive to enter the profession, improved capacity to increase quality and future international collaboration) Modern technology makes test taking and assessment less costly than it has been in the past.

Inputs

4) Build teaching capacity. In addition, the physical capital there is a dearth of qualified instructors, these two inputs important "rate-limiting" institution constraints on the production of health workers. Consideration should be given to limited incentives for outstanding teaching, student placement, and course improvement. It may be possible to attain donor support for this type of activity.

Models

5) Promote cross-subsidization models. Many universities in developed countries use profit generating educational units such as business school to subsidize the initial losses associated with capital costs for medical and health institutional development. Similarly, many medical schools subsidize their doctor training programs. Cross-subsidization makes sense because there is some predictability of revenues and a degree of control over where they will come from and how they will be used. Social entrepreneurship activities, such as subsidizing teacher salaries through stipends from the company can create much good at limited cost.

6) Don't start from scratch — support branch campuses. Models which leverage existing institutions (branch or even franchise models) may improve quality and also operate more efficiently (these

organizations have long histories of operating successfully, albeit in different environments — some lessons are likely transferrable). Excellent examples of this may be found in European business schools opening branch campuses in China and using these to offset declining revenues at home. This benefit should be weighed against the costs of increasing regulatory oversight and developing institutional capacity.

Finance

7) "Level the playing field" for financial resources to support both public and private high-quality institutions. If private institutions cannot compete for government funding for education, the appeal of the market is naturally reduced. It is best to have a policy that all are welcome to apply and to use evaluative mechanisms in which the money "follows the student" or tracks results (e.g. financing according to number of students enrolled or even outcome measures such as graduates passing qualifying exams). Competition in this context can have desirable side effects.

8) Evaluate individuals' capacity to finance their own education. The state is heavily involved in financing higher education for health on the basis that health is an important public good. However, in many cases (not just high-cadre jobs), individuals gain a substantial return on their training. Finding the appropriate level of subsidy is not easy, but the price paid by individuals for their education should bear some relation to their expected future private income benefits.

9) Seek novel financing sources for both fixed capital costs and recurrent expenditures. Both private and non-profit organization should consider leveraging their capabilities to extract revenue from firms or organization in the health business. These may include developed-country institutions (US National Institutes of Health) and private firms (pharmaceuticals) seeking to conduct research and development in LMICs.

Appendix 10A.1 Virtual and/or Distance Education Universities in Sub-Saharan Africa

Country	Institutions
Cameroon	University of Dschang
Ethiopia	Addis Ababa University (AAU)
	Jimma University (JU)
	Mekelle University (MU)
Ghana	Ghana Institute of Management and Public Administration (GIMPA)
	University of Cape Coast (UCC)
	University of Education
Lesotho	National University of Lesotho (NUL)
Madagascar	National Distance Learning Centre of Madagascar (CNTEMAD)
Niger	University Abdou Moumouni
	University of Ibadan (UI)
Nigeria	Abia State University
	Abubakar Tafawa Balewa University
	Ahmadu Bello University
	Institute of Management and Technology (IMT)
	Obafemi Awolowo University (OAU)
	University of Abuja (UNIBUJA)
	University of Calabar (UNICAL)
	University of Lagos
Rwanda	Kigali Institute of Education
South Africa	INTEC College
	University of South Africa
	University of the Free State
Sudan	Omdurman Ahlia University
Swaziland	University of Swaziland
Tanzania	Institute of Finance Management (IFM)
	The Open University of Tansania (OUT)
Togo	University of Lome
Uganda	Kyambogo University (KYU)
	Uganda Martyrs University (UMU)
Zambia	University of Zambia

Note: The African Virtual University (AVU) is a consortium of centers across Africa.
These institutions identified themselves as having virtual/distance learning programs in the World Higher Education Database (WHED, 2007) from the International Association of Universities.
Source: OBHE (2009b).

Appendix 10A.2 Some Definitions for Novel Educational Organizations

Virtual university · (institution or consortium)	A virtual university is dedicated to a teaching, learning, and research environment in which it connects its teachers and students solely by electronic, technological means. Virtual and distance universities are considered synonymous, but the latter may use other forms of technology to transmit knowledge (see correspondence-based). Some entities require a short-term presence to take a test in each course.
Distance learning	This term identifies any form of learning that is conducted when both teacher and student are at a distance. As Keegan states, "Distance learning systems used technology to separate the learner from the teacher, and the learner from the learning group, while maintaining the integrity of the education process".
International distance education programs	International distance education programs are degree-granting programs delivered by a home institution to other locations throughout the world by satellites, computers, correspondence, or other technological means. They may also be delivered in face-to-face formats (e.g. via inter-institutional partnerships and branch campuses).
Open university	Any university that offers open entry for admissions through distance and online learning programs.
Mixed-mode blended instruction	This term attempts to characterize a balanced pedagogical approach of face-to-face teaching with online instruction. Blended may include face-to-face and e-learning or an integration of other technologies (e.g. print).
Bridging and twinning programs	Bridging programs, also known as foundation courses, allow for prerequisite courses to be undertaken in preparation for a qualifying degree program. Twinning programs refer to agreements made between institutions in different countries to offer portions of their degree programs at both institutions (e.g. 1 + 3 and 2 + 2 year models).
Satellite or extension (branch) campuses	Satellite campuses are physical entities established by a home institution that offer the same degree and/or courses at a distance. This classification also includes overseas branch campuses that may not necessarily take on the same characteristics of the host culture in which they operate.

(Continued)

Appendix 10A.2 (*Continued*)

Correspondence-based education	"Correspondence education is defined as providing teaching via the written world by means of so-called self-instructional texts combined with communication in writing (i.e. correspondence between students and tutors)".
Open educational resources (OER)	"[Arefian, #1] refers to the open provision of educational resources, enabled by information and communication technologies, for consultation, use and adaptation by a community of users for non-commercial purposes". It usually takes the form of open source software, which is intended for the development and delivery of resources (content management systems, development tools, social software, and learning management systems); courseware, and other materials published online for reference; and implementation sources (licensing tools, interoperability, and best practices).
Online education	Online education refers to the provision of education and training utilizing the Internet and the WWW. Although synonymous to e-learning, online education generally includes the use of a learning management system that provides both structure and guidance.

Source: OBHE (2009b).

Appendix 10A.3 Glossary of Terms for Composite Financial Index

Composite Financial Index (CFI) combines four core high-level ratios: Primary reserve ratio, net income ratio, return on net assets ratio, and viability ratio into a single score. Developed by Prager, McCarthy & Co., LLC and KPMG LLC, the CFI is useful in helping governing boards and senior management understand an institution's financial position in the marketplace. CFI is also useful in assessing future prospects of the institution's functioning as an "affordability index" of a strategic plan.

CFI scores are interpreted as follows:

- −1–1 = Assess the institution's viability to survive
- 1–3 = Reengineer the institution

- 3–5 = Direct institutional resources to allow transformation
- 5–7 = Focus resources to compete in future state
- 7–8 = Allow experimentation with new initiatives
- Above 8 = Deploy resources to achieve a robust mission.

CFI has been adopted by many leading institutions and has found great acceptance by senior management and boards of trustees in the United States.

Primary reserve ratio measures financial strength by comparing expendable net assets to total expenses. The ratio represents the percent of a year the institution could meet financial obligations with assets readily available. A primary reserve ratio of 0.40x or better is advisable to give institutions the flexibility to transform the enterprise. The implication of a 0.40x ratio is that the institution would have the ability to cover about five months of expenses. Generally, institutions operating at this level are able to carry on a reasonable level of activities and appear capable of managing modest unforeseen and adverse financial events.

Return on net assets ratio is a measure of the overall asset return and performance; the ratio shows whether the institution's total assets, restricted and unrestricted, are growing or shrinking. This ratio should fall in the range of 3–4 percent above the inflation rate.

Net operating revenues ratio is computed as the ratio of operating income to revenue. It is a measure of operating performance results and tells if an institution has a balanced budget or not. A positive net income ratio indicates that the institution experienced an operating surplus for the year. Generally speaking, the larger the surplus, the stronger is the institution's financial performance. However, if surpluses are obtained by underspending on mission-critical investments, the surplus should be questioned. A negative ratio indicates a loss for the year. A ratio of 0.02 is regarded by Strategic Financial Analysis for Higher Education to be adequate to keep pace with or slightly exceed the growth in operating expenses.

Viability ratio is the ratio of expendable net assets to long-term debt. It measures the ability of the institution to manage its debts. A ratio of less than one, where debt obligation and expendable assets are equal, is poor and may identify an institution as a credit risk; the range from 1.25 to 2.0 is acceptable; and greater than 2.0 is a strong indicator of financial health.

Methodology for Computing the CFI

The four-step methodology is as follows:

- Compute the values of the four core ratios;
- Convert these figures to strength factors along a common scale. The strength factors provide standardized measurements of each ratio for comparative purposes;
- Multiply the strength factors by specific weighting factors; (primary reserve and viability ratios at 35 percent; return on net assets ratio at 20 percent; and net operating revenues ratio at 10 percent). For institutions with no long-term debt in a given year, the weighting is altered to reflect the absence of a viability ratio; primary reserve ratio at 55 percent; return on net assets ratio at 30 percent; and net operating revenues ratio at 15 percent; and
- Total the resulting four numbers to reach the single CFI score.

Age of facilities ratio calculates the average age of plant facilities measured in years. It is computed as the ratio of accumulated depreciation to depreciation expense. A low ratio is better, since it indicates that an institution has made recent investments in its plant facilities.

Physical asset reinvestment ratio is relatively new; it calculates the extent capital renewal is occurring compared with physical asset usage, represented as depreciation expense. A ratio above 1:1 indicates an increasing investment in physical assets, whereas a lower ratio potentially indicates an underinvestment in campus facilities.

Current ratio is an indication of a company's ability to meet short-term debt obligations; the higher the ratio, the more liquid the company is. Current ratio is equal to current assets divided by current liabilities. If a company's current assets are more than twice its current liabilities, then that company is generally considered to have good short-term financial strength. If current liabilities exceed current assets, then the company may have problems meeting its short-term obligations.

Endnotes

1. Needs-based estimates are taken from WHO (2008). Demand-based estimates are taken from Scheffler *et al.* (2008).
2. These include the Global Health Workforce Alliance, The Capacity Project (USAID), The World Federation for Medical Education, and The Foundation for Advancement of International Medical Education and Research (FAIMER).
3. It is beyond the scope of this chapter to examine these constructs in detail, but the reader can review the references for additional detail.
4. African Virtual University (AVU.org), accessed March 5, 2010.

References

Adcock, D., A. Halborg, and C. Ross, *Marketing: Principles and Practice*, 4th (ed.). Upper Saddle River, NJ: Prentice Hall/Financial Times Press, 2001.

Altbach, P. G. and J. Knight, "The internationalization of higher education: Motivations and realities", *Journal of Studies in International Education*, **11**(3/4), 290–305, 2007.

Barney, J., "Firm resources and sustained competitive advantage", *Journal of Management* **17**(1), 99–120, 1991.

Beciu, H. and D. Haddad, *Scaling Up Education of Health Workers in Ghana: A Country Assessment*, Washington, DC: World Bank, 2009.

Beciu, H. and R. P. Jacob, *Global Trends in Tertiary Medical Education: Policy Recommendations for Sub-Saharan Africa*, Washington, DC: World Bank, 2009.

Birdsall, N., "Public spending on higher education in developing countries: Too much or too little?" *Economics of Education Review*, **15**(4), 407–419, 1996.

Clemens, M. and G. Pettersson, "Medical leave: A new database of health professional emigration from Africa", Washington, DC: Center for Global Development, 2006.

Dierickx, I. and K. Cool, "Asset stock accumulation and sustainability of competitive advantage", *Management Science*, **35**(12), 1504–1511, 1989.

Dranove, D. and M. A. Satterthwaite, "The industrial organization of health care markets", In *Handbook of Health Economics*, (eds.). by A. J. Culyer and J. P. Newhouse, pp. 1093–1143, Amsterdam: Elsevier, 2000.

Gaynor, M. S., "Issues in the industrial organization of the market for physician services", NBER Working Paper 4695, National Bureau of Economic Research, Cambridge, MA, 1994.

Harden, R. M., "International medical education and future directions: A global perspective", *Academic Medicine*, **81**(12), S22–S29, 2006.

Higher Education Almanac 2009–2010 (database), Chronicle of Higher Education, Washington DC (accessed June 26, 2013), accessed at http://chronicle.com/section/Almanac-of-Higher-Education/141/.

IFC (International Finance Corporation), *The Business of Health in Africa: Partnering with the Private Sector to Improve People's Lives*, Washington, DC: International Finance Corporation, 2007.

Johnstone, D. B., "The economics and politics of cost sharing in higher education: Comparative perspectives", *Economics of Education Review*, **23**(4), 403–410, 2004.

Johnstone, D. B., "Higher education finance and cost sharing profiles by country", *International Comparative Higher Education and Finance Project*, 2009, accessed at http://gse.buffalo.edu/org/intHigherEdFinance/project_profiles.html.

Kapur, D. and M. Crowley, "Beyond the ABCs: Higher education and developing countries", CGD Working Paper No. 139, Center for Global Development, Washington, DC, 2008.

Katz, M. and H. S. Rosen, *Microeconomics*, Boston, MA: Irwin, 1994.

Kotler, P., G. Armstrong, V. Wong, and J. Saunders, *Principles of Marketing*, 5th European (ed.). Upper Saddle River, NJ: Financial Times/Prentice Hall, 2008.

Kwoka, J. E. and C. M. Snyder, "Dynamic adjustment in the US higher education industry, 1955–1997", *Review of Industrial Organization*, **24**(4), 355–378, 2004.

Levinthal, D. A., "Adaptation on rugged landscapes", *Management Science*, **43**(7), 934–950, 1997.

MacDonagh, R., M. Jiddawi, and V. Parry, "Twinning: The future for sustainable collaboration", *BJU International*, **89**(s1), 13–17, 2002.

Mahal, A. and M. Mohanan, "Medical education in India: Implications for quality and access to care", *Journal of Educational Planning and Administration*. **20**(4), 173–184, 2006.

Materu, P., "Re-visioning Africa's tertiary education in the transition to a knowledge economy", Paper presented at the World Bank Conference on Knowledge for Africa's Development, "Innovation, Education and

Information and Communications Technology", Johannesburg, South Africa, 2006, May 8–10.

OBHE, *Arise For-Profit, and Go Forth Global? Kaplan and Apollo among the Private Providers Making New Inroads*, London: The Observatory on Borderless Higher Education, 2009a, accessed at http://www.obhe.ac.uk/ documents/download?id=779.

OBHE (Observatory on Borderless Higher Education), *Higher Education by Distance: Opportunities and Challenges at National and International Levels*, (ed.). by B. D. Denman, Consultant report, London: OBHE, 2009b, 2013, July 15, accessed at http://www.obhe.ac.uk/documents/view_ details?id=730.

Oketch, M. O., "The growth of private university education in Kenya: The promise and challenge", *Peabody Journal of Education*, **78**(2), 18–40, 2003.

Osterwalder, A. and Y. Pigneur, *Business Model Generation — A Handbook for Visionaries, Game Changers, and Challengers*, New York, NY: Wiley, 2010.

Pauly, M. V., "Insurance reimbursement", In *Handbook of Health Economics*, (eds.). by A. J. Culyer and J. P. Newhouse, pp. 537–560, Amsterdam: Elsevier, 2000.

Porter, M. E., *Competitive Strategy*, New York, NY: Free Press, 1980.

Poterba, J. M., "Government intervention in the markets for education and health care: How and why?" NBER Working Paper 4916, National Bureau of Economic Research, Cambridge, MA, 1995.

Prager, Seally & Co., LLC; KPMG, LLC; BearingPoint Inc., *Strategic Financial Analysis for Higher Education*, 6th edn., New York, NY: Prager, Seally and Co., LLC, 2005.

Psacharopoulos, G. and H. Patrinos, "Returns to investment in education: A further update", Policy Research Working Paper 2881, Washington, DC: World Bank, 2002.

Psacharopoulos, G., J. P. Tan, and E. Jimenez, *Financing Education in Developing Countries: Exploration of Policy Options*, Washington, DC: World Bank, 1986.

Rumelt, R. P., "Towards a strategic theory of the firm", In *Competitive Strategic Management*, (ed.). R. B. Lamb, pp. 556–570, Engelwood Cliffs: NJ: Prentice-Hall, 1984.

SAMSS *Sub-Saharan African Medical School Study*, 2010, accessed at http:// samss.org/display.aspx?twinning.

Scheffler, R. M., J. X. Liu, Y. Kinfu, and M. R. Dal Poz, "Forecasting the global shortage of physicians: An economic- and needs-based approach", *Bulletin of the World Health Organization* **86**, 516–523, 2008.

Scherer, F., "The pharmaceutical industry", In *Handbook of Health Economics*, (eds.). by A. J. Culyer and J. P. Newhouse, pp. 1297–1336, Amsterdam: Elsevier, 2000.

Schmalensee, R., M. Armstrong, R. D. Willig, and R. Porter, *Handbook of Industrial Organization*, Amsterdam: North Holland, 2007.

Sloan, F. A., "Not-for-profit ownership and hospital behavior", In *Handbook of Health Economics*, (eds.). by A. J. Culyer and J. P. Newhouse, pp. 1141–1174, Amsterdam: Elsevier, 2000.

Sosale, S., "Trends in private sector development in World Bank education projects", Policy Research Working Paper 2452, Washington, DC: World Bank, 2000.

Tilak, J. B. G., "Higher education in developing countries", *Minerva*, **38**(2), 233–240, 2000.

Teece, D. J., G. Pisano, and A. Shuen, "Dynamic capabilities and strategic management", *Strategic Management Journal*, **18**(7), 509–533, 1997.

UNESCO (United Nations Educational, Scientific and Cultural Organization), UNESCO Data Centre, Institute for Statistics, Montreal, Canada, 2013.

UNESCO (United Nations Educational, Scientific and Cultural Organization), Brain gain initiative: A digital infrastructure linking African and Arab region universities to global knowledge, Paper read at World Conference on Higher Education, Washington, DC, 2009.

Universities UK, "The growth of private and for-profit higher education providers in the UK", (ed.). by J. Fielden, Consultant report, 2010, accessed at https://chronicle.com/article/The-Growth-of-Private-and/66301/.

WHO (World Health Organization), "Forecasting the global shortages of physicians: An economic and needs-based approach", *Bulletin of the World Health Organization*, 2008.

Wilson, R., "For-profit colleges change higher education's landscape", *Chronicle of Higher Education*, **56**(22), A1–A19, 2010.

Winston, G. C., "For-profit higher education: Godzilla or Chicken Little?" *Change: The Magazine of Higher Learning*, **31**(1), 12–19, 1999.

Winston, G. C., J. C. Carbone, and E. G. Lewis, "What's been happening to higher education? A reference manual", Williams Project on the Economics of Higher Education, 1998, accessed at http://siher.stanford.edu/documents/pdfs/DP-47.pdf.

Zweifel, P. and W. G. Manning, "Moral hazard and consumer incentives in health care", In *Handbook of Health Economics*, (ed.). by A. J. Culyer and J. P. Newhouse, pp. 409–459, Amsterdam: Elsevier, 2000.

Appendix

Innovations in Tertiary Education Financing: A Comparative Evaluation of Allocation Mechanisms*

Jamil Salmi and Arthur M. Hauptman

Contents

---

*This Appendix was originally published by the World Bank. Rights to republish the research presented in this Appendix was granted by the Authors and the World Bank. At the time of the original publication, the authors were respectively Coordinator of the World Bank's Tertiary Education Thematic Group and Consultant to the World Bank. The findings, interpretations, and conclusions expressed in this paper are entirely those of the authors and should not be attributed in any manner to the World Bank, the members of its Board of Executive Directors or the countries they represent. The authors wish to thank all the colleagues who kindly reviewed earlier drafts and offered invaluable suggestions, in particular Bahram Bekhradnia, Roger Brown, Luis Crouch, John Fielden, Luciano Galán, Rick Hopper, Norman LaRocque, Kurt Larsen, Paul Lingenfelter, Benoît Millot, Harry Patrinos, Kristian Thorn, and Alex Usher. Full responsibility for errors and misinterpretations remains, however, with the authors. An abbreviated version of this paper was published in the first volume of the GUNI Series on the Social Commitment of Universities, Higher Education in the World 2006: The Financing of Universities, Palgrave MacMillan, Houndmills and New York, 2006.

1. Introduction

In recent decades, a growing number of countries have sought innovative solutions to the substantial challenges they face in financing tertiary education.[1] One of the principal challenges is that the demand for education beyond the secondary level in most countries around the world is growing far faster than the ability or willingness of governments to provide public resources that are adequate to meet this demand.

There are three main reasons for this rapid increase in demand. First, the economic value of attaining a tertiary education in virtually all countries, as measured by rates of return or other indicators, is growing faster than the economic returns accruing to those who receive a secondary education or less. Secondly, in many cultures there are strong social pressures on students for moving beyond the secondary level of education for non-monetary reasons such as greater social standing and prestige in the community — sometimes even better marriage prospects for girls. Thirdly, many countries are attempting to make their tertiary education curricula more relevant as governments and tertiary education institutions de-emphasize certain fields with low levels of labor force demand such as public administration and education in favor of emerging fields such as information technology, engineering and science.

Competing demands on public resources are growing more intense as governments around the world face challenges across the board in providing more and better public services, including health care, housing, transportation, agriculture, and the full range of education. In this context, tertiary education is often far from the highest priority for public funding in both industrial and developing countries.

Countries and institutions have responded to the mismatch between available public resources and the growing demand for tertiary education in several broad ways. The most frequent response has been to mobilize more resources principally by introducing or raising tuition fees as a way of increasing cost sharing. Another related response has been to seek additional private resources through the commercialization of research and other private uses of institutional facilities and staff. A third, perhaps less commonly found response, has been an increased reliance on bond issuance and other forms of creative financing that allow for greater public/private partnerships in providing services related to tertiary education activities.

This paper focuses on the trend towards innovative allocation mechanisms that allow both public and private funds to go farther in meeting the challenges that tertiary education systems face around the world. Such groundbreaking mechanisms cover a broad range of approaches, including:

- the evolution of public resource transfer mechanisms for recurrent expenses and capital investment in a number of countries from the more traditional negotiations of budgets between governments and public institutions toward increasingly sophisticated funding formulas that aim to insulate allocation decisions from excessive political pressures and encourage positive institutional behaviors.

- the creation of a 'demand-side' voucher system, such as the one recently launched in the state of Colorado (US), in which institutional operating subsidies will be distributed through a voucher given to all undergraduates, or the consideration of possibly using voucher-like incentives by allocating formula funds to institutions based on student characteristics, an approach which might be referred to as 'supply side vouchers'. Such vouchers can be limited to public tertiary institutions, but can also cover students in private institutions.
- the adoption of a variety of performance-based allocation mechanisms in a number of countries including: setting aside a portion of funding to be distributed to institutions on the basis of a series of performance measures; performance contracts negotiated between governments and institutions; competitive funds that encourage innovation, greater academic quality, and strengthening institutional management capacity; and financing mechanisms that directly pay for results, either as part of the basic funding formula or as a separate set of government payments of institutions.
- the development of alternatives to the most traditional way of financing university-based research that jointly funds it with instruction and operations, including approaches that fund research separately from instruction, the creation of centers of research excellence on selected campuses and the use either of 'blue skies' approaches that encourage broad based experimentation in basic and applied research or of competitive project-based funding.
- the substantial expansion of financial aid for students with high levels of financial need and/or academic merit to allow for financing strategies that anticipate higher fees to increase overall resource levels to institutions and to help students pay for their housing, food, and other living expenses while enrolled, including the provision of student aid in the form of vouchers as a means of stimulating greater competition among institutions as an alternative to more traditional government funded but institutionally administered student aid programs the creation of tax incentives (credits, deductibles, etc.) in a number of countries to help students and their families offset the expense of tuition fees and tax-based family allowances that primarily cover the living costs associated with attendance in tertiary education.[2]

- the growth of student loans in many countries, to help students pay for the higher tuition fees entailed in cost recovery strategies and for living expenses, including the development of income contingent repayment schedules in which repayment levels are tied to the amount borrowed and the income of borrowers once they complete their education, as well as a series of creative financing arrangements by which the initial funding of mortgage-type student loans is leveraged to provide higher capital levels through modern financing techniques.

As the list above indicates, the search for innovative mechanisms applies both to the funding of institutions and the funding of students. In the case of institutional support, the allocation mechanisms apply to the financing of instruction, operations, and capital investment as well as university-based research. In terms of the support of students, the mechanisms include the provision of grants and scholarships, the use of tax benefits to offset the current expenses of tuition fees and living costs, and the continuing growing reliance on student loans in many countries around the world.

The primary purpose of this paper is to review the scope and potential impact of these various innovative resource allocation mechanisms. Such a review can help policymakers, institutional leaders and stakeholders in tertiary education identify and explore the most effective ways to improve the equity and efficiency of public resource transfers to institutions and students. The paper begins by proposing a typology that describes both traditional and innovative approaches to resource allocation that are being used or considered in various countries. This typology includes approaches that fund institutions directly and indirectly through students as well as those that fund students and their families. Chapter 3 examines how these various allocation mechanisms meet important policy objectives such as expanded access and improved equity, better external efficiency such as enhanced quality and relevance, and increased internal efficiency through cost containment and better throughput. Chapter 4 identifies the various conditions required for the successful implementation of the various innovative approaches. The paper concludes, in Chapter 5, by drawing some lessons from international experience with both traditional and innovative allocation mechanisms.

2. Typology of Allocation Mechanisms

This section describes two general types of allocation mechanisms for tertiary education that are used in countries around the world: (i) those that make resource transfers directly to institutions for the support of recurrent expenses, capital investments, specific purposes, and research, and (ii) those that indirectly support institutions through resources transfers, vouchers and subsidies provided to students or their families in the form of grants and scholarships, tax benefits, and subsidized loans to defray or delay the cost of tuition fees or related non-educational expenses such as housing, food, and other living expenses.

The chart presented as Annex 1 summarizes the allocation mechanisms that are described in this section. It also indicates examples of countries and sub-national units such as states or provinces where these mechanisms are in use, being implemented, or have been proposed in a serious way. An effort is made to indicate which of these mechanisms are more traditional and which qualify as being more reform-oriented or innovative. A more detailed description of these mechanisms and examples of countries where they are now being used or contemplated is provided below.

Part I. Direct Funding of Institutions

Governments typically provide public support of universities for two principal purposes: (i) to finance the cost of instruction, operations, and investment; and (ii) to pay for the conduct of university-based research including investment in research facilities and equipment.

1. *Funding instruction, operations and investment* — Governments around the world use a number of different approaches to help tertiary education institutions pay for their expenses related to instruction, operations, and capital investment in academic and related facilities and equipment. These payments typically apply only to public institutions, although in a few countries such as New Zealand and Chile some private institutions are also eligible for public forms of institutional support.

In examining mechanisms that support institutional activities, it is important to distinguish between how the level of public funding for tertiary education is determined and how those public funds are allocated. The decision on the level of funding can be taken in a number of ways including: constitutional provisions, appropriations legislation, and negotiations among key government policy makers and stakeholders.

A key issue addressed in this paper is how the level of public funds for tertiary education, however determined, is allocated among various institutions. Countries have traditionally used variations of the following three allocation mechanisms to support these basic activities:

- Negotiated or *ad hoc* budgets
- Categorical or earmarked funds
- Funding formulas

1.1. *Negotiated or ad hoc budgets.* Negotiations between government and tertiary education institutions are the most traditional way in which the funds for the operations and investment plans of public providers are allocated to individual institutions. The levels of funding decided through the negotiations process, usually primarily based on historical trends, are then typically distributed to institutions in one of the two following ways:

i) *Line-item budgets* — Negotiated budgets very often are implemented through line-item allocations to institutions. These line items typically entail relatively rigid restrictions on how institutions can spend the public funds they receive from governments or other public bodies. The extent to which institutions can switch or reallocate between budget headings in some instances is controlled centrally while in other cases institutions have greater discretion.

ii) *Block grants* — Providing a single block grant to each institution is another way that negotiated budgets can be implemented. Block grants tend to give institutions more flexibility and autonomy than line-item arrangements in determining how public funds are to be spent. Nepal is an example of country that is currently considering moving from line-item budget to block grant financing as part of a reform aiming at giving tertiary education institutions more autonomy. Australia, on the other hand, has recently adopted reforms that move in the opposite direction: in exchange for enhanced public funding levels over a several year period, university officials agreed to move away from block grants toward a more regulated, line-item approach. Countries considering a transition from line-item to block-grant financing must consider the various laws and regulations that may need adjustment to accommodate such a step.

In some countries, the negotiation process takes places within the framework of a budget calculated on the basis of set guidelines. In several Central American and Andean nations (Bolivia, Peru, Ecuador), for example, the Constitution stipulates that the public universities should receive 5 to 7 percent of the national budget every year. In Costa Rica, the allocation for tertiary education is determined as a percentage of GDP. In Jordan, the budget of the universities represents a set percentage of import/export duties.

1.2. *Categorical or earmarked funds.* Categorical funds are another traditional means of allocating public funds to tertiary education institutions. These usually involve the government designating or 'earmarking' a particular institution or group of institutions to receive funds for a specific purpose. Frequently, categorical or earmarked funds are established in an attempt to correct or ameliorate real or perceived past under-funding for a group of institutions most often characterized by their geographic location or the types of students they serve. For example, institutions located in rural areas might be deemed by the government as eligible to receive funds to expand opportunities for distance learning. Or institutions that serve large numbers of chronically underserved students might be eligible for grants to upgrade their facilities or equipment.

The United States and South Africa are examples of countries that have used categorical funds for this latter purpose. In the US, the so-called Title III program for decades has provided funds for institutions that serve high proportions of minority students. In South Africa categorical funds for libraries, academic facilities, and equipment needs were set aside for predominantly black institutions before widespread mergers occurred post-apartheid.

Experience suggests that categorical funds are best suited for targeting funds on specific institution or groups of institutions with an identified set of needs, particularly for specific physical resources or services such as libraries or laboratories. The distribution of earmarked funds to participating institutions may be accomplished in one of several ways: the allocation can be specified in legislation, based on an assessment of need for the designated activities or services, or based on enrollment or some other formula basis. As a general rule, categorical funds seem better suited at funding capital investment projects than operational expenditures. Categorical funds can also be particularly useful to fund activities in which benefits spill over beyond the university and its students to the broader community. On the other hand, categorical funds have the disadvantage of only influencing those institutions eligible for funding. Institutions ineligible for the earmark have little or no incentive to improve or address the expressed government priorities since they are not allowed to compete for funds.

1.3. *Funding Formulas*. Many governments over time have moved away from negotiated budgets and earmarked funds toward some type of formula as the primary means to allocate funds to institutions for their recurrent expenses. These formulas vary on the basis of the factors used in their development and the type of organization that develops the formula. Examples of factors often used to determine funding formulas include:

i) *Inputs such as staff or students* — Most funding formulas are based at least in part on inputs in the form of staff or students. The most elemental type of funding formula utilizes the number of staff or staff salaries at each institution as a basis for allocating funds. Nepal is an example of a country currently using such a funding formula. Sometimes, more refined staff-based measures are used such as the number of professors with a PhD. Staff-based formulas are still used by many governments, particularly in Eastern Europe.

As funding debates have become more sophisticated over time, formula designers have tended to move to using numbers of students rather than the number or qualifications of staff as the basis for distributing funds. The number of students may be calculated on a prospective or retrospective (actual) basis. Retrospective allocations, by their nature, tend to be more based on actual data while prospective formulas typically require mid-year adjustments to reflect reality (see description, below, of chargeback arrangements. In some cases, staff-based formulas have been combined with formulas based on the number of students enrolled. In Poland, for example, the allocations are based on a combination of the number of students enrolled and the number of full-time teaching staff with PhDs.

One of the big issues that policy makers must resolve, when using enrollment-based formula systems, is how to define what course load constitutes full-time status and how to differentiate between full-time and part-time students. There is great variety in how countries address these questions although in almost all cases full time students, however defined, are given a different weight than part-time students in calculating per student costs, student/faculty ratios, and other measures. Another common convention is to convert part-time students to full-time equivalency based on their course load.

Another key issue in developing enrollment-based allocation systems is whether the number of students that will be funded is capped. Most countries do limit the number of students they will fund principally through a planning process as a means for controlling budgetary exposure. A few countries have a more demand-driven funding system in which funding caps are not imposed and all qualified students are funded albeit often it at lower per student spending levels than would apply under a capped system. New Zealand is perhaps the most prominent example of such a demand-driven funding system, although budgetary realities are leading to reconsideration of these open-ended arrangements.

- *Charge back arrangements* — When funding formulas are based on prospective estimates of student numbers and/or costs, charge back arrangements allow for initial allocations to be reviewed mid-year or ex-post to reflect actual spending levels, and funding may then be adjusted. Most countries that use formulas based on prospective numbers of students now recognize that they should use charge-backs to correct for erroneous projections in the numbers of student or costs per student. This kind of mid-course correction substantially reduces the amount of 'gaming' that is likely to occur when institutional officials are asked to estimate figures for the upcoming year rather than reporting actual enrollments or spending per student in the previous year. Another approach is for the government or funding body to project enrollments and to take the "risk" of projecting incorrectly. This reduces the potential for "gaming" while allowing for growth. South Africa uses this kind of planned approach.

ii) *Costs per student* — Most funding formulas now are based on some measure of the number of students enrolled at a point in time multiplied by a cost per student calculation. The cost per student figures are typically calculated retrospectively for an obvious reason — institutions should not be funded on the basis of the costs they think they will incur — and are based on one of several enrollment figures as shown below:

- *Actual costs per student* — The most traditional form of formula funding occurs when allocations to institutions are based on actual costs per student as reported by the institution. Most states in the US use actual costs per student in their funding formulas; many countries also seek to use actual costs in calculating their institutional allocations.
- *Average costs per student* — In this approach, which constitutes an alternative to using actual costs per student at each institution, allocations to institutions are based on system-wide average costs per student, usually calculated from aggregate statistics on spending and enrollments.
- *Normative costs per student* — Perhaps the most innovative way of calculating costs per student in funding formulas is to base the calculation on normative costs. Under this approach, optimal staff/student ratios and other standardized efficiency measures are used to calculate what costs per student *ought* to be, rather than what they are on an actual or average basis. Thus, formulas using normative costs have the potential for improving efficiency by tying how much institutions will be paid for their expenses to a more efficiency-based standard. Among industrial countries, England is one of the main countries where normative costs have become part of the funding formula calculation. Often at the urging of the World Bank, normative costs have recently been introduced into funding formulas in a number of developing and transition countries as well, for example in Bulgaria, Hungary and the Czech Republic.
  - o *Benchmarking* — One form of normative costs used in some countries is one in which the cost figures and structure are pegged to a

'benchmark' institution or set of institutions. A number of states in the US, for example Kentucky, use the cost structures of comparable institutions in other states to help establish the costs per student in their funding formulas.

○ *Differentiating costs per students by level and field of study*. The question of whether to differentiate costs by field and level of study is an important consideration regardless of what type of cost per student calculation is used. For example, should undergraduate costs per student be calculated separately from graduate student costs? Should distinctions be made between relatively low cost fields in the humanities and education and typically higher cost fields in the sciences and engineering? Most governments do make such distinctions in their allocation systems but in a wide variety of ways. One approach is to 'band' certain fields of study into cost categories, 'x' cost for a humanities student and a larger 'y' cost for an engineering student. These bands can become quite numerous. At one time the UK had a matrix of 44 cells in its cost per student formula, although that structure has been simplified under more recent reforms. Australia has recently announced that it will move to an allocation system in which fixed sums per student will be used in eight subject groupings, and that the number of students to be funded in each group will also be set, representing a step forward in control.

iii) *Priority-based funding* — Another basis for funding is one in which adjustments are made to cost-based considerations to reflect national and regional priorities such as critical labor force needs. This approach might also be referred to as "funding for relevance" since fields of study designated as being of greatest relevance tend to receive the highest level of funds. The traditional way for funding relevance occurs when central bodies determine which programs to fund based on their determination of relevance. In the more innovative approach now being introduced in some countries, the 'price' paid by the government or the funding body to institutions for a seat in a high priority field is higher than what is paid for seats in lower priority fields of study. In some cases, the full cost per student or even more might be paid to institutions for seats determined to be in high priority fields of study. Or payments might be increased for those institutions that are deemed to be of higher priority than other institutions. For example, institutions in rural areas might be paid more for their seats than more urban institutions if there is a desire to ensure a more dispersed distribution of students. The special per capita grants for students in 'scarcity subjects' used in England would be one example of priority-based funding.

- *Supply-side vouchers*. One form of priority-based funding occurs when public funds are distributed to institutions based primarily on the characteristics of the students who enroll in them rather than the more traditional method of funding based on institutional characteristics such as costs per student. This kind of formula could be referred to as *'supply side vouchers'* as funds would be distributed to institutions based on which kinds of students enroll at different institutions. There are relatively few examples where supply side vouchers have been implemented or even seriously proposed by governments. For a number of years England has paid a premium in its funding formula for students from postal codes with high concentrations of families with low socioeconomic status, although the government is now considering abandoning this policy. Ireland is moving in the opposite direction, now paying institutions about one-third more for disadvantaged students in its funding formula. In Chile, seven percent of public funding for tertiary education is linked to the ability of universities to attract students receiving the highest scores in the national university admission exam.[3] Jordan and the Palestinian National Authority have are considering allocation schemes based on student characteristics with some of the funds then being used as grants for targeted groups of students, thereby improving the equity of the tertiary education system.

iv) *Performance-based formula components* — Another nontraditional funding approach occurs when institutional performance measures are built into funding formula, e.g. by paying institutions on the basis of the number of year-end completers or degree recipients rather than the number of students enrolled. This approach is discussed in greater detail below under the section on performance-based funding.

v) *Organizations developing and maintaining formulas.* A number of organizations may take responsibility for how public funds are allocated at the national or sub-national level, including relevant ministries or an agency that acts as a buffer body to negotiate between government and tertiary education institutions. The two principal options are:

- *political entities* — In most countries politically elected entities such as chief executives or legislatures, or the bureaucracies that report to them, design and implement the funding formula and/or are responsible for negotiations. Mexico, Chile, South Africa and India are countries where non-elected administrators have considerable independence in devising allocation processes and procedures. In many other countries, elected officials have more authority over funding and allocation decisions.
- *buffer bodies* — In a minority of countries, groups known as buffer bodies develop and implement the formula. Buffer bodies are institutions such as the University Grants Commission in India or the Higher Education Funding Council of England (HEFCE). These buffer bodies represent the link between governments and institutions and are intended to insulate the funding process from excessive political pressures. The Higher Education Council in Turkey (YOK) is one of the more independent buffer bodies deciding on the allocation of funds to tertiary institutions.

Decisions about the level of public funding allocated to tertiary education should rest with political bodies to ensure that the public interest is best served. In contrast, decisions regarding how public funds or appropriations are to be distributed to institutions should be insulated as much as possible from the political process to a large degree. The funding system administered by the Higher Education Funding Council of England (HEFCE) is a prime example of a buffer funding body that distributes funds on a priority- and performance-basis, as institutions are paid more for students enrolled in high priority fields of study, bands of normative costs are used to determine per student payment levels to institutions, payments are based on the number of students who complete a year of study rather than their enrollment, and institutional payments are higher for students who live in districts with high concentrations of low income families.

vi) *Higher Education or Tertiary Education?* Another issue relating to the organizations that develop or maintain formulas is whether they govern higher education, i.e. primarily academic colleges and universities, or the broader range of tertiary education institutions including more vocationally oriented colleges or institutes, open universities, etc.. The traditional approach has been for separate entities to govern the funding of universities and other tertiary institutions. The funding councils in England, Ireland, Pakistan and Turkey and in most US states are examples of this traditional approach. With the creation of the Tertiary Education Commission in 2002, New Zealand was among the first countries to establish funding bodies that cover the full range of tertiary education. Ireland is following the New Zealand lead by incorporating polytechnics into its higher education agency as are a number of other countries.

1.4. *Performance-based funding.* In contrast to negotiated budgets, earmarked funds or funding formulas that focus on inputs or numbers of students enrolled, performance-based funding represents one of the more recent and growing innovations in tertiary education allocation mechanisms in recent decades. By linking funding levels to some measure of outputs or outcomes, performance-based funding represents a clear shift from traditional funding approaches. Performance-based allocation mechanisms differ from most other allocation approaches in that they tend to use performance indicators that reflect public policy objectives rather than institutional needs. They also typically include incentives for institutional improvement, not just for maintenance of the status quo that is often the characteristic of more traditional allocation mechanisms.

Performance-based allocation processes can be based on a number of criteria that recognize institutional performance or student performance. Systems using performance indicators to measure the exam scores of students would be an example of a student-based approach while a process that uses completion rates would be considered institution-based.

Four types of allocation mechanisms might be considered performance-based funding:

- *Performance contracts* — governments enter into regulatory agreements with institutions to set mutual performance-based objectives.
- *Performance set asides* — a portion of public funding for tertiary education is set aside to pay on the basis of various performance measures.
- *Competitive funds*, which support peer-reviewed proposals designed to achieve institutional improvement or national policy objectives.
- *Payments for results* — output or outcome measures are used to determine all or a portion of the funds that institutions receive either through a formula or as a separate set of payments.

Table A.1 indicates how these performance-based allocation mechanisms differ from more traditional approaches.

Table A.1. Traditional and Performance-Based Allocation Mechanisms

Traditional	Performance-based
Negotiated Budgets — allocations of public funds are negotiated between government agencies and institutions	**Performance contracts** — governments enter into binding agreements with institutions to reward them with resources linked to the achievement of mutually determined performance-based objectives
Categorical Funds — categories of institutions designated as eligible for funds for specific purposes including facilities, equipment, and programs	**Performance set asides** — a portion of public funding for tertiary education is set aside to pay institutions on the basis of their achieving various performance targets
Funding Formulas — funds are allocated to institutions on the basis of staff numbers or enrollment levels and unit costs	**Competitive funds** — institutions or faculty compete on the basis of peer reviewed project proposals against a set of policy objectives
	Payments for results — output or outcome measures are used to determine all or a portion of distributions from a funding formula, or institutions are paid for the number of students graduating in certain fields of study or with specific skills

i) *Performance Contracts* — Despite their name, performance contracts typically are not legally enforceable documents. Instead, they are more often non-binding regulatory agreements negotiated between governments or buffer bodies and tertiary education institutions which can take a number of forms. The agreements may be with entire systems of institutions or individual institutions. All or a portion of funding may be based on whether institutions meet the requirements in the contracts. The agreements can be prospectively funded or reviewed and acted upon retrospectively. In some instances, such contracts can be viewed as a punitive instrument rather than as incentives, as failure to meet goals may result in reduced funding.

Examples of performance contracts include:

- *France* which since 1989 has devoted one third to half of the recurrent budget to 4-year performance contracts. Payments are made when the contracts are signed, with a post-evaluation to assess the degree and effectiveness of implementation.
- *Finland and Denmark* which have contracts that set out general goals for the entire tertiary education system as well as specific goals for each institution.[4]
- *Colorado* (US) which as part of its new voucher scheme is setting up performance contracts that would penalize institutions that do not meet standards as part of broader reform effort that includes demand-side vouchers and fee for services.
- *Virginia* (US) which is developing contracts with its public universities in which increases in autonomy are exchanged for reduced funding levels from the state. The model evolved from a request by the three top universities in the state to swap reduced public funding for greater autonomy in how public funds are spent to the final version that applies to all public institutions in the state.
- *Quebec* (Canada) which used performance contracts beginning in the mid-1990s, but has dropped them as a policy mechanism in recent years.
- *Switzerland* which started to introduce performance contracts in the mid 1990s as part of a reform to grant universities greater autonomy. A recent evaluation of the reform (Schenker-Wicki, 2006) indicates

that, in the absence of complementary changes within the universities themselves, the performance contracts have not yielded significant efficiency gains.

- *Spain* where some provinces have recently developed an interesting variation on this model called a "contract program" ("contrato-programa marco de financiación global") as a result of the new decentralization policy which delegates significant powers to the autonomous regions of the country. The first "contract program" in Spain was signed in 2005 between the autonomous government of Madrid and the six public universities operating in the Spanish capital city. This agreement combines the elements of a funding formula and a performance contract with a multi-year horizon (five years). Not only does the formula allocates resources for both teaching and research, amounting to 85 percent of the total budget contribution, but it also provides funding against a number of policy objectives (restructuring of studies in accordance with the Bologna process, better deployment of teachers, improvement in pedagogical practices and use of education technologies, continuing education, etc.).

Box A.1 Performance Contracts in Spain: The "Contract Program" in Madrid

The first "contract program" in Spain was signed in 2005 between the autonomous government of Madrid and the six public universities operating in the Spanish capital city. This agreement combines the elements of a funding formula and a performance contract with a multi-year horizon (five years). Not only does the formula allocates resources for both teaching and research, amounting to 85 percent of the total budget contribution, but it also provides funding against a number of policy objectives (restructuring of studies in accordance with the Bologna process, better deployment of teachers, improvement in pedagogical practices and use of education technologies, continuing education, etc.). The "contract" includes as well a clause for compensatory payments to the universities less favored by the new allocation model in order to reduce past resource disparities.

Source: Interview with Rector of Universidad Autónoma de Madrid, 28 November 2005.

ii) *Performance Set Asides* — In countries and sub-national units that use performance set asides, a portion of funding for recurrent expenses is set aside to be allocated on the basis of a number of performance measures. The set aside typically is less than 5 percent of total funding but in some cases may be nearly 100 percent of recurrent funding. The number of indicators varies from single to multiple (as many as twelve or more). The performance measures are typically decided through negotiations between government agency or buffer body and institutional officials: the allocation of funds is usually not done on a formula basis.

- South Africa has for a number of years set aside most of its core budget for teaching, research, and other services based on multiple performance measures. This performance funding is supplemented by a competitive fund.
- In the US, more than a dozen state governments have used performance set asides over the past decade or more. Examples include:
  - o Tennessee which sets aside six percent of funds based on multiple criteria — four standards and ten indicators — with each of these given a certain weight. Institutions compete against their own record; and
  - o South Carolina which for a number of years based most of its recurrent budget allocations on a wide variety of performance criteria. The South Carolina experience is instructive in that it represents an extreme in performance-based funding as the state decided to allocate almost its entire recurrent budget on the basis of performance measures. The general evaluation of the South Carolina performance-based funding experience is that it failed because there were too many indicators and standards and thus the signals provided to institutions were mixed and confusing.

iii) *Competitive Funds.* One of the more prominent innovations in tertiary education finance over the past several decades, competitive funds represent an alternative to the more traditional approach of categorical funds. Typically, under such systems, tertiary education institutions and/or individual departments within institutions are invited to formulate project proposals that are reviewed and selected by committees of peers according to transparent procedures and criteria. Argentina, Bolivia, Bulgaria,

Chile, Ghana, Hungary, Indonesia, Mozambique, Sri Lanka are examples of countries that have established competitive funds in the past decade or so, often with financial and technical support from the World Bank.

Competitive funds are typically established for the purposes of improving quality and relevance, promoting innovation, and fostering better management — objectives that are difficult to achieve through funding formulas or categorical funds. The actual eligibility criteria vary from country to country and depend on the specific policy changes set out by governments. In Argentina and Indonesia, for instance, proposals could be submitted by entire universities or by individual faculties or departments. In Chile both public and private institutions are allowed to compete for

Box A.2   The Contribution of Competitive Funds

Well-designed competitive funds can greatly stimulate the performance of tertiary education institutions and can be powerful vehicles for their transformation and innovation. Argentina's Quality Improvement Fund (FOMEC) has encouraged universities to engage in strategic planning for the strengthening of existing programs and the creation of new interdisciplinary graduate programs. Within universities, faculties that had never worked together started cooperating in the design and implementation of joint projects. In Indonesia a series of World Bank projects that began in 1993 has succeeded in stimulating ownership within the entire academic community of new paradigms in tertiary education. In Egypt the Engineering Education Fund was instrumental in introducing the notion of competitive bidding and peer evaluation in the allocation of public investment resources. The fund promoted in an effective manner the transformation of traditional engineering degrees into more applied programs with close linkages to industry. The new competitive fund in Jordan has detailed guidelines which are described in an operations manual, and it relies on international peer reviewers for projects of national interest. In Chile a second wave of tertiary education reforms is being supported by a competitive fund for diversification (development of the non-university sector, including private technical institutes) and quality improvement of all tertiary institutions.

Source: World Bank (2002), pp. 104–105.

public funding. In Egypt a fund was set up in the early 1990s specifically to stimulate reforms within faculties of engineering.

A fundamental prerequisite for the effective operation of competitive funds — and one of their significant benefits — is the practice of transparency and fair play through the establishment of clear criteria and procedures and the creation of an independent monitoring committee. In countries with a relatively small or isolated academic community, it is desirable to draw from a regional or international pool of peer reviewers to reduce the danger of complacency and subjective evaluation among a limited group of national colleagues. Use of a transnational pool is a long-standing practice in Scandinavian countries and the Netherlands. One of the added benefits of competitive funding mechanisms is that they encourage tertiary education institutions to undertake strategic planning activities which help them formulate proposals based on a solid identification of needs and a rigorous action plan.

International experience with competitive funds has shown the need to consider three operational questions when designing a new fund: (i) How to create a level playing field in diversified systems with strong and weak tertiary education institutions? (ii) Should private institutions be eligible? (iii) Is it desirable to closely link access to funding with accreditation or similar quality assurance requirements?

To deal with the heterogeneity of institutions and capacity, there may be a compelling argument for opening several financing windows with different eligibility criteria and funding ceilings or for setting up compensatory mechanisms to increase equity among institutions with varying levels of capacity. In Indonesia, for example, three different windows of competition were designed to serve universities according to their actual institutional capacity. This decision helped to prevent the strongest institutions from winning all of the funding while leaving the weaker institutions out of the game and unable to tap into significant public resources for important investments in quality improvements. In a recent tertiary education project in China, the strongest universities with the greatest capacity were required to form a partnership with a weaker university located in a poor province as a condition for competing for resources from a curriculum reform fund. In Egypt the competitive fund initiated under the World Bank-supported Engineering Education Reform project had a special window for technical assistance to help less experienced engineering schools prepare well-formulated proposals. Also in Egypt, proposals that included a partnership agreement between a stronger university and a weaker one received additional points for evaluation purposes. In Chile a special grant window was recently opened to provide preparation funds for universities requiring assistance in strategic planning and subproject formulation.

Governments that wish to encourage the growth of high quality private institutions can use competitive funds to support investments in these institutions. A competitive fund for engineering education in the Philippines had this feature in the 1980s and ongoing innovation funds in Sri Lanka, Chile and Ghana make public resources available to private institutions.

Finally, one of the strengths of competitive funds is that they are more likely to be effective in improving quality than broader-based approaches such as negotiated budgets or funding formulas. Therefore, one way in which competitive funds can improve quality is to link eligibility for funds to participation in the accreditation process, either on a voluntary basis (Argentina) or in a compulsory way (Chile). Another approach is to use quality improvement as a criterion in evaluating proposals and selecting recipients.

iv) *Payments for Results* — There are two ways in which some governments pay for results. One approach uses some set of performance measures to calculate institutional eligibility for all or part of their formula funding of recurrent expenses. The second occurs when governments or private entities agree to pay institutions for each student who completes a year of study or receives a degree in certain fields of study or with specific skills.

Examples of countries that have built performance into their funding formulas include:

- England where the recurrent expenses formula is paid on the basis of the number of students who complete each year of study;
- Denmark which has a 'taximeter model' in which 30 to 50 percent of recurrent funds are paid for each student who passes exams;
- Netherlands where half of recurrent funding is based on number of degrees awarded;

- South Africa where the funding formula takes both the number of students enrolled and the number of graduates into consideration; and
- Norway where some funding has been based on the number of credits obtained and beginning in 2007 a portion of funding will be based on the number of graduates.

Payments for results can also occur outside of the regular funding formula. In Colorado (US), for example, the state now purchases through a fee-for-service contract a specific number of subsidized graduate credit hours for resident students to complement the demand-side vouchers scheme for undergraduates. Another type of payment for results takes place within the community college systems in the US and Canada, whereby the government contracts with private firms to train employees.

2. *Funding of Research*[5] — Basic and applied research is one of the essential functions of a comprehensive university. The responsibility of the government with respect to academic research is to help ensure that public funds allocated for this are spent efficiently and effectively to meet the policy objectives of generating relevant findings and improving the quality of research capacity and academic offerings. A number of arrangements exist around the world for the funding of university-based research including the payment of overhead costs. These comprise instances in which instruction and research are funded together, project-based funding, and block grant funding for research. The sources of funding research are also varied and include: national research bodies/councils, government departments, charities, industry and commerce as well as the education ministry or the funding buffer body.

2.1. *Instruction and research funded together.* Combined funding of instruction and research is perhaps the most common approach for funding campus-based research, whereby institutions use some of the public resources they receive to pay for the conduct of research on campus in addition to expenditures for academic instruction and institutional operations. Most states in the US and many countries around the globe fund research together with instruction as part of their negotiated budgets or funding formulas. Joint funding of instruction and research arguably is the easiest to administer as it does not require additional entities such as a

Appendix

research council or similar body to make allocation decisions. At least in theory, joint funding of teaching and research also has the strength of being the research funding method most likely to integrate teaching and research efforts, which many tertiary education officials and analysts to believe is a desirable outcome.

In spite of the many positive attributes of combined funding of teaching and research, one of the strongest arguments against it is that it may remove public officials from setting their country's research agenda. Many observers would rightly view it as a strength that politicians are kept apart from decisions about what research gets funded. But joint funding of research and instruction essentially places decision-making responsibility in the hands of institutional officials and faculty who may or may not have national objectives in mind when making these internal allocation decisions. As a result, national relevance objectives may not be well served when research and instruction are funded together. In addition, the internal efficiency objective of moderating costs is probably not well served when research is funded jointly with instruction. When they are funded separately, the government may also gain certain flexibility to address changing priorities more readily.

2.2. Research project funding. Another common way to allocate public funds for research occurs when faculty or other staff are funded for specific projects, usually based on peer reviews of proposals. The federal system of funding research in the US, which is employed by multiple funding agencies such as the National Institutes of Health and the National Science Foundation, extensively uses a peer review process to determine which proposals receive funding. By measuring the quality and potential of proposals in an objective way, the process is somewhat insulated from inevitable political pressures. Multiple agencies are responsible for funding peer-reviewed research projects in a number of other countries as well. Funding is sometimes provided on a matching grant basis, whereby government funds are complemented by institutional or private sources. This matching grant approach is used in Singapore (3 from government to 1 from private sector) and New York State in the US, for instance.

Peer reviewed funding of research projects has a number of advantages over joint funding of teaching and research. Assuming the peer review process is conducted properly, the objective of maintaining and improving quality of research should be achieved. Peer reviewed projects also often have the best potential of combining relevance and quality — politicians deciding what level of funding to provide to different disciplines but kept away from selecting which projects and institutions are funded.

But the strengths of peer-reviewed projects can also be their weaknesses. Homogeneity in the selection of peers — with those in the establishment excluding dissenters — certainly could stifle innovation, result in narrow research agendas and detract from the quality and relevance of the projects funded. Similarly, breakdowns in budgeting processes can lead to inefficiencies and even controversy when there is a perception that the funds were inappropriately spent.[6]

2.3. *Block grant funding for research*. Under this less traditional mechanism for allocating research funds, institutions receive a block grant allocation that is not differentiated or earmarked by project; institutions or faculties then have wide latitude in setting their own priorities for the expenditure of these funds. In some instances, eligibility for the block grant may be based on *institutional demonstrated capacity*. The amount of public research funding for each university is based on a periodic peer-reviewed assessment of collective faculty capacity to conduct research in an innovative fashion. In England, for example, the "blue skies" approach for allocating research funds is based on the results of the Research Assessment Exercise (RAE) conducted every 5 to 7 years, which attempts to measure the quality of the research produced at different universities although this assessment may be in the process of being phased out. Scotland also utilizes block grants to fund research and Australia is introducing a similar system of funding research based both on measures of the quality of research and its impact on society.

Another way to allocate research funds through block grants is to fund *centers of research excellence* at particular institutions that often specialize in certain fields or endeavors. In the US, the federal government and a number of states have adopted this approach as a way to supplement the research funding embedded in their core funding. New Zealand and the Netherlands are examples of OECD countries that have funded much or all of their academic research through centers of excellence, although New Zealand is moving toward an RAE-type system that would shift some funds previously allocated through the research centers. The China '211' project, the Brain 21 program in South Korea, and the Millennium Institutes recently established in Chile and Venezuela with World Bank funding are examples of how some other countries have established or boosted centers of excellence. In some cases, notably the CNRS in France, the centers function as independent research entities largely disconnected from university administration and operations.

Funding research through block grants can be an effective way to meet important policy objectives. Centers of research excellence have the potential of improving the relevance of research if the focus of the centers accurately reflects national and regional needs. Processes such

---

Box A.3   Multiple Approaches to the Funding of Research in the Netherlands

The Netherlands is an example of a country that has adopted a number of different allocation approaches when it comes to the funding of university-based research. Methods of allocation vary for the five components of the Dutch research structure:

- Basic funding of research facilities based on a fixed amount per university
- Funding of PhDs is allocated on the basis of the number of PhD dissertations and related degrees at each university
- Basic research centers are funded on the basis of resources received in several other components
- Centers of research excellence are funded in a number of different disciplines; Minister decides on the allocation of funds after consultations with research stakeholders
- A strategic consideration component is also allocated on the basis of fixed amounts per university.

Source: CHEPS (2003), *Higher Education Reform: Getting the Incentives Right.*

as the 'blue skies' approach in the English research funding system seem more likely to stimulate innovation and creativity than many other research allocation methods because they allow for greater flexibility and autonomy in the selection of research projects. To the extent care is taken in budgeting for block grants, internal efficiency goals may also be well met. On the negative side, one of the greatest concerns is that the awarding of block grants will not be sufficiently insulated from political pressures. If grants are awarded to universities based more on political considerations than on demonstrated capacity, then the goals of improved efficiency are not well served. A key issue for policymakers to consider is how much to allocate through peer-reviewed projects and how much to provide with greater flexibility through block grants.

2.4. *Demand Side Funding of Research.* In a number of countries, university-based research is funded indirectly through the provision of scholarships, fellowships, and research and teaching assistantships provided to graduate students. To the extent the government or private sector are the source of this assistance, it reduces the financial burden on the institutions themselves and thus is viewed properly as an indirect source of support for institutions. The US is a prime example of this demand side approach in which the multiple agencies that fund research each typically have various programs of graduate student support. This is discussed further in the following part of this paper that examines the various allocation mechanisms that provide indirect support of institutions as well as direct support to students and their families.

Part II. Indirect Funding of Institutions and Direct Support Provided to Students and Families

While the large share of public support of tertiary education in most countries is provided directly to institutions, most countries also provide some portion of the public funds for tertiary education to students and their families. One of the more innovative student-based approaches is demand side vouchers which finance the recurrent expenses of institutions indirectly through vouchers provided to the students. More typically, some portion of public funds is allocated directly to students and/or their families in the more traditional form of non-repayable aid such as grants and scholarships, tax-based benefits for current expenses and savings for future, and a variety of government-subsidized or sponsored student loan models. In a few countries, support is provided to students in the form of grant/loan in which the aid begins in one form and, over time, transforms into the other.

1. *'Demand Side' Vouchers*. Around the world, voucher debates are much more common in basic education and some other government functions such as public support of housing than as a means of paying for tertiary education. But in all public functions, the purpose of adopting vouchers is basically the same: to promote greater competition among providers of a good or service by providing public support indirectly through the consumers rather than directly to providers.

A number of definitions could be used to describe how vouchers might work in tertiary education. A narrow definition would include:

- students and/or families receive a coupon (voucher) which represents a certain amount of money to be used exclusively for tertiary education related expenses.
- students carry the voucher to the institution in which they enroll, and the institution then redeems the value of the coupon from the government. This allows for portability and consumer choice.

A broader definition would include vouchers being utilized to defray all or a portion of the recurrent expenses of institutions, particularly those which rely primarily on public funding to fund their operations. These might be referred to as demand side vouchers as they serve as an alternative to more traditional methods of allocating public funds directly to institutions to help meet their recurrent expenses. In developing both kinds of vouchers for tertiary education, policymakers must consider and resolve a number of key issues:

- Do vouchers cover the full cost of education, or will tuition fees be used to pay some of the costs?

- Do vouchers cover the full public cost of tertiary education, or is there a mix between supply side and demand side approaches?
- Are vouchers available to all students, or only to specific groups of students?
- Are the vouchers the same amount for all students, or do students from disadvantaged families receive more?
- Are students at private institutions eligible to use the vouchers, or are they restricted to those at public institutions?
- How are seats allocated to voucher holders at institutions that are oversubscribed?

Demand side vouchers are so innovative that there are few examples of countries or states that use them. The most prominent example can be found in the state of Colorado (US) which began implementing a voucher scheme in 2004 to pay a portion of the recurrent expenses of undergraduates in both public and private institutions. A law passed in 2004 in the former Soviet Republic of Georgia creates the framework for a similar demand-side voucher system.[7] The recently launched Universities for All program (ProUni) in Brazil constitutes an interesting variation of a voucher scheme. Under that new program, the Brazilian government uses tax incentives to "buy" places in private universities for deserving, academically qualified low income students who were not admitted in the top public universities. An innovative scheme recently set up in the Colombian Department of Antioquia is also worth mentioning in this context. A public-private partnership bringing together the local authorities, a group of private universities and a number of private sector employers offers qualified low income students who could not find a place in a public university the opportunity to study in one of the local private universities. The students get a scholarship equivalent to 75 percent of the tuition costs and receive a loan from the National Student Loan Agency (ICETEX) for the remaining 25 percent. Finally, the new *Iskolar* scheme in the Philippines will provide a two to four-year scholarship of about $200 annually for one student of each low-income family.

Box A.4   The Tertiary Voucher Experiment in Colorado

Under the Colorado plan, all undergraduates at public and private institutions in Colorado are scheduled to receive a uniform voucher (officially referred to as 'stipend') that covers a portion of the average cost per student at Colorado public institutions. Students then submit the voucher to the institution they choose to attend (including private institutions in the state) to be used to defray an equivalent amount of their tuition fees and related expenses. Students and their families are responsible for paying the tuition fees over and above the amount of the voucher although these costs can be covered through student financial aid with no effect on the amount of voucher received.

In the first year of the plan (academic year 2004-05), the vouchers were worth $2,400 per student, which covered about half of the estimated costs of educating undergraduates in that year. The $2,400 value of the voucher was substantially below the initial estimates of the program because actual funding fell short of levels projected at the time the legislation was enacted. Colorado students attending private institutions were eligible for $1,200 in the first year of the program; unlike the benefits for public school students, however, vouchers for private sector students are limited to those from low income families, effectively making it a student aid voucher. The amount of tuition fees that voucher recipients are responsible for paying varies depending on the type of institution attended.

The Colorado tertiary voucher experiment was created in conjunction with two other financing components:

- Performance contracts have been negotiated with each public institution in Colorado in which institutions face the risk of losing public funding if they fail to meet the goals set out in the contracts.
- The State will pay public universities for each graduate student they enroll, as the demand side voucher applies only to undergraduates.

Source: O'Donnell, R. (2005) Presentation at joint World Bank/Korean Education Development Institute conference, April 2005, Seoul, South Korea.

2. *Government Grants and Scholarships* [8] — Most countries provide non-repayable aid to their students, but how this aid is provided varies on a number of dimensions, including: program administration modalities, which students are eligible, and which expenses are covered:

2.1. *Program administration.* Grants and scholarships are provided to students in two basic ways: direct and indirect provision. In France and most Francophone countries, eligible students receive the money directly from a specialized government agency, for example CNOUS in France. But in most countries, the traditional way of administering non-repayable aid involves an indirect transfer whereby officials in tertiary education institutions make the basic decisions on who is eligible and how much they receive, often with guidance or limits set by the government. The degree of government regulatory intervention tends to be influenced by the manner in which the grants and scholarships are financed. If institutions are using their own funds to provide discounts, the role of government in determining eligibility is typically small. In the more typical case where public funds constitute the bulk of funding for scholarships and grants, then the degree of government regulation and authority generally increases. Hungary, Lithuania, Poland, Portugal (merit-based program) are a few examples of the many countries that rely on universities and colleges to administer publicly funded scholarship programs.

In some cases, governments require institutions to match public funds by providing waivers or discounts to selected students. In the US, for example, the Supplemental Education Opportunity Grant (SEOG) program has regularly expected participating institutions to match a portion of the funds provided by the federal government.

The more innovative way in which grants and scholarships may be provided is in the form of student aid vouchers rather than relying on institutions to administer the aid programs and to determine eligibility. When student aid is provided through vouchers, eligibility is typically determined in a more centralized fashion: students receive vouchers, or chits, from the government or its agents that they then present them for redemption against tuition fees and other direct costs at the institution in which they enroll. Typically, the institutions then are able to redeem the value of the vouchers with the government. Student aid vouchers thus can be contrasted with more centralized student aid programs in which students apply directly to government once enrolled in an institution, or more decentralized programs that use institutions to administer funds, usually within government guidelines. Examples of countries that use student aid vouchers include:

- US, where since the end of the Second World War, the GI Bill has provided benefits to veterans solely on the basis of the length of their military service. Since the early 1970s, in the Pell Grant program, students receive means-tested vouchers on the basis of centrally calculated financial assessment.
- France, where students at public and state private institutions are eligible for social scholarships based on the student's and parents' income. Similar voucher systems are in use in many African francophone countries.
- Denmark, where all university students are eligible to receive up to 70 monthly vouchers to cover living expenses related to their tertiary education attendance. An interesting feature is that students can save their vouchers early in their tertiary careers and 'double up' near graduation.

Need-based grants and merit-based scholarships can be a critical component in any country's financing structure for tertiary education. Properly designed and implemented, they represent a means for promoting greater access, equity, and quality. Such financing mechanisms can also represent an important component in any broader effort to increase cost sharing as they can offset the effects of higher fees for academically qualified students who don't have the financial means to pay for them. This contribution to greater cost sharing occurs regardless of whether the grants and scholarships are funded through public funds or are internally financed by having students with greater means pay more than students with less family resources, as long as the amount of the grants and scholarships provided is less than the overall increase in the amount of tuition and other fees.

In comparing mechanisms for allocating funds to students and/or their parents, student aid vouchers have a number of advantages over institutionally administered grants and scholarships. They allow institutions to compete for students and provide students with much greater choice of institutions than they might otherwise have. Student aid vouchers also can be more effective in promoting equity by establishing uniform rules of eligibility rather than leaving that critical decision to the institutions that typically may be less likely to promote national objectives of promoting greater equity. On the other hand, many countries may simply not have the administrative capacity to implement student aid voucher systems effectively, an issue which is discussed in greater detail in section 4 of this paper.

3. *Tax Benefits* — An increasing number of countries are providing tax-related benefits to families or students for tertiary education expenses. The tax benefit may be in the form of a credit against tax or a deduction from income for either current expenses or savings for future expenses. In this paper, only those tax benefits related to current tertiary expenses are examined. This kind of tax benefits is typically provided for one of two purposes:

i) *Tuition offsets* — Students or their families receive a tax benefit that offsets a portion of tuition fees paid. Ireland and the US are two examples of countries that have used the tax system to provide this form of benefit. In the US, two different tax credits and a tax deduction have been available since 1997 to offset a portion of tuition expenses at accredited postsecondary institutions. The province of New Brunswick in Canada recently established a "Tuition Tax Cash Back Credit" in which students enrolled in New Brunswick institutions are eligible to receive up to half of tuition fees up to a maximum of $10,000, provided they reside in the province after completing their educational program.

ii) *Family allowances* — Provided through the tax system, these tax provisions help parents offset the expenses of supporting children while they are enrolled in tertiary education. Austria, Belgium, Czech Republic, France, Germany, Latvia, Netherlands, and Slovenia are examples of the growing number of countries providing tax benefits in the form of family allowances for students attending tertiary education.

4. Student Loans — A number of different models exist in the more than 60 countries around the world where student loan programs have been developed.[9] The various student loan models can be defined in the first instance by the type of repayment terms that are applied. Yet, student loan schemes also vary on other important dimensions including: the source of capital, the type of expenses covered, student eligibility rules including applicability to private and distance institutions, and the level of subsidy.

4.1. Repayment plans. One of the principal decisions that policy makers must make in developing a student loan plan is how the loans are to be repaid. In this regard, there are two basic approaches: mortgage-type loans and income contingent repayment plans.

i) *Mortgage-type repayment.* Mortgage-type loans, which represent the more traditional student loan repayment arrangement, are reimbursed on an amortized (equal) basis over a fixed period of time. This equal payment approach reflects the way that banks around the world typically deal with mortgages on homes or with a variety of consumer-type loans. The period of time for each payment is most typically a month, although quarterly or even annual payments are not unusual. The amount of time required for full repayment may range from as little as three years to as much as fifteen; the more typical length of repayment is seven to ten years.

- *Graduated and Extended Repayment Plans* — As a way of providing borrowers of mortgage-type loans with greater flexibility than what is allowed under fixed amortized repayments, student loan authorities in some countries permit graduated payments (smaller earlier in the repayment period and larger later payments) and/or extended beyond the normal fixed term to reflect more adequately the evolution of a student borrower's income over the course of his/her working life. The US graduated and extended repayment program is an example of this approach. The national Student Loan Agency in Venezuela (FUNDAYACUCHO) and the Mexican Student Loan Institute in the Northern State of Sonora (ICEES) have also moved to graduated repayment plans in recent years, following technical advice from the World-Bank.

ii) *Income Contingent Repayments*. One of the more innovative financing approaches for structuring student loans consists in calculating borrower repayments as a function of the amount borrowed and a percentage of the income of graduates once they complete their education. The theoretical basis for income contingent student loan repayment can be traced at least back to 1945 with an article written by Milton Freedman in which he argued that the prices charged for higher education should more accurately reflect the private economic benefits that accrue to the individuals receiving that education and suggested income contingency as an appropriate means of repayment. The first experiment with income contingent loans did not occur until a quarter century later when Yale University instituted such a plan that was then disbanded within a decade. Over the past two decades, half dozen countries have established versions of income contingency.

- *Mandatory Income Contingent Repayment* — The most common form of income contingent repayment occurs when all borrowers repay based on their income after graduation, although even under mandatory arrangements, borrowers may still have an option to prepay. Within the framework of mandatory income contingency, there are two principal approaches relating to who pays the initial fees:
  ○ *Fees initially paid by students and families*. This approach combines a traditional fee structure in which students and/or their parents initially pay the fees and then borrow to pay all or a portion of those fees and, possibly, related living expenses. Repayment on those loans is based on the income of the student borrower once they complete their education. South Africa, Sweden, New Zealand, Germany, and Hungary are examples of countries in which at least some loans have this kind of repayment arrangement although the scope of the loan program and the particulars of how repayment is administered varies considerably in each of these countries.
  ○ *Fees initially paid by government*. The more innovative method for introducing income contingent repayment for student loans is for the government to pay the initial fees for participating students and for student "borrowers" then to repay as a percentage of their income and amount borrowed once they graduate and enter the tax system. This form of mandatory income contingency can include

some borrowers being exempted because their incomes fall below some standard. Australia introduced the earliest example of this kind of income contingent approach in 1988 through its Higher Education Contribution Scheme (HECS). Scotland also has had an operational HECS-like student loan program for the past half decade. England and Thailand are introducing similar schemes in 2006.

- *Optional Income Contingent Repayment* — An alternative to mandatory income contingent repayment is that borrowers with mortgage-type repayment obligations are provided the option of repaying on the basis of their income after graduation. In the US, borrowers since 1994 have been provided with an option to repay on an income contingent basis. But usage of this option for income contingency has been modest in the US, limited largely to borrowers who have defaulted on their student loans and have been moved into income contingency repayment plans. Chile is another example of a country where student loan defaulters are moved into tax system to enhance their repayment levels.

iii) *Graduate Tax* — Students pay for their education as a percentage of their income through taxes paid throughout their working life once they complete their education. Income contingency differs from graduate taxation in that repayment for the loan is required only until the value of the loan has been fully repaid; it is not required for a lifetime or even until retirement as with the graduate tax. While this is a novel concept, no government is known to have instituted a pure graduate tax at this time.

iv) *Human Capital Contracts* — Student participants agree to repay a portion of their incomes to private sector investors who purchase an 'equity stake' in the student's education. This is paid as a percentage of the student's post-graduation income. Under some versions, investors would be able to depreciate from their taxable revenue the economic value of the students whose education they have financially supported. Such a practice, however, remains controversial. While these contracts previously were mostly a theoretical construct, private companies are now establishing pilot experiences in Chile, Colombia, Germany and the US. These private contracts represent in many ways the logical extension of the arguments made more than a half century ago by Milton Friedman, that students should repay based on the private benefit success that their education produces in the form of higher incomes. By contrast, the sharpest critics of human capital contracts argue that they are based on principles that appear too closely related to slavery.

Box A.5   The Experience with Income Contingency Loans in Australia and New Zealand

Australia and New Zealand, which both charged little or no fees at their public institutions in the late 1980s, adopted similar strategies to increase cost sharing. Both decided to increase fees while introducing student loan programs that would allow students to pay for these higher fees over an extended period of time based on their incomes once they completed their education. But the two countries took somewhat divergent approaches in how they imposed fees and in the characteristics of the income contingent repayment schedules they adopted:

- In 1988, Australia through its Higher Education Contribution Scheme (HECS) adopted a very innovative approach to cost sharing. Faced with prospective widespread student opposition to imposing tuition fees, Australian policy makers decided to use public funds to pay the fees while students were enrolled. All students participating in HECS were then obligated to repay these fees once they completed their tertiary education as a percentage of their incomes, although students with below average incomes were exempted from repayment. HECS applies only to fees, not living expenses.
- Beginning in 1990, New Zealand took the somewhat more traditional approach of imposing fees at their public institutions that students and their families would be required to pay upfront when they enrolled. Beginning in 1992, students could borrow to cover the cost of these fees

(Continued)

Box A.5 *(Continued)*

as well as a substantial amount of living expenses. Repayment of these loans would then occur through the income tax system based on a percentage of students' income once they completed their education and the amount borrowed.

New Zealand and Australia have moved in different directions since they first adopted their income contingent student loan plans nearly two decades ago. New Zealand began with a more market-based approach in which virtually all borrowers (who then constituted a small share of students) repaid on the basis of their income and there was only modest reduction in interest rates below market levels. Over time, New Zealand has moved away from market-based principles by increasing subsidies, including exempting more lower-income students from making repayments and forgiving interest on most loans. As a result, borrowing has grown substantially over time. The overriding policy concern now seems to be that high debt levels of graduates are leading an increasing number of them to emigrate from New Zealand to avoid their loan repayment obligations. This concern may be somewhat overblown as default in New Zealand is low by international standards. Nevertheless, the government has responded by making repayments for borrowers who remain in New Zealand interest-free beginning in 2006.

Australia's HECS system, on the other hand, created a public expenditure challenge as the government found it difficult to pay for both operating subsidies along with the initial HECS fees. To meet this challenge, Australia in 1997 moved toward the market by reducing HECS subsidies and introducing three bands of HECS tuition fees as well as reducing the level of income exempted from HECS repayment. In addition, more market-based loan programs have been developed for the more than one-quarter of students who do not participate in HECS, including growing numbers of foreign students and domestic students enrolling in fields of study not covered by HECS. So as Australia has moved to a more market-based student loan system, New Zealand has moved away from a market-oriented approach. It could be argued that the two systems now have crossed in their devotion to market principles.

Sources: Chapman, B. *Australian Higher Education Financing*, and LaRocque, N., *Who Should Pay?*

4.2. *Sources of funds.* A principal variable in the structure of student loans around the world is how they are financed. This is particularly true for loans with mortgage-type repayments as income contingent student loans are typically funded ultimately through public sources since repayments will be made to public agencies, usually those associated with tax collection. Sources of funds for mortgage-type loans include:

- *Private sources* — Commercial banks and other private sources of capital fund most mortgage-type student loan programs around the world, including in: Canada, Chile, China, (commercial), South Korea, US (guaranteed program)
- *Public sources* — One recent innovative trend is for countries to shift from private to public funding of mortgage-type loans. Examples of countries that use public sources of funds to pay for mortgage type loans include: Canada, China (subsidized program), Hong Kong, Thailand, US (direct student loan program)
- *Internally financed student loans* — In this much less utilized way to finance student loans, tertiary institutions use the fees paid by some students to finance loans that help other students pay their fees. IESA, a private business school operating in Venezuela in collaboration with Harvard Business School, has implemented a scheme along these lines. The first student loans in China, after the government introduced tuition fees in the late 1990s, operated along similar lines. These internally financed student loans may entail little or no government involvement although they can be financed by private funding that allows institutions to finance their current operations until loans are repaid. They also allow more innovative repayments including:
- *Deferred payment plans* — fee payments spread out over a period of time that begins while the borrower is still in school. This system can be found at some private institutions in the Philippines.
- *Privately financed and serviced* — Institutions sell loans or contract with private servicers when borrowers begin to repay. There are a number of private firms operating in the US that offer these kinds of financial services to tertiary education institutions.

- *Creative Financing* — A number of innovative financing mechanisms have been considered and implemented to facilitate the provision and expansion of mortgage-type student loans, including:
  - o Secondary markets in which existing student loans are sold or used as collateral to create new loan capital. The US (Sallie Mae and other entities) and Colombia are examples of countries that have developed secondary markets for student loans.
  - o "Securitization" is a financing process in which bonds are secured by the projected flow of funds from student loan repayments. The US and Chile are examples of countries that have employed securitization techniques in financing student loans.

4.3. Expenses covered. One way in which student loan programs can vary is on the type of expenses which they cover.[10] The three basic approaches to eligible expenditures are programs that allow the loan proceeds to be used for tuition fees only, living expenses only, or tuition fees and living expenses. Examples of countries that have these different arrangements include:

- Loans for tuition fees only — Lithuania, South Korea (all programs), Japan, Philippines (all programs)
- Loans primarily for living expenses only — Denmark, Finland, Germany, Hong Kong (subsidized), Lithuania, Poland, Slovakia, England, Scotland
- Loans to pay for both tuition fees and living expenses — Canada, China, Estonia, Hong Kong (non subsidized), Malta, Mexico (Sonora), Netherlands, Thailand, US (all student loan programs)

The primary argument for limiting student loans to tuition fees is that fees represent the investment component of what students and their families spend for tertiary education and therefore should be the purpose of student borrowing. In addition, opening up student borrowing to cover living expenses can be very costly and subject to abuse as students borrow to support their life style rather than their further education. The rapid growth of borrowing in the US and New Zealand can be attributed in part to how much students are allowed to borrow against their living costs. The opposing argument is that living costs (and for that matter opportunity costs) represent a real cost of continuing one's education and student loans should be available to help students meet their responsibilities.

4.4. *Eligibility for loans.* Student loan programs also vary widely in terms of which students and, in some cases parents and other key family members, are eligible to borrow. One of the key issues with regard to student loan eligibility is whether participation is means-tested. Most countries with student loan programs do not require students to meet a means test in order to borrow, but in some countries including Austria, Italy, and Poland, only students who meet certain means tests are eligible to borrow. In other cases, only students who meet a means test are eligible for subsidies (see below), but students without financial need can still borrow at unsubsidized or less subsidized terms and conditions.

Course load and level of study are other conditions of eligibility. Most countries limit borrowing to full-time students although there are a number of countries including England, Poland, and the US that allow part-time students to borrow as well. In some countries such as Scotland, loans are limited to undergraduates. In other instances, loans are made available only to graduate or professional school students on the theory that these are the students who may benefit the most from borrowing and are the most likely to repay than undergraduates. In most countries with student loan programs, however, both undergraduates and graduate/professional school students are eligible to borrow.

Another key issue with regards to loan eligibility is whether students attending private institutions are eligible to borrow in the publicly funded or publicly guaranteed student loan programs. Many governments have decided that loans should be made available only to students in the public sector. The overriding principle of such a policy decision is the belief that public subsidies should be applied only to public tertiary education institutions. A number of governments, however, permit their student loan proceeds to be used by students at private institutions either on the grounds that the government wishes to assist needy students to study at the institution of their choice, or that the governments wish to have public resources flow to the institutions with the higher demand in an effort to reward quality or meeting demand. This latter rationale presumes that the best tertiary education institutions (public or private) will attract the best students. In many Asian countries students are able to borrow for studies in both the public sector and private sector including South Korea, the Philippines, and Thailand. Loan eligibility for students in private institutions is less prevalent in other regions of the world but does exist in a number of countries including Norway, Palestine, Poland, and the US (all programs).

Another way that governments encourage socioeconomic equity at private sector institutions is through the application of mandatory grants. The provision of grants and scholarships in private universities is sometimes regulated by the State without direct financial contribution. In Mexico and Syria, for instance, private universities must give scholarships to at least 5 percent of their students to offer access opportunities to low income students. The Philippines also has a long tradition of requiring private institutions to provide enough scholarships or loans to needy students to maintain their accreditation.

A more specialized issue is whether students who are distance learners should be eligible to borrow. The argument for permitting borrowing is simple: distance learners are students who have costs of attendance just as other students do and therefore should be eligible to borrow. If one is serious about promoting the concept of lifelong learning, it is difficult to argue against broad eligibility for distance learners for a wide range of student financial aid programs. One argument against distance learners being equally eligible for student aid programs including loans as more traditional students revolves around the question of how living costs are treated in calculating eligibility. How countries vary in how they treat the living costs of distance learners can produce interesting comparisons. In the US, for example, distance learners are eligible to receive grants and to borrow to cover their living expenses to the same extent as students in more traditional modes of learning.

4.5. *Subsidy Levels.* The question of whether to subsidize student loans is directly tied to the purpose that the program is intended to serve. Student loans typically serve one or both of two policy purposes: increasing the degree of cost sharing in the system and improving access for the more economically disadvantaged students. To the extent that the primary purpose of the student loan program is to increase cost sharing, subsidies are less justified than in a program designed to increase access for the disadvantaged. This leaves open the question of whether it is better to subsidize borrowers while they are still enrolled as a student based on their family's financial circumstances or to focus the subsidy during the repayment period though an income contingent repayment arrangement in which borrowers with lower incomes do not repay the full value of what they borrowed.

One form of subsidy is for the government to pay the interest of borrowers while they remain enrolled. This subsidy is usually provided to students who meet some form of means test to prove that they are financially needy and would benefit from additional government support, although in some cases this benefit is extended to all borrowers (at a relatively high budgetary cost). In some instances, this interest-free feature applies only while the borrower is in school; the US and Canada are examples of countries that do not charge at least some of their borrowers interest during the in-school period. Germany is an example of a country that traditionally has not charged interest on its student loans throughout the course of the loan, both while borrowers are still students and during repayment. With recent reforms, New Zealand has now moved to a student loan system to one that is much more highly subsidized throughout the life of the loan.[11]

Another form of interest subsidy occurs when student or parent borrowers are charged an interest rate that is lower than prevailing market-based rates — the government then covers the financial shortfall resulting from this lower-than–normal interest rate or lenders agree to charge a lower than market rate to meet societal obligations.[12] By charging the government rate of borrowing to student loan borrowers, countries like the Netherlands are in effect providing a subsidy to their borrowers. This is done to make borrowing for education more attractive and to reduce the financial burden on graduates.

A third type of subsidy is provided when the governments choose to cover any financial shortfall caused by deferred repayment. Governments sometimes allow students to defer payment on their loans during their period of full-time study. This lowers the financial burden on full-time students who presumably cannot undertake simultaneous full-time employment. In income contingent repayment systems, a common form of subsidy is exempting some borrowers from having to make their income contingent repayments when their incomes fall below some pre-determined level.

To summarize these different kinds of subsidies, student loan programs can be characterized according to whether they carry a relatively high level of subsidy — say, 10 percent of more of the value of the loans provided — or lower levels of subsidy where the value of the subsidy is below 10 percent of the face value of the amount borrowed.

- Means-tested and highly subsidized — Eligibility for subsidies is means-tested and interest subsidies exceed 10 percent of loan value. Examples of means tested loan programs that carry a high level of subsidy include: China (subsidized), New Zealand, Philippines (study now pay later), Thailand, US (subsidized).
- Little or no subsidy — In loan programs where eligibility is broad-based, subsidies would typically constitute less than 10 percent of loan value. Examples include China (commercial) or the US (non subsidized).

Guarantees and Insurance. The issue of whether loans charge a 'market rate' of interest is tied to whether the student loans are guaranteed or insured against the risk of default and loss. A true market interest rate on an unsecured loan to a student would be so high that it would essentially be unaffordable to all but a few students in most countries. The market is simply not willing to take such a high risk and charges interest according to the level of risk. That is why most student loans carry some form of guarantee or charge a fee to offset some of the costs of default. It is the government that generally provides this guarantee in order to encourage lenders to develop loan programs at rates attractive to student borrowers and their families; thus, his guarantee represents another form of government subsidy for student loans.

5. *Grant/Loan Arrangements.* In some countries, a portion of student financial aid is provided partially as grants and partially as loans. The Basic Grant in the Netherlands is one example of such a scholarship/loan program. All regular full-time students are eligible for a basic scholarship that varies with the student's living circumstances; student living with their parents are eligible for a smaller stipend than those living away from home. For all students, the award is initially a loan, but if students demonstrate satisfactory academic progress the loan over time becomes a scholarship. Norway and Sweden are other countries that have introduced scholarship/loan structures.

6. *Loan Forgiveness.* Another form of loan/grant arrangement occurs when some or all of what borrowers owe on their student loans is forgiven or waived if they accept certain types of employment after they graduate. An example of loan forgiveness is in the US which for several decades has forgiven loan repayments for teachers or doctors who agree to practice in underserved geographic areas such as rural settings or inner cities for an extended period of time. Typically the loan forgiveness is in the form of excusing a portion of loan repayment for each year of service, often until the full interest and principal is forgiven. In Norway, the government has put in place an internal efficiency incentive which allows part of the loan to be converted to a scholarship if the student finishes his/her studies on time.

3. Assessing the Effectiveness of Innovative Allocation Mechanisms

The underlying reason for governments to contemplate and implement reforms in how they allocate funds for tertiary education is to advance the goals of public policy. The following discussion, summarized in the two charts presented as Annex 2, draws from recent international experience to indicate which allocation mechanisms seem more effective at meeting various important public policy objectives. Basically there are three main

policy goals that countries around the world seek to achieve with regard
to tertiary education:

- *increasing access to, and equity in, tertiary education as measured by*:
  - o increasing overall participation rates for students of traditional enrollment age who enter a tertiary education institution in the year following their graduation from secondary school
  - o expanding the number and range of lifelong learning opportunities particularly for older students and other nontraditional groups of students including distance learners
  - o reducing disparities in participation rates between students from low income and high income circumstances as well as other important dimensions of equity such as gender and racial/ethnic group
  - o increasing private sector investment and activity in the provision and support of tertiary education activities
- *increasing the external efficiency of tertiary education systems by improving both*:
  - o the quality of the education provided, assessed in a number of ways including measures of what students learn and how effectively teachers teach
  - o the relevance of programs and of graduates in meeting societal and labor market needs
  - o the relevance of basic and applied research programs in addressing critical national and regional needs
- *improving the internal efficiency and sustainability of tertiary education systems by*:
  - o reducing or at least moderating the growth over time in a range of measures of funding effort, most especially costs or expenses per student
  - o improving how resources are allocated, both among tertiary education institutions and within institutions, to make the system more efficient and sustainable
  - o decreasing repetition and raising degree completion rates

Objective 1: Increasing Access and Equity

A fundamental policy issue everywhere is how to increase access to the tertiary education system. In most countries around the world traditionally only a small percentage of the population has been able to benefit from extending their education beyond the secondary level. As governments are evermore concerned with moving from elite to mass tertiary education, they seek a variety of incentives to ensure greater tertiary participation of all levels of society. Although the degree of access has increased markedly in many countries to levels that in some cases do represent mass or even universal systems of tertiary education, ensuring equity remains a constant struggle.

Even in countries that have achieved unprecedented and previously unimaginable levels of access, other equity problems remain including large disparities in the participation rates of different groups of students. Frequent disparities include the differences in participation between students by their socioeconomic status, by gender of the student, and by ethnic/racial differences. Another disparity often exists between students of traditional university age and older individuals who wish to pursue lifelong learning opportunities.

1) *Increasing Participation Rates of Traditional Age Students.* A fundamental goal in most countries is to increase the participation rates among traditional age students who have satisfactorily completed their secondary education. An examination of the experience in many countries suggests that three overall strategies seem to be most successful in raising the participation rates of these students:

- Growing funding of public tertiary education to increase the supply of seats combined with relatively low tuition fees to stimulate demand. Examples of where this strategy has been successfully pursued and much higher levels of participation have been achieved include most US states in the 1950s and 1960s and a number of Scandinavian countries over the past quarter century.
- Higher fees to increase resources combined with greatly enhanced levels of scholarships and loans to help students and families pay for

the higher fees. Countries that have achieved much higher levels of participation by pursuing this approach include the US and Canada over the past quarter century and Australia and New Zealand since the late 1980s.

- Expanding private sectors of tertiary education that reduce pressure on public funding to finance expansion of the system. Examples of this approach include a number of countries in Asia (Japan, the Philippines, South Korea, Taiwan, India), Latin America (Dominican Republic, Colombia, Brazil), Portugal, and a growing number of Middle Eastern and Eastern European nations.

An examination of international experience also reveals a number of examples of financing strategies that have not been as successful in achieving higher levels of participation, particularly among traditional age students. These include countries in which:

- relatively low public funding levels for tertiary education are combined with low fee levels to create elite tertiary education systems with low participation rates by traditional age students
- moderate overall funding levels combined with high levels of spending per student and low commitment to financial aid result in low participation rates as well
- low public funding levels, high fees, and low amounts of financial aid to students also tend to lead to elite tertiary systems albeit at high expenditures per student.

2) *Expanding Lifelong Learning Opportunities.* A trend in many countries over the past several decades has been the increasing proportion of enrolled students who are older than the traditional enrollment age, that is the age when students usually complete their secondary education. This trend toward larger numbers of older students enrolling in tertiary education is a function of many factors. Key among these are the global pressures for participants in the labor market to upgrade their skills and complete periodic retraining over a lifetime, along with the greatly increased availability of distance learning and other educational delivery modes that are more flexible and sometimes more suitable to the needs of older, non-traditional students.

International experience suggests that traditional resource allocation mechanisms such as funding formulas tend not to work well in expanding lifelong learning. Most formulas and other mechanisms that provide direct funding to institutions are generally not designed to meet the specific needs of older students. Demand side vouchers also appear unlikely to promote lifelong learning as it is harder to identify older students and distance learners who would become potential voucher recipients: such students are quite varied and they are not obvious consumers of tertiary education in any given year.

Perhaps a more effective mechanism to encourage lifelong learning would be for countries to redesign their funding formulas or categorical funds so that they pay a higher premium to institutions according to the level and intensity of their distance learning activities. Under such a system of supply side vouchers, institutions would have the financial incentive to recruit greater numbers of older, non-traditional students.

Demand-side mechanisms that directly fund students would seem to have a better chance of promoting lifelong learning than those that fund institutions, especially student aid programs that are portable and could be better tailored to meet the needs of older students. But most student aid programs are not well designed for older students either — they tend to be primarily intended to meet the needs of traditional age students and their families. Reportedly one of the main reasons why the US Open University launched in the early 2000s failed after only a few years of existence was the lack of financial aid opportunities for its students who tended to be older and non-traditional.

Three examples of student support programs that suggest a greater potential for expanding lifelong learning opportunities are:

- grants and scholarships that provide support for the tuition fees and living expenses of students who are financially independent of their parents
- student loans with liberal eligibility rules designed to serve borrowers from a broad range of incomes and circumstances pay for their tuition fees, including income contingent repayment arrangements that would allow students of all ages repay on the basis of their situation after they complete their education

- tax benefits that are designed to help meet the fees and current expenses of students who are or have been in the work force.

3) *Closing Equity Gaps for Disadvantaged Groups of Students*. Improving the equity of tertiary education is another public policy objective in most countries. It is hard to find any country that does not have some participation gap among groups of students according to their socioeconomic status, gender, religion, ethnicity, race, and/or language. As is the case with lifelong learning, mechanisms that allocate funds to institutions are unlikely to help much in closing equity gaps in student participation. Negotiated budgets and funding formulas are not conducive to recognizing the special needs and costs associated with educating certain groups of students. One exception could occur with various supply side vouchers when institutions are paid more for certain categories of students such as what England and Scotland do in paying premiums for students from areas with high concentrations of low income families. Thus, proposals to create supply side vouchers in which allocations to institutions are distributed based on student characteristics rather than institutional factors could prove be effective in this regard.

If demand side vouchers are differentiated by income, they also can help improve socioeconomic equity. A powerful model would be one in which demand-side vouchers that pay equal amounts for all students are supplemented by targeted student aid vouchers for needy or disadvantaged students. Under such an approach, all students could carry a voucher to cover a portion of their education and non-education expenses; those students who have demonstrated academic merit and/or high financial need could receive an additional amount of funding through a second voucher that would advance the goals of equity and quality. If not differentiated inversely by family income, however, demand-side vouchers can decrease equity as they would provide no additional resources to students who most need help to pay for the higher fees that might be entailed in implementing such a system. Thus, to be successful in promoting equity, demand side vouchers must be adequately funded and include a substantial student aid component as well.

Debates in most countries regarding the need for greater equity typically recognize that programs providing support to students and their families are more likely to be effective in closing equity gaps than mechanisms that provide financial support to institutions. International experience suggests that need-based scholarships represent the primary policy vehicle used in most countries to close equity gaps. The expectation is that such scholarships help to support economically disadvantaged students to overcome the significant financial barriers they face in continuing their education. This practice has worked well in a number of countries where need-based scholarships have indeed contributed to increased participation rates and helped narrow gaps among various socioeconomic groups.

Student loans are also viewed as a primary means for closing equity gaps in many countries. The general theory underlying this view is that, to be effective in promoting equity, loans must be substantially subsidized to encourage low-income students to enroll. But an examination of the actual experience in a number of countries suggests that loans with lower levels of public subsidies often are more effective in closing equity gaps. It appears that students from a wide range of socioeconomic backgrounds are actually willing to borrow to pay for their tertiary expenses, as illustrated by the US experience.

How to explain this seemingly counterintuitive observation that unsubsidized loans can be more effective in promoting equity than loans that carry high subsidy costs? First, one must recognize that student loans are implemented for one of two principal purposes: (i) to enhance cost sharing efforts by allowing students to borrow to meet higher fees and other expenses, and (ii) as a vehicle for promoting greater social equity by allowing students with limited family resources to borrow to pay for tuition fees as well as living expenses. The problem is that these two objectives often may be in conflict: student loan programs designed to enhance cost sharing are more likely to focus on alleviating the cash flow needs of middle class students than on providing resources or subsidies to impoverished students. In Malaysia, for instance, where the student loan program has no family income condition of eligibility, a significant proportion of the loans granted have benefited students from wealthy families who take advantage of the 3% concessional interest rate to support expenditures not directly linked to their studies. Second, a student loan program with high levels of public subsidy will not provide loans to as many students as a program with smaller levels of subsidy per loan.[13]

Another explanation of how more subsidies in student loans can lead to less equity could begin with the recognition that most countries simply do not have the public resources to provide the student loan capital needed to fund a student loan program of adequate proportion. As a result, they must rely, at least initially, on private sources of funds such as commercial banks to provide the capital for student loans. The problem with this approach, as international experience indicates, is that private providers of loan capital usually demand high levels of public subsidies in order to provide the initial funding and participate actively in student loan programs. This use of public subsidies in various forms — paying lenders to keep interest rates below market levels and

Box A.6   The Student Loan Experience in Thailand

Thailand provides a good example of a country which is radically changing its approach in student loans based on an initial unsuccessful effort. The student loan program that was established in Thailand in 1996 was viewed as a leading example of an approach in which loans would be used to improve access by targeting loans to low income students with a high level of subsidy during repayment. But flaws in the program design — including not targeting subsidies well on lower income students, allowing students to borrow mostly for living costs, and allocating loan funds to institutions based on enrollments rather than in a strategic way — led to an inequitable program that failed to meet its intended objectives.

In response, the Thai government decided to introduce a new student loan scheme that is designed more to facilitate cost recovery than to promote access. To do this, it has adopted a plan that draws heavily on the experience in Australia with HECS. Fees would be paid initially by the government and repayment would be conducted by tax authorities and be set as a percentage of income. Access concerns would be addressed through an expanded program of need-based grants. A key issue is whether the substantial differences between Thailand and Australia can be overcome to make this approach successful.

Source: Ziderman. A. (2006) Student Loans in Thailand: From Social Targeting to Cost Sharing, *International Higher Education*, Winter.

public payment of interest while borrowers remain enrolled — can be very costly and detract from the efficiency of the effort. A number of analysts also make the point that because of political pressures public subsidies in student loans tend to be distributed in less equitable ways than optimal. This reality leads to the conclusion that unsubsidized student loan programs may be more likely to meet the objectives of improving equity and efficiency that the highly subsidized programs that exist in many countries.[14]

The US experience in this regard is instructive. Government payment of interest while borrowers remain enrolled applies to borrowers with family incomes in the highest income quartile because of the way in which financial need is defined. In 2000, New Zealand introduced a similar interest benefit for borrowers while in school and more recently extended it to the repayment period; it, too, is poorly targeted on the neediest students and, thus, seems an ineffective policy intervention at least for purposes of improving equity.

One of the advantages of income contingent and other innovative repayment schemes tied to the income of the borrower once they complete their education is that they may be more effective in expanding access to a broader range of the population than up-front interest subsidies that often are difficult to target on the most disadvantaged students. The equity effect of income contingency is perhaps more powerful because such systems are designed precisely to have the subsidies applied when borrowers need them the most — during repayment.

Utilizing creative financing sources to provide capital for student loans represents another way to increase efficiency without necessarily sacrificing equity objectives. One type of creative financing is to use mechanisms such as secondary markets and securitization to expand the uses of private capital. Another is to use private sources of capital to allow institutions to initially fund student loans by using the fees paid by some students to pay. Still another is having privately funded entities deal directly with tertiary institutions that are willing to receive discounted flow of funds from investors in exchange for immediate cash flow. Policy makers in developing and transition countries should explore these creative financing solutions as they may allow for higher student loan volume than more traditional means of finance.

Tax benefits seem less likely to help in closing equity gaps as they accrue to those citizens who are most likely to pay taxes in the first place. Tax benefits that help students and their families pay for tuition fees and other expenses or tax incentives that encourage more savings for tertiary expenses are more likely to help middle and upper income families. But to the extent that the availability of tax benefits may allow policymakers to focus more need-based grants on the most disadvantaged students, they can indirectly help in improving the equity of the overall support system as well.

4) Expanding Private Sector Provision of Tertiary Education. One of the key issues in developing public resource allocation mechanisms and strategies is whether to permit those public funds to be transferred to private institutions and the students who attend them. One rationale for public support to the benefit of private institutions is that it is less expensive and therefore more efficient for a government to pay for a portion of a private college or university seat than to create and pay for a new one in the public sector. Policy support for these programs in the US is buttressed by studies in several states indicating that students in the public sector have a higher family income than students attending private institutions.

Very few countries provide direct public support of the recurrent expenses of private institutions. New Zealand, Chile, the Palestinian Authority, and a few countries in Asia including the Philippines provide public funds to their private institutions for their recurrent expenses (mainly faculty and staff salaries).[15] In the US, a handful of states traditionally make payments to private institutions over and above portable student financial aid. New York has the oldest and largest program of this kind; it pays private institutions in the state for every graduate from a private college — so much for a baccalaureate, more for a master's degree, and more for a PhD. Another way that governments transfer public resources to private colleges and universities is through the use of competitive funding for investment projects. To the extent that demand side-vouchers are made available to students enrolling in private institutions as well as public institutions, in principle they should be a good vehicle for promoting private sector development.

In general, resource allocation mechanisms that support students should be much more effective in promoting private sector development than mechanisms that support institutions, especially loan schemes that focus on helping students pay for tuition fees which tend to be higher in the private sector. In such portable, flexible systems, students may apply the proceeds from their student loans for tuition fees at either public or private colleges and universities. A number of countries provide public support to the students who attend private tertiary education institutions in the form of grants or loans, including South Korea, the Philippines, Thailand, Ivory Coast and the United States. Similarly tax benefits that are designed to offset the costs of tuition fees may be more effective in promoting greater private sector development than tax benefits for living expenses such as family allowances.

Objective 2: Increasing External Efficiency — Improving Quality and Relevance

Another major public policy objective in tertiary education is the improvement of the external efficiency of the system. There are two related ways to consider external efficiency. One indicator is the level of quality that can be measured in a variety of ways. Another way to assess external efficiency is to examine the relevance of the education being provided by the tertiary system — the extent to which the system is meeting the needs of society in general and the labor force in particular. Various resource allocation mechanisms attempt to embed incentives to improve external efficiency.

1) *Improving Quality.* In most countries, assuring and improving quality in tertiary education is an important policy objective — though the definition of quality can vary widely. At a minimum measuring quality may simply mean ensuring that students are learning. However, some governments seek to ensure or augment the level of academic standards in their tertiary education systems and put in place regulatory or funding mechanisms to ensure that standards are met. In a number of cases quality is defined or measured in terms of spending per student or by completion rates, though in this paper such measures are regarded as indicators of internal efficiency.

In tertiary education policy debates, quality has been largely viewed as a supply concept — one that is strongly in the hands of the institution. Mechanisms that allocate funds to institutions are therefore considered a more direct way to achieve improved quality than mechanisms that allocation funding to students. One very common practice to ensure some linkage between quality and funding is to require tertiary education institutions to have achieved some level of accreditation status as a condition for any resource transfers.

Even with a solid accreditation system in place and with linkage to funding, not all institutional allocation mechanisms are equally effective at ensuring or improving quality. Negotiated budgets, for instance, are not conducive to promoting quality objectives because they are based on static line item allocations. Funding formulas are also considered weak mechanisms for improving quality because there are few if any measures of quality that are readily adaptable to formula components or calculations. Competitive funds and other similar allocation mechanisms are therefore more likely to be effective in promoting quality improvement because they allow for a more sophisticated assessment of what it takes to improve quality and they can be more easily designed to reward whichever aspect of quality improvement is being sought. The practice of competitive funding also has the added benefit of touching more squarely on organizational behaviors within institutions, creating a strong financial incentive for quality improvement.

Funding mechanisms that support students are typically not considered as effective in ensuring quality as institutional support mechanisms. However, there are ways in which student funding mechanisms can support quality improvements. Merit-based scholarships that reward the best students are the most obvious example of student support programs that can promote quality. It is also widely believed that portable grants and student loans allow students to vote with their feet, and spend their funding allocation at the institution of their own choice. The underlying link to quality is that students will tend to spend their money on the best quality programs whenever possible, thereby rewarding institutions for good performance.

In spite of the various possible linkages between funding and quality, there is little substitute for regulatory efforts such as maintaining admissions standards at selective institutions or creating quality assurance procedures to ensure minimal levels of quality in the teaching and learning functions. A strong quality assurance system forms the bedrock of quality control in any tertiary education system. Funding mechanisms may generally influence improvements in quality at the margins through indirect means, yet they rely on incentives that touch on important organizational behaviors related to quality.

2) *Improving Relevance.* Although quality is perhaps the most obvious form of external efficiency, ensuring that tertiary education is relevant to the needs of society and responsive to the pressures of the market place is an equally important and related measure of external efficiency. Quality and relevance are inextricably linked as low quality programs are unlikely ultimately to be relevant to employers and other so-called consumers of tertiary education outputs.

A common measure of relevance is to determine whether the graduates of tertiary institutions are meeting the labor force needs of the marketplace. Are institutions graduating students in fields of study that match up well with the demands of employers? Do graduates have the requisite skills needed by the labor market? Similarly, is the research being conducted at universities relevant to the key challenges at hand?

International experience suggests that the goal of improving relevance can be addressed through the transfer of funding to both institutions and students. Several institutional funding mechanisms seem particularly appropriate at improving relevance:

- Priority-based funding formulas that allocate more money for seats in high priority fields of study combined with low tuition fees in those priority fields to encourage greater student demand. In the Netherlands, the three-year non-university professional training institutions (HBOs) have recently been allowed to set up master's programs as part of the Bologna process restructuring. But the government has committed to finance only master's programs in fields that are not already covered by the universities' postgraduate programs, thereby supporting the development of new programs rather than paying for existing ones. Having governments pay more for seats in high priority fields of study can serve as a powerful incentive for institutions to shift resources and attention into those fields, but such allocation mechanisms are more difficult to administer because they require additional data on labor markets that are difficult to collect. It is also difficult to use such data to project into the future labor market needs.

- Competitive funds that include relevance (improved labor market outcomes) as a key criterion in the selection of winning proposals can serve as an important incentive to achieve progress toward that objective.
- Supply-side vouchers are a more flexible tool for promoting relevance than demand-side vouchers because adjusting the prices paid to institutions for seats in relevant disciplines is straightforward. Demand-side vouchers are not well designed to improve relevance because they tend to pay institutions the same amount for each student. Thus, formulas structured as supply side vouchers have a much better chance of improving relevance.

On the student financing side, mechanisms that have a high chance of leading to improved relevance include:

- Scholarships for students enrolling in high priority fields of study.
- Favorable terms and conditions for loans made to students enrolling in higher priority fields of study.
- Loan forgiveness for student borrowers who enter employment in high priority fields or designated areas of public service.

Objective 3: Increasing Internal Efficiency and Sustainability

Increasing internal efficiency and ensuring sustainability is the third principal policy objective in tertiary education. Internal efficiency has several components. One is the need to moderate costs to conserve resources. Another is to maintain or increase the rate at which students complete their programs and receive degrees. These and other measures of internal efficiency ultimately are linked to notions of sustainability — policies will prove unsuccessful if they are not financially sustainable in the longer term.

1) *Cost Containment and Moderation.* Well-designed funding formulas are one of the most important elements in institutional allocation policies to help ensure overall cost containment and moderation. Funding formulas that utilize average costs per student or normative costs are more likely to lead to a moderation in institutional costs per student than formulas that use actual costs per student. The reason is that basing formulas on actual costs may encourage inefficient institutions to either spend more or restrict enrollments to increase their expenditures per student.

Another way in which resource allocation mechanisms can play a major role in moderating the cost of tertiary education has to do with how funds are distributed among tertiary sectors, a concept that economists refer to as allocative efficiency. One strategy for improving system efficiency is to allocate a disproportionate share of funds to those sub-sectors with lower costs per student. Under this approach, institutions such as community colleges and other types of institutions with relatively low costs per student receive a higher proportion of public funds than their share of enrollments would generally dictate. This was an essential element of the much touted success of the California (US) master plan for higher education in the 1950s and 1960s. By allocating a larger share of funds to low cost institutions, the state was able to leverage average levels of public resources to fund each sub-sector at above average levels, thus building an excellent system of higher education in California. Movement away from this approach is one reason the California system today may not be regarded as being as good anymore as it was in earlier decades.

Performance-based allocation mechanisms such as performance contracts or payments for results also hold the prospect of moderating costs if this goal is included in the contracts or payment agreements. Other institutional allocation mechanisms such as input-based funding or categorical funds are less likely to be effective in moderating costs because they lack incentives for institutions to increase efficiencies. While institutional mechanisms are likely to be the most effective in containing costs, student support programs can also play a role in achieving this important objective. For example, a student's eligibility for student financial aid — scholarships, loans, or tax credits — should not be tied to their total costs of attendance in order to minimize the potential impact of aid availability on institutional pricing strategies.

The US experience in this regard is instructive. When the GI Bill to pay for the higher education of returning military veterans was first implemented after the Second World War, the benefit was intended to cover the total tuition fees that students would pay. To implement this objective, a maximum benefit level was set that corresponded to the highest price then charged by any institution. But many institutions then raised their tuition fees to that maximum level to fully capture this new source of federal funding. The policies of the GI Bill were then changed to provide a monthly benefit of a fixed amount that included living expenses to introduce more of a market test since participating veterans could pocket the difference between the fixed benefit and the tuition fee that was charged. By contrast, the terms of the US federal student loan programs permits students to borrow up to the total cost attending higher education. Some argue that this availability of loans may have inadvertently contributed to the dramatic rise in tuition fees in the US which grown at twice the rate of inflation for more than two decades while student loan availability has grown ten fold in real terms during that same time. Perhaps for this reason, when tuition tax credits were introduced in the US in the late 1990s, they covered only a portion of the tuition up to a fixed dollar maximum.

One of the strengths of demand-side vouchers when compared to more traditional ways of funding recurrent expenses is that they have the potential of introducing more competition among institutions, thus increasing system efficiency by forcing institutions to compete for students more than under other allocation mechanisms. This kind of competitive mechanism should lead to greater efficiency and lower costs per student, at least in theory.

Supply-side vouchers as a form of formula funding do not appear to stimulate the same market response as demand-side vouchers in terms of encouraging student choice or competition for funds. On the other hand, a supply side voucher in which payments are based on normative costs could be a mechanism that promotes internal efficiency as well as equity.

2) *Improving Throughput.* Another aspect of internal efficiency is the throughput of the system as measured by degree completion rates or how many students complete the educational program they start, and the speed at which students graduate. As in the case of cost moderation, improving throughput can be achieved through institutional or student financing policies. Unlike cost issues, however, discussions of throughput often focus on what can be done to encourage students to complete their education more quickly. These debates typically address the question of whether student aid should be limited to the normal duration of the course of study.

Paying institutions through funding formulas or separately for the students they graduate can be a powerful incentive to improve throughput rates. However, there is a concern that institutions could sacrifice quality by reducing standards in order to qualify for more performance-based funding. One way to address that concern is to not pay too much for results or to mix payments for enrollment with payments for degree completion. Having adequate quality assurance mechanisms in place is another critical policy means for allowing institutional incentives to work properly.

Supply-side vouchers can also be used to pay institutions more for student performance, thereby encouraging greater throughput. The Governor of Michigan (US) has recently proposed to replace the state's merit-based program of college scholarships with a pledge to automatically give $4,000 to students who complete two years of postsecondary education or apprenticeship training. By paying for graduates or year-end completers, supply side vouchers as a funding formula can lead to improve throughput while demand side vouchers by their nature are more linked to the enrollment decision of students.

3) *Ensuring Sustainability.* In many countries, especially developing nations, the most important consideration in ensuring that policies are effective in the long term is to ensure their sustainability. The principal kind of sustainability, of course, is a financial one: can a country afford to pay for policies over the longer term? But this issue of sustainability applies not only to financial considerations but also to cultural issues: are the mechanisms that are put in place compatible with the traditions of a particular country or region?

A prime example of this is the question of introducing student loans in a culture that is unused to borrowing for a wide variety of needs including housing and automobiles. In China, for example, when the central government introduced compulsory fees for all tertiary education students in the late 90s, some universities set up their own student loan schemes to help students from low income families. But there was limited interest on the part of students and their families because there was no tradition of borrowing from "strangers", i.e. people or institutions outside the family circle.

In the case of allocating funds to institutions, a primary issue in countries around the world is whether public funds can keep up with the growth in demand and enrollments. In those instances where the growth in enrollments exceeds the ability of governments to fund this growth, relying on a funding formula based on enrollment may result in a sharp decline in per student decline or enrollment caps imposed by the government.

Australia's HECS program, for all of its success, is an example of a student funding allocation mechanism that may not have been sustainable at least in its initial form. To achieve political feasibility, the government of Australia initially agreed to pay the fees of all participating students with the plan that the repayment stream would be sufficient to replenish these funds except for the forgiveness of the repayments of borrowers with incomes below the average wage. But over time this arrangement proved to be too costly even for a country as wealthy as Australia and the subsidies have had to be reduced over time. This issue of over subsidization arises in a number of student loan programs as reductions of interest rates below market levels and other features are simply unaffordable.

Ghana, which also tried to introduce an income-contingent student loan scheme in the 1990s, encountered similar difficulties. Contrary to the Australian scheme that was linked to the income tax system, in Ghana loan payments were collected through the social security system. But as an increasing number of graduates started to default, the financial pressure on the social security system became unbearable and the government had to abandon the student loan scheme in the early 2000s.

Competitive funds are another example of allocation approach that can enhance long term financial sustainability. While competitive funding mechanisms have often been created as part of World Bank projects or under projects by other development agencies, it is important to ground them in a sustainability plan. Governments need to consider how they will sustain such mechanisms after the project funding is expended. In Indonesia, for example, the government committed to not only include matching funds during the project, but also to gradually transfer to the competitive funding mechanisms a percentage of the government's own investment budget for higher education. Today about 30 percent of the investment budget for public universities is distributed through a competitive process.

4) *Using Performance-Based Allocation Mechanisms to Improve Equity, Effectiveness, and Efficiency.* The potential effectiveness of countries shifting to performance-based allocation mechanisms is one of the principal topics of this report. The limited experience with performance-based funding thus far suggests that program design issues are important in ensuring the successful adoption and implementation of policies. Deciding which kind of performance-based funding to use may be the most important decision that will determine success. Issues of program design that policy makers should consider include:

• What proportion of public funds should be based on outputs or outcomes rather than more traditional measures such as numbers of staff or students, or costs per student?
• How many and which measures should be used to allocate performance-based funding?
• Should poor performing institutions be punished or encouraged to do better?

Various kinds of performance-based funding mechanisms have the potential to be effective public policy tools in a number of countries, although so far relatively few countries have adopted this kind of approach. The strengths of performance-based funding approaches relative to other more traditional allocation mechanisms include that they:

• Tend to be more transparent than many other financing mechanisms if performance indicators are publicly developed and readily available
• Allow for greater linkage between funding and public policy objectives

- Encourage greater accountability in the expenditure of public funds by linking results to funding levels.

The weaknesses of performance-based funding relative to other mechanisms include that they:

- Tend to be more inflexible in their application
- Can lead to greater year-to-year variation in funding if performance results vary, thus possibly contributing to instability in the system
- May discourage institutional diversity if many institutions collectively pursue similar incentives and often are linked to reduced institutional autonomy in the expenditure of public and private funds relative to other financing methods.

In comparing the strengths and weakness of different specific types of performance-based approaches, the following may be helpful for policy makers to consider:

- *Performance Contracts*:
  - These are the most regulatory of the performance-based approaches and therefore require a strong governmental body to develop and enforce the contracts
  - A key issue of design and implementation is whether the contracts should be established as incentives for good performance or penalties for underachievement
  - Another key implementation issue is that the contracts tend to be difficult to enforce or to use for incentives.

- *Performance Set Asides*:
  - These performance-based categorical funds create more competition for funds among institutions than the more traditional use of inputs.
  - What percentage of funds is set aside on a performance-basis is an important decision?
  - Policymakers have to be careful not to use too many indicators and confuse signals.

- *Competitive Funds*:
  - o These may be one of the best allocation mechanisms for funding quality improvement and innovation. The peer review process often associated with competitive funds seems to be an effective means for getting institutions to think through their needs and to look for innovative solutions to problems.
  - o Competitive funding mechanisms are flexible tools because eligibility criteria, calls for proposals, and selection criteria can be altered easily. Governments must be careful to make any changes in a systematic, fully transparent manner and broadcast the information on any changes to the system widely.
  - o They are typically not good for funding facilities construction or renovation because funding levels of competitive funds tend to be inadequate to meet the full range of facilities needs of a tertiary education system.
  - o They require more adequate administrative structures to ensure fairness and competitiveness. Competitive funds can put too much emphasis on whether institutions have good proposal writers than on whether they have worthy projects and needs.

- *Payments for Results*:
  - o These are the most market-based performance approach, thus care should be taken to prevent market abuses such as bogus or very low quality institutions being created primarily to be eligible to receive government payments.
  - o These payments need to be designed so as not to create perverse incentives that would reduce quality, relevance, and efficiency.

4. Ensuring Successful Implementation of Innovative Mechanisms

The preceding discussion indicated which generic types of allocation mechanisms tend to be better in meeting the broad objectives of improving access, quality, and efficiency. But this kind of policy assessment may not be sufficient for policymakers trying to decide which specific allocation approach is likely to be most effective in the context of their particular country. The following discussion seeks to identify the critical elements that will ensure a successful implementation of the various innovative allocation mechanisms.

In considering the applicability and appropriateness of different allocation mechanisms, particularly in the context of a developing or transition country, policymakers should raise and seriously address three critical questions related to the process of implementation, including:

- the administrative capacity of the government and the tertiary education institutions, including the degree to which different mechanisms promote flexibility of institutions to change and adapt rapidly and the capability of the system to collect necessary data;
- the transparency and perceived objectivity of the proposed allocation mechanisms and the potential for leakage and corruption of the system; and
- the political dimensions of adopting new or reformed allocation mechanisms, particularly the risks and difficulties involved in the transition from existing to new approaches.

In addition to addressing each of the three questions listed above, policy makers should also seek to prepare for possible unforeseen and often unpredictable consequences of implementing reforms in allocation policies. All of these issues are addressed below.

Gauging the Administrative Capacity of Government and Institutions

Simply put, a key implementation issue is whether governments and tertiary institutions have the capacity to administer whatever set of policies are enacted. This question of administrative capacity covers a broad range of issues, including the size and experience of staff in administering similar programs and the capacity to collect and process accurate data. This question applies to a series of allocation mechanisms for both institutions and students.

In terms of funding institutional activities, negotiations between government and institutional officials are not only the most traditional way of paying for recurrent expenses and capital investment, they are also the type of allocation mechanism that is easiest to implement. Negotiated budgets involve representatives of the government and the institutions meeting to determine how public funds are to be allocated. Categorical funds also tend to be relatively easy to administer, especially if the criteria for selecting institutions to participate are straightforward.

By contrast, funding formulas require greater administrative capacity than either negotiated budgets or categorical funds, in large part because they rely on accurate data to produce the appropriate allocation figures. For example, it would not be advisable for a country to move to a formula based on actual costs per student if those cost figures are not regularly collected or verifiable. Formulas based on average costs or normative costs tend to be easier to administer because they do not require as much detailed information from institutions as actual cost figures.

As a general matter, the availability of appropriate data is a critical element for success of any performance-based allocation mechanism. Funding formulas work best when the measures used to allocate financial resources to institutions are readily available and easily verifiable, and there is agreement about the relationship between the measures used and the results sought. In Argentina, for example, when the government started to reform the tertiary education system after 1995, audits revealed that several universities had inflated their enrollment figures to receive more funding. In the following years, a comprehensive management information system was designed and introduced within the context of a World Bank-supported project to provide the entire university system and the government with adequate and reliable information to monitor progress in reform implementation.

As noted in earlier sections of this paper, demand-side vouchers represent a real innovation financing. A primary strength of demand side vouchers relative to more traditional funding approaches is that they can expand the choice of students through enhanced competition, thus encouraging greater access and internal efficiency, as well as more private sector development if vouchers are made available to students who enroll in private institutions. One weakness of demand-side vouchers, however, is that they are more difficult to administer than more traditional allocation approaches such as negotiated budgets or funding formulas, thus possibly adding to system inefficiency. For instance, the process of identifying eligible students before they enroll in order to provide them vouchers requires a much stronger government structure than more traditional approaches that allocate funds directly to institutions. Another key to the successful implementation of demand side vouchers is the provision of adequate information to consumers. Demand side vouchers are more likely to be effective if students have a good knowledge of their educational options. Supply side vouchers, however, are easier to administer because of the direct relationship between the government and tertiary education institutions.

The administrative capacity of governments also is a critical variable in determining the potential success of various schemes that involve payments to students. Two particular issues with regard to administrative capacity are the possible use of student aid vouchers and determining the means of repayment of student loans. Both of these allocation mechanisms require a strong governmental structure in order to be successful.

Student aid vouchers represent an important policy alternative as they hold the promise of improving access, choice, and competition relative to institutionally-administered aid programs. While vouchers offer a number of advantages as a means for providing student financial aid, many developing and transition countries simply may not be in a position to use them as a means for providing student grants and scholarships. The conditions for successful implementation of student aid vouchers and other demand-driven approaches include:

- strong governmental structures as administrative requirements are high;
- good quality assurance procedures to prevent the proliferation of low quality institutions and programs in response to the availability of vouchers; and
- good information systems to allow students to take advantage of real choices afforded by vouchers.

It is also important for policy makers to recognize the weaknesses of vouchers as a means for providing student aid. Vouchers tend to place higher administrative responsibilities on governments than decentralized student aid programs that institutions administer. Moreover, for tuition fee and aid policies to be well coordinated, which is an important condition for successful implementation of policies, tertiary education institutions should have at least some discretion in deciding which students receive aid and how much aid they receive. For these reasons, many developing and transition countries may be better served by relying on their tertiary education institutions to administer their student aid programs than moving to a voucher system despite its several advantages in promoting greater choice, competition and system efficiency.

In order to ensure that student loans are effective policy tools, policy makers must address and resolve a number of key issues entailed in implementation, including source of funds, levels of subsidy, and the means of repayment. Perhaps most important, student loan agencies need to have the capacity to calculate and monitor the debt accumulated by its student clients. For example, in Venezuela, during the years of transition from a grant to a student loan agency in the early 1990s, the Student Loan Foundation FUNDAYACUCHO often was unable to tell graduates returning from their overseas studies how much they owed.

A second, critical determinant of successful implementation of student loan schemes is to utilize repayment mechanisms that best fit the situation of the country. Putting a student loan program in place without a reasonable expectation that the loans will be repaid sharply reduces the credibility of the effort as well as its financial sustainability. A more effective approach for achieving adequate repayment levels is to have the government collect from student borrowers once they complete their education through their tax systems on an income contingent basis. The conditions for success of income contingency include: strong government structures to administer the program; viable tax structures to collect income-based repayments, and adequate public resources to wait for the income-contingent repayment streams to materialize and be returned (with interest) to the public treasury. Few developing countries (and not that many industrial countries) can meet these criteria for successful implementation of income contingent repayment of student loans.

Without these conditions, countries may need to rely on more traditional amortized repayment arrangements, with banks or other private sector entities with experience in debt collection being responsible for loan servicing and collection.[16] This private sector servicing of loans can best be accomplished in one of two ways: either the banks or private entities own the loans and service them within proper industry norms or through government contracting of servicing to private firms that submit competitive bids. Student loans serviced and collected by banks or other private entities in accordance with generally accepted processing procedures often have the best chance of achieving levels of repayment acceptable to investors. But many developing countries do not have a banking sector or other private groups with a reasonable chance of achieving repayments that are both financially and politically acceptable. There is also the question of whether the income of young graduates is sufficient to repay the level of loans they may have borrowed. In many countries, the answer to this question is no.

Thus, for many developing countries, the two principal ways of ensuring adequate repayment levels may not be realistic options. For these countries, if student loans are viewed as an important component of their financing strategy for tertiary education, then identifying private firms with international experience in capitalizing student loans and providing the necessary repayment services may be the only realistic way to implement an effective student loans program.

Ensuring Transparency and Objectivity

One of the key elements in successfully implementing various public policies is that they are transparent to all stakeholders including students and their families as well as faculty and institutional officials. Transparency is critical to achieving the other objectives for successful implementation discussed in this section, especially reaching an adequate degree of political agreement. Without transparency in the allocation of funds to either institutions or students, policies ultimately will fail to achieve the objectives of increased equity, quality, and efficiency. A related aspect of transparency is to minimize the potential for corruption in the expenditure of funds. Even for well conceived policies, if the perception or reality is that funds are not being distributed in a fair and acceptable way, then the policy is likely to fail.

There is considerable variation in the transparency of institutional allocation mechanisms. One of the greatest weaknesses of negotiated budgets is their lack of transparency as the criteria for how funds were distributed are typically unclear to all but those involved in the negotiations. By the same token, one of the strengths of moving from negotiated budgets to funding formulas is that formulas by their nature tend to be more transparent than negotiations that typically are conducted outside of public view.

The biggest risk of corruption may be in the distribution of funds through categorical funds of one form or another. The risk is greatest if the criteria for how funds are to be distributed are unclear or if certain institutions are able to 'game' the system to increase the level of their allocations. While it is more likely to occur in poorly performing programs or policies, it can also occur in policies that are relatively strong. One example is federal research funding in the US which is highly regarded as a model of peer reviewed projects. But more than a decade ago, widespread revelations that some of the best research universities were improperly charging for the indirect costs of doing research severely undercut the credibility of this longstanding activity.

With regard to transparency, the policy question frequently raised during implementation of student aid programs is the capacity to determine a student's and family's ability to pay for tertiary education. Should the process be a simple one, asking only a few questions to determine family resource levels, or should the determination of eligibility for student aid be a more complicated process trying to make sophisticated distinctions among families as a means to achieve greater equity in the distribution of financial aid?

Defining eligibility for aid is an important question that policy makers in many countries may not have addressed in a systematic way. The options range from a simple system in which a few key verifiable questions are asked of students and their families to much more complex systems in which application forms can consist of many pages and detailed instructions. Simple systems can be found in a number of countries where students and their families petition for aid and are asked a limited set of questions about their own and their family's financial circumstances, including possibly income or wages. Often, though, the questions asked may not relate directly to income but rather to lifestyle issues that help to define a student's economic circumstances.

The US is an example at the other end of the spectrum with aid application forms that number many pages and which may require substantial amounts of time to complete. Some Catholic universities in the Philippines have used a complex system on the assumption that only needy students would be motivated enough to go through the time consuming process of filling the lengthy application form; that approach was reinforced by random checks of the veracity of the declaration by social workers visiting the family home of the applicants.

Compliance is another key issue with regard to the successful implementation of student aid systems. If students and their families come to believe that they can manipulate the results by providing inaccurate answers, the aid system will lose credibility over time. To ensure greater compliance and accuracy, especially in countries with weak or nonexistent tax systems or large black market economies (where income cannot be easily verified), officials in most countries should strive to establish relatively simple systems that require easily verifiable information. Examples of such questions include what high school did the student attend (especially if schools are ranked by the socioeconomic profile of their students or in countries with a significant proportion of students enrolled in private institutions), where does he/she live (if postal codes are ranked by low income concentrations), whether the family owns a car, has indoor plumbing, or even the size of the family's electricity bill.

While complexity of the aid process can yield additional equity in making greater distinctions among the capacities of students and their families to pay for tertiary education, most developing and transition countries are probably better served by opting for simpler aid systems that ask fewer questions and make less sophisticated distinctions. Complexity can be a substantial barrier to greater equity if students and their families are intimidated by the aid application process.

Addressing the Political Feasibility of Reform

Achieving political agreement among a broad range of stakeholders is another critical component in the successful implementation of tertiary education policies, especially financing reforms. One of the chief issues with regard to the political feasibility of implementing possible reforms is the degree of displacement or disruption in how funds have been traditionally allocated. The potential for large-scale disruption exists for both institutional and student allocation schemes. The success of implementing policies that entail redistribution of funds is directly proportional to the ability of ensuring smooth transitions from old to new policies.

The imposition or substantial raising of fees is the clearest example of a politically explosive tertiary policy that creates large transitional issues. But fees are more of a resource mobilization strategy and therefore fall outside the scope of this paper on allocation mechanisms. There are, however, a number of allocation mechanisms for both institutions and students that also result in large-scale changes in the distribution of funds and therefore raise substantial transitional issues.

When looking at institutional funding patterns, a primary disruption can occur when funding methodologies are altered. For example, when moving from negotiated budgets that tend to favor the most politically entrenched institutions to categorical funds or funding formulas that provide greater percentages of funds to institutions that are less well entrenched politically, it is important to recognize the difficulties that these changes may produce for institutional budgets of the most favored institutions. Similarly, changes in the components or the weighting of different elements of a funding formula can lead to the redistribution of funds among institutions. Moving from a system in which actual costs per student are reimbursed to one in which normative cost calculations would become the standard for allocating funds means that less efficient institutions with higher than average costs per student will most likely lose in the share of funds they receive while those institutions with relatively low costs per student will gain. This is exactly what happened in Colombia after the government modified the funding formula in 2004 to introduce elements of performance in the allocation criteria. Up to 12 percent of the budget was going to be distributed on the basis of performance indicators such as degree completion time and dropout rates.[17] But three universities filed a complaint with the Constitutional Court, which reversed the government's decision in 2005 and even forced the State to reimburse these universities for the "lost" income.

To deal with these disruptions, it may be advisable to introduce 'grandfather' provisions or minimal funding levels that guarantee all institutions a proportion of the funds they would have received under previous arrangements at least for some period of time. In the extreme, institutions could be assured that they would not lose funds for a sustained period of time to increase political acceptability. Under this approach, change would come through any growth in funding being distributed on a different basis than existing funding patterns. This is how it was done in Pakistan, where the newly established Higher Education Commission (2002) designed a funding formula to replace the traditional negotiated budget system, with an equalization component intended to compensate for past disparities in budget allocations. To avoid antagonizing the more powerful universities that would lose under the new formula, the equalization part of the formula was applied only to the additional resources during the first two years. But as of 2006, the new funding formula is applied to calculate the entire budget allocation.

Another aspect of political feasibility occurs when political pressures are introduced into systems that previously were largely insulated from the political process. The history of the FIPSE competitive fund in the US, as described in the box below, provides a good example of how politically neutral organizations can become politicized and as a result may lose credibility in the broader population.

Neutralizing political pressures also is the reason why it is important for countries to have a strong buffer body to make allocation decisions while leaving decisions on the level of funding to the appropriate political bodies. Funding formulas are likely to be more successful in meeting policy objectives if they are well insulated from the political process. This is why it is preferable to have buffer bodies decide on the allocation of funds once the more politically charged individuals and organizations have decided on the overall level of funding.

An important lesson is that it is much easier to impose redistribution measures when there is additional funding than when it is carried out

Box A.7   Fund for the Improvement of Postsecondary Education (FIPSE)

Possibly the first competitive fund in the world for tertiary education was the Fund for the Improvement of Postsecondary Education (FIPSE) established in the US in 1972. FIPSE, which has awarded grants to institutions or individual faculty members on a highly competitive basis for projects that promote innovation in teaching and research, operates as an office within the federal Department of Education. But FIPSE has traditionally been granted more flexible hiring and operational practices than the rest of the Department, including hiring faculty and institutional officials on exempted and limited term basis rather than as civil servants. In its more than three decades of existence, FIPSE has established a reputation for independence within the federal structure and as a constructive and effective means for stimulating innovation and quality improvement in the higher education community. However, one of the more disturbing trends in the past decade to many observers is the increasing tendency of Congress, the legislative branch of government, to designate specific projects for funding as part of the legislative appropriations process. This dramatic increase in "earmarked" projects has greatly increased funding of FIPSE but at the cost of less insulation from the political process and reduced credibility as an independent agency.

under a constrained budget. When the Minister of Higher Education attempted to change the funding formula in the Netherlands in the early 1990s, with the objective of reallocating resources from the oldest, richest universities to the younger, less favored universities, the former revolted and sued the Ministry. The courts sided with them and the Minister had to drop his plan. By contrast, Pakistan's recent reform to replace the traditional negotiated budget with an objective and transparent funding formula that includes a compensatory element has been accepted much more easily by the universities because the reallocation process concerns only the additional funding part of the tertiary education budgetary envelope.

In the area of support for students, one of the most politically controversial issues in many countries is the distribution of funds by the socioeconomic status of the recipients. Whether the benefits of student aid programs are well targeted on low income students and other groups of underserved students helps to determine the success of their implementation. Student aid programs in most countries when initially begun are intended to help students from the lowest economic strata to increase their rates of participation. But over time there is a tendency for benefits to be stretched up the income scale to gain greater political acceptance from middle class voters or the political elite. In many francophone African countries, for example, scholarships tend to be given to all students for lack of political will to fight corruption and nepotism. This kind of shift often results in higher financial costs at the expense of effectiveness in achieving greater equity in the tertiary education system. Thus, in this case and many others, making policies more politically acceptable may detract from their effectiveness in meeting the objectives they were supposed to address.

Anticipating Unintended Consequences

One of the most frequent barriers to the successful implementation of policies is the inability or unwillingness to consider the full range of possible consequences of enacting reforms or changes in existing policies. It is therefore important for policy makers to try to anticipate possible consequences both in the policy development process and in the putting together of implementation plans. In the arena of tertiary education, there are many examples of unintended consequences both in the funding of institutions and in providing aid to students and their families that ought to be considered.

In terms of funding institutions, there are a number of instances in which policies designed to achieve one goal may have unexpected adverse consequences on another important objective. Take, for example, those countries such as the Netherlands or England that have developed funding formulas in which institutions are paid for the number of students they graduate or complete a year of study rather than on the basis on the number of students who enroll. An obvious concern that should be monitored is that such a shift does not result in reduced quality as institutions seek to gain more funding by lowering their standards and graduating more students or allowing more students to complete their year of study. Another unintended consequence is when institutions choose to compete more aggressively for the top ranked students rather than seeking to improve the quality of the overall pool of students. By the same token, there should also be a consideration of whether the traditional policy of paying institutions on the basis of the number of students who enroll contribute to degree completion rates that are lower than in countries where funding is provided or distributed more of a performance basis.

For mechanisms that support students, a number of adverse consequences also exist that should be anticipated and avoided if possible. One concern is that insufficient supply of seats will blunt the effects of increasing demand by lowering the net price that students face through the provision of student aid. If seats are too limited, financially needy students will likely lose out to students with more family resources who also may have better grades or other measures of academic achievement.

Another concern with providing student aid in many countries is that institutions might raise their fees and other prices more if aid becomes more readily available. This has been a hot topic of debate in the US for nearly a quarter century as fees and other charges have grown at more than twice the rate of inflation at the same time that the volume of student aid, particularly loans, has grown multiple fold. In the US, those who make this connection point to the correlation between aid availability and price hikes while those on the other side make the point that no causal relationship between prices and aid availability has been established in the literature.

Similarly, students might choose nicer life styles if student grants or loans that pay for living costs are not capped or if the amount provided is sufficient to allow for excesses. In the late 70s, for example, Venezuelan students benefiting from a generous FUNDAYACUCHO grant to study in the North America were known by university administrators in the US or Canada as "the richest students in town". The rapid growth in debt burdens in New Zealand has been largely fueled by the amount that students are borrowing to pay for living costs, and the exodus of university graduates (perhaps more perceived than real) to avoid their student debt repayment obligations would surely qualify as an unintended consequence of the decision to raise fees in the early 1990s and rely on student loans to pay for the additional cost recovery. Another not fully anticipated effect from the US experience is the apparent shift of institutional discounts up the income scale as many universities and colleges are increasingly relying on government funded aid to meet the needs of the most disadvantaged students, thereby enabling institutions to use their own aid to 'market' to middle income students.

These possibly unforeseen effects apply to more than strictly financial considerations. For example, if a scholarship program does not require recipients to maintain satisfactory academic progress towards a degree, then one might find students dropping out of school prematurely or with little intent to graduate. Similarly, relatively low tuition fees might allow students to take longer to graduate or to drop out of school as the size of the amount invested in the student by the family or the student is relatively small.

One of the primary responsibilities of policy makers is to try to anticipate these possible adverse effects of new policies and to take the steps necessary to offset the negative incentives and consequences. Maintaining quality in the face of payments to institutions on the basis of the number of students who graduate might require maintaining adequate academic standards. Or it could entail not paying institutions "too much" for their graduating students, thus reducing the degree of financial incentives arising out of such a policy. In the case of possible 'price' effects of student aid, one policy response would be to provide student aid only for a portion of the fees and living expenses rather than covering the total costs of attendance as is often the policy in place.

5. Conclusion: Some Lessons Learned

Many reforms and innovations reviewed in this paper are very recent, as a result in-depth impact evaluations have yet to be conducted. Nevertheless, the experience of a number of countries over the past two decades provides a set of preliminary, lessons that can help policy makers formulate strategies for increasing the effectiveness of resource allocation mechanisms.

- *Rely on a combination of resource mobilization and allocation mechanisms to achieve the desired policy objectives.*
  A primary lesson from international experience in recent decades with resource mobilization in tertiary education is the importance of not relying on a single source of funding. The growing diversity of funding sources has been an important and effective response by many governments and institutions to the mismatch between demand and resources. Similarly, it seems clear that most countries should rely on a mix of allocation mechanisms to achieve the objectives they seek for their tertiary education systems. Funding formulas appear to be a good instrument for allocating core resource levels but may not be as good at rewarding quality or stimulating greater equity. Student aid programs often are the best mechanism to help promote better access and equity, but they should not be relied upon exclusively for achieving this important objective. Policy makers should also explore innovative ways to use institutional allocation mechanisms to improve equity of the system. By the same token, improving quality and relevance should not be the sole province of institutional allocation mechanisms. There are several ways in which student aid can be used to improve both quality and relevance as well.

- *Consider adopting performance-based mechanisms to achieve better results in tertiary education.*
  The experience with performance-based allocation mechanisms in various countries over the past decade or more suggests that tying policies to results can have the beneficial effect of improving key indicators such as degree completion rates or lowering costs per student below projected levels. This is perhaps the most telling trend examined in this paper — tying the distribution of funds to institutions or students to performance measures can make a real difference in the ability of tertiary systems to achieve the goals of improved equity, quality, and efficiency. Whether the policies achieve this

potential appears to depend in large measure on how the policies are designed and which performance mechanism is adopted. Competitive funds seem well suited for promoting innovation and quality improvement, performance contracts represent an improvement over negotiated budgets in defining the financial relationship between institutions and governments, while paying for results through funding formulas or other arrangements can positively change the incentives for institutions to improve equity, relevance, or efficiency. By the same token, a chief concern in adopting performance-based procedures should be to avoid adverse consequences such as reduced quality that might result from efforts to provide incentives for greater access or throughput.

- *Choose the most appropriate mix of allocation instruments to meet the policy objectives sought.*
  While linking allocations to improving equity, quality, and performance should be a guiding principle, the selection of allocation instruments must depend in great degree on the balance of policy objectives being sought. As discussed in the paper, some allocation mechanisms are much better at achieving certain objectives than others. In general, the particular circumstances of the country matter a lot in determining the most appropriate set of allocation mechanisms on which to rely. What works well in one country will not necessarily work well in another. Many allocation mechanisms require strong government structures and adequate public resource bases to be effective. Many developing and transition countries lack these basic essentials and thus must look to other approaches that do not have these requirements for success. Even industrial countries often lack the policy structures and resources bases that make certain approaches work in other countries. In some cases, changes within the institutions themselves are needed to accompany the effective implementation of new allocation mechanisms. Furthermore, what worked well at a given moment in time may not be adequate anymore ten years later to address a different set of policy challenges and objectives.

- *Be careful in defining and prioritizing the policy objectives that are being sought.*

  Policy discussions in many countries tend to devolve into general discussions of the need for more access or better quality or greater efficiency. Without precise and accurate definition of the objectives being sought and the indicators that can be used to measure progress, these policy discussions can easily slide into advocacy exercises in which more of everything is better, with little or no prioritization of goals or objectives. These kinds of discussions are ultimately disappointing and counter productive as they fail to inform policy makers with a plan for making the inevitable tough choices about how to utilize scarce resources most effectively.

- *Avoid linking allocation mechanisms and systems of quality assurance and performance too rigidly.*

  Governments should be cautious and not try to establish too rigid a relationship between the results of evaluation / accreditation and performance and the amount of funding going to tertiary education institutions. A related concern is that too much emphasis may be placed on achieving certain performance measures with the result of diminished quality or equity. A more effective approach may be to make participation in evaluation and accreditation exercises or achievement of certain performance measures a criterion for access to additional public funding, rather than a determinant of the amount of that funding. Argentina, for instance, linked eligibility to the Competitive Fund to participation in the accreditation process. Chile has just introduced a new law to extend the eligibility of student loans to students enrolled in private tertiary education institutions that have accepted to participate in the accreditation process.

- *Guarantee stable funding over the medium terms.*

  Any allocation mechanism such as a competitive fund or a performance contract that guarantees funding over several years is preferable to year-to-year allocations. Multi-year funding allows tertiary education institutions to plan their investment and reform programs over the medium to longer term in accordance with their strategic plan. To avoid the political fallout that can occur from large-scale shifts in the distribution of funds that often are the result of reforms, policymakers should consider 'grandfather' provisions to produce more gradual shifts or using new funds to implement reforms.

- *Address the political feasibility of reforms through appropriate expert studies, stakeholder consultations, public debates and press campaigns to minimize the risks of opposition and resistance.*
  Many financing reforms, including establishing or increasing tuition fees, replacing grants and scholarships with student loans, or authorizing private tertiary education institutions to operate are controversial measures. Political difficulty should not be used, however, to delay implementing important and necessary reforms.

- *Make anticipating the unforeseen consequences of policies a key component of the implementation process.*
  An examination of the experience in many countries indicates that policy makers tend to shift their attention away from policy areas once policy decisions have been taken and before implementation has begun. This tendency contributes to the situation where the unintended consequences of policies detract from their eventual effectiveness in addressing the critical goals of improving equity, quality, and efficiency. One way to deal with these unanticipated consequences is to build models and other analytic techniques that might predict the direction and the magnitude of these consequences, and to rely on monitoring systems that allow policy makers to identify problems early on and make the necessary adjustments.

6. Annex 1 — Typology of Allocation Mechanisms

Type of allocation	Examples of where practiced
I. Direct Public Funding of Institutions — Countries typically provide public support of institutions to finance: their instruction, operations and investment expenses, including recurrent expenses and for a variety of specific purposes; and university-based research.	
1. *Funding instruction, operations and investment* — Countries use a number of different approaches to help institutions pay for expenses related to instruction and operations as well as financing capital investment. These payments of public funds generally apply only to public institutions, although in a few countries private institutions also are eligible for this type of support.	
1.1. *Negotiated or ad hoc budgets* — Allocations of public funds are negotiated between government and institutions and thus are largely a function of historical or political factors, either the amount received the year before or the political power of the institution. Negotiated budgets typically are allocated to institutions either as:	The most traditional form of funding recurrent expenses, still in effect in many countries
i) *Line-item budgets* — Negotiated budgets often are implemented through line-item allocations to institutions.	Nepal
ii) *Block grants* — Providing a single block grant to each institution is another way that negotiated budgets can be implemented.	Malaysia
1.2. *Categorical or earmarked funds* — More traditional form of funding in which categories of institutions are designated as eligible for funds for a specific set of purposes; these funds may often be distributed on a formula basis among the designated institutions	Title III program in US, funds for predominantly black institutions in S. Africa

(Continued)

(Continued)

Type of allocation	Examples of where practiced
1.3. *Funding formulas* — Many countries now use some type of formula to allocate funds to institutions for their recurrent expenses. These formulas vary on the basis of what factors are used in the development of the formula and what type of organization develops it. The factors used in determining funding formulas include:	
i) *inputs such as staff or students* — Most funding formulas contain a component based on inputs such as number of staff or students	
• *staff* — Once the most typical funding formula, based on inputs such as the number of staff or staff salaries at each institution, and occasionally other more sophisticated measures such as number of professors with a PhD.	No longer the most frequently formula, still used in some countries, especially in Eastern Europe
• *number of students* — More typical formula, based on the number of students rather than the number or qualifications of staff. Enrollment figures used can be retrospective (actual) or projected	Countries with formulas use some measure of number of students as a key component for making allocations
ii) *costs per student* — Most funding formulas now are based on the number of students enrolled multiplied by one of the cost per student calculations described below:	
• *actual costs per student* — The most traditional way to allocate funds to institutions based on actual costs per student as reported by the institution	Actual costs are used in funding formulas in most countries
• *average costs per student* — Allocations to institutions based on system-wide average costs per student, usually calculated from aggregate statistics on spending and enrollments	Some countries use average costs per student in their funding formulas
• *normative costs per student* — Allocations are based on the calculation of normative costs, using optimal staff/student ratios and other standardized efficiency measures	Bulgaria, Czech Republic, England, Hungary

(Continued)

(Continued)

Type of allocation	Examples of where practiced
• *benchmarking* — One form of normative costs in which the cost figures and structure are pegged to a 'benchmark' inst or set of institutions	Kentucky (US)
• *Charge back arrangements* — In cases where funding is based on prospective estimates of student numbers and/or costs, allocations are reviewed mid-year to reflect reality and funding levels are then adjusted	Most countries w/ formulas based on prospective enrollments use charge-backs
iii) *Priority-based funding* — Formulas where adjustments are made to reflect national and regional priorities such as critical labor force needs; also referred to as funding for relevance, e.g. a price higher than full cost might be paid to institutions for seats determined to be in high priority fields of study.	England inserts priorities into part of its funding formula; selected US states also make similar adjustments
• *Student-based allocations* — One form of priority funding, funds could be distributed to institutions based primarily on the characteristics of the students who enroll instead of the more traditional institutional characteristics such as costs/student; this kind of formula could be referred to as 'Supply side' vouchers	England and Ireland pay institutions more for low-income students they enroll. Jordan and Palestinian Authority have proposed student-based allocations.
iv) *Performance-based formula components* — Performance measures are built into funding formula, e.g., institutional allocations are based on the number of year-end completers or degree recipients rather than the number of students enrolled.	Denmark, England, Israel, and the Netherlands base all or some formula on end-of year completers or graduates
v) *Organizations developing formulas* — Another important consideration in describing the use of formulas is what kind of group develops the particulars of the formula. Two basic options include:	
• *Political entities* — Entities run by politically elected officials design and operate formula and allocate funds	This is the approach in most countries around the world

(Continued)

(Continued)

Type of allocation	Examples of where practiced
• *Buffer bodies* — Groups known as buffer bodies develop refine the formula and allocate funds. These buffer bodies represent the link between governments and institutions and are intended to insulate the funding process from excessive political pressures	Pakistan, England, India and Sri Lanka have higher education buffer bodies. New Zealand and now Ireland have tertiary education agencies.
1.4. *Performance-based funding* — A number of countries in recent years have adopted performance-based funding mechanisms to fund all or a part of operating budgets or capital investment. Four types of performance-based funding are:	
i) *Performance set asides* — A percentage of funds outside of the basic funding formula are distributed based on a set of performance measures. Typically only a small portion of funds for recurrent expenses are distributed on this basis; although in a few cases most funds are allocated based on performance measures.	South Africa; more than a dozen states in US, including Missouri, New Jersey, Tennessee, South Carolina, and Ohio
ii) *Performance contracts* — Regulatory agreements between governments and systems of institutions or individual institutions in which various performance measures are used to benchmark progress. These contracts are typically more punitive than incentives as institutions would be penalized for not meeting the agreed upon performance-based standards.	France, Finland, Denmark, and Austria now have contracts. Colorado and Virginia in the US are also implementing contracts.
iii) *Competitive Funds* — These are usually funded on a project-by-project basis, typically for the purposes of improving quality, promoting innovation, and fostering better management — objectives that are difficult to achieve through funding formula or categorical funds	Argentina, Bolivia, Bulgaria, Chile, Ghana, Hungary, Indonesia, Mozambique, Sri Lanka, US (FIPSE)
iv) *Payment for results* — A small number of countries now pay for performance results in one of the two ways:	
• *Performance-based formula components* — discussed above in 1.3(iv)	Denmark, England, Israel & the Netherlands

(Continued)

(*Continued*)

Type of allocation	Examples of where practiced
• *Fees for services* — Institutions enter into contracts with governments to produce certain numbers of graduates and are paid based on whether they meet the contract specifications	Colorado implementing system to pay for each post-baccalaureate student enrolled
2. *Funding of Research* — A number of arrangements exist around the world for allocating funds to support the conduct of university-based research including overhead costs. These arrangements include: funding instruction and research together, block grant funding, and project funding.	
2.1. *Instruction and research funded together* — Perhaps the most common approach for funding research, some of the funds that governments provide to institutions are used to pay for research rather than for instruction and operations	Many countries fund research and instruction together via negotiated budgets or formulas
2.2. *Research Project funding* — faculty or other staff receive funding for research for proposed projects, usually based on peer reviews	US federal funding of research
• *Matching funds* — governments provide funds for specific purposes if matched by institution or private sources	Singapore, New York (US)
2.3. *Block grant funding for research* — Institutions receive a block grant allocation specifically for research activities but typically not differentiated or specified by project; institutions or faculties set priorities. The size of the block grant may be based on:	
• *Institutional demonstrated capacity* — Block grants in which the amount of funding provided to each university is based on an assessment of its collective faculty's capacity to conduct research — 'blue skies' approach	England, Scotland, Australia (Proposed)
• *Centers of research excellence* — Block grants to particular institutions that specialize in certain fields of research	Chile, China, New Zealand, Netherlands, South Korea, Venezuela

(*Continued*)

(Continued)

Type of allocation	Examples of where practiced
II. Support of Students/Indirect Funding of Institutions While most public support of tertiary education around the world is directly provided to institutions, in many countries a growing share of public funds are provided to students and their families in the form of grants and scholarships, tax benefits, and various types of student loans. Students may also be the vehicle for indirect support of institutions in the form of demand side vouchers.	
1. *'Demand Side' Vouchers* — Public funds in support of the operating expenses of institutions are distributed to students in the form of vouchers; institutions then are reimbursed by government based on number and/or amount of vouchers they submit.	Colorado (US) now uses vouchers to pay recurrent expenses of undergraduate students. The Republic of Georgia is considering a similar system
2. *Government Grants and Scholarships* — Most countries provide non-repayable aid to their students, but how this aid is provided varies on a number of dimensions, including: how the programs are administered, which students are eligible, and which expenses are covered.	
2.1. *Program administration* — A key policy variable in describing grant and scholarship programs is how they are administered:	
i) *administered by institutions* — Public funds are provided to institutions who are then responsible for distributing funds to students, often according to rules set forth by government	Hungary, Lithuania, Poland, Portugal (merit-based)
• matching funds — Govts may require institutions to match public funds by providing waivers or discounts to targeted groups of students	US (institution-based program)

(Continued)

(Continued)

Type of allocation	Examples of where practiced
ii) *student aid vouchers* — Students and families apply to a centralized source and are provided vouchers based on an assessment of their financial need and/or merit. In some cases institutions receive government payments to reflect vouchers they receive from students or students may receive the money directly.	Denmark; France & other Francophone African countries; US (GI Bill, Pell grant), Chile (merit-based vouchers for best secondary school graduates)
2.2. *Eligibility and Coverage* — Grants and scholarships vary greatly in the criteria for how eligibility for non-repayable aid is determined and which expenses are covered:	
i) *Means-tested (Grants)* — In most countries, eligibility for grants is based primarily on assessments of the financial need of the student and/or family. This form of non-repayable aid may be used:	
• solely or primarily for tuition fees	U.K. (until 2006)
• solely or primarily stipends for living expenses	Austria, Belgium, Estonia, France, Finland, Germany, Ireland, Italy, N. Zealand, Norway, Poland, Slovenia
• available for both tuition and living expenses	Portugal, US
ii) *Merit-based (Scholarships)* — In a number of countries, eligibility for scholarships is based primarily or partially on the academic merit or other accomplishments of the student. This form of non repayable aid may be:	
• primarily for tuition fees	US (in a number of states)
• primarily stipends for living expenses	Austria, Estonia, France, Hungary, Poland
• available for both tuition fees and living expenses	Netherlands
iii) *Need-based and merit-based* — Eligibility is based on both financial need and the academic merit of student	Czech Republic, France, Malta, Slovakia (stipends)

(Continued)

(Continued)

Type of allocation	Examples of where practiced
3. *Tax Benefits* — Families or students receive a tax benefit either as a credit against tax or a deduction from income for either tuition fees or living expenses:	
3.1. *Current tuition fees* — Students and/or families receive tax benefits to offset all or portion of tuition fees	Ireland, US, New Brunswick (Canada)
3.2. *Family allowances* — Provided through the tax system, these provisions help parents offset the expenses of supporting children while they are enrolled in higher education	Austria, Belgium, Czech Republic, France, Germany, Latvia, Netherlands, Slovenia
4. *Student Loan Models* — Student loans are now provided in more than 50 countries around the world. A key difference in these models is the type of repayment schedule employed. Approaches also vary according to the source of capital; type of expenses covered; and eligibility and level of subsidy provided:	
4.1. *Repayment plans* — Student loans generally are repaid as mortgage-type loans and income contingent repayments.	
i) *Mortgage-type loans*. The most traditional type of student loan repayment plan, loans are repaid on an amortized (equal) basis over a fixed period of time.	In most countries with student loans, repayment is on an amortized basis, usually lasting 7 to 10 years
• Graduated and Extended Repayment Plans — fixed amortized repayments are graduated (smaller earlier payments and larger later payments) and/or extended beyond the normal fixed term	US (option), Sonora (Mexico), Venezuela
ii) *Income Contingent Repayments*. A more innovative financing approach for student loans occurs when repayment is based on the amount borrowed and a percentage of the income of borrowers once they complete their education	

(Continued)

(Continued)

Type of allocation	Examples of where practiced
Mandatory Income Contingent Repayment — All borrowers repay based on their income after graduation and amount borrowed; plans vary depending on who pays fees initially:	
• Fees initially paid by students and families — Income contingent repayment is combined with traditional fees in which students or their parents pay fees while borrowing to pay those fees	South Africa, Sweden, New Zealand
• Fees initially paid by government — More innovative approach in which govts pay the fees for students initially which are then repaid through the tax system once students complete education	Australia, Scotland, Thailand (in 2006), U.K. (in 2006)
• Optional Income Contingent Repayment — Borrowers who have amortized repayment obligations are provided the option of repaying on the basis of their income after graduation. This may also entail moving borrowers who are having trouble meeting their repayment obligations in an amortized system into a tax-based repayment system.	US since 1994 has provided income contingent repayment option for borrowers; in Chile, student loan defaulters are moved into tax system
iii) *Graduate tax* — students pay for their education as a percentage of their income through taxes once they complete their education. Income contingency differs from graduate tax in that repayment is not required for lifetime or until retirement, just until loan has been fully repaid	No country really has an operating graduate tax
iv) *Human Capital Contracts* — Student participants agree to repay a portion of their incomes to investors who have an 'equity stake' in the student's post graduation income. Under some versions, investors able to depreciate the economic value of the students on their taxes.	Pilots in Colombia, Chile, Germany, and US

(Continued)

(Continued)

Type of allocation	Examples of where practiced
4.2. *Sources of funds* — Student loans can be financed through a variety of sources including:	
i) Private sources — commercial banks and other private sources of capital provide the capital in most mortgage-type student loan programs around the world:	Canada, Chile, China, (commercial), Korea, US (guaranteed)
ii) Public sources — One recent trend is for countries to shift from private to public funding of mortgage-type loans	Canada, China (sub), Hong Kong, Thailand, US (direct)
iii) Internally-Financed Student Loans — A less utilized way to finance and structure student loans, institutions use the fees paid by some students to finance loans to help other students pay their fees. These loans, which can entail little or no government involvement allow more innovative repayments including:	
• *Deferred payment plans* — fee payments spread out over a period of time that begins while borrower is still in school	Philippines
• *Privately financed and serviced* — Institutions sell loans or contract with servicers when borrowers begin repayment	US (Sallie Mae and other entities), Colombia
iv) Creative Financing — A number of creative financing mechanisms have been considered to facilitate the provision and expansion of mortgage-type student loans, including:	
• *Secondary markets* — existing student loans are sold or used as collateral to create new loan capital	US (Sallie Mae and other entities), Colombia
• *"Securitization"* — Bonds are secured by the projected flow of funds from student loan repayments	US, Chile

(Continued)

Type of allocation	Examples of where practiced
4.3. *Expenses covered* — Like grants, student loan programs also vary in terms of whether they cover tuition fees only, living expenses only, or both tuition fees and living expenses:	
i) tuition fees only — students can borrow only for tuition fees	Lithuania, Korea, Japan, Philippines
ii) primarily for living expenses only — loans are available to students to cover their living expenses	Denmark, England, Finland, Germany, Hong Kong, Poland, Slovakia
iii) cover both tuition fees and living expenses — In a number of countries student loans are available to cover both tuition fees and living expenses of students while enrolled	Canada, China, Estonia, Hong Kong, Malta, Netherlands, Thailand, US
4.4 *Eligibility to borrow* — Mortgage-type loans vary in terms of which groups of students are eligible to borrow including by:	
• *Means testing* — Some countries limit borrowing to students who meet a means test, although more often means tests are used to determine whether the loan will be subsidized (see below)	Austria, Italy, Poland
• *Course load* — Most countries limit borrowing to full-time students but some countries extend borrowing to students who are enrolled on less than a full time basis	England, Poland, and US
• *Level of study* — Most countries allow borrowing by both undergraduate and graduate students but some countries limit borrowing to certain groups of students such as:	
• *Undergraduates only*	Scotland
• *Private sector eligibility* — In a number of countries public sector and private sector students are both eligible to borrow.	Norway, Philippines, Poland, South Korea, Thailand, US

(Continued)

Type of allocation	Examples of where practiced
4.5. *Level of subsidy* — There is also considerable variation in whether student loans are subsidized relative to market terms and conditions	
i) *Means tested and more highly subsidized* — Countries in which eligibility for subsidies is means-tested and interest subsidies and default costs exceed 10% of loan value	Canada, China (subsidized), Germany, New Zealand, Philippines (study now pay later), Thailand, US (sub)
ii) *Little or no subsidy* — In loan programs where eligibility is broad-based and subsidies are less than 10% of loan value	China (commercial), US (non subsidized)
5. *Part Grant/Part Loan* — In some countries student financial aid is provided partially as grants and partially as loans, including:	
5.1. *Loans that become grants* — Loans that students initially borrow are converted to grants if students demonstrate satisfactory academic practice	Netherlands (Basic Grant), Norway, Sweden
5.2. *Loan forgiveness* — Another form of Grant/Loan is to forgive all or a portion of repayments for borrowers likely to earn less in public service positions such as those entering certain employment fields particularly in underserved geographic areas such as rural settings or inner cities.	US — forgives portion of loan repayments for teachers or doctors who agree to practice in underserved areas

7. Annex 2 — Assessing the Effectiveness of Allocation Mechanisms

A. Possible effects by policy objective							
	Access and Equity				External Efficiency	Internal Efficiency	
Type of Allocation Mechanism	Increase Level of Access	Improve Equity of Access	Promote Lifelong Learning	Private Sector Expansion	Improve Quality & Relevance	Contain Cost Growth	Increase Throughput
I. Direct Public Funding of Institutions							
1. *Funding Instruction, Operations, and Investment*							
1.1. Negotiated Budgets	–	–		–		+	–
1.2. Categorical/Earmarked	–				+		
1.3. Formula Funding							
i) Input-based					–	+	
ii) Cost-based							
- Actual costs/student			–	–	–	—	
- Average costs/student						+	
- Normative costs/student					+	+ +	
iii) Priority-based			+		+ +		
iv) Performance components				+			+ +
1.4. Performance-Based Funding							
i) Performance set-asides							
ii) Performance Contracts							
iii) Competitive Funds					+ +		
iv) Payment for Results		+				+	+ +
2. *Public Funding of University-Based Research*							
- Funded w/instruction					–		
- Block grants					+	+	
- Projects peer reviewed			+		+	–	
II. Public Funding of Students and Families/ Indirect Funding of Institutions							
1. *Demand Side Vouchers*	+	–	–	+ +		+	–
2. *Grants and Scholarships*							
- administered by institutions				+/–			
- student aid vouchers		+		+ +		+/–	
- means-tested	+	+					
- merit-based		–			+		
- need and merit-based	+	+			+		
3. *Tax Benefits*							
- tuition fee offsets	+	–	+	+	–	–	
- family allowances	+	+/–					
4. *Student Loans*							
i) Mortgage-type	+					–	
ii) Income contingent	+	+ +	+			+/–	
5. *Grant/Loan Arrangements*							

Notes: + = positive impact; –= negative; =/– = depends on specific program design.

B. Which allocation mechanism is more effective?

Policy objectives pursued

- improving access and equity
- improving external efficiency (quality and relevance)
- improving internal efficiency (cost moderation and throughput) and sustainability

Improving access and equity

- traditional age students
  — increased cost sharing with more student grants, scholarships and/or loans to offset adverse effects of higher fees
  — income contingent student loan repayments
  — enrollment-based funding formula
- disadvantaged students
  — expanded need-based grants and scholarships
  — pay institutions premiums for enrolling and graduating disadvantaged students
- lifelong learning opportunities
  — needs-based grants and merit-based scholarships
  — student loans
  — tax benefits for workers enrolled in tertiary programs
  — lifelong learning vouchers
  — savings accounts

Improving external efficiency

- improving quality
  — competitive funds
  — merit-based scholarships
- increasing relevance
  — formula with differential weights for high priority fields
  — competitive funds with priority for relevance
  — grants and scholarships in priority fields
  — student loans in priority fields
  — loan forgiveness for employment in high priority fields or public service

Improving internal efficiency and sustainability

- cost containment
  — funding formula based on normative costs
- improving throughput
  — output-based formula
  — pay for results
  — performance contracts

Endnotes

1. This paper adopts the OECD definition of tertiary education as "a level or stage of studies beyond secondary education. Such studies are undertaken in tertiary education institutions, such as public and private universities, colleges, and polytechnics, and also in a wide range of other settings, such as secondary schools, work sites, and via free-standing information technology-based offerings and a host of public and private entities." (Wagner, A. 1999. "Lifelong Learning in the University: A New Imperative?" In W. Hirsh and L. Weber, eds. Challenges Facing Higher Education at the Millennium. 134–52. American Council on Education. Phoenix, Arizona: Oryx Press. p. 135).

2. Several countries also use their tax system to provide incentives for greater levels of saving for future expenses related to tertiary education. These tax incentives for savings are more of an example of resource mobilization than resource allocation that is the focus of this paper.

3. Thorn and Holm-Nielsen, 2004.

4. In Denmark, these contracts are called "development contracts" to reflect the long term strategic perspective of the activity.

5. In many countries, some or most of the research conducted within universities or related institutions is funded through private sources but in this report the focus is on how public funds are allocated for research.

6. For example, in the US in the 1990s, the practice of some universities attributing excessive expenses to their indirect cost pool of resources led to heightened media attention and calls for reform of the funding campus-based research.

7. Pachuashvili, M., "Dual Privatization in Georgian Higher Education", *International Higher Education*, Fall 2005.

8. The terms used to describe non repayable forms of aid vary widely among countries; they include grants, bursaries, scholarships, fellowships, and others. This paper uses the convention of referring to need-based aid as grants and merit-based aid as scholarships, recognizing the problems in making these definitions including that the term grant does not exist in French or Spanish.

9. Salmi, J. (2003). "Student Loans in an International Perspective: The World Bank Experience." LCSHD Paper Series number 44, Washington DC: The World Bank.

10. Much of the information on the specifics of student loan models around the world are drawn from Vossensteyn, *Student financial support, an inventory*

in 24 European countries, CHEPS and Ziderman, *Policy options for student loans schemes: lessons from five Asian case studies*, UNESCO Bangkok.

11. See Usher A. (2005) for a summary of loan programs and subsidies in eight industrialized countries.

12. Some analyses measure the subsidy as the difference between the student borrower rate and the government costs of borrowing, see, for example, discussion of subsidy levels in Usher, A. (2005). But most economists would argue that the market interest rate, to the extent it can be measured or estimated, is the appropriate standard to use in calculating subsidy levels. There is also a question of which rate to use to calculate the present value of subsidies over the life of the loan; on this question most economists would say that the government cost of borrowing is appropriate to measure the present value of government subsidies.

13. Ziderman. A (2006). "Student Loans in Thailand: From Social Targeting to Cost Sharing," International Higher Education, Number 42, Winter 2006.

14. This argument can be found, for example, in Barr N. "Higher Education Funding" in *Oxford Review of Economic Policy*, 2004.

15. In the case of Chile, only a restricted number of private institutions are eligible for this form of public funding of institutions.

16. The convention in loan administration seems to be that servicing refers to the regular repayment of loans whereas collection is the activity that occurs when loans are in arrears or have been defaulted.

17. Uribe, C. (2006). "New Developments in Colombia's Higher Education." International Higher Education. Number 42, Winter 2006, pp. 20–22.

References

Barr, N., Higher Education Funding, *Oxford Review of Economic Policy*, 2004.

Burke, J. *et al.* (2002), *Funding public colleges and universities for performance: popularity, and prospects*, Albany, New York, The Rockefeller Institute Press.

Center for Higher Education Policy Studies (Netherlands), (2003), *Higher Education Reform: Getting the Incentives Right*, CHEPS, Enschede, the Netherlands.

Center for Higher Education Policy Studies (2001), *Public funding of higher education: A comparative study of funding mechanisms in ten countries*, Enschede, the Netherlands.

Chapman, B. (2001). Australian higher education financing: Issues for reform. *The Australian Economic Review*, **34**(2), pp. 195–204.

Department of Education, Science, and Technology (Australia). (2002). *Higher education at the crossroads: An overview paper.* Canberra, Australia: Author.

Department for Education and Skills (England) (2003). *Higher Education Funding: International Comparisons* (monograph).

Fehnel, R. (2004). Higher education reforms and demand responsive innovation funds: Dimensions of difference, A report to the World Bank (monograph).

Hauptman, A. (1998). Linking funding, student fees, and student aid. *International Higher Education* 13 (Fall), pp. 10–11.

Hauptman, A. (1999). Student-based higher education financing policies. *International Higher Education* 17 (Fall), pp. 5–6.

Hauptman, A. (1999). Internal financing of student loans. *International Higher Education* 16 (Summer), pp. 4–5.

Hauptman, A. (2004). Using institutional incentives to improve student performance. In R. Kazis, J. Vargas, and N. Hoffman (eds), *Double the numbers: Increasing postsecondary credentials for underrepresented youth.* Cambridge: Harvard Education Press.

HEFCE (2003), *Funding higher education in England — How hefce allocates its funds*, London: Higher education funding council for England.

International Institute for Educational Planning, UNESCO (2005). *EdSup Info link: resources on student support schemes, loans, grants and scholarship policies, Database.* http://lst-iiep.iiep-unesco.org/wwwisis/studsup_form. htm.

Jongbloed, B. and J. Koelman, (2004), *Vouchers for higher education?* Center for Higher Education Policy Studies, Netherlands.

Larocque, N. (2003). *Who should pay? Tuition fees and tertiary education financing in New Zealand.* Wellington, New Zealand: Education Forum.

Leslie, L. and P. Brinkman, (1998). *The economic value of higher education.* New York: ACE/Macmillan Series on Higher Education, Macmillan Publishing Company.

McPherson, M. and M. Schapiro, (1991). *Keeping college affordable.* Washington, DC: Brookings Institution.

Organization for Economic Cooperation and Development. (2003). *Education at a glance*, 2003. Paris: OECD.

Pachuashvili, M. (2005). "Dual privatization in Georgian higher education", *International Higher Education.*

Palacios, M. (2004). *Investing in Human Capital: A Capital Markets Approach to Student Funding.* Cambridge: Cambridge University Press.

Salmi, J. (2003). "Student Loans in an International Perspective: The World Bank Experience." LCSHD Paper Series number 44, Washington DC: The World Bank.

Salmi, J. (1992). "Perspectives on the Financing of Higher Education". Higher Education Policy, volume 5, number 2.

Schenker-Wicki, A. and M. Hürlimann, (2006). "Performance Funding of Swiss Universities — Success or Failure? An *ex post* Analysis. Higher Education Management and Policy, volume 18, No. 1.

Thorn, K., L. Holm-Neilsen, and J. Jeppesen, (2004). *Approaches to Results-Based Funding in Tertiary Education*, World Bank, Latin American and Caribbean Region.

Usher, A. (2005). *Global debt patterns*, Educational Policy Institute, (Canada).

Vossensteyn, H. (2004). *Student Financial Support: An Inventory in 24 European Countries*, Center for Higher Education Policy Studies, (the Netherlands)

World Bank (1994). *Higher education: The lessons of experience*, Washington DC: The World Bank.

World Bank (2000). *Higher education in developing countries.* Report of the Task Force on Higher Education and Society (TFHES). Washington DC: The World Bank.

World Bank (2002). *Constructing Knowledge Societies: New Challenges for Tertiary Education.* Washington D.C.

Ziderman, A. (2003). Policy options for student loan schemes: lessons from five Asian case studies, UNESCO Bangkok.

Ziderman, A. (2006). Student loans in Thailand: From social targeting to cost sharing. *International Higher Education*, 46 Winter, pp. 6–8.

Author Index

Subject Index

Organization–Place Index

CPSIA information can be obtained
at www.ICGtesting.com
Printed in the USA
BVHW040201240819
556602BV00005B/6/P